Industrial Relations

Text and Cases

Attention Authors

Manas Publications is fighting a war to tell the world that India can win the battle not only by the bullet but also by pen. There is no dearth of intellectuals in our country, but their knowledge is confined to them only. No sincere effort has been made by any other publisher to channelise their knowledge in national interest, which is why the talent of large number of intellectuals remain latent. An author always gives the raw material in the shape of a manuscript and it is the job of the publisher to convert it into a beautiful book. Manas always motivates the intellectuals by publishing their manuscripts since more than four decades and would like to publish your manuscript too. If you or your colleagues have any manuscript ready for publication or are working on it, kindly contact us with a detailed synopsis and list of contents for its best publication. If you wish, we can also suggest you a suitable title for writing related to your area of expertise. Manas is known for its publishing quality and commitments. We take utmost care in production and give wide publicity to the book as well as its author through our national and international distribution network.

Industrial Relations
Text and Cases

Dr Ajit Kumar Ghosh
University of Burdwan

Manas Publications
(We Convert Fighters into Writers)
New Delhi-110002 (INDIA)

MANAS PUBLICATIONS
(Publishers, Library Suppliers, Importers & Exporters)
4402/5-A, Ansari Road (Opp. HDFC Bank)
Darya Ganj, New Delhi-110 002 (India)
Off. ✆ 23260783, 23265523, Res. ✆ 23842660
Fax: 011-23272766
E-mail: manaspublications@vsnl.com
manaspublications@yahoo.com
manaspublications@gmail.com

Second Impression 2012

ISBN 978-81-7049-415-7
₹ 695/-

Designed by
Manas Publications

Printed in India at
IYN Graphics, Delhi
and published by Mrs Suman Lata for
Manas Publications, 4402/5-A, Ansari Road
(Opp. HDFC Bank),
Darya Ganj, New Delhi-110 002 (INDIA)

CONTENTS

Dedicated to my Mother

PREFACE

Change, continuous change and radical change is a regular phenomena. It is prevalent in every field of activities, be it in the social, economic, cultural or political. The abrupt change in industrial activities in India has started after the implementation of the new economic policy in July 1991 that has brought a significant departure from controlled, regulated and protected (CRP) economy to the liberalized, privatized and global (LPG) economy.

In the LPG economy a fierce, stiff and hyper competitive environment exists as a lot of MNCs and TNCs enter into market and strive hard to show their strength and competence to face challenges and capture market through delivery of goods and services to the delight of customers.

Competitors know that customers demand for quality goods and services at a reasonable price, as they are very much aware that today's market is buyers' market, not sellers'. In order to face challenges, survival in the market, obtain competitive advantages, attain business excellence and achieve goals, organization needs reservoir of people who are satisfied, contented and have developed high degree of morale, a sense of belonging, 'we-feeling' 'togetherness', a spirit of co-operation and collaboration. It is not difficult for the organization to have such kind of human resources that help to survive, grow, develop and attain business excellence if congenial, conducive and harmonious industrial relations exist in the organization. So, sound industrial relations are necessary for the growth, development of the organization and achievement of goals through delivery of quality goods, services at a reasonably lesser price and providing delightment to the customers. It occurs that in healthy industrial relations system both labour and management come close, interact with each other, develop sound dyadic relationships and establish a state of mutuality (i.e., mutual understanding, mutual faith, mutual trust and mutual confidence). All this helps to achieve organizational goals.

There is no denying the fact that industrial relations play a pivotal role to make the organization achieve its goals. So, organization can fulfil its mission, objectives, goals if it has dynamic, committed, loyal and contented workforce. And this can be possible in healthy industrial set-ups where much emphasis is laid on promoting better human relations between boss and subordinates, expeditious disposal of employees' grievances, and disputes individually by boss or collectively under collective bargaining approach between employer's representatives/associations and employees' representatives/ trade unions, generating a climate of discipline in the organization and involving people in organizational activities to put in their spontaneous efforts to face challenges in macro-environment to achieve its goals through employee empowerment, employee participation and introduction of quality circles.

This book is designed to introduce the readers to the conceptual perspectives ofindustrial relations and its practices in Indian organizations. It comprises ten chapters. Chapter 1 provides an understanding on human relations. In the organization, people work with boss and with members in group/team. In the process of working/work activities they interact among themselves and develop some relationship which is termed as human relations. Human relations make a significant contribution to promote better industrial relations in organizations.

Chapters 2, 3 and 4 present the roles of trade unions and employers' association and the importance of collective bargaining to settle problems/ issues of the people at work through joint participation, interaction and discussion. All this helps develop industrial relations through generating a climate of mutuality. It happens that some find it difficult to hold negotiations under collective bargaining process for amicable settlement of issues because of ambiguity and complexity inherent in the system itself. The indepth discussion deliberated in chapter 4 on collective bargaining may give a crystal clear idea to the readers to remove the doubt if any, in such specific field of human behaviour.

Chapter 5 attempts to provide enrichment of knowledge with respect to grievances and its effective ways to deal with such grievances. Employees may have problems, complaints, and grievances while working in the organization and they expect that their grievances should be disposed off expeditiously. But, in reality it may not happen all the time and it occurs that grievances are piled up, and people feel dissatisfied, and aggrieved. All this effects dyadic relationship and the industrial relations as well.

The organizations frame rules, regulations and procedures to carry on their tasks in an orderly and systematic way. It is expected that all people at work should follow such rules. But, it occurs that some follow spontaneously and some do not. They violate and resort to indisciplined activities. In such a situation management takes constructive, preventive and motivating measures to correct their behaviour, and improve their conduct so that they do not repeat the same pattern in future; but when they do not improve their conduct and again resort to acts of misconduct, the disciplinary action is taken against them. Today, rapid growth of trade union solidarity, a change in the traditional concept of management prerogatives and authority and enacting employee oriented labour laws that usher in equity and social justice make the discipline management complicated. Chapters 6 and 7 discuss discipline and disciplinary action respectively with the objective of providing some guidelines, practical suggestions regarding procedures to deal with disciplinary cases. These chapters give a great emphasis on the behavioural and procedural aspects of issues with a view to understand the perspective clearly.

No organization can survive, grow, develop and obtain the competitive advantages if the industrial relations are unhealthy, disharmonious and uncoducive. The detailed analysis in such areas of IRs is made in chapter 8.

Chapter 9 focuses on the most important area of industrial relations. People feel happy and contented if organization settles disputes immediately in an amicable and systematic manner and takes necessary measures to prevent disputes. So, origin of industrial disputes, their forms, machineries to settle and prevent them, role of HR/IR specialists to settle disputes and importance of tripartite bodies to prevent them are discussed in this chapter.

Organizations cannot function without people. Now, only the functioning is not sufficient to stay in the market in changing competitive scenario. Organizations need to face competition and win over challenges. For that it needs a reservoir of different kinds of people that help companies to exist, grow, develop and achieve excellence. In such case, the contribution of the schemes like employee empowerment, employee participation and quality circle cannot be underestimated. All these schemes make the employees psychologically and mentally involved in their jobs and help them display a much greater degree of identification with the company and its goals, to generate a climate of mutuality, to promote the degree of morale and loyalty and to establish sound industrial relations in the organization. A thorough and analytical deliberation on employee empowerment, quality circle and workers' participation in management is made in chapter 10 with particular emphasis on the relevant areas that have greater linkage to providing healthy industrial relations of the company.

There has been a great need for an introductory text in industrial relations with emphasis on practical exposure/applications in industrial settings. Students of various business schools, institutes have also expressed the need for such kind of book. Looking into this aspect and particularly to meet up the needs of the students, practicing managers, and research scholars, the text is designed to provide authoritative and accurate information with regard to the subject matter covered. However, it is not intended to be a source oflegal/professional advice for any purpose. This book can be of great use for the students of MBA, MCom, MHRM, MBA(HR), BBA and also the students prosecuting studies in technical and professional education programmes. It can be used effectively as the main text book as it covers the topics prescribed for the above course curricula.

The book has been written in a clear and concise style. It presents an analysis and reflection on both theoretical and practical issues cropped up in the field of labour-management relations. At the end of each chapter, at least one 'real case' has been given. And all these cases are drawn from the real life situations the author has faced/managed, in the event of his performance/discharging responsibilities as functional head of the personnel department (now HRM department) in service industry and manufacturing industry for about 27 years. These case studies are used to enrich knowledge/understanding of the reader on the subject and also to develop a thought process to find the link between the relevant body of knowledge (theoretical issues) and its application (practices).

While I am of course exclusively responsible for the contents in Industrial Relations (Text and Cases), I want to thank several personalities for their assistances. This includes first, the senior management personnel and the executives of Bank of Boroda who extended support, co-operation to me to prepare this book: Mr TKM Das, Corporate Deputy General Manager (HRM), Mr KC Pati, Deputy General Manager, Mr Rajkumar Jotsinghani, Asstt General Manager (Recruitment) and Mr Victor Vincent Chief Manager (Coordination and HRM) as well as the officers who persistently helped in various ways to write the book: Mr NK Mallik, Sr Manager (HRM), Mr Gopal Mondal, Sr Manager, and Mr SR Kuchlan, Sr Manager.

I express my heartiest gratitude to Prof P Das my respected teacher, former Professor, Deparment of Commerce, Burdwan University and also to Prof AK Mallick, former Vice Chancellor of Burdwan University for their constant assistance, guidance and support extended to me to prepare this text.

I express my thanks to my colleagues of the Centre for Management Studies, Burdwan University, faculty members of the Department of Business Administration NIT, Durgapur and faculty members of the Department of Business Administration, Kalyani University for their advice, support and encouragement.

It is needless to mention that it would not have been possible to make this book if the students of MBA (HR) and MBA of Burdwan University and also the students of MBA of NIT Durgapur and Kalyani University would not have insisted that I write such a book. I would like to express my appreciation to them.

I am thankful to research scholars who carried /have been carrying out PhD work under my supervision for their encouragement and invaluable assistance to write this book: Dr Debasis Baidya, Dr Swapan Roy, Dr Parimalendu Banerjee, Prof P Dutta, Prof Amiya Nayak, Prof Suvarun Goswami, Prof Soma Bose and Miss Arpita Banerjee.

I cannot forget the help my student Sandip Sen extended to me to write the book, I appreciate his efforts.

I want to thank Mr Somen Banerjee and his team for the hard work and efforts put in to complete the typing and other jobs for making the book complete within a short period of time.

At home, I want to acknowledge the support and patience of my wife Dr Bhabani Ghosh as she spent many hours working on preparing the text. My son Dr Nilmadhab Ghosh and my daughter Dr Ananya Ghosh who were sources of inspiration and helped me in various ways to write the book.

Dr Ajit Kumar Ghosh

I

Human Relations: A Perceptual Exposition

Meaning of Human Relations

People work in the organization to satisfy their needs through organizational rewards by contributing towards attainment of organizational goals and also individual goals. They do it through team work. In the process of developing such team work people need to interact for accomplishment of individual goals, team goals and organizational goals. Hence, the relationship developed through the interactions people make amongst themselves can be termed as human relations. Human relations have a significant role in the establishment of promoting industrial relations in the organization.

In the narrow sense, the term 'human relations' denotes relation between human beings. Such relationship arises between humans in all activities of life, may be in school, homes, business, clubs and in other activities. When the relationship exists in the organization, it is termed as 'employee – human relations' or simply 'human relations' and when it exists in any place or activity outside the organization it is referred to as 'public human relations'.

In layman's view 'human relations' means 'being nice to people'. In other words, it is used to denote interest in their work and their group behaviour.

In the organizations people work with boss and in group/team. In the process of working/work activities they interact amongst themselves, that means, they interact with boss and group members and develop a relationship. This relation is human relation.

Derek French and Heather Saward (1977) defined human relation 'as an approach to the theory of management and of organization that emphasizes the individual worker's needs for satisfactory relationship with other members of his work group and his need to participate in decisions that affect his work'.

It is basically a pattern of interaction that the bosses in an organization make with their subordinates for satisfaction of their needs, desires, expectations. And in the process they build an effective team work and motivate the people for higher performance.

Macfarland (1970) opined that 'Human relations is the study and practice of utilizing human resources through knowledge and through an understanding of the activities, attitudes, sentiments and interrelationships of people at work.

Keith Davis (1980) observes "human relations is motivating people in organizational settings to develop team work which accomplishes individual as well as organizational goals effectively"

So, from the perusal of above definitions it becomes transparent that human relations is the art of getting along with people as individuals or as a group to achieve individual/group goals (i.e., satisfaction of human needs) and organizational goals (i.e., maximum production, quality production, greater productivity).

Salient Features of Human Relations

The important characteristics of human relations include the following.

- It is a necessity to have two or more persons to establish human relations.
- Individuals develop human relations through interactive process. They interact among themselves on various issues and in the process, a state of human relationship is generated. So, interaction is a necessity in human relations – building exercise.
- Human relations may have positive manifestations or negative manifestations. Positive manifestation indicates sound human relations and reverse is the case when manifestation is negative.
- Individual values, beliefs, attitudes, culture, ethical standard influence pattern and outcome of interactions between persons that may result in human relations.

- In organizational settings human relations can be developed at various levels, viz., individual level, dyadic level, group/team level and organization level.
- Human relation is an effective means to achieve organizational goals. Better the human relations, brighter is the chance of developing industrial relations. This may facilitate achievement of company goals.
- Human relation has direct link to the need satisfaction of individuals. Hierarchy of needs demands prompt and timely satiation to make the people happy, contented, and satisfied. This may help develop human relation.
- Individuals who have great desire to satisfy the higher order needs are inclined to establish sound human relations. So, establishing a state of human relation among the people in an organization cannot be ruled out if they can satiate their psychological needs.
- A climate of mutuality (mutual understanding, mutual faith and mutual confidence) among the people can be prevalent in the organization where people at various levels develop positive human relations.

Objectives of Human Relations

Human relations play a contributary role for smooth and effective functioning of organizational activities. The main objectives of human relation are discussed in brief.

1. Generating a climate of congeniality

People work in the organization at different levels viz., dyadic level, team level, organization level, etc. To make their work meaningful, effective and result oriented they need to develop understanding among themselves; and it is possible if they can generate a climate of sound human relations in the organization.

2. Promoting a high degree of morale

Better human relation helps create a congenial and conducive work climate through positive and complimentary interactions with boss, peers and other members of the organization. This may boost the level of morale of the employees.

3. Making organization effective

One of the objectives of human relation is to ensure that organization runs smoothly and effectively. Sound human relations generate a state of mutuality (i.e., mutual faith, mutual confidence and mutual trust) amongst the people that helps improve production, sales, services, and profit in the organization.

4. Providing customers' delight

Each and every company strives its best to provide excellent service to the customers to increase its share and to make a dominating hold in the market. Customers want quality goods and service at a competitively lesser price at the time they desire. That means customers delight is a necessity to increase business. And it is possible through better human relations.

5. Reducing industrial conflicts

A healthy human relations situation helps create a climate of cooperation, support, facilitating and agreeability that taken together brings peace and harmony in the work place. In a situation like this frequency of industrial conflicts gets reduced.

6. Promoting sound industrial relations

One of the prerequisites for introduction of industrial relations programme in a company is prevalence of better human relations amongst the people in the organization. Human relation is a means to promote industrial relations. So better the human relations, healthier is the industrial relations in the company.

7. Achievement of organizational goals

Every organization has its mission, vision, objective and goals. So, all companies give its all out efforts to ensure that goals are achieved. Positive human relations help create a situation for uninterrupted functional activities in the organization that tends towards achievement of goals.

8. Creating a positive work environment

Objective of human relation is to ensure that people's needs and aspirations are fulfilled and organization's goals are achieved. This may be possible through creation of positive work environment.

9. Obtaining competitive advantage

Organization needs to face the challenge and obtain competitive advantage for survival, growth and development. This may be possible through generation of group cohesiveness, team building, team commitment and promoting a feeling, of 'we-ness', 'togetherness' and 'belongingness'. Human relation programmes may make the process effective to overcome the competitive situation and to make a dominating place in the market.

Factors Necessitating Human Relation Movement

Promoting human relation is a necessity for smooth and effective running of the organization. Organization needs to achieve its goals for its survival, growth and development. This is possible if a climate of better human relations between individuals in the organization is created through developing understanding, faith and confidence in a state of mutuality. But initially up to first quarter of twentieth century no importance was given on developing human relation. Human aspect was totally ignored by the management. It was not even perceived that human relations could contribute to the achievement of the organizational goals. So human relation did not appear/exist in industrial setting as an important component to bring success to the organization. But subsequently human relation originated and developed. The following factors are responsible for the origin, growth and development of human relations.

1. Non-recognition of human values

Non-recognition of human values by the management brings the people close to each other to develop better understanding amongst themselves. Every human being wants recognition of human values; and for getting it everybody strives his best. When human values were not recognized by the management, people felt the necessity of coming into close proximity of each other to develop mutual ties amongst themselves.

2. Formation of trade union

Trade union takes care of the people's problem and ensures that they are not deprived of their legitimate benefits. Formation of trade union in early period of twentieth century generated new hopes, and aspirations in the mind of the people that helped develop inter–personal relations in the organizations. Further, enactment of Trade Union Act in 1926 inspired them to form trade union to get justice from the management.

3. Victimization of workers

Victimization of workers by management action compels the working community to come close and face the situation through concerned efforts. In the process it creates a state of mutuality (i.e., mutual faith, mutual understanding and mutual confidence) amongst individuals.

4. Management philosophy towards workers

Management attitudes, philosophy, thought process and style

of functioning affect the worker's activities that influence to form an indifferent paradigmal state to confront situation. A negative outlook, attitudes of management make the workers feel uncomfortable, insecure, helpless; and it becomes impossible for them to continue their activities if they are not united. Hence, such situation prompts workers to develop group cohesion and efforts.

5. Change in worker's needs

It is not that workers desire only to satiate their physiological and safety needs, they want to satisfy their social needs, esteem needs and self-actualization needs. Dissatisfaction concerning such needs creates a gap between what they want and what they get resulting in generating industrial disharmony, and unrest in organizations. All this requires to promote unity, and solidarity among the workers.

6. Non-professionalism in utilization of employees

Non–professional handling of employee issues creating un-congenial and un-conducive work climate and utilization of employees for the benefit of the company only develops a feeling among the employees that the management is not concerned about their well-being.

7. Educational level of employees

An increase in educational level of companies' workers makes them conscious about their rights. So, this they feel the necessity of team formation in work place to develop human relations.

8. Technology advancement

Use of new technology in the production system requires restructuring of work activities, job roles and responsibilities of companies. This creates a situation in work environment resulting in strained relationship between supervisors and employees. This develops an urge for promoting group relationship.

An Overview of Human Relations Movement

People at work were considered commodities or cogs of machines that could be purchased or sold out in the market. There was no place for human elements in the organization. The whole concept of worker was based on material perspective because workers were highly keen to satisfy their financial needs. But the thought process and the perceptions of the owners of organizations about worker started changing after the scientific management movement laid the foundation of modern industrial management in the latter part of the nineteenth century. It was

FW Taylor who felt that production could not be increased if the standard of living of the workers remained low. He developed a link between productivity and workers wellness. He made a proposition that standard of living could be improved by increasing earnings of the workers through higher production. So, he advocated the use of technology in the production system.

A change with regard to the image of workers in the organizations was noticed in first quarter of the twentieth century. The owners/ management of the companies developed ideas that workers were complex and unique beings and had a role in contributing in the development of the organizations. So, they felt that quick disposal of workers' problems with human face was a necessity.

Some organizations started giving recognition to the workers as human beings and took initiative to develop mutual understanding with workers through interactive process. The importance of workers as human beings was accelerated when a group of researchers conducted studies at the Hawthorne plant of Western Electric and developed human relations theory in the process of research activity undertaken by Elton Mayo and his team associates. Various studies established the role of people at work in the organization for the achievement of goals. So, the importance of human relations was accepted by most of the organizations. A series of research work on human resource management in the twentieth century particularly in the last quarter of the century focused on the contributory role of human relations towards organizational excellence through goal achievement.

A Bird's Eye View of Hawthorne Studies

The Hawthorne works of the General Electric Company revealed an un-encouraging trend in production of the factory in the first quarter of the twentieth century. The company introduced various schemes for providing fringe benefits and social security measures to motivate the employees in the production activities. But there was no indication of improvement in the overall production/performance of the employees. To find out the cause of such state of production activities and also to explore remedial steps, a series of studies were conducted in the Hawthorne Plant. Some of these include:

- Illumination Experiments
- Relay Room Experiments
- Plant-Wide Interview Programme
- Bank Wiring Room Study

The Illumination Experiments

- This experiment was made to find the relationship between intensity of illumination and productivity. That means to see whether any change in illumination can make any effect on productivity.
- Workers were selected for two different groups – Some for experimental group and others for control group.
- In control group the workers enjoyed the same intensity of light while, the control group had different intensity of light.
- Initially, the researchers enhanced the intensity of light in the experimental group. Then they noticed that productivity had increased in the experimental group. But the control group workers who were not effected by the increase in intensity of light increased their production.
- In the next step researchers decreased intensity of light to see whether productivity decreased or not. But the experimental group workers increased their productivity.

The study concluded that intensity of light was not a driving factor to make any effect on productivity. Some other factor was operating.

The result of experiments are shown in the Table 1.1

Table-1.1

Effect of change in intensity of light on productivity

Intensity of light	Productivity of the experimental group	Productivity of the control group under constant intensity of light
Increase in intensity	Increased	Increased
Decrease in intensity	Increased	Increased

The Relay Room Experiment

After illumination experiment, relay room experiment was conducted mainly during 1927 to 1931/32 under the active guidance of Elton Mayo. The main characteristics of relay room experiment are given below:

- The purpose of the experiment was to determine the effects of changes in work and other working conditions (like rest break, early departure, and refreshment) on productivity.
- Experimental group with six girl workers (including four girls selected by other two girls of the group) was formed and these

girls did their work from a test room. The main activities of the girls were assemblance of telephone relays.

- One observer (member of the research team) was associated with the experimental group to record all that happened, to make the girls aware of the experiment, to provide assistance when needed and to get to know their problems through active listening.
- A lot of changes were introduced to ascertain the effects of changes on productivity.
- All this is given in the Table 1.2

Table-1.2

Effects of changes on productivity

Type of changes	Details of changes	Result/effects
Time-rated work	Duty hours 48 in a week, no rest pause	Produced 2400 relays a week.
From time/rated work to piece-rated work	Duty hours 48 in a week.	Productivity increased.
Providing rest breaks	2 breaks 5 minutes each and then 2 breaks 10 minutes each	Productivity increased
Providing more rest breaks	6 breaks 5 minutes each	Productivity decreased
Providing hot meal	Hot meal at free of cost	Productivity increased
Allowing early departure from work place	Early departure from work place at 4. 30 p.m. instead of 5 p.m.	Productivity increased
Allowing much more early departure from work place	Departure from work place at 4 p.m. instead of 5 p.m.	Productivity neither increased nor decreased, remained constant
Restoring to earlier situation i.e., withdrawal of allamenities	Returned to original working condition with no rest pause, no hot meal, no early departure	Productivity increased to 3000 relays per week

Source: *Compiled from Human Relations and Organizational Behaviour by RS Dwivedi (Oxford & IBH Publishing Co Pvt, Ltd New Delhi 1987)*

- The study highlighted the change of attitudes of girl employees to excel performance as
    - they developed team spirit and unity with 7 members including the one who originally belonged to research group.
    - they felt that the company realized their importance in the company activities and solicited their cooperation and help.
    - they observed that they were not treated as commodities or saleable products by the company, they were rather treated as co-partners.
    - they developed a sense of belongingness, togetherness and 'we-ness' that generated a sense of responsibility.

Plant wide Interviewing Programme

- This is one the phases of the Hawthorne Studies.
- The interview programme was carried out during 1928 and 1930.
- Under this programme 20, 000 interviews were conducted.
- Both direct and non-direct questions were administered for collecting information, but more emphasis was given on 'non-directive' interviewing that allowed interviewers to listen instead of talk, advice and argue.
- The purpose of administering interview through 'non-directive' method was to generate a feeling of openness and trustworthiness amongst the interviewees to enable them to express their views, ideas, and factual occurences to the interviewer.
- The study through Interviewing Programme revealed that
    - the decision of the informal group had a great impact on the individual behaviour for performance of work.
    - the social group pressure in some cases was effective to restrict production and other activities of the group members
    - the workers perception about the status enjoyed by them in the company tended to be deciding factor of their satisfaction/ dissatisfaction with work.
    - providing opportunity to interviewee to talk, to express grievances under 'non-directive' method had a positive impact on their morale.

Bank Wiring Room Study

- This study was conducted between November 1931 and May 1932.
- This was the fourth phase of the Hawthorne Studies.

- The objective of the study was to find whether group pressure could restrict the production activity.
- In order to ascertain group pressure on the individual workers, observational analysis of the informal work- groups was made.

Some Relevant Information Concerning Study

i. Nine wiremen, three solder men and two inspectors were engaged on bank wiring.

ii. One observer who was friendly but appeared non-committal had been in the bank-wiring room along with the employees.

iii. The other person whose job was of an interviewer remained as an outsider and did his work under strict confidence in a different part of the factory. His primary task was to get to know the Mindset, feelings, attitudes, values, and thought process of the workers through interview method. He also maintained a constant linkage/touch with the observer to take stock of the behavioural manifestation of the group from time to time.

iv. The job of the employees in bank-wiring room involved attaching wires to switches for certain parts of the telephone equipment.

v. The observer was well accepted by the employees and became a member of the group. He earned confidence of the employees.

Observation Made by the Study

- The group emerged as an effective team with informal leaders.
- The group fixed the target of production which was 6000 units per day.
- The optimal capacity for production was much more then 6000 units; it was 7000 units per day.
- The factory introduced the incentive scheme for higher performer who would cross the limit set.
- Nobody could dare to produce more than the standard set by the group. If anybody attempted to produce more, he had to immediately return to his original quota so determined.
- The group decision was much more vital than the factory decision. So the group members did not think of producing more and getting financial incentive disregarding the group norms.
- The group fixed the target of production less than the capacity of production to protect the low performer, to check the raised

standard of the factory, to ensure continuance of employment in the factory.

- The group activity generated an unwritten code of conduct that helped identify the people on the basis of behavioural manifestation of the group members:
  - Rate buster who turned out too much
  - Chiseller who turned out too little work
  - Squealer submitted information/data to supervisor that could harm another member.

Conclusions

- Group activity is a necessity to achieve individual goals, team goals and organizational goals.
- Incentives fail to influence the group productivity.
- Group feeling and cohesiveness make the members ensure that the standard of output fixed by the group is maintained without regard to the standard set by the management.

Criticisms of the Hawthorne Studies

The human relations concept and the findings of the Hawthorne Studies have been criticized by various authors, experts. Some of the criticisms are mentioned below.

1. Scientific validity

Most of the conclusions drawn from the human relations studies are not supported by adequate scientific evidence (Brown, 1954). Company environments selected for study are not typical of industry generally.

According to some experts much of theoretical underpinning of human relations depends upon findings in clinical psychology which is concerned primarily with treatment rather than scientific research. So, main conclusion of the studies are based upon 'clinical insight' rather than upon controlled experiments (HJ Eysenek, 1953).

2. Maintaining the superiority of group decision over individual decision

Human relationists are criticized for maintaining the superiority of group decision over individual decision. Much more emphasis is laid on group activity. So, the individual loses his personality in stifling conformity to group norms.

3. Attitudinal perspectives

Attitudinal values of the people have not been given due importance by the researchers but in reality the attitudinal pattern of the individuals influences performance activities.

4. Financial support

Financial support/benefit satiates the people's physiological need that can act as motivator. This aspect has been neglected by the Hawthorne researchers. No doubt informal organization may help to satisfy social need and can act as one of the motivating tools but in no way can act as a substitute for it.

5. Role of trade union

Trade union plays an important role to influence the behaviour of the people at work. The workers are much more directed for work behaviour by the union than the group leader. This is quite obvious in strongly unionized industry.

6. Paternalistic activities of the management

It happens that management with expert ideas and thought process manipulates group activities through counselling, communication and other ways, and makes group leader ineffective in influencing the role behaviour of the group members.

7. Perception of researchers towards the people at work

The Hawthorne researchers look upon the workers as means to an end not as end in themselves.

Sound Human Relations: Some Important Steps

Sound human relations are an important requirement for achievement of organizational goals. Organization cannot achieve goals if the relationship between boss and subordinates in the organization is not positive. Positive dyadic relation generates a climate of mutuality, mutual understanding, mutual trust and mutual faith between boss and subordinates. This sort of human relationship facilitates the establishment of healthy industrial relations.

The following steps if adopted by the management can help improve human relation in the organization.

1. Attractive compensation package

Workers are happy and develop feeling of contentment when their services are compensated by attractive monetary and non-monetary package. People desire to satisfy their physiological and also psychological needs. They want to satisfy their physiological needs first and after that they go for satisfaction of psychological needs. So if the compensation package is well-planned, lucrative and excellent workers can meet their physiological needs easily to their greatest satisfaction, they reflect the same in their behavioural activities.

2. Higher degree of job satisfaction

Higher degree of job satisfaction makes the workers contented, committed and develops a sense of belonging to the company. Workers generate a feeling that they are treated as part and parcel of the company. So, they strive their best to increase their production and services for achievement of the company goals.

Human relations can be improved by enhancing the level of job satisfaction of workers through introduction of various measures like promotion, supervision, working conditions and others. Higher the job satisfaction, better are the human relations.

3. Grievance procedure

Human relations can be improved through introduction of a well-defined grievance procedure and its systematic functioning in the organization. Industrial employees may have a lot of grievances that need to be settled at the earliest. If there is no system of the disposal of the grievances, all these get accumulated to turn into bigger issues subsequently. Now the formulation of the grievance procedure and its implementation is a necessity for generating confidence amongst the employees with regard to company's concern for worker's problem.

4. Promotional opportunity

Employees need promotion to go up in the hierarchy. Nobody wants to remain in the same cadre for years together. The company should develop a career planning and development system to promote its employees.

If the employees are happy with promotional opportunities provided by the company, they feel proud of being the members of the company. They become loyal, committed to the work and to the organization, and develop better understanding, and rapport with the management which help improve human relations.

5. Supervisors' attitude

Supervisor's attitude plays an important role to develop human relations. If the employees are happy with the attitudes/activities of the supervisors, they come close to their bosses/supervisors and develop a great understanding with them. In the process a healthy dyadic relationship is established. Supervisor's attitude affects the group functioning/activities also. If the group members feel that a congenial working environment exists because of positive activities/attitudinal functioning of supervisors, they develop harmonious group relations tending towards sound human relations in the organization. So, greater the degree of positive attitudes of supervisor, better are the human relations.

6. Working environment of the organization

Working environment of the organization influences the human relation pattern. If a climate of openness, trust, authenticity and cohesiveness (OTAC) exists in the organization, there is the possibility of promoting healthy human relations. Openness includes climate where employees are free to interact with bosses, discuss problematic issues, and seek guidance, advice as and when required. The climate of trust indicates a situation where both boss and subordinates or employees amongst themselves believe each other. Authenticity gives the expression of the climatic situation where people do the same what they say. In a way it is of higher order than trust. That means there is a perfect understanding between stimulus givers and respondents. Cohesiveness environment creates a situation where all the employees think and work identically treating them as un-separated entity. This sort of OTAC environment helps develop sound human relations in the organization.

7. Recognition of employees

As a step toward promoting human relations it is vital to see how the employees are treated in the organization, that is, to find whether they are considered assets/resources or simply marketable commodities. If employees feel that they are given recognition by the company as assets, important partners for achievement of goals, the possibility of establishing healthy human relation exists. Employees cannot develop sound human relation when they are not considered as human beings. So, for promoting human relations, acceptance of employees as assets, human resources is a must.

8. Morale of employees

Human relations are developed if the employees do have higher degree of morale. So, improvement of morale is one of the requirements for promoting human relations. Greater the degree of morale of employees, better are the human relations.

9. Employee empowerment

It is one of the needs of the human beings that they should have power, authority, responsibility in the organizations where they work. So, if the employees are given authority with responsibility to structure/ design their job for effective and efficient performance, they will develop a sense of interest to work, a sense of belonging to the organization and commitment to the work. All this will help improve human relations.

10. Employee participation and involvement

Employees will feel happy if they are allowed to participate in the decision making process and are involved in various activities. This will improve human relations pattern of the employees because employees start feeling that they contribute to the achievement of organizational goals through their active participation and involvement in various activities.

11. Other measures

The following measures can promote human relations

a) Using positive stroking in presence of people like praise, appreciation, a word of thanks for excellent performance, activities, etc.

b) Empathetic activities of the management to sort out problems of the subordinates.

c) Developing effective communication channel for the employees in the organization.

d) Adopting various motivational techniques by the management.

e) Rational and just treatment of the workers by the management where there is place for nepotism, favouritism, and double standards in their activities.

Differences Between Industrial Relations and Human Relations

The differences between industrial relations and human relations are given in Table 1. 3.

Table: 1. 3

Differences between Industrial Relations and Human Relations

Dimension	Industrial Relations	Human Relations
1. Concept	It is the relationship between employer, employees and government.	It is the relationship arising out of interaction between the people in the organization.
2. Step	It is the next step towards establishment of relationship between parties, after human relation.	It is the first step towards industrial relation.
3. Destination	It is an end in itself.	It is a means to an end.
4. Parties	In a broader sense it needs three parties– employer/employers' association, employees/ employees' union and government/ government agencies.	It needs two or more persons.
5. Emphasis	Emphasis is given on employer-employees relationship.	Emphasis is given on group behaviour in work teams.
6. Trade union	Union plays an important role to contribute to the development of industrial relations.	Union has no/less contribution to the promotion of human relations.
7. Group Dynamics	Group dynamics is not much effective to shape the industrial relations pattern of the organization.	Group dynamics influences to promote human relations.
8. Impact	Impact of industrial relations is far reaching. It affects employer, employees, society and the nation.	Impact of human relations is not far reaching. It affects the particular organization only. That means people at work in the organization.

9. Multi-dimension	It is multi-dimensional.	It is not so multi-dimensional.
10. Factors	Factors like technological advancement, market, government interference, international relation, economy, trade union, etc., have direct bearing on industrial relations.	Factors like technological advancement, market, international relation, economy, trade union, etc., do not have direct bearing on the human relations.
11. Individual grievances	It includes varied problems.	Individual grievances predominate.
12. Solution	Solution of problems needs expertise, competency, special tact and other qualitative attributes.	It is comparatively easy to solve problem.
13. Consequences	Sound industrial relations promote all round development/ improvement and reverse is the case when industrial relations is unhealthy.	Sound human relations tend to promote mutual understanding, mutual faith, and mutual trust with consequential effect. Unsound human relations generates a feeling of suspicions, confusion, apprehension, uncertainty, hatred and helplessness. Human relations effect on congenial work place environment.
14. Approach	It is a people centred approach	It is an individual person- centred approach.
15. Application	It has a wider application	It has comparatively less application.

Books Recommended

1. Jack Halloran: *Applied Human Relations – An Organizational Approach* (Prentice- Hall of India Private Limited, New Delhi, 1998)
2. D Katz: *Morale and Motivation in Industry in Current Trends in Industrial Psychology* (Pittsburgh, University of Pittsburg Press, 1949)
3. French Derek and Heather Saward: *Dictionary of Management* (Pan Books, London 1977)
4. DE Mac Farland: *Management: Principles and Practice* (Macmillan & Co, New York 1970)
5. Keith Davis: *Human Behaviour at work Organizational Behaviour* (Tata McGraw Hill Publishing Company Ltd, New Delhi, 1980)
6. RS Dwivedi: *Human Relations and Organizational Behaviour* (Oxford and IBH Publishing Co. Pvt Ltd, New Delhi, 1987)
7. SG Huneryager and IL Heekmans: *Human Relation in Management* (DB Taraporevala Sons & Co Private Limited Mumbai 1, 1972)
8. AK Ghosh: *Managing Human Resources: Strategic Approach to Win* (Manas Publications, New Delhi, 2002)
9. JL Latham: *Human Relations in Business* (Columbus, Ohio; Charles E Merrill Books, Inc 1964)
10. F Luthans: *Organizational Behaviour* (McGraw Hill Publishing Company, 1981, New Delhi)
11. JAC Brown: *The Social Psychology of Industry* (London, Penguin 1954)
12. HJ Eysenek: *Uses and abuses of psychology* (London, Pelican, 1953)

Questions

1. "Human relations is motivating people in organizational settings to develop team work which accomplishes individual as well as organizational goals effectively". – As a student of MBA do you justify this statement? Explain.
2. Discuss briefly the salient characteristics of human relations.
3. Human relations play an important role to contribute to the smooth and effective functioning of organizational activities. Do you endorse it? Produce your arguments in support of your views.
4. What is human relations? Discuss in some detail the factors that necessitated the human relations movement.
5. Give a brief overview of human relations movement.
6. What were the major phases of the Hawthorne Studies? Discuss in brief the procedures and findings of each phase.

7. As an IR executive of a company what steps will you suggest to improve human relations in the organization?
8. Some say Human Relations and Industrial Relations are the same. As a student of MBA, how will you explain this?
9. Write short notes on:
   i. Objectives of Human Relations
   ii. Illumination Experiments
   iii. Relay Room Experiment
   iv. Interviewing Programme
   v. Bank Wiring Room Study.

Case Study

Mrs Sulochana is a clerk attached to Regional office of a nationalised Bank in Bangalore. She is intelligent and particular about her assigned task. She completes her allotted job much earlier than the usual time. Her output is more than average. She is smart, obedient and polished. She excels in communication. Normally, she commits no mistake in her work. She enjoys positive strokes from her immediate boss, Mr Naresh Kumar for perfection and accuracy in her work. She can grasp her assigned job in no time and renders service to the utmost satisfaction of her boss. She never says no to her superior whenever any additional task is given.

Mrs Sulochana has some shortcomings. She likes leisure period. She cannot work for long at a stretch. After doing some work, she feels bored, uneasy and fatigued. She cannot remain in her seat after the assigned task is finished and she moves to other colleagues who remain engaged at their job. She starts gossiping and disturbs their work.

She has the habit of remaining absent frequently without taking prior permission. She sends messages to her boss about her not coming to office. On resumption of duties she submits application for sanction of leave. She frequently leaves office with permission from her boss before the scheduled time of departure on flimsy pretexts.

She keeps her immediate boss happy who appreciates her and gives her recognition for quality work. Since she does not keep allotted jobs pending, her boss gives her some relaxation for attending/departing office. She has developed a good understanding with the boss and has earned confidence in her work. She is responsible and accountable to her immediate boss, Mr Naresh Kumar for her work performance but her attendance, punctuality, salary and leave administration are controlled by Mr Chanakya Bhat, Senior Manager (Office Administration). Mr Bhat keeps a close watch on her mobility and attendance activities at the office.

Mr Bhat is a non-acceptable person. He is a negative personality. He never helps people. He does not believe in the motivational approach. He does not treat people as human beings. He perceives people as non-performers and leisure seekers. He is an autocrat in his behaviour and activities.

In the instant case Mrs Sulochana resumed her duties after three days of absence. All these three days she informed office about her absence. Mr Bhat was away from headquarters during those three days. The day Mrs Sulochana came to report for duties, Mr Kumar was present. On seeing Mrs Sulochana, Mr Bhat started firing her. The following transactions/ exchange of stimuli and responses occurred between them.

Mr Bhat: Why have you not submitted your leave application?

Mrs Sulochana: Sir, our office hour starts from 10 a. m. It is now 5 munutes to 10 a. m. I have just come to attend office after my illness.

Mr Bhat: On earlier occasions also you delayed submission of your applications for sanction of leave of absence.

Mrs Sulochana: Sir, it had not happened in my case. Everytime I got my leave sanctioned before I proceeded for privilege leave or I sent a communication to office about my inability to attend office when it was a casual or sick leave.

Mr Bhat: No, no, you are not correct. You are in the habit of not submitting leave applications on time. This time also you have repeated the same thing. You did not bother to inform us about your not coming to office.

Mrs Sulochana: Sir, I telephoned at the office. I wanted to talk to you but you were out of headquarters three days ago. I gave the information to Mr Kumar, my boss about my indisposition. I also told him that I would not be able to join duty for three or four days. I never delayed submitting my application for sanction of leave of absence. I know the rules as I have rendered 20 years of service with the organization.

Mr Bhat: Don't talk about 20 years' service. I know how to set the thing right. You have no casual leave to your credit and for sanctioning privilege leave, one has to apply 30 days ahead of the date of availing of privilege leave.

Mrs Sulochana: Since I have no casual leave credit balance, you will have to sanction privilege leave.

Mr Bhat: You have become over smart. You do not know how to talk? Are you commanding me to sanction privilege leave? I will teach you a lesson.

Mrs Sulochana: Sir, I did not mean that. I simply wanted to say that if my casual leave was exhausted, it is you, my superior boss, to see how my absence period would be adjusted, may be by debiting privilege leave. (Then she started crying.)*

Read the above case thoroughly and answer the following questions.

1. What sort of relationship is established between Mrs Sulochana and Mr Kumar?
2. Do you think the relationship between Sulochana and Mr Bhat arises out of interpersonal conflict?
3. If you were the Head of HR Department at Bangalore Regional office of the bank how would you tackle such problem?
4. If the relationship between supervisors and subordinates in an organization is almost the same as that of relationship established between Mrs Sulochana and Mr Bhat, do you think it will have an adverse effect on promoting harmonious industrial relations? Why?
5. As a Student of MBA what suggestions will you preserbe to improve industrial relations in the bank?

---

*[*Source: AK Ghosh: Human Resource Management (with cases), Manas Publications, New Delhi, 2006, PP 383-386*]

II

TRADE UNIONISM

Introduction

People get employed in different organizations, institutions, hospitals, and clubs to perform their jobs assigned to them. But it happens that sometimes they cannot give their best because their problems, grievances remain unattended by the management. Such people feel dissatisfied, discontented, insecured, uncared, and develop an urge to consolidate their strength to protect their interest jointly, and collectively. So, they form associations. The formation of such an association by the people at work for maintaining and improving their working conditions and protecting their interest through joint and collective action is known as a trade union.

Meaning of Trade Union

The term 'trade union' has been defined by various authors, experts differently. The dictionary meaning of trade union is society of workers formed to protect their interest (Collins Gem English Dictionary). Sydney Webb and Beatrice Webb expressed that a 'trade union' is continuous association of wage earners for the purpose of maintaining or improving the conditions at work. Dale Yoder has defined trade union as continuing, long term association of employees formed and maintained for the specific purpose of advancing and protecting the interest of members in their relationship. The trade union is, therefore, defined as an association of people at work formed to protect and promote their interest through generating a climate of mutuality, mutual understanding, mutual trus' and mutual confidence. Under the Trade Unions Act 1926 the term 'tra' union' is defined as any combination, whether temporary or permanent, formed primarily for the purpose of regulating the relations between workmen and employers or between workmen and workmen or between employers and employers or for imposing restrictive conditions on the conduct of any trade or business, and includes any federation of two or more trade unions.

Characteristics of Trade Union

The important characteristics of trade union include the following:

- It is an association either of employers or of employees
- The trade unions particularly workers' union are usually formed permanently.
- The trade union is formed to protect and promote the interest of its members.
- It is a continuous associations of workers.
- It settles issues of the workers through direct negotiation with management (that means through collective bargaining mechanism).
- It regulates, and promotes labour management relations of the company.
- It includes federation of two or more unions.
- It has a changing nature of activities.
- The trade unions are influenced by a number of ideologies.
- The prime interest with which a trade union is formed is economic.

Objectives of Trade Unions

The objectives of trade unions are discussed below:

1. Economic conditions

One of the main objectives of trade union is to ensure adequate wages or salaries to the workers for the services rendered by them in the organization. The trade union, on behalf of workers places the charter of demands including the demand for higher wages/salaries before the management and initiates for the settlement of issues through collective bargaining mechanism. Thus, arranging to enhance wages/salaries of the employees, the trade union leadership helps improve the economic conditions of the employees.

2. Redressal of grievances

Workers may have a lot of problems, grievances while working in the organization. Trade union officials demand for setting up grievance redressal process for expeditious disposal of grievances. The trade unions make the workers happy, contented through effective and smooth working of grievance redressal procedure.

3. Working Condition

Working conditions like ventilation, temperature, rest rooms, drinking water, lighting, safety appliances, etc., affect health of employees that influences production a great deal. All these are required to be provided to the employees by the companies in terms of provisions of various laws. In case of non-compliances/not providing the benefits, trade union puts pressure on the management for compliance.

4. Welfare and social security

Trade union leadership demands for providing welfare and social security benefits to the employees as per laws, agreements and launches various agitational measures against the management till such benefits are provided. The benefits like canteen facilities, housing accommodation, transport arrangement, medical facilities, retiral benefits, etc., come under the purview of welfare and social security benefits.

5. Disciplinary activities

It happens that management in some organizations takes disciplinary action against the employees not in conformity with laws, rules, standing orders. Under such situation trade union restrains management from taking disciplinary action against employees which is unfair, unjust, illegal and irrational.

6. Implementation of agreement, award, policies

Some organizations do not honour agreement, court verdict, awards; do not implement personnel policies formulated by them. All this makes the workers unhappy, discontented and creates a climate of suspicion, distrust between employees and management. Trade union submits such issues to the management and pressurizes them for immediate implementation.

7. Healthy industrial relations

One of the objectives of the trade unions is to develop sound industrial relations in the organizations. Trade union plays a pivotal role to sort the conflicting issues emerged in the process of negotiation with the

the management and to reach an amicable settlement. Such settlement arising out of mutual understanding, consensus helps promote healthy relations between employer and employees.

8. Congenial and conducive climate

Constructive activities of the trade union ensure smooth and effective functioning of the organization where a situation like go slow, work-to-rule, strike is a remote possibility. In the process of working, employees develop a mutual understanding, mutual faith and confidence with their bosses and feel comfortable to work in such environment. All this makes the organizational climate congenial and conducive to work.

9. Helping and supporting

Helping the workers at the time of necessity through financial and mental support is one of the objectives of trade union. It happens that during strike and in difficult situation the workers may need support, help to strengthen their mental base and energy to face the crisis situation.

10. Psychological need satiation

Every employee wants status, recognition, authority, responsibility, challenging job and also self-actualization. All this is possible through implementation of a well-designed promotion policy and creation of a climate of mutuality. In this case a trade union with its supportive, facilitative and rational outlook can contribute a lot.

11. Industrial democracy

One of the objectives is to ensure that industrial democracy is achieved. That means workers will have a say in running the industry.

Trade Union Movement: Some Conceptual Differences from Labour Movement

It may appear that trade union/labour union and labour movement are not separate entities; but interwoven ones. Some say trade union is the outcome of labour movement. So, both are interrelated, and there is no difference between trade union and labour movement. But on thorough examination of various perspectives of trade union and labour movement it gives the idea that there are differences between trade union and labour movement. The Table 2.1 depicts a clear picture of difference between trade union and labour movement.

Table 2.1

Differences between trade union movement and labour movement.

Dimension	Trade union movement	Labour movement
Concept	It is an association of the people at work formed to protect and promote their interests.	It is a movement of the working class for the common cause and interests of the workers.
Scope	It has a limited scope. It looks to the interest, benefits of small number of people.	It has a wider scope. It looks to the interest, benefits of the entire working class.
Nature	The movement is made by the workers.	The movement is made for the workers.
Period of origin	It started much later, may be during second decade of twentieth century.	It started much early, may be during last quarter of nineteenth century.
Objective	Its objective is to protect and promote the interests of the employees through generating a climate of mutuality–mutual understanding, mutual trust and mutual confidence.	Its objective is to generate and promote a feeling of association, class consciousness, self-reliance and solidarity.
Emphasis	Emphasis is given mainly for the well-being of the workers/ employees who are members of the concerned union.	Emphasis is given to develop a spirit of combination, solidarity amongst workers that may help to change the mindset of the employees for overall betterment of the working class.
Result	Its activities may bring immediate result.	It takes a long time to achieve results.

Formation	It is formed with the employees of the concerned organization	It is composed of many forms of organizations having common need to serve a common interest of the workers.
Degree of consciousness	It does not convey a high degree of consciousness amongst workers.	It gives the massage to manifest higher degree of consciousness amongst workers.
Basis	It is an essential basis of labour movement.	It has a separate entity. But it cannot exist without trade unions, because they are the principal schools in which the workers learn the lesson of self-reliance and solidarity. (GDH Cole)
Control	Its activities are regulated/controlled by statutes, laws.	The statutory control is less in its normal activities.

Rationality of Joining Trade Unions

A question may arise, 'why do employees join trade unions?' or 'what is the rationality of joining trade unions?' It is sure that employees get some benefits, help, assistance, support from trade unions if they become their members. And these they cannot get if they do not join trade unions. Now, let us see how the trade unions benefit the employees. The trade unions help the employees in the following manner.

i. Trade unions help the employees to get fair and rational wages. Trade unions through collective bargaining process negotiate with the management for fair and rational wages and arrive at a settlement. The employees, therefore, can satisfy their physiological needs.

ii. Trade unions ensure healthy working conditions for the employees.

iii. The employees desire to have security of job and this they can have if strong trade unions exist in the organizations. The employers find it difficult to arbitrarily exercise 'hire and fire' policy because of strong trade unions.

iv. Every employee wants promotion in the career activity. Trade unions demand for better promotion policy for the employees of the organization.

v. Employees want a sound industrial relations climate in the organization. Trade unions play an important role to establish healthy industrial relations through active participation in the disputes settlement exercise.

vi. Trade union help in designing and developing better HR/IR policies in the organization.

vii. Employees want a higher degree of quality of working life (QWL) and this is possible when trade unions with positive values, constructive activities help management to run organization smoothly, effectively and achieve its goals.

viii. It is the trade union that can change the mindset of the employees to give quality production, quality service, to face challenges and help the company to obtain competitive advantages. So, in the process of company's growth and development, employees growth and development is also ensured.

ix. Trade unions help the employees to satiate their social needs by making them official members of the union and involving them in union activities.

x. Employees have a desire to participate in the decision making process, to secure some power, authority to involve in the company's policy making exercise and to be part and parcel of the company. Trade unions help the employees to fulfill their desire in all such activities by creating pressure on the management.

xi. Employees want to make the management know about their problems, demands and difficulties and they find the trade union is an appropriate platform for such purpose.

Functions of Trade Unions

Trade unions need to perform a lot of functions looking to the interest of its own organizations, its members, the industrial organizations where the members are working, society and the nation as a whole. To discuss in detail the functions of trade unions, it is pertinent to have some ideas about the functions as mentioned in the Trade Unions Act 1926, Report of the First National Commission on Labour and the First Five-Year Plan.

Functions of Trade Unions as per Trade Unions Act, 1926

According to Section 2(h) of the Trade Unions Act 1926 the primary purpose of formation of trade union is, interalia, to regulate the relations between workmen and employer and to impose restrictive conditions on the conduct of any trade or business. Here, union activities for regulating relations and imposing restrictive practices are made basically for protecting and promoting interests of the workers and conditions of their employment. So, protecting and promoting interests of the workers and conditions of their employment are the main functions of the trade union.

Functions of Trade Union as Recommended by the National Commission on Labour

- To secure fair wages for workers.
- To safeguard the security of tenure and improve conditions of service.
- To enlarge opportunities for promotion and training.
- To improve working and living conditions.
- To provide for educational, cultural and recreational facilities.
- To cooperate and facilitate technological advancement by broadening the understanding of workers in the issues involved in their jobs.
- To promote identity of interests of the workers with their industry.
- To offer responsive cooperation in improving levels of production and productivity, discipline and high standards of quality.
- To promote individual and collective welfare.

Functions of Trade Union as Emphasised in the First Five–Year plan

- To present plans to workers so as to create enthusiasm among them for the plans.
- To exercise the utmost restraint in regard to work stoppage.
- To formulate wage demands which are attuned to the requirements of economic development and are in keeping with consideration of social justice.
- To assume greater responsibility for the success of the productive effort.

Functions of Trade Union for the Benefits of its Members

Trade unions put in all-out efforts and strive hard to benefit its members in the following ways.

- To secure wages/salaries, incentives, bonus and other benefits in terms of agreement, award, settlement, laws, etc.
- To enhance standard of living in the changing situation when organizations obtain competitive advantages and make considerable profit, by putting pressure in collective bargaining discussions.
- To ensure that statutory provisions of rest shelter, canteen services, working hours, health and safety measures and working conditions are complied with.
- To protect from unfair labour practices by employers.
- To ensure that grievance redressal procedure is set up and functions effectively.
- To protect from exploitation, victimization by employers.
- To generate a feeling of being an important partner in the organization.
- To help introduce schemes like employee empowerment, employee participation in decision making in organizations.
- To create awareness concerning rights and duties.
- To raise status in the organization and in the society as well.
- To make them know the usefulness of grievance settlement mechanism/methods like collective bargaining, joint negotiation/ discussion, voluntary arbitration.
- To provide financial and mental support during strike, lockout, lay-off, sickness and in other difficult periods.
- To provide adequate welfare and social security measures.

Function of Trade Unions for the Benefits of the Company

- To help the company run it smoothly, uninterruptedly and effectively.
- To ensure that workers will give maximum production of quality goods through observance of norms laid down jointly by the management and trade union.
- To raise the company's stature, image in the market by promoting a culture of joint consultation, cooperation and mutuality.
- To help the company make the people committed, satisfied and contented by enhancing the degree of quality of working life (QWL) and promoting healthy industrial relations in the

organization to enable it to face challenges emerged in the hypercompetitive market, and obtain competitive advantage.

- To ensure maintenance of discipline in the organization.
- To help develop a congenial and conducive climate in the organization and to explore the alternatives to punitive action against the delinquent employees.
- To create a good image about the trade union and its members in the minds of the management.
- To help the organization introduce schemes, programmes for the growth and development of the employees and the organization as well.
- To create opportunity for empowerment of employees and also for participation in management decision making process.
- To develop an understanding with the company for expeditious disposal of employee grievances through setting up grievance redressal procedure and ensure effective working of the grievance procedure.

Functions of Trade Union for the Benefits of the Union Organization

- To create a positive image in the minds of the public about trade union and its constructive activities in the society.
- To educate the members to promote loyalty towards union organization.
- To take steps to create a solid financial strength by ensuring regular collection of subscription and also by enhancing the rate of subscription of members.
- To develop a sound database in the various areas like socio-economic conditions of workers/societal people, job satisfaction and moral level of employees, desires, expectations and attitudes of workers; and take some measures to guide to follow right dimension.
- To publish periodicals, bulletin for promoting understanding, knowledge of the employees in the various fields of activities.
- To create a good linkage between the company and union organization.
- To introduce a system of union democracy in the administration of the union organization with the objectives to make an impact on industry administration.

- To remove inter union rivalry by promoting the urge to solidarity and unity amongst all workers irrespective of their attachment to the union.
- To change the union strategy to achieve its objectives in the hyper changing socio-economic situation.
- To ensure that union organization is not used as a tool to meet the needs of some vested interested persons.
- To develop competencies of members who can be assigned the role of leadership in future.

Functions of Trade Union for the Benefits of the Society

- To take measures to eradicate communalism, casteism through launching various programmes in the society.
- To ensure uninterrupted supply of domestic goods and other necessities by keeping the production activities running and effectively functioning.
- To create opportunity for employment of local people by putting pressure on the management.
- To put in efforts to stop unsocial and corrupt practices like increasing price by hoarding, smuggling, black-marketing, giving and taking dowry, etc., through launching campaigns and generating awareness amongst societal people against such activities.
- To help the unorganized working class to organize itself.
- To help maintain social peace and harmony by creating a congenial and conducive climate in industry.

Functions of Trade Union for the Benefits of the Nation

- To help the government implement the schemes/programmes like family planning, afforestation, national integration by creating awareness amongst the people.
- To ensure increase of revenue of the government by keeping the industrial activities functioning smoothly and effectively.
- To participate actively on the development programme of the country.
- To help the government to enact legislation for the development of the country by giving suggestion on the matter.

Theories of Trade Unionism/Approaches to the Origin of Trade Union

Various authors and experts studied, examined and explored the factors that led to the origin of trade unions. So there is no one theory of trade unionism. Multiple theories have originated. Some of the important theories of trade unions are given below:

1. Theory of Industrial Democracy/Webbs' Theory of Industrial Democracy
2. Socio – psychological Theory of Robert Hoxie
3. Revolution Theory of Karl Marx
4. Protest Theory of Kerr and Associates
5. Frank Tannenbaum's Socialist Theory
6. Mahatma Gandhi's Trusteeship Theory

All the above theories are discussed in brief:

1. Theory of Industrial Democracy/Webb's Theory of Industrial Democracy

According to Sydney Webb and Beatrice Webb, trade unionism is an extension of democracy from the political sphere to that of industry. It may equalize the bargaining power of labour and capital. Hence, it would be possible to establish uniform rules, which they called as common rules, in respect of wages, working hours and working conditions. Webbs asserted that 'trade union movement is not an instrument of revolution to overthrow the capitalistic order'. They felt that the solution of class conflict could be made in equality of bargaining power and collective negotiation. According to Webbs the methods of collective bargaining, mutual insurance and legal enactment would help improve the economic status of the workers and also to infuse industrial democracy[1].

2. Socio-Psychological Theory of Robert Hoxie

Robert Hoxic gave the idea that trade unionism grew out of socio-psychological environment of workers. Economic consideration was not the only reason for the origin of trade union. He asserted that 'workers, who are economically and socially associated and not too divergent in temperaments and training, will tend to develop a common interpretation of the social situation and a common solution of the problem of living'. [2] This makes them unite to form trade union. According to him, unionism

1 Webb, Sydney and Webb, Beatrice, *Industrial Democracy*, Longmans, Green & Co., London, 1897.

2 Hoxie, R.H, *Trade Unionism in the United State*, 1923, p6.

is the result of group psychology generated from environmental situation and temperamental characteristics of its members. Differences of environment cause different unions to develop. Hoxie classified 5 types of unions on the basic of structure and functional operations. His classifications include.

- Business unionism also known as bread and butter unionism for protecting the interests of various craftsmen through the use of collective bargaining mechanism.
- Friendly or uplift unionism for promoting moral, intellectual and social life of members such as association of sales engineer
- Revolutionary unionism for replacing the capitalist system by the socialistic system through political and violent means like strike, sabotage, etc.
- Predatory unionism which does not subscribe to any ideology can adopt any method that may deliver the goods.
- Dependent unionism that appears in two forms – company unionism relying upon the support of the company and label unionism depending upon the union label imprinted on the product made by union members.

3. Revolutionary Theory of Karl Marx

According to Karl Marx trade unions represent a prime instrument for abolition of the capitalist class and the origin of trade unionism lies in the growth of industrial capitalism. Both Karl Marx and Engels admitted that with the development of industry the proletariat not only increased in number, it became concentrated in greater masses, its strength grew, and it felt much stronger. The competition among industrial capitalists increased, commercial crisis appeared and wages of the workers fluctuated. The collision between individual workman and individual employer took more and more character of collisions between two classes. Then workers felt the necessity to form association. They clubbed together in order to keep up the rates of wages and found permanent association. To Karl Marx, trade unions by themselves cannot do more than carry on the economic struggle of workers and can continue to bring about a revolutionary transformation of working class.

4. Protest Theory of Kerr and Associates

According to C Kerr, John T Dunlop, FH Harbinson and CA Myres workers' protest is inherent in industrialization. The process of industrialization creates a new environment in industrial setting. It makes a change in relationship between man and his work and also between man and his cultural-setting. A kind of discipline is imposed on him that circumscribes his freedom. He often finds the task distasteful, his compensation is not adequate to his needs and never commensurate with contribution[3]. Formation of union is one of the organized form of protest – a manifestation of workers' resentment over the prevailing industrial system.

5. Frank Tannenbaum's Societal Theory

Frank Tannenbaum observed that 'the emergence of unionism is spontaneous, unpremeditated. It is inherent in the growth of capitalism. It reflects the urge of human beings to create a society'.[4] According to him, workers migrated from rural background to urban industrial location, they developed a feeling of loneliness, loss of community and alienation. At this crucial point of time union formed to give back to his workers their society and code of conduct by which they can live in. So, unions are reflections of worker's sentiment, urge, desire to reestablish their identity and to get back to their social life.

6. Mahatma Gandhi's Trusteeship Theory

Mahatma Gandhi considers trade unions as essentially reformist organizations and economic institutions, and they should be organized on the basis that labour and capital are not antagonistic but are supplementary to each other. His philosophy is based on the principles of truth, non-violence and trusteeship in which class harmony prevails

Gandhiji observed that labour and capital should be a great family living in unity and harmony; capital should not only be looking to the material welfare of the labourers but their moral welfare also. The capitalist should be the trustee of the welfare of the labouring classes under them. Trade Unionism is not anti- capitalist. It wants due share of labourers, nothing more, and this not by paralysing capital but by reform among labourers form within and by their own self- consciousness[5].

According to Gandhiji, workers should treat the business of their employers as if it were their own business. They have the right to get justice done to their reasonable demands, and grievances. They should submit their demands before the employers for redressal and if their just, and reasonable demands are not redressed, they should go for a strike in a peaceful and non-violent way, but the strike should be the last resort

3 Kerr, C; Dennlop JT; Harbinson FM; and Myres CA *The Labour Problems in Economic Development*, International Labour Review, Volume 46, P6.

4 Tannenbaum, FA: *Philosophy of Labour*, 1951, P 14.

5 Quoted in *The Ahmedabad Experiment in Labour Management Relations*, (International Labour Review, 1959)

when all other means of persuading the capitalists to concede to their just demands are exhausted.

Growth and Development of the Trade Unions in India

The development of trade unions in India is seen after the factory system of operation had started, particularly in the second half of the nineteenth century. The growth and development of the trade unions in India can be divided into the following periods, each of them manifesting characteristics different from others.

1. Early Period of Trade Unions
   (The period upto 1918)
2. Post-World War 1 Period of Trade Unions
   (The Period from 1919 to 1923)
3. Leftist's Trade union Period
   (The period from 1924 to 1934)
4. Trade Union's Unity and Activity period
   (The period from 1935 to 1947)
5. Post-Independence Period
   (The period after 1947)

Now, the growth and development of Indian trade unions is discussed in brief.

1. Early Period of Trade Unions (Upto 1918)

Large scale industries started coming up in India after 1850. The textiles mills in Bombay had begun to operate from 1851 while Jute mills in Kolkata started functioning from 1854. The railways started its operation in 1853. The working conditions of the workers in factories were appallingly low. Workers did not enjoy job security. The situation like excessively long hours of work, poor wages, employment of women and children in factories, poor housing were common in all factories during this period. There were no trade unions existing in Indian industrial settings. In 1875, Sorabjee Shahpurjee Bengali led a movement in Bombay for legislative measures against the sufferings of the workers. The first trade union in India called the Bombay Mill Hands Association was set up in Bombay in 1890 by the honest and active initiative of Mr NM Lokhande to pressurize the then Government foramending the Factories Act, 1881 and also to improve the working conditions of workers. Subsequently this Act was amended and a new Act was passed in 1891. However, in real sense, the Bombay Mill Hands Association was not a trade union, for it had no membership, no fund, no rules and it did not organize any real sort of working class struggle against the employers. Mr Lokhande was a philanthropic promoter of labour legislation and workers' welfare not a pioneer of labuor organization or labour struggle[6].

After 1891, a large number of labour unions were formed in the country, the most important of them being

- The amalgamated Society of Railway Servants of India, 1897
- The Printers' Union, Calcutta, 1905
- The Bombay Postal Union, 1907
- The Kamgar Hitvardhak Sabha, 1909
- The Social Service League, 1910

All these labour organizations were not trade unions in the true sense. They worked as labour welfare associations to improve the lot of workers through government measures. After the grievances were settled, unions' functions ceased. These organizations could not generate class consciousness among the people at work. They did not have definite aims, strategy, and lacked constitution.

Some labour unions were mostly sectarian in nature. The majority office bearers of the unions like Bombay Mill Hands' Associations and Kamgar Hitvardhak Sabha hailed form the backward Maratha communities while the members of the amalgamated Society of Railway Servants of India came from the Anglo-Indian and European communities in India.

This period witnessed a chain of strikes in the major industries in the country, some of them are given below:

- Strike resorted to by the weavers in Ahmedabad in 1895
- Strike in jute mills in Calcutta in 1896
- Mill-workers strike in Bombay in 1897
- Strike in Madras Press in 1903

The workers experienced the power of united action through measures of strike, but in effect no trade union in real sense was prevalent during this period.

2. Post-World War I Period of Trade Unions (1919 to 1923)

The real beginning of the labour union movement in India started after the outbreak of World War I. Between 1919 and 1923 many unions came into existence in the country. The factors influencing the growth of trade unions in India during this period were as follows:

6 Dutt, Palme R : *India Today*, People's Publishing House, Bombay (1949) p – 375

- Formation of International Labour Organization (ILO) in 1919 to protect the interests of working class at the international level.
- Setting up of occupational unions like 'Spinners' union and weavers' union at Ahmedabad, federated into the industrial union known as Textile Labour Association, Ahmedabad in 1920.
- Formation of the All India Trade Union Congress (AITUC) in 1920.
- Political disturbance in the country that made an impact on the working class. The repressive measures of the Government of India like Jallianwala Bagh massacre, Martial Law, non-cooperation movement launched by Mahatma Gandhi, mass movement started by Lokmanya Tilak, Annie Beasant made the working class serious for launching labour movement.
- Enactment of the Indian Trade Unions Act 1926 providing legal protection to the workers.
- Unprecedented rise in prices of essential commodities during world war without corresponding rise in wages that prompted workers to organize union.

3. Leftists' Trade Union Period (1924–1934)

The revolutionary waves generated by the Russian Revolution influenced the Indian leaders to take interest in trade union activities. The publication of the English weekly 'Socialist' by SA Dange in 1923 in Bombay and a Bengali weekly 'Janawani' by Muzaffar Ahmed in Calcutta intensified the trade union movement. A number of violent and long-drawn out strikes were held in several industrial areas in 1924 which resulted in prosecution, imprisonment of many communist leaders. The communists held the control of the General Council and Executive Committee of the AITUC. A difference of opinion was generated between rightists and leftists in the trade union organizations. The moderates under the leadership of NM Joshi and the representatives of 24 affiliated unions seceded from the AITUC and formed a separate union All India Trade Union Federation (AITUF) in 1929. Another split took place in the AITUC when a section of union members led by SV Deshpande and BT Ranadive broke away at the Calcutta congress session in 1931 and formed the All India Red Trade Union Congress (AIRTUC).

Looking to the trend of continuous split in the AITUC that had affected the solidarity of trade union movement, the Railwaymen's Federation came forward to unite the AITUC and AITUF. For such purpose Trade Union Unity Committee was formed in 1932. Alternatively, a body with a new name was suggested and the National Trade Union Federation (NTUF) was formed in 1933. The unions affiliated to AITUF and railway union joined NTUF. However, efforts were made to unify the AITUC and the NTUF. In 1934, the AIRTUC (All India Red Trade Union Congress) was disbanded and the unions affiliated to AIRTUC came back to the AITUC.

During this period a number of important Acts were passed viz., the Workmen's Compensation Act, 1923, the Trade Unions Act, 1926, the Trade Disputes Act, 1929 and all these Acts stimulated the trade union leaders to intensify their movement for the betterment of the labour community.

In July 1929, the Royal Commission on Labour was appointed by the Government to enquire into and report on the existing conditions of labour in industrial undertakings and plantation in respect of health, efficiency, standard of living and also the relations between workers and employers. A substantial increase in union membership and number of trade unions were found. The number of registered trade unions rose to 170 in 1932-33 while the total membership of the unions stood to 237369 covering 147 unions that submitted returns to the Registrar of Trade Unions.

4. Trade Unions' Unity and Activity Period (1935-1947)

This period showed a phenomenal growth of trade unions in Indian industrial undertakings. The number of registered trade unions rose to 1837 in 1946-47 and the total number of membership of 998 unions which submitted returns increased to 13, 31962. [7] The following factors contributed to the growth and development of trade unionism in India during this period:

- Introduction of the Government of India Act, 1935 which provided for the labour/trade union constituencies for election of representatives to the legislatures. This made the labour unions united to promote unity and solidarity for the upliftment of working community.
- "Giri proposal"as made by. VV Giri to unite NTUF and AITUC was agreed upon by the two federations in 1938. The proposal provided that question of strike and political resolutions would be sorted by 3/4th majority of the central organization. In April 1938 at a special session at Nagpur the NTUF was affiliated as a separate unit to the AITUC and in 1940 NTUF was dissolved

7 *Indian Labour Year Book*, Government of India, Ministry of Labour, 1951-52 p 152

and merged with the AITUC. This made the AITUC very strong to achieve its goals.

- Formation of popular ministries in 1937 in most of the provinces brought a new era in the history of trade union movement in India. The Congress Election Manifesto inspired the working class as it had promised to the working community "to secure them a decent standard of living, hours of work and condition of labour in conformity, as far as the economic conditions in the country permit, with international standard, suitable machinery for the settlement of disputes between employers and workers and protection against the economic consequences of old age, sickness and unemployment and the right of workers to form unions and to strive for protection of their interests" New ministries provided a congenial and conducive atmosphere for smooth functioning of trade union activities.
- Price spiralling and scarcity of essential commodities due to Second World War made the union leaders feel to intensify their agitational Programmeme through concerted efforts. In 1941, Radicals left the AITUC with 200 unions approximately and formed a central federation known as the Indian Federation of Labour with Jamuna Das Mehta as president and MN Roy as General Secretary.
- Launching Quit India Movement by the Indian National Congress under the leadership of Mahatma Gandhi generated a feeling of 'we-ness', 'togetherness' amongst the industrial workers to protest against injustice, oppression made by employers.
- The promulgation of the Essential Service (Maintenance) Ordinance in 1941 brought a high hope and aspiration in the minds of the industrial workers to carry on union activities without being afraid of harassment and victimization as the ordinance prohibited dismissal of workers in some specified industries.
- Holding of Indian Labour Conference in Delhi in 1942 with 22 representatives of Central and Provincial Governments and also with the representatives each of employers' and workers' organizations provided recognitions to the trade unions in the country's socio-economic situation.
- The enactment of the Industrial Employment (Standing Orders) Act, 1946, the Industrial Disputes Act, 1947, the Bombay Industrial Relations Act, 1946 and the Indian Trade Union (amendment) Act, 1947 gave impetus to the trade union leaders

to continue their trade union activities with fullest zeal and vigour for betterment of the working class.

- Splitting in the AITUC and formation of the Indian National Trade Union Congress in May 1947 gave an appropriate platform to the leaders of the Indian National Congress to work for the well-being of the workers and to adopt peaceful means consistent with truth for furtherance of its objectives.
- The efforts ofleaders helped the freedom fighters, political leaders to make our country independent on 15th August 1947. But trade union movement got a great jolt because of the partition of the country; particularly the Indian Federation of Labour (IFL) that had significant following in Punjab, Sind and East Bengal was worst sufferer from the point of view of number of unions and number of memberships. IFL also lost more than one lakh members belonging to Bengal Chamber of Labour, who migrated to Pakistan.

5. Post–Independence Period (The period after 1947)

The INTUC was recognized as the representative body of the working community, in 1948. A split in AITUC took place in 1948 when the socialists broke away from the AITUC and formed the Hind Majdoor Sabha (HMS). The Indian Federation of Labour (IFL) merged with the Hind Majdoor Sabha (HMS). Some trade union leaders of HMS did not agree with the principles, objectives of the HMS and they seceded from the HMS and formed United Trade Union Congress (UTUC) on 30th April 1947. In 1955, the Bharatiya Majdoor Sangha (BMS) was set up by Bharatiya Jan Sangh and subsequently the BMS came under the influence and domination of the Bharatiya Janata Party. A division in the communist movement took place in 1964. The Communist Party of India (Marxist) seceded from the Communist Party of India. AITUC could manage a split for some period but in 1970 the CPM leaders broke away from the AITUC and formed a new central organization called the Centre of Indian Trade Union (CITU). After separation of CPM leaders from the AITUC, the organizational strength of AITUC reduced substantially.

The INTUC suffered a jolt in its strength of membership in 1972 when 112 trade unions from Gujarat seceded from it because of a rift in the Congress Party, and formed the new central organization called the National Labour Organization (NLO).

Some other central unions were also established. For obtaining cooperation from employers and trade unions and developing understanding and trust between unions and employers so as to maintain peace and harmony in industrial settings Industrial Truce Resolution was adopted by the tripartite Indian Labour conference immediately after independence.

A number of labour legislations had been enacted to protect the working class from arbitrary and whimsical act of employers in respect of payment of wages/salaries, bonus, providing social and welfare benefits, retiral benefits, promotion, maintenance of better industrial relations and so on. Some of the important labour laws are:

The Minimum Wages Act, 1948.

The Factories Act, 1948

The Employees' State Insurance Act, 1948

The Employees' Provident Fund and Miscellaneous Provisions Act, 1952.

The Maternity Benefit Act, 1961.

The Payment of Gratuity Act, 1972.

In 1966 the first National Commission on Labour was set up to investigate the matter relating to trade unions, industrial relations and other aspects like wages, bonus, living conditions, working conditions, social security, etc. In 1999, the Second National Commission on Labour was appointed the terms of reference of which, inter alia, included "to suggest rationalization of existing laws relating to labour in the organized sector".

The Government of India adopted planning as a measure to develop the economic strength of the country and the First Five-Year Plan was launched in April, 1951. It had implemented some Five-Year plan and a few annual plans; and in all plans labour had been given much more importance to attain strategic goals of the policy formulations. In various plans it had been categorically stressed upon the role of trade unions for increasing production and productivity of workers, smooth and effective functioning of organizational activities; for prompting industrial relations, creating a climate of industrial peace, harmony and generating congenial and conducive atmospheres of mutuality in industrial settings. All these plans had encouraged trade union leaders to carry on their trade union activities. After independence various industrial policy resolutions had been taken with the objective of developing country's all round growth in different perspectives through industrialization process. With impetus to industrialization a number of new units in different industries were set up resulting in growth of trade unions and its activities in the area of manpower procurement, compensation, grievance settlement, industrial relations, conciliation, adjudication and other disciplinary activities.

The period 1951 onward (that is, after introduction of First Five-Year Plan) has shown a tremendous growth in trade union movement as is revealed from the number of unions, registered number of unions submitting returns and membership of unions submitting returns, shown in Table 2.2.

Table 2.2

Showing growth trend of trade unions

Year	No of registered trade unions	No of unions submitting returns	Membership of unions submitting Returns (in '000)		
			Men	Women	Total
1950-51	3766	2002	1649	107	1756
1951-52	4623	2556	1847	136	1983
1956-57	8554	4399	2097	280	2377
1961-62	11614	7087	3607	370	3977
1966	14686	7244	4078	314	4392
1971	22484	9029	5083	387	5470
1976	29757	9102	5751	400	6151
1981	37539	6682	5012	385	5397
1985	45067	7815	5831	602	6433
1986	45030	11365	7368	819	8187
1987	49329	11063	7211	748	7959
1988	50048	8730	6334	739	7073
1989	52210	9758	8207	1088	9295
1990	52016	8828	6181	838	7019
1991	53535	8418	5507	5594	11101
1992	55680	9165	5148	598	5746
1993	55784	6806	2636	498	3134
1994	56872	6277	3239	855	4094
1995	57952	8162	5675	863	6538
1996	58805	7309	4259	1354	5613
1997	59968	10016	6498	910	7408

Source:

a) Various issues of *Indian Labour Year Book* and *Pocket Book of Labour Statistics*, Govt of India, Ministry of Labour.

b) Sinha, PRN and others: *Industrial Relations: Trade Unions and Labour Legislation* (Pearson/Education) 2006, P 86.

Cont.

Table 2.2 shows a significant growth of trade unions over the period from 1950-51 to 1997. In all spheres growth registers viz., number of registered trade unions, number of unions submitting returns and union memberships. Though women membership has substantially increased from 107 in 1950-51 to 910 in 1997, the growth rate of membership is low in 1990s. The same trend is also prevalent in case of men's membership growth rate.

Factors Inhibiting Growth of Trade Union in India

Trade Union in India has not developed as required. Number of registered trade unions has not increased substantially. Average membership per union submitting returns is poor, it remains over the years between 500 and 900 memberships per union approximately. Some factors inhibit the growth of trade unions in India. They are:

1. Union leadership

Union leaders play an important role to promote the growth and development of trade unions. In industrial settings union leaders can make things happen if they are leaders in the real sense and work selflessly for the wellbeing of the followers/masses in right direction. But, union leaders in Indian industries have not been successful to make substantial growth of trade unions. Some of the important reasons for dismal growth may be

- Lack of farsightedness of leaders to prepare strategic course of action adapted for attainment of union goals, objectives.
- Selfish attitudes of leaders in the power game activities.
- Generating a climate of distrust, misunderstanding amongst the leaders that result in split, divisions in unions.
- Failure of leaders to keep the whole fabric of working masses united within a single thread.
- Obtaining short term gains by the leaders at the cost of long term benefits.
- Attaining personal gains by leaders.
- Lack of professionalism in dealing with union problems by leaders.

---

c) It also includes information relating to employers' organizations registered under the Trade Unions Act, 1926 and it will reflect the trend of trade union growth because number of employers' organizations is insignificant as compared to workers' organizations between 1950-51 and 1997, the numbers of employer's organizations on the whole less then 2% of the total number of trade unions and their membership less then 1% of the total membership of the unions in the country.

- Disproportionate/unbalanced ego-status of leaders making them uncompromising, stubborn, biased, prejudiced for addressing conflicting situations.
- Loss of confidence on leaders by the rank and file.
- Indifferent attitudes of leaders to solve workers' problems, and grievances.
- Arbitrary, unjust and whimsical decision taken by leaders to keep the masses in the dark (viz., decision for resorting to strike, gherao, go-slow programmes) resulting in severe hardship of workers.

2. Multiplicity of Unions

A large number of unions in an industry creates a great problem to achieve its objectives. Multiplicity of unions inhibits the growth and development of unions in the following manner:

- It crushes the solidarity of workers.
- It lessens the bargaining strength of unions.
- Employers ignore unions because they become very much aware of workers' unity and strength.
- Union leaders cannot take drastic steps against employers, for the just and right cause as there remains every possibility to utilize other union's services by the employers for their own benefit.
- It creates more disharmony than harmony in the atmosphere of union activities.
- It weakens the pecuniary support of the unions in situations where stable and sound financial health is a necessity to settle disputes through arbitration/adjudication process.
- It cannot generate a feeling of 'we-ness', 'togetherness', 'belongingness' amongst the workers which is one of the pre-requisites for establishing a foundation of unity and solidarity amongst them.
- It creates unfavourable working situations where unions with different ideologies, philosophies indulge in unethical activities that result in inter-union rivalry.

3. Outsiders in unions' key posts

It happens that unions' key posts like general secretary, president are held by outsiders who are not the employees of the organizations but are the key decision makers of the unions. Outside leaders can make much headway in the trade union activities considering their level of leadership qualities, linkage with different high profile personalities in the society and other factors but in reality there is no growth in trade unions as such. Rather, outside leaders inhibit the growth of trade union movement as is seen from the following:

- Objectives of trade union organizations differ from the objectives of outside trade union leaders who make an entry into the trade union fields in industrial settings.
- Outside union leaders are not well acquainted with various processes of industrial activities that hinder them to make effective bargaining with the employees.
- Casual approaches of outsiders to look at the workers' problems.
- Outside leaders are much more interested in achieving personal goals than unions goals.
- They use the union organizations as platforms to show their strength for obtaining political gains that help the political parties to which they belong but not the working masses who make them leaders.
- Wide difference in social status, standing between workers who are illiterates, innocent and union leaders makes two distinct classes, though they belong to the same union organizations.
- Infrequent visit of outside leaders to industry, devoting less time/ no time to know the organizational climate, working problem and living conditions of workers make it difficult to effectively present the workers' issues in various forums like conciliation, adjudication.

4. Poor pecuniary strength

One of the reasons for low growth of trade unions is dearth of adequate fund of union organizations. The main source of income of trade union is membership subscription but the money collected from the union members on account of membership subscriptions is meager. Financially weak unions face a lot of difficulties

- to contest labour cases in the court/tribunals.
- to take appropriate steps to help the workers in danger, distress.
- to conduct welfare and social security programmes.
- to provide financial help to the workers during strike, lockout.
- to provide training to the workers to develop their level of competency, to promote team spirit, to make them aware of

various products launched, schemes framed and other company activities.

- to create and promote union information system that can provide necessary data/information to the union organizations as and when required.
- to carry on research activities on labour related issues.

5. Small size of unions

Size of unions is a crucial factor to determine the growth of trade unions. It decides the bargaining strength of unions. Bigger the size of union, higher is the bargaining strength and reverse is the case when size of union is small. In trade union scenario size of unions in India is very small. Heterogeneous composition of workers makes the size small. Working class in Indian industries belongs to different religions, castes, creed; and they come from different parts of the country having different mother tongues. All this makes the people form unions as per their convenience on the basis of geographical location, religion, caste, languages and so on. The Trade Unions Act, 1926 also makes it easy for them to form union and get it registered if they have seven members for such purpose. Small size of unions in Indian industries stands in the way of promoting growth of unions. Some of the important reasons are given below:

- Small size of unions cannot have bargaining strength.
- Employers can ignore the unions and the problems raised by them as well.
- Unions with low membership may not be encouraged to launch agitational movement for fulfillment of their demands.
- Unions cannot have sufficient funds to meet up essential expenses like conducting welfare programmes, helping the workers at the time of strike, lockout, etc.
- It may create a situation of inter-union rivalry particularly amongst the trade union leaders that result in multiplicity of union.

6. Other factors inhibiting growth of trade unions

The following factors create obstacles in the growth of trade unions:

- Unwillingness of workers to go against employers.
- A large number of workers consider their employers as protectors, giving them bread and butter to maintain their livelihood and it will not be fair to revolt against them.

- Absence of full time paid persons to help the trade union leaders by providing necessary information regarding worker's problems/ issues, living and working conditions of workers, conciliation, adjudication cases, etc.
- Employers' negative values, beliefs, attitudes and autocratic leadership style create a great hurdle in the development of trade unions. Such employers consider workers as commodities, and they do not like to give any opportunity to grow through development of trade unions.
- Emergence of a hire and fire situation particularly after the introduction of liberalization, privatization and globalization (LPG) makes it difficult for the unions to grow.

Classification of Trade Unions

Different types of trade unions are prevalent in Indian industrial settings. Workers come close and form unions on the basis of common understanding; may be, on the basis of ideology/purpose, or trade. So classification of trade unions may be made as follows:

1. On the basis of ideology/purpose
2. On the basis of types of worker members
3. On the basis of agreement for union membership

1. On the basis of ideology/purpose

Under this classification trade unions may be (a) reformist unions (b) revolutionary unions and (c) other unions.

a. Reformist unions

Workers form the union with the objective of making changes as needed within the existing social, economic and political structure of the state. It aims at preserving the capitalist society and continuance of employer-employee relationship with some modification that provides recognition to labour in society. The unions affiliated with American Federation of Labour (AFL) belong to this type of union in the USA.

RF Hoxie (1928) has classified this type of union into (i) Business unions and (ii) Uplift unions. Business unions are basically craft-conscious rather than class-conscious. Such unions try to bring economic advantages for their members through reforming process. Economic advantages may include increase in wages, allowances and also an improvement of living and working conditions.

Uplift/Friendly unions are generally interest-conscious but not craft-conscious. Such unions attempt to elevate the moral, intellectual and social life of workers and advocate extensive reforms for social regeneration. They give much emphasis on the need of mutual insurance, profit sharing and cooperative schemes.

b. Revolutionary unions

Revolutionary unions believe in destruction of the present structure completely and substitution of a new one. Workers form unions to destroy capitalist form of industry, to destruct private property, to abolish wage system, social and economic order, and to replace it with another system, generally socialist/communist. Revolutionary unions are of two types:

- Anarchist Unions
- Political Unions

Anarchist unions believe in destruction of the existing economic system by revolutionary means. Workers form such unions with the objective of destroying the present economic structure completely through revolutionary process.

Political unions believe in gaining power through political process. The main objectives of such union are:

- to minimize wage differentials
- to give effective power to workers
- to eliminate the power of capital and capitalist
- to redistribute the wealth

Unions get these objectives through political action and enactment of suitable legislations.

c. Other unions

There are some unions which are formed for certain purposes but they do not specifically belong to reformist unions or revolutionary unions. They are

- Predatory Unions
- Hold-up Unions
- Guerrilla Unions
- Dependent Unions

Predatory unions

These unions are formed to achieve its goals by whatever means seem appropriate. Such unions have not any specific ideology, principles or ethical values to get its purpose served.

Hold-up unions

Hold-up unions are those unions which make an agreement with unscrupulous employers to control market through setting excessive prices for the services they render to the public. This is one kind of union that represents a combination of unethical, unscrupulous business agents of labour organizations with employers who are equally unethical and unscrupulous. Such unions do not look at the interest of the masses.

Guerrilla unions

Guerrilla unions do not believe in cooperation with employers. Such unions do not hesitate to use any extreme means like act of terrorism, to enforce its demands. The leaders of guerrilla unions are aggressive, militant, violent. Their aim is to exploit whatever and whatsoever they can.

Dependent unions

It happens that some employers sponsor and support some unions as a means of preventing organization of their employees by outside affiliated unions. Such sponsored unions are called dependent unions. The existence of the dependent unions is wholly or partly dependent on others.

2. On the basis of types of worker members

Classification of trade unions can also be made on the basis of types of workers that unions include as members. On such basis unions may be of.

- Craft union (or occupational union)
- Industrial union (or common employment union)
- General union
- Staff union

Craft union/Occupational union

Craft unions are those unions which seek to organize all employees in a single or two or more related occupations/crafts/trades. It is not a point of consideration for such unions to see that the employees should be from the same industry or from any other industry. Such unions are found mostly amongst professional employees and non-manual employees.

Since craft union is formed with skilled employees whose jobs are relatively secured it contributes to the growth and development of trade unions. The United Patternmakers Association in UK, the International Wood Carvers' Association and the Indian's Pilots' Guild are some of the examples of crafts unions.

Industrial union/common employment union

Industrial unions are those unions which include workers with a variety of skills employed in a particular industry. Such union is formed on the basis of an industry rather than a craft. It seeks to organize all workers-skilled, semi–skilled, unskilled engaged in a single industry into one homogeneous organic unity. Some of the important industrial unions are Rashtriya Mill Majdoor Sangh; Bombay; Tata Workers' Union and Textile Labour Association of Ahmedabad.

General union

General unions include all workers without distinction as to industry or craft. Such unions cover various industries and workers having different types of skills. National Union of General and Municipal Workers in Great Britain and Jamshedpur Labour Union, Jamshedpur are examples of general unions.

Staff union

Staff Unions are generally formed in non-manual sectors where people from different strata join together with the objective of showing their solidarity amongst themselves.

Such union is used to refer both craft union and industrial union. Staff union comprising members like supervisors, clerks, computer operators, draftsmen, stenographers, etc., carries on activities under common goals.

3. On the basis of agreement for union membership

Trade unions can be classified on the basis of agreements made by unions and employers with regard to membership in a union as one of the conditions of employment. Accordingly following types of unions can be found in the industrial settings.

a. Union shop

This type of union is very much common in the USA. Union shop is found in the organization where all new recruitees become members of the union before or after they join the organization, in terms of agreement. Union shop has following important characteristics:

- Obtaining union membership is compulsory.
- There must be agreement in the company regarding union membership.
- This is applicable for each and every recruitment made by the company.
- New recruitees may become union members before they join the

organization or may become members of the union after the close of the probationary period.

The union shop is desirable for the contribution it can make to stabilize industrial relations. A union whose security is beyond question, can afford to be more reasonable on other matters such as promotions, lay-offs and other points of which discrimination might be practical against union members[8].

b. Closed shop

Under closed shop union enjoys the authority of supplying labour to the organization. Union supplies labours to the organization who are their own members. So closed shop means providing labours to the organizations by the union under an agreement and such labours are their member. In a narrow sense, 'closed shop' means a shop remains closed to non-unionists for the purpose of employment. In the USA, the Taft Hartley Act, 1947 bans closed shop agreement, but in printing and construction sector closed shop still exists.

The important characteristics of closed shop are:

- All new recruitees are union members.
- Union supplies labour to the organization as and when required. It happens that union acts as an employment agency for the organization.
- The supply of labour is made on the basis of closed shop agreement reached between union and management.
- Employees maintain their union membership in good standing.
- It dominates the workers through exercise of influence over them that creates a problem for the supervisor to maintain discipline in the plant.
- The worker loses his job if he ceases to be a member of the union.

In India closed shop agreement is not prevalent. The First National Commission on Labour expressed that the practice of closed shop is neither practicable nor desirable[9].

c. Agency shop

Under agency shop a worker who does not want to be a member of the union needs to pay the subscription of the union which is equivalent to a member's subscription. So all employees in an organization need to

8 Sharma, GK: *Labour Movement in India* (1963, Pp 7 and 166)

9 *Report of the National Commission on Labour*, Government of India (1969, page 293).

pay dues to the union for continuance with the job. Joining the union as member is not a must.

Agency shop is similar to Rand Formula in Canada but it is not like free riders who share the benefit gained by negotiation without contributing. According to section 11 of the British Industrial Relations Act, 1971 a union and an employer might come to an agreement laying down that membership of the union was a part of the terms and condition of employment and a worker, who objected to joining the union, woud have to agree to pay appropriate contribution to the union in lieu of membership or agree to pay equivalent contribution to a charity.

d. Preferential shop

When under an agreement management gives first chance to union members for employment, it is called preferential shop. Important characteristics of preferential shop are mentioned below:

1. There must be an agreement between employer and employees regarding recruitment.
2. It must be mentioned in the agreement that union member be given first chance to fill a vacancy.
3. It is a right of the union to urge upon the management to fill in vacancy first through its member.
4. It is an additional recognition granted to the union by agreement.

e. Maintenance of membership shop

In maintenance of membership shop if an employee joins union as a member he remains as a member during his whole tenure of employment with the particular employer. This sort of shop gained popularity in the USA during Second World War. It was a compromise settlement of union demand for closed shop, made by the War Labour Board. Union membership is not compulsory for employment. It is up to the discretion of the employees to choose or not to choose membership. All employees who are or who become members of the union on or after a specified date must remain members in good standing for the full term of the agreement. The arrangement includes an escape period of ten to fifteen days after contract negotiations during which members may resign if they wish[10].

Some of the important features of the shop are:

- An agreement is made between employer and trade union with regard to union membership.

10 Yoder, Dale: *Personnel Management and Industrial Relations* (Sixth Edition, Prentice-Hall of India Private Limited, New Delhi, 1972, P-443).

- Employer can hire persons without regard to membership or non-membership of the union.
- It is left to the employees concerned to decide whether they want to become union members or not.
- Once an employee becomes member he must have to continue his membership so long he remains in service with the same employer.
- An escape period is given after contract negotiation during which any member can resign if he so wishes.

f. Open shop

- It means that no restriction is imposed on employees from employment from the perspective of union membership.
- Union membership is not compulsory for the employees before and after recruitment.
- It involves 'right to work' having no relationship with union membership for employment.
- The concept of 'open shop' originated when some employers refused to recognize any union or bargaining agent for employees or members and they insisted on their right to deal with employees individually not through union or agency.
- It is not liked by unions as some employers intend to keep union and union members out of their plants.

Some Important Issues Under the Trade Unions Act, 1926

Registration of Trade Union

Registration of trade unions is not compulsory under the Trade Unions Act, 1926. It is voluntary. So, it is up to the union to decide whether it intends to get registered or not. It is, however, better for the union to seek registration because the Act provides legal status and protection to the members of trade union and ensures application of same standard of obligation to all unions

Section 4 (i) of the Trade Unions Act, 1926 provides that seven or more members of a trade union may by subscribing their names to the rules of trade union and by otherwise complying with the provisions of this Act with respect to registration, apply for registration of trade union.

The application for registration needs to be sent to the Registrar of Trade Unions. This application must be accompanied by a copy of the rules of the trade union and a statement of the following particulars:

i. the names, occupations and addresses of the members making the application

ii. in the case of a Trade Union of workmen, the names, occupations and addresses of the place of work of the members of the Trade Union making the application

iii. the name of the trade union and the address of its head office

iv. the titles, names, ages, addresses and occupations of the office bearers of the trade union and

v. where a trade union has been in existence for more than one year before making of an application for its registration, a general statement of the assets and liabilities of the trade union prepared in such a form and containing such particulars as may be prescribed[11].

A trade union is not entitled to registration unless its executive is constituted in terms of the provisions of the Act and its rules provide for the following particulars:

- the name of the trade union.
- the whole of the objects for which the trade union is established.
- the whole of the purposes for which the general funds of the trade union are to be applicable (The Act prescribes the purposes on which the funds are to be sent).
- the maintenance of a list of the members of the trade union and adequate facilities for its inspection by the office–bearers and members of the trade union.
- the admission of ordinary members who are the persons actually engaged or employed in an industry with which the trade union is connected and admission of the number of honorary or temporary members as office-bearers in accordance with the provisions relating to the formation of executive of the trade union.
- the payment of a subscription by members of the trade unions which is not to be less than one per annum for rural workers, Rs 3/- per annum for workers in other unorganized sectors and Rs 12/- per annum for workers in any other cases.
- the conditions under which any member is entitled to any benefit assured by the rules and under which any fine or forfeiture may be imposed on the members.

11 Section 5 of the Trade Unions Act, 1926

- the manner in which the rules may be amended, varied or rescinded.
- the manner in which the members of the executive and other office-bearers of the trade union shall be elected and removed.
- the safe custody of the funds of the trade union, and annual audit, in such manner as may be prescribed, of the accounts thereof, and adequate facilities for the inspection of the account books by the office-bearers and members of the trade union, and
- the manner in which the trade union may be dissolved.

If the Registrar is satisfied that the trade union has complied with all the requirements of the Act with regard to registration, he will register the trade union by entering in a register the particulars relating to the trade union contained in the statement accompanying the application for registration. The registrar then issues a certificate of registration in the prescribed form. This is conclusive evidence that the trade union has been duly registered. The registered trade union enjoys the following privileges:

i. It becomes a corporate body.
ii. It gets a perpetual succession and a common seal.
iii. It acquires a legal personality separate from its members.
iv. It can acquire and hold both movable and immovable property.
v. It can enter into contract.
vi. It can sue and be sued in its registered name.

Cancellation of Registration

The registration of the union can be withdrawn or cancelled by the Registrar:

- on the application of the trade union to be verified in such manner as may be prescribed, or
- if the Registrar is satisfied that the certificate has been obtained by fraud or mistake or that the trade union has ceased to exist or has wilfully and after notice from the Registrar contravened by any provisions of this Act or allowed any rule to continue in force which is inconsistent with any such provision, or has rescinded any rule providing for any matter provision for which is required to be made by section 6, or
- if the Registrar is satisfied that a registered Trade Union of workmen ceases to have the requisite number of members.

It is, however, required that not less than two month's previous notice in writing specifying the ground on which it is proposed to withdraw or cancel the certificate should be given by the Registrar to the Trade Union before the certificate is withdrawn or cancelled by him. However, such notice is not required when the registration is withdrawn or cancelled on an application by the union itself.

Minimum Requirement for Membership

A registered Trade Union must at all times continue to have not less than 10% or 100 of the workmen, whichever is less, subject to a minimum of seven members, engaged or employed in an establishment or industry with which it is connected[12].

Appeal

Any person aggrieved

a. by any refusal of the Registrar to register a trade union or

b. by the withdrawal or cancellation of a certificate of registration may prefer an appeal within 60 days of the date on which the Registrar passed the order against which the appeal is preferred.

The appeal is to be made to the High Court if the head office of the trade union is situated within the limits of a presidency town. Where the head office of a trade union is situated in an area, falling within the jurisdiction of a Labour Court or an Industrial Tribunal the appeal is to be made to that Court or Tribunal, as the case may be. Where the head office of a trade union is situated in any other area the forum of appeal is such court not inferior to the court of an additional or assistant judge of a principal civil court of original jurisdictions as the appropriate Government may appoint in this behalf for that area.

The appellate court may dismiss the appeal or pass an order directing the Registrar to register the trade union and to issue a certificate of registration under the provisions of section 9 or set aside the order of the withdrawal or cancellation of the certificate. In the event of the dismissal of an appeal by a court appointed by the government, the aggrieved person may appeal to the High court.

Rights of Registered Trade Unions

A registered trade union enjoys a number or rights. The rights of registered trade unions are discussed herein:

---

12 Section 9A of the Trade Unions Act, 1926.

1. Immunity from criminal conspiracy

Office bearer or member of a registered trade union is not liable to punishment under section 120 B (2) of the Indian Penal Code in respect of any agreement made between the members for the purpose of furthering any object prescribed under the Act unless the agreement is designed to commit an offence[13].

2. Immunity from civil suits in some cases

No suit or other legal proceeding is maintainable in any civil court against any registered trade union or any office bearer or member in respect of any act done in contemplation or furtherance of a trade dispute to which a member of the trade union is a party on the ground only that such act induces some other person to break a contract of employment or that such act is an interference with the trade, business or employment of some other person or with the right of some other person to dispose off his capital or his labour at his will[14].

3. Immunity from tortious act

A registered trade union is not liable in any suit or other legal proceeding in any civil court in respect of any tortious act done in contemplation or furtherance of a trade dispute by an agent of the trade union if it is proved that such person acted without the knowledge of, or contrary to express instructions given by the executive of the trade union.

4. Enforceability of agreement

An agreement between the members of a registered trade union is not to be void or voidable merely by reason of the fact that any of the objects of the agreement is in restraint of trade. A civil court is not authorized to entertain any legal proceeding instituted for the express purpose of enforcing or recovering damages for the breach of any agreement concerning the conditions on which any members of a trade union shall or shall not sell their goods, transact business, work, employ or be employed[15].

5. Right to inspect books of trade union

The office bearer or a member of the trade union has the right to inspect account books and the list of members of the registered trade union.

---

13 Section 17 of the Trade Unions Act, 1926

14 Section 18 of the Trade Unions Act 1926.

15 Section 19 of the Trade Unions Act, 1926.

6. Rights of minors to membership of trade unions

Any person who has attained the age of fifteen years, may become a member of registered trade union subject to rules of the trade union to the contrary. Such a member may enjoy all rights of a member and execute all instruments and give all acquittances necessary to be executed or given under the rules. (Section 21 of the Trade Unions Act, 1926)

Liabilities of Registered Trade Unions

A registered trade union has a right to maintain general fund. The Section 15 of the Trade Unions Act specifies that the general fund of a registered trade union cannot be spent on any other objects than the following:

i. the payment of salaries, allowances and expenses to office-bearers of the trade unions,

ii. the payment of expenses for the administration of the trade union, including audit of account of the general funds of the trade union,

iii. prosecuting or defending a legal action to which the union or any of its members is a party, when such prosecution or defence is undertaken for the purpose of securing or protecting any rights of the trade union as such or any rights arising out of the relations of any member with his employer or with a person whom the member employs,

iv. the conduct of trade disputes on behalf of the trade union or any member thereof,

v. the compensation of members for loss arising out of trade disputes,

vi. allowances to members or their dependants on account of death, old age, sickness, accidents or unemployment of such members,

vii. the issue of, or the undertaking ofliability under, policies of assurance on the lives of members or under policies insuring members against sickness, accident or unemployment,

viii. the provision of educational, social or religious benefits for members (including the payment of the expenses of funeral or religious ceremonies for deceased members) or for the dependants of members,

ix. the upkeep of a periodical published mainly for the purpose of discussing questions affecting employers or workmen as such,

x. the payment, in furtherance of any of the objects on which the general funds of the trade union may be spent, of contributions to any cause intended to benefit workmen in general, provided that the expenditure in respect of such contributions in any financial year shall not at any time during that year be in excess of one-fourth of the combined total of the gross income which has up to that time accrued to the general funds of the trade union during that year and of the balance at the credit of those funds at the commencement of that year, and

xi. Subject to any conditions contained in the notification, any other object notified by the appropriate government in the official gazette.

The union is liable to refund the amount to the member if received by it on behalf of him, on resignation from the union[16].

Constitution of a separate fund for political purposes

A registered trade union may constitute a separate fund for political purposes, from contributions separately levied for or made to that fund.

The political fund may be spent in furtherance of any or the following civil and political objects:

i. the payment of any expenses incurred, either directly or indirectly, by a candidate or prospective candidate for election as a member of any legislative body constituted under the Constitution or of any local authority, before, during or after the election in connection with his candidature or election, or

ii. the holding of any meeting or the distribution of any literature or documents in support of any such candidate, or

iii. the maintenance of any person who is a member of any legislative body constituted under the Constitution for any local authority, or

iv. the registration of electors or the selection of a candidate for any legislative body constituted under the Constitution or for any local authority, or

v. the holding of political meetings of any kind, or the distribution of political literature or political documents of any kind.

No member can be compelled to contribute to the political fund and a member who does not contribute to the fund cannot be excluded from any benefits of the trade union, or placed in any respect either directly or indirectly under any disability or at any disadvantage as compared with other members of the trade union (except in relation to the contort or management of the said fund) by reason of his not contributing to the

16 In GS Dhara Singh vs EK Thomas (Air 1988 SC 1829) the Hon'ble Supreme Court has given this judgment.

said fund; and contribution to the said fund cannot be made a condition for admission to the trade union.[17]

Disqualifications of Office-bearers of Trade Unions

A person is disqualified for being chosen as, and for being a member of the executive or any other office-bearer of a registered trade union, if

i. he is below 18 year or

ii. he has been convicted by a court in India of any offence involving moral turpitude and sentenced to imprisonment, unless a period of 5 years has elapsed since his release.

Any member of the executive or other office-bearer of a registered trade union who, before the commencement of the Indian Trade Union (amendment) Act, 1964 has been convicted of any offence involving moral turpitude and sentenced to imprisonment, shall on the date of such commencement cease to be such member or office-bearer unless a period of five years has elapsed since his release before that date.[18]

Proportion of Office-bearers to be connected with the Industry

Not less than one-half of the total number of office-bearers of every registered trade union in an unorganized sector must be person actually engaged or employed in the industry with which the trade union is connected but the appropriate government may make exempting orders in this regard. The unorganized sector is to specified by the appropriate government by notification in the official gazette.

In all other cases, all office-bearers of a registered trade union, except not more than one third of the total number of office-bearers or five, whichever is less, are to be persons actually engaged or employed in the establishment or industry with which the trade union is connected.

No member of the Council of Ministers or a person holding an office of profit (not being an engagement or employment in an establishment or industry with which the trade union is connected), in the Union or a State, is to be a member of the executive or other office-bearer of a registered trade union.[19]

Dissolution of Registered Trade Unions

For dissolution of a registered trade union a notice signed by seven members of the trade union and by the secretary has to be sent to the

17 Section 16 of the Trade Unions Act, 1926

18 Section 21 A of the Trade Unions Act, 1926

19 Section 22 of the Trade Unions Act, 1926

Registrar of Trade Union within 14 days of the dissolution. If the Registrar is satisfied that the dissolution has been made in accordance with the rule of Trade Union, he is required to register the dissolution which is to come into effect from the date of dissolution. If the trade union is dissolved and the rules of the trade union do not provide for the distribution of funds of the trade union on dissolution, the Registrar shall divide the funds amongst the members in such manner as may be prescribed[20].

Books Recommended

1. CB, Mamoria, S Mamoria and SV Gankar: *Dynamics of Industrial Relations* (Himalaya Publishing House, Mumbai, 2003)
2. PRN Sinha, IB Sinha and SP Shekhar: *Industrial Relations, Trade Unions and Labour Legislation* (Pearson/Education, Delhi, 2008).
3. Allan Flanders: *Trade Unions* (The English Language Book Society and Hutchinson University Library, London, 1963)
4. Sydney Webb and Beatrice Webb: *Industrial Democracy* (Longmans, Green & Co, London 1897)
5. TN Chhabra and RK Suri: *Industrial Relations: Concepts and Issues* (Dhanpat Rai & Co (P) Ltd 2005, Delhi).
6. PC Tripathi: *Personnel Management & Industrial Relations* (Sultan Chand & Sons, New Delhi, 1978)

Questions

1. What is a trade union? State the salient characteristics of a trade union.
2. Explain, in brief, the objectives of trade union.
3. Some say 'trade union movement' and 'labour movement' are the same—As a student of MBA do you endorse this view? Explain.
4. Why do employees join trade unions? Submit your views.
5. Briefly discuss the various functions of trade union.
6. 'There is no one theory of trade unionism. Multiple theories have originated'—What are those theories? Discuss any two.
7. Write a historical account of Trade Union movement between 1919-1934.
8. Write a critical note on Trade Union movement after Independence and compare it with the period of 1935-1947 movement of Trade Union.

20 Section 27 of the Trade Unions Act, 1926.

9. What are the factors inhibiting growth of Trade Unions in India? Discuss.
10. What are the impacts of outside leadership on the working of trade union?
11. Define 'trade union' according to Trade Unions Act, 1926. What are the conditions to be satisfied to get a trade union registered?
12. State and explain various types of trade unions.
13. What are the rights, privileges and statutory obligations of a registered trade union?
14. Can a Registrar refuse to register a trade union? State the circumstances when a trade union is not entitled to registration.
15. The registration of the union can be withdrawn or cancelled by the Registrar. Discuss in this context the circumstances when the Registrar can cancel or withdraw the registration of the union.
16. Write short notes on:
    a. Disqualification of office-bearers of trade unions
    b. Appeal
    c. General Fund of a registered trade union
    d. Dissolution of a registered trade union
    e. Political fund of a registered trade union
    f. Proportion of office-bearers of be connected with the industry

Case Study

Mr RKR Sundaram is the Chief Manager (HRM) of the Eastern Region of Universal Bank Limited. The Eastern Regional office of the bank is in Kolkata. Mr DR Putnis, Dy General Manager is the Regional Head of the bank.

1. The bank has 70 branches (30 metropolitan, 25 Urban and 15 semi urban branches), 1350 employees (including officers, clerical staff and subordinate staff of all 70 branches and regional office) under Eastern Region.
2. The bank has started operations in Eastern Region from 1975. However other regional offices, viz., Northern Regional office in New Delhi, Southern Regional office in Chennai and Mumbai Regional office have started functioning from 1965, 1970 and 1974 respectively. The bank's Head office is situated in New Delhi.
3. The union composition looks like this:

a. Three Unions namely Universal Bank Workers' Union, Universal Bank Employees' Union and Universal Bank Workers' Solidarity Union are having members in branches and regional office in Kolkata.

b. The Universal Bank Workers' Solidarity Union is majority union of Universal Bank Limited. The corporate management has recognised this union as a sole collective bargaining party, but this union is minority union in Eastern Region from the membership point of view.

c. The Universal Bank Employees' Union ranks third from the view point of union membership in the Universal Bank Ltd. as a whole, but in Eastern Region it has about 55% membership.

d. The Universal Bank Workers' Union has 35% membership in the Eastern Region. The membership strength of this union (taking into account of membership strength of all regions and head office together) is next to the strength of Universal Bank Workers' Solidarity Union.

4. Some of the bank's salient activities over which union leaders launched agitational programmes against management are under mentioned.

a. The bank's eastern regional authority in consultation with Head office made an agreement with Universal Bank Employees' Union (minority union in terms of all India union membership strength) in 1985 to provide canteen facilities to the employees at branches and administrative offices. Under this agreement the bank authority requires to appoint canteen boys (on permanent employee roll), provide utensils, furniture, room space, fuel at free of cost and arrange to serve the employees food, tea, snacks at subsidised rate (on 'no profit, no loss' basis). Mentionably, only the bank employees of eastern region are enjoying such benefits. The other unions started agitation to extend such benefit to all the bank employees in other regions. Looking into different perspectives top management in the corporate level agreed to provide a canteen allowance for all employees of the bank at different rates (Rs. 15 per day per officer, Rs. 10 per day per clerk and Rs. 5 per day per subordinate staff) linked to month's attendance of employees. The payment of such allowance came into effect from April, 1991. The Universal Bank Employees' Union was called by the management of eastern region in May 1992 for discussion on the 'canteen boy' issue in the context of introducing a similar benefit scheme for the employees of the bank. The management informed them about justification for discontinuance of 'canteen-boy engagement' system and told them that existing canteen-boys would be converted into peons. The management expressed their views that this practice of engaging/recruiting canteen boys would be stopped forthwith. The union leaders vehemently protested over the management's desire/intention to discontinue the system of appointing canteen boys in bank. They informed management that if, such practice is discontinued they would cease to work for an indefinite period.

The practice of engaging canteen boys in bank's branches/offices under Eastern Region continues and the employees are getting subsidised 'canteen facilities' and also canteen allowance.

b. In Universal Bank Ltd. non-officers (clerks and subordinate staff) were continuing with the same branch/office till their retirement, promotion or exit from the bank. No job rotation from one branch/ office to other branch/office was in practice. In August 1986, the bank issued a circular in respect of job rotation scheme for clerks and substaff (i.e., for award staff members) of the bank for implementation from 1st September 1986. The scheme provided that in the first phase the staff members (including substaff) who had been working for 10 years and above would fall under job rotation and in the 2nd phase those staff members who had been working for 5 years and above in the same branch/office would be transferred under job rotation w. e. f. 2nd February 1987. In normal situations union leaders of different unions did not have good understanding, relations amongst themselves. Inter union rivalry was a common cause to disturb industrial peace. After the issuance of management circular with regard to job rotation of staff, all the three unions joined together to launch agitational programme. They threatened management that they would face dire consequences if, job rotation scheme was implemented. The local management, in terms of circular, prepared a list of employees falling under job rotation scheme and gave one copy of the same to each union seven days before the date of effect, for information.

The unions gave deputation, demonstration, wore black badges, staged dharna in front of the chamber of Dy. General Manager and resorted to different forms of industrial disputes except strike. All these the unions did in the month of August 1986 when they came to know the management decision through circular.

On 31st August 1986, branch managers were advised to transfer the concerned staff members at the respective branches and confirm action of having complied with to HRM Department of eastern regional office. The concerned award staff members were issued transfer orders with the instructions to report to branches on 01. 09. 1986 as mentioned in the orders.

On 1st September, 1986, the staff members in eastern region, belonging to respective unions ceased to work and declared an indefinite period of strike if transfer orders were not withdrawn by the management. The strike continued for some days and with the intervention of the State Government and the efforts put in by the top management the employees withdrew strike.

Additional Information

i. The Universal Bank Ltd. has introduced a system of holding discussion/negotiation on the issues raised by three unions separately in structured meetings twice an year in Regional Office and once a year in the Head Office.

ii. The branches developed a practice to hold staff meeting on personnel as well as non-personnel issues of the branches where free and open discussions are held to sort out differences/problems and promote understanding, faith amongst them.

iii. For cleaning, sweeping the branch/office premises the bank has permanent sweepers at a different time rate (viz., 1/3, 1/2, 3/4, full rate of scale) depending upon the floor space of the premises. The bank engages casual sweepers (from the enlisted panel of casuals) on a temporary basis when permanent incumbents go on leave.

You are required to form some groups with 5 to 6 members in each group, select group leader, discuss among the members the following issues/points, prepare group views to present before all the members by the leaders one by one. The rest of the members (other than leaders) are also required to present their views.

Q. 1

(a) Do you think the agreement extending the canteen benefit to the employees of eastern region is a right step to promote industrial relations?

(b) What would happen if management would not have agreed to reach such an agreement meant for a section of employees of the bank?

(c) Is it violating norms of natural justice that deprives a majority of employees from getting canteen facilities simply because they are working in other parts of the country?

Q. 2

(a) What could be the reasons for expression of such attitudes of the union on the issue of discontinuance of appointment system of canteen boys?

(b) As IR Specialist of the bank how would you tackle this issue concerning appointment of canteen boys?

(c) Do you think management's proposal to stop engaging canteen boys is justified and proper particularly in the light of the agreement that still exists?

Q. 3

(a) Do you think job rotation has any effect on improving quality of services of employees who are transferred under this scheme?

(b) How could you justify management action to implement job rotation scheme?

(c) Do you feel it is desirable to discuss with the unions on the matter of job rotation before such scheme is framed and implemented by the management?

(d) Can unions go for strike on such issue? What are the legal implications?

Q. 4

(a) What could be the roles of Regional HRM professionals before strike and after strike?

(b) As, CM (HRM) of the eastern region of the bank point out your plan of action during strike.

Q. 5

(a) Do you think structured meetings at regional and corporate level facilitate healthy industrial relations? Do you feel the necessity of such meeting?

(b) Do you think appointment of sweeper on permanent basis at different time scales is justified in the context of obtaining competitive advantages as also social concept? What are other alternatives to appointment of permanent part time sweepers?

Q. 6

As CM (HRM) of the bank what would be your suggestions to promote industrial relations in the eastern region?

III

National Federations

National level federations exist in industrial settings. Both employers' organizations and employees' organizations have their national level federations. These are central trade union organizations and central employers' organizations. A number of such national federations have been formed. They are discussed separately.

Central Trade Union Organizations/National Federations

In order to have a thorough understanding of central trade union organizations in India it is felt necessary to know the structural pattern of unions that can give an idea about the relationship the national federations/central trade union organizations are having with other federations.

The following three types of federations are prevalent in Indian trade union spheres of activities.

a. Local level federations

b. Regional level federations and

c. National federations

The relationship pattern between various union federations is depicted in Figure 3. 1

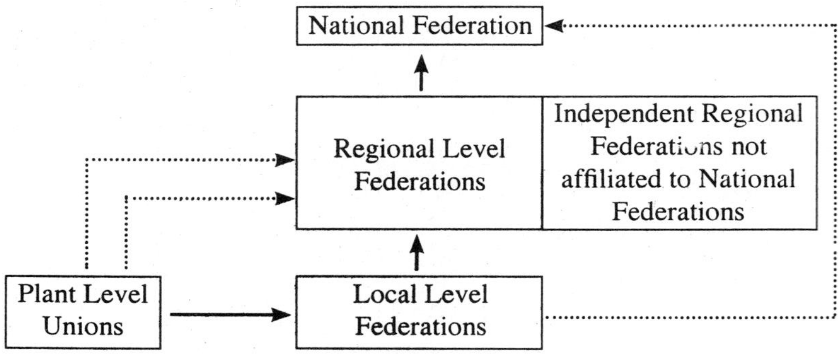

Figure 3. 1: Pattern of relationships between unions/federations.

a. Local level federations

Local level federation is formed for a particular craft and industry in a local area. It brings the plant level trade unions operating in a craft or industry in a locality, under its fold. It is the second layer next to plant level trade unions, in the organization structure of unions. These local level federations are affiliated to regional level federations or national level federation.

b. Regional level federations

Regional level federation is the third layer of union structure next to local level federation. This federation is formed with local level federations and also the plant level unions that are not affiliated to local level unions but are indirectly routed through them. It operates in a state or region for a particular craft and industry. Regional level federation may be affiliated to some national federations or they may remain as independent structure of federations.

c. National federations

National federation is the apex structure of trade unions. It may have the following constituents under its affiliation:

- Plant level trade unions
- Local level federations
- Regional level federations

It occurs that some regional level federations get themselves affiliated to the national federations while others do not.

The important central trade unions/national federations which are recognized by the Government are:

- All India Trade Union Congress (AITUC)

- Indian National Trade Union Congress (INTUC)
- Hind Majdoor Sabha (HMS)
- United Trade Union Congress (UTUC)
- Centre of Indian Trade Unions (CITU)
- Bharatiya Majdoor Sangh (BMS)
- United Trade Union Congress – (Lenin Sarani) (UTUC-LS)
- Nation Labour Organization (NLO)
- National Front of Indian Trade Unions (NFITU)
- Trade Union Co-ordination Committee (TUCC)

A few of national organizations such as National Federation of Post and Telegraph Workers, Indian Railwaymen's Federation, All India Port and Dock Worker's Federation, All India Bank Employee's Association, Indian Federation of Working' Journalists, etc., are not affiliated to any central trade unions as aforementioned. They are operating as independent organizations. The national organizations like Hind Majdoor Kisan Panchayat and Indian Confederation of Labour have stronger regional affiliations than a national coverage.

Some of the important central trade unions/national federations recognized by the government for the purpose of representation at various bodies, meeting, conferences at national and international level and also for giving advice, suggestions, consultancy services to the government and other agencies as and when required, are discussed in brief.

All India Trade Union Congress (AITUC)

This union serves as a labour forum of Communist Party of India. It was formed in 1920 in consequence upon a resolution passed by the organized workers of Bombay and the delegates in a conference on 31st October, 1920. It had 9,24, 000 members which was 7.7% of total members of central trade unions as on 31.12. 1989.[1]

Organizational Structure

The organizational structure of AITUC is as follows:

a. Unit level/Local level affiliated unions.

b. State level/provincial bodies.

c. General council including office bearers (which incorporates the working committee of the general council).

d. Delegates to the general or special session.

1 Indian Labour Year Book, 1995

Objectives

The aims and objectives of AITUC as mentioned in its constitution are

- To establish a socialist state in India
- To socialize and nationalize means of production, distribution and exchange
- To ameliorate the economic and social conditions of the working class
- To watch, promote, safeguard and further the interests, rights and privileges of the workers in all matters relating to their employment
- To secure and maintain for the workers
  - freedom of speech
  - freedom of press
  - freedom of association
  - freedom of assembly
  - right to strike and
  - right to work and maintenance
- To coordinate the activities of trade unions affiliated to the AITUC and
- To establish political or economic advantage based on caste, creed, community, race or religion.

The AITUC is affiliated to communist dominated World Federation of Trade Unions with its headquarters in Paris.

Indian National Trade Union Congress (INTUC)

The moderate leaders having faith and belief in the ideology of the Indian National Congress seceded from the AITUC and formed this union through a resolution passed on 17th November, 1947. This union enjoys the active support and encouragement from Congress leaders.

This union believes in industrial democracy. One of the important objectives of this union is to bring about harmony and peace in industry and settle disputes through existing disputes settlement machineries. It may go for arbitration if settlement by present machineries does not yield any result.

It had 27,06, 000 members which is 22.75% of total membership of all recognized central federations as on 31.12.1989.[2]

2 Indian Labour Year Book 1995 and the *Hindustan Times*, 7th August 1989.

This union is most dominant among all the central trade unions. It recommends workers' delegates to the International Labour Conference. This is affiliated to International Confederation of Free Trade Unions with its Headquarters in Brussels.

Organizational Structure

INTUC is an industry level federation. Plant level unions or units are grouped together for the negotiation at the industry level. Regional branches and councils provide support services. The structure may be like

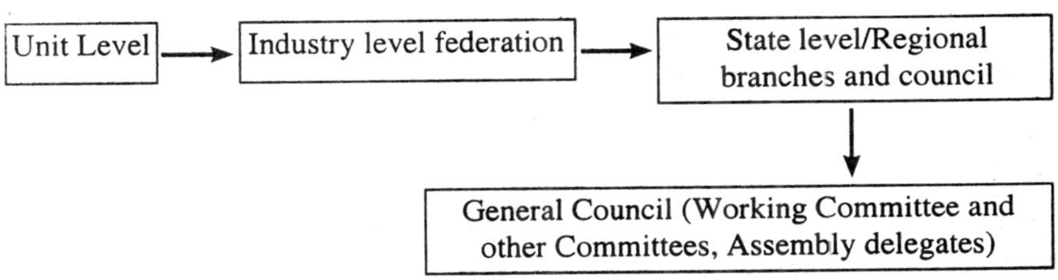

Figure 3. 2: Organizational Structure of INTUC

Objectives

The aims and objectives of INTUC which are mentioned in its constitution are

- To establish an order of society which is free from social, political and economic exploitation and inequality and antisocial concentration of power in any form
- To place industry under national ownership and control
- To secure increasing association of workers in the administration of industry
- To organize society in such a manner as to ensure full employment and the best utilization of its manpower and other resources
- To promote generally the social, civic and political interest of the working class
- To establish just industrial relations
- To secure a living wage for all workers
- To secure suitable legislative enactment for ameliorating the conditions of workers.
- To raise the workers' standard of efficiency and discipline[3]

3 Banerjee, RN; *Organizational Behaviour* (New Central Book Agency(P) Ltd, Kolkata, 1994)

The aforementioned objects are to be achieved by all legitimate, democratic and peaceful methods like negotiation, conciliation, arbitration and adjudication and in the last resort when all methods fail, by peaceful strike.

Centre of Indian Trade Unions (CITU)

This union was formed in 1970 with the members of the Communist Party who seceded from the AITUC. This is a national federation that had 1474 affiliated unions in 1980 and 17,76, 000 members as on 31.12.1989[4].

Organizational Structure

The organizational structure of CITU is given below:

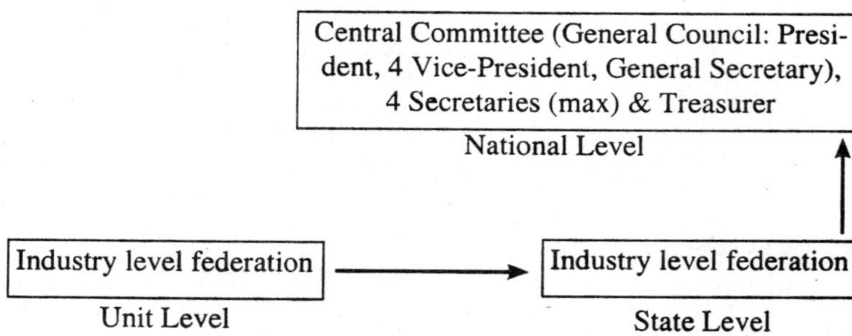

Fig-3. 3 Organizational Structure of CITU

Objectives

The objectives of CITU as mentioned in its constitution are

- To socialize all means of production, distribution and exchange
- To establish a socialist state.
- To stand for the complete emancipation of the society from all exploitation.
- To fight against all encroachment on the economic and social rights of the workers and enlargement of their rights and liberties including the right to strike, for winning, defending and extending the freedom of the democratic trade union movement.
- To demand for nationalization of all foreign monopoly concerns and also the concerns owned by Indian monopolists.
- To fight against the repressive policy of the government towards the democratic and trade union movement.

4 Govt of India, Ministry of Labour, Labour Bureau's Labour (1989) Pp 128-136 and office of the Chief Labour Commissioner (Central)

- To fight against government's economic policy of safeguarding the interests of capitalists and landlords.
- To adhere to the position that no social transformation can be brought about without class-struggie and to repel attack constantly to take the working class along the path of class collaboration.

Hind Majdoor Sabha (HMS)

This union was formed in 1948 with socialist philosophy. It has linkage with socialist parties. It had 14,81,000 members in 1989. It is dominated by Praja Socialists and Socialist Parties.

Organizational structure

The general council of HMS is constituted with

President	
Vice-Presidents:	5 maximum
General Secretary	
Secretaries:	2 maximum
Treasurer	
Members	

Objectives

The main aims and objectives of HMS are mentioned in its constitution. The objectives are

- To promote the economic, political, social and cultural interests of the workers
- To improve the terms and conditions of employment of workers
- To guide and coordinate the activities of affiliated unions and to help them
- To form a federation of unions from the same industry or occupation at the national level.
- To watch, safeguard and promote the interest, rights, privileges of workers.
- To promote the formation of cooperative societies and to foster workers' education.

Employers' Federations/Central Organizations of Employers

Industrial relations pattern of our industry is greatly influenced by the attitudes, values, beliefs and the philosophy held by the unions and the employers' associations. In industrial relations system employers' association and trade union organizations are two major actors. Like trade unions employers' associations are important in industrial relations scenario. It is very much evident from the Trade Unions Act, 1926 that employers' organizations are included under the purview of trade union. The importance of employers' organizations was also felt by Mr Naval Tata for

- development of healthy and stable industrial relations.
- promoting collective bargaining at different levels.
- bringing a unified employers' viewpoint on the issues of industrial relations to the government in a concerted manner
- representing at the meetings of Indian Labour Conference and Standing Labour Committee the employers' approach to labour matter
- Both the parties take active role in the formulation of guidelines, principles, rules, policies through participation on equal representation basis in bipartite and tripartite bodies and also for providing consultancy services to the government and other agencies. In this context it is felt pertinent to have a thorough idea on unions and employers' associations. (The details of some important central trade union organizations have already been discussed in the previous deliberations).

Employers' association was first formed in 1875 on local basis by the textile mill owners in Bombay in the name of Bombay Mill Owners' Association to look after the needs of the mill owners and to promote sound industrial relations between them. The local organizations like this operate through local Chambers of Commerce.

The employers' organizations such as Employers' Federation of Southern India, the West Coast Employers' Federation, the Employers' Associations, Calcutta have regional bases. They offer consultancy services to their members, provide supervisory training to the identified supervisors and organize safety and welfare activities on behalf of their members. They are affiliated to central employers' organizations.

Employers' organizations have apex bodies such as All India Organization of Employers (AIOE), Employers' Federation of India (EFI) and All India Manufacturers' Organization (AIMO).

A separate organization to represent public sector undertakings known as Standing Conference of Public Enterprises (SCOPE) was set up in 1970.

To develop better condition between AIOE and EFI, the Council of Indian Employers was formed in 1956.

Some of the employer's federations are discussed in brief.

All India Organization of Employers (AIOE)

All India Organization of Employers (AIOE) was set up in 1953. It is an associate organization of FICCI and an apex body of employers in India. The principal objectives of the organization are

- to promote and protect the legitimate interests of employers engaged in industry, trade and commerce.
- to initiate necessary steps to oppose, support or promote legislative measures that may affect/likely to effect industries.
- to educate employers so that sound and healthy industrial relations can be established.
- to take organized action on the matters that involve the interest of its members.
- to gather and disseminate information affecting employers and to advise members on promoting industrial relations.
- to promote and protect the industrial development of India.
- to take all steps to establish harmonious relations between employers and employees.
- to promote and support all well-considered schemes that will increase productivity and also the earning of the employees.
- to nominate delegates representing Indian employers at the International Labour Conference and other international bodies.

Membership

It has two types of members – Association members and Individual members.

Association members include any Association/Chamber representing industry, trade or commerce in the country. Individual members mean any individual, firm or joint stock company engaged in any industry, trade or commerce.

Organizational Structure

The organizational structure of AIOE consists of General body, Executive Committee and Secretariat. The general body is the apex policy making body, executive committee is responsible for execution/implementation of policies and objectives of the organization and the Secretariat is responsible for carrying the decision of the general body.

The meetings of general body are held once a year to elect office-bearers, to receive the annual report and to have discussions on various activities of the organization.

The executive committee consists of

- President
- Vice-president
- Treasurer
- Nominee of each association
- Other members elected by delegates representing individual members: 6
- Coopting from industries not represented: 6

The President is elected every year by the annual general meeting, Vice-president and treasurer are elected by the Executive Committee.

Finance: The main source of income is subscription from member employers. Approximately one-fourth of the income comes from membership subscriptions. The other source of income is from the interest on corpus/deposit, publication, conferences, etc. The AIOE spends a major part of its income towards payment of secretariat services, to FICCI, subscription to the International Organization of Employers (IOE) and for publication of weekly periodical *Labour News*.

Employers' Federation of India (EFI)

Employers' Federation of India is one of the central employers' organizations in India. It was formed in 1933 with the aim of protecting the interest of employers who are members of the organization and engaged in trade, commercial and industrial activities in India.

Objectives

The important objectives of EFI as mentioned in its constitution are

- to promote and protect the legitimate interest of employers engaged in industry, trade and commerce
- to maintain harmonious relations between management and labour and to initiate and support all well-considered schemes that will increase productivity and at the same time will give labour a fair share of the increased return
- to gather and disseminate information affecting employers and advise members on industrial relations and other ancillary problems

The consideration of broad economic problem is not excluded within the purview of objectives. However, in the matter of commercial questions of customs, taxation and the like EFI generally does not comment, as all these fall within the jurisdiction of Associated Chamber of Commerce and Industry.

Membership

EFI has three types of members namely association members, ordinary members and honorary members. Association members include associations of employers having not less than 1000 employees. Ordinary members constitute firms undertaking business in India employing not less than 500 members and honorary members are individuals who join the federation having some special skills or experience such as leading lawyers, etc.

Organizational structure

The organizational structure of EFI is shown through diagrammatical presentation in figure 3. 4

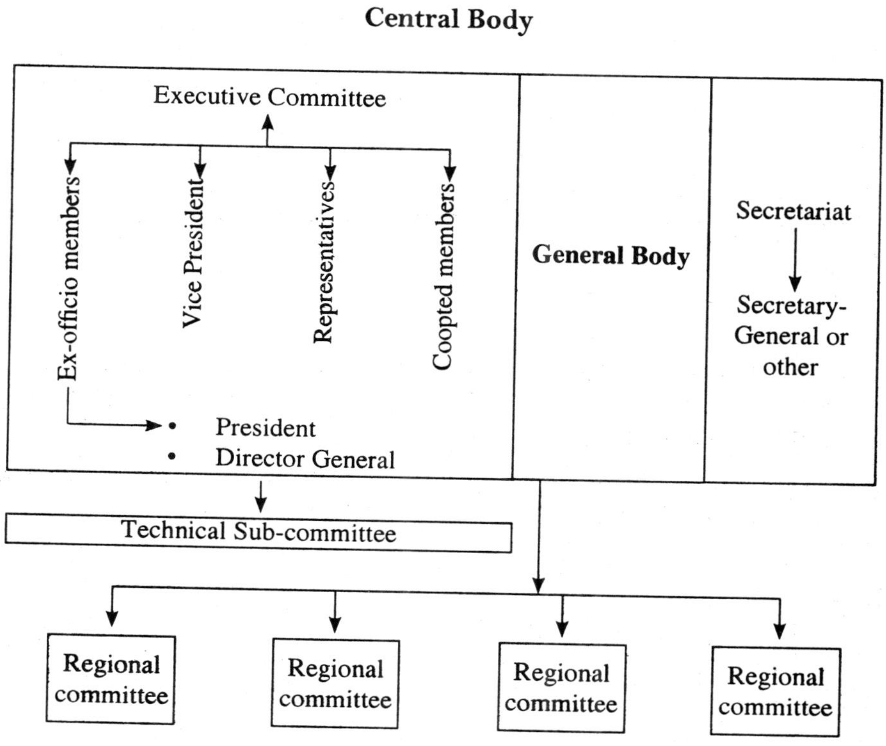

Figure-3. 4: Organizational structure of EFI

EFI was registered under Trade Unions Act, 1926 in 1963. **Its** activities are performed through four regional committees and a central body comprising of executive committee, general body and secretariat.

Executive Committee

It includes

- President } Ex-officio members
- Director General of the Federation }
- Vice-President : 4 or more
- Representatives : 8
- (2 from each regional committee)
- Co-opted member : Maximum 6

(Not more than 6 from among honorary members)

Vice presidents and other members are appointed by the annual general meeting after nominations by regional committees. The executive committee meets 4 or 5 times an year. Technical Sub-committee was set up in 1959 consisting of industrial relations officers to consider matters put up by the secretariat. This Sub-committee acts as a technical advisor to the executive committee.

Regional Committees

Regional Committee is set up for a period of one year. That means the tenure of such committee is one year. Four such regional committees operate to act as a forum for discussing national issues, for raising and discussing local matters.

The general body is the policy-making body, the executive committee is responsible for implementing the policies and objectives of the organization and the secretariat is responsible for carrying out the decisions of the general body.

Finance

The main source of income of EFI is subscriptions from member employers. Nearly half of the income is from membership subscriptions. Other sources of income are from the interest on corpus/deposit, publication, conferences, etc.

All India Manufacturers' Organization (AIMO)

All India Manufacturers' Organization (AIMO) was set up in 1941 under the leadership of M Vishwesvarayya, a renowned engineer to represent both the trade and labour interests of the member firms in the medium and small sectors. This is one of the central employers' organization in India.

The aim of AIMO is to promote economic development through sustained dialogue between trade and industry and government agencies. The motto of AIMO is 'prosperity through industry'. This organization basically consists of domestic entrepreneurs and has secured recognition from the government of India for representation at the national level and also for representation at the International Labour Conference in 1980s. It has links with the Federation of Indian Chamber of Commerce and Industry (FICCI).

Objectives

The important objectives of AIMO as mentioned in its constitution are given herein below:

- to bring about rapid industrialization of the country through sound and progressive policies.
- to enhance the people's standard of living through effective utilization of national resources and talents available in the country.
- to assist in increasing aggregate output in India.
- to serve as a source of valuable information for the Indian and foreign manufacturers.
- to act as a liaison agency between the manufacturers and the government.
- to play positive role in reducing pressure of population on land.

Organizational Structure

AIMO is organized at the following levels:

- **Local Organizations/Associations**

They are formed to look into the interest of the local small and medium sized firms.

- **Regional Organizations/Associations**

They are affiliated to Central Employer Organization. They offer consultancy services; provide welfare and safety measures on behalf of their members.

- **Apex Organization**

AIMO operates as apex body governing the affairs of regional and local associations.

Finance

The primary source of income of the federation is the subscription fee paid by member employers.

Books Recommended

1. BD Singh, *Industrial Relations: Emerging Paradigms* (Excel Books, New Delhi, 2004)
2. PC Tripathi, *Personnel Management & Industrial Relations* (Sultan Chand & Sons, New Delhi, 1978)
3. CB Mamoria, S Mamoria and SV Gankar, *Dynamics of Industrial Relations* (Himalaya Publishing House, Mumbai, 2003)
4. SC Srivastava, *Industrial Relations and Labour Laws* (Vikas Publishing House Pvt Ltd, New Delhi, 2007)

Questions

1. What is an employers' organization? State and explain, in brief, any two central organizations of employers.
2. State the organizational structure and objectives of central organizations of employers in India.
3. What is central trade union organization? Mention the central trade union organizations in India. Discuss, in brief, any one central trade union organization recognized by the government of India for the purpose of representation at various bodies and giving consultancy services to the government.
4. State the objectives and organizational structure of any four central trade union organizations in India.
5. Write short notes on:
   a. CITU
   b. AITUC
   c. EFI
   d. AIMO
   e. UTUC

IV

COLLECTIVE BARGAINING

An Introduction

Collective bargaining is one of the mechanisms used in organization to make an amicable settlement between the parties (i.e., worker's representatives and employer's representatives) in the organization. It helps develop healthy industrial relations through generating a climate of mutuality. (i.e., mutual understanding, mutual responsibility, mutual confidence and mutual trust). People become happy, contented and satisfied if they get what they want. Collective bargaining process aims at fulfiling the expectations of the people in a systematic way.

Meaning of Collective Bargaining

In the narrow sense, collective bargaining means negotiating the terms of agreement by a group of people representing employees and employer in the organization. That means it is a 'group bargaining'. Both employer and employees act as a group, and negotiate with the various terms of agreement each other. In such process of negotiation both employer and employees work as a group and that is why it is called 'collective'. It is known as 'bargaining' because the process of reaching an agreement involves proposals and counter proposals, offers and counter offers.

The term 'collective bargaining' was first used by Sidney Webb and Beatrice Webb in 1891.[1] But subsequently the importance of collective

1 Webb, Sidney and Webb Beatrice: *Industrial Democracy* (Seaham Divisional Labour Party, London, 1920,p-173)

bargaining for determining the terms and conditions of employment was laid by Samuel Gompers.

According to Dale, Yoder, "collective bargaining is the term used to describe a situation in which the essential conditions of employment are determined by a bargaining process undertaken by representatives of a group of workers on the one hand and of one or more employers on the other".[2]

It is a process of discussion and negotiation between two parties, one or both of whom is a group of persons acting in concert. The resulting bargain is an understanding as to the terms and conditions under which a continuing service is to be performed. More specifically, collective bargaining is a procedure by which employers and a group of employees agree upon the conditions of the work.[3]

So, collective bargaining is a mechanism used by both unions' representatives and employer's representatives to settle the issues relating to terms and conditions of employment collectively as a group through discussion and negotiation between each other.

Hoxie defines collective bargaining 'as a mode of fixing the terms of employment by means of bargaining between an organized body of employees and an employer or an association of employers usually acting through organized agents. The essence of collective bargaining is a bargain between interested parties and not a decree from outside parties'.[4]

Features of Collective Bargaining

Salient features of collective bargaining are discussed herein below:

1. Parties in the collective bargaining

Two parties – employer and employees – are involved in the collective bargaining process. Some management personnel represent employer while trade union officials represent employees in the collective bargaining activities.

2. Group process

It is a group process. The representatives of both the parties – employer and employees – act as a group. They sit together, discuss together and negotiate terms of employment as a group.

2 Yoder, Dale: *Personnel Management: Principles and Policies* (Prentice-Hall, New York, 1959, p- 97)

3 *Encyclopedia of Social Sciences* Vol-iii, 1951, p 628

4 Hoxie, RF in Shister, J (ed) *Readings in Labour Economies and Industrial Relations* (Harper & Row, New York, 1962, p 148)

3. Interactive process

Discussion and negotiation involves interaction between the representations of the parties. So, settlement of issues is made through interactive process.

4. Role of trade union

Trade union plays an important role towards reaching an agreement or contract in the bargaining activities. If the trade union is supportive, constructive, facilitative and positive to the growth and development of the employees and the organization as well, the possibility of successful collective bargaining in the organization occurs; and reverse is the case if the trade union is negative, destructive and does not rely on collective bargaining mechanism.

5. Outcomes of collective bargaining

Outcomes of collective bargaining are reflected in production both in quantity and quality, profit, market share, etc.

6. Issues in collective bargaining

Issues in collective bargaining basically relate to economic issues and non-economic issues governed by service rules, standing orders, bipartite settlements, etc. Most of the issues settled through collective bargaining process are connected with employment, terms of employment, unemployment and condition of labour.

7. Process activity

Collective bargaining is a process activity. It follows a number of steps starting from the stage of submission of charter of demands to the concluding stage of reaching of an agreement or contract.

8. Flexibility

One of the important characteristics of effective collective bargaining activity is flexible attitudes of the members representing the parties. It occurs that the parties need to go for a compromise arrangement or to surrender some rights/privilege in exchange for some other consideration. So, all this needs a flexible thought process amongst the persons representing the parties in bargaining.

9. Climate of industrial relations

Collective bargaining determines the state of labour-management relationship in the organization through the process of negotiation and reaching of an agreement. Effective collective bargaining process helps develop labour-management relation resulting in generation of a congenial climate in the organization. Successful collective bargaining process brings the parties close to each other and promotes understanding amongst them. All this makes the working environment conducive that facilitates establishment of better industrial relations in the organization.

10. Industrial democracy

Decisions on vital issues are taken through collective bargaining forum where representatives from both the parties--employer and employees interact and negotiate. So, workers play an important role in such policy decision process in the organization. This indicates that collective bargaining introduces democratic practices in the organization.

11. Process of adjustment

Through collective bargaining process both the parties – union and management adjust themselves to maintain peace and harmony in the organization. It may happen that the parties need to sacrifice some interest for amicable resolution of issues through the process of compromise, adjustment and accommodation.

12. Continuity in communication process

Collective bargaining in its entirety does not mean that it ends immediately after agreement or contract is reached; it goes through different phases like administration, interpretation and enforcement of agreement. So, for all such activities continuous communication/ interaction between labour and management is a necessity.

13. Variance in results

Representatives of workers and management interact and negotiate in the collective bargaining forum. The results of interaction and negotiation between leaders emerge into an agreement that may be satisfactory or unsatisfactory to the employees. If the leaders actively participating in collective bargaining exercise hold positive values, beliefs, attitudes, thought patterns, balanced ego states, there is the possibility of better results in the negotiation, and reverse is the case if the leaders do not possess the desired level of attributes, ego states, values, and attitudes.

14. Complementary process

Collective bargaining is a complementary process. Both the parties-- management and labour need each other for their existence and growth. Labour can give the service, efforts for production and management can compensate in exchange for service. So, 'give and take' activity is carried on through collective bargaining system.

Objectives of Collective Bargaining

Objectives of collective bargaining are to run the organization smoothly, effectively so that it can face challenges, obtain competitive advantages through making the people dynamic, contented, satisfied and committed, and generate a climate of healthy industrial relations in the organization.

Since collective bargaining needs two parties--union and management – to interact, discuss, negotiate and reach an agreement, they may have objectives of their own. So, to have a better understanding on the objectives of collective bargaining it is felt pertinent to discuss objectives separately from the view point of union and management.

Objective of Collective Bargaining from the Union's Point of View

The trade union of employees accepts collective bargaining as a mechanism to settle disputes, to develop understanding with the management that helps make changes in organizational process activities in favour of the employees and promote the status and identity of the employees as inseparable part of the whole organization system. So, the trade unions have some objectives in collective bargaining. Some of the important objectives of collective bargaining are:

- to make sound pecuniary condition of the employees through negotiation on economic issues with the management in the collective bargaining forum and reaching of an agreement.
- to introduce an industrial democratic set-up in the organization where workers' contribution is properly assessed and focused in the right place.
- to bring a change in perception of management about role, importance and worth of employees in smooth and effective functioning of activities in the organization.
- to make a solid and strong organizational sub-system by entering into an employee-oriented bipartite settlement to enable it to interfere with activities that come exclusively under management prerogative.
- to give maximum comfort, concession, privileges, benefits to the employees through collective bargaining settlement in order to make the members loyal, disciplined that helps to take decision in subsequent period, against management.
- to ensure employees that there is no threat of losing jobs.

- to make the union dedicated for the cause of employees and to use collective bargaining as an exclusive machinery to address grievances, settle disputes and to make the management adopt various ameliorative and motivating measures in terms of settlement.
- to bring a change in societal activities and to help implementation of various schemes undertaken by the management under corporate social responsibility (CSR).

Objectives of Collective Bargaining from the Management's Point of View

One of the main objectives of the management in collective bargaining is to ensure that the organization grows, develops and confronts challenges to attain business excellence and to obtain competitive advantages.

However, the important objectives of management in collective bargaining are discussed. They are

- to ensure uninterrupted functional activities of the organization by way of establishing a state of mutuality – mutual understanding, mutual faith and mutual confidence between trade union representatives and management under a collective bargaining system.
- to maintain dominance over the working people and to retain the prerogatives of the management.
- to ensure achievement of organizational goals and fulfillment of company's mission with and through the people in a situation when union representatives extend their support to the management under collective bargaining agreement.
- to delight the customers through delivery of the quality goods and services to them at a lesser price by the contented, committed work force and to make an important place in the market.
- to make a strong enterprise to face challenges and to obtain competitive advantages by developing team spirit and creating a culture of OCTPAC ('O' stands for 'openness', 'C' stands for 'confrontation', 'T' stands for 'trust', 'P' stands for 'proactive', 'A' stands for 'autonomy', and 'C' stands for 'co-operation') in the organization.
- to reduce industrial conflicts, to increase production, profit, to improve standard of living of the employees and to establish healthy industrial relations

- to ensure growth and development of the enterprise and to promote stability in collective bargaining relations.

Benefits of Collective Bargaining

Collective bargaining is an effective device to bring both the parties—union and management together and to compromise their conflicting interests. It plays an important role to improve labour management relation and to ensure peace and harmony in industry. An effective collective bargaining system benefits both employees and employers.

Benefits to Employees

Employees are benefited through collective bargaining in various ways. They are:

1. Pecuniary condition of the employees

Collective bargaining agreement improves the financial conditions of employees. It fixes higher rates of wages/salaries and allowances for the employees under an agreement and ensures a minimum level of earning.

2. Standard of living

Since employees' earnings are increased, standard of living gets improved. Employees can have money to meet some necessities of their lives that becomes impossible in absence of positive collective agreement.

3. Security of jobs

Collective bargaining process ensures that the employees' jobs are secured, protected and stable. This makes them happy and relieved from mental worries, agony, and anxiety of loosing jobs.

4. Quality of working life

Collective bargaining helps promote the quality of working life of employees by improving economic condition, ensuring stability of jobs and other measures.

5. State of mutuality

It makes the people happy, contented and committed; and promotes a healthy relationship between boss and the subordinate in the organization. This, in the process develops a climate of mutuality—mutual understanding, mutual responsibility and mutual faith between boss and subordinates.

6. Industrial democracy

It brings industrial democracy by making proper forum in organizations for participation of employees in discussion, interaction exercises with employer(s) on various important issues.

Democratic set up in organization is built-in under collective bargaining process through various measures such as employee participation, employee involvement, employee empowerment, gain sharing and the like.

7. Self-respect

Employees develop a feeling of self-respect, self-importance when a tradition of effective collective bargaining system is built in the organization.

8. Morale

Collective bargaining improves the level of morale of the employees. This motivates them to give their best and surpass the targets set by the management.

9. Fair and judicious action of the management

Employees receive fair and judicious treatment from the management. Management remains abstained from taking whimsical and arbitrary action against employees.

10. Trade union strength

It increases the strength of union when a culture of successful collective bargaining is generated in the organization. This helps strengthen labour movement.

Benefits to Employers

Collective bargaining benefits the employers in the following ways:

1. Uninterrupted production

Employees give maximum production and ensure that production activities are not disturbed.

2. Company image

It helps enhance company's stature and image in the market through delivery of quality goods and services at a comparatively lesser price by the employees who remain happy, and contented under effective collective bargaining agreement.

3. Existence, growth and development

In a hyper-competitive market collective bargaining occupies a pivotal role to make the people committed, loyal and competent who strive their best for existence, growth and development of the organization.

4. Zero conflict or less conflict

Since most of the issues of the employees are settled through collective bargaining and the employees feel satisfied, they may not have major issues for raising industrial conflicts. So the organization functions smoothly and effectively in a situation where there is 'zero conflict' or less conflict.

5. Industrial jurisprudence

It establishes a system of industrial jurisprudence through introduction of a code that defines the rights and obligations of the parties in their employment relations. It creates a 'discipline climate' based on mutual understanding of the union and management.

6. Disposal of issues

It is an effective means of disposal of issues collectively. It occurs when issues are settled individually by the management, not under collective bargaining system the settlement process creates a lot of misunderstanding between management and complainants and takes lot of time to dispose issues.

7. Implementation of decisions

The management does not find it very difficult to implement the decisions taken under collective bargaining system because employees know that decisions are taken by them, not by the management themselves only.

8. Competitive advantage

Company can obtain competitive advantage by capturing market through a change in quality of product, service, delivery and also the Mindset of the people. All this is possible in a 'collective bargaining climate' that makes the people dynamic, proactive and competition-oriented to face any emerging challenges in the market.

9. Peace and harmony

It makes the people happy, contented; and establishes healthy dyadic relation, human relation and develops a sense of 'belonging', and 'togetherness'. All this helps bring peace and harmony in the organization.

Pre-requisites for Successful Collective Bargaining

To make the collective bargaining successful there are some essential pre-requisites. They are:

1. A climate of mutuality

If the collective bargaining needs to be effective, a climate of mutuality should exist in the organization. The climate of mutuality is based on mutual understanding, mutual faith, mutual responsibility and mutual trust between the boss and the subordinate. If the supervisor and subordinate are close, open and respect each other there is the possibility of developing better dyadic relationship. This helps make the bargaining system effective.

2. A solid and strong trade union

The trade union must be solid and strong from the perspectives of membership and finance. If the union is strong financially and organization-wise, it is easier for the management to take decision on the issues. Strong trade union can make it possible to honour the agreement as the union has a control over the members. Weak union, on the contrary does not have adequate followers and it is unstable to carry on union activities effectively. Under such situation management can make any agreement with the weak union. So for effective collective bargaining a solid, strong and stable union is a necessity.

3. A changed mindset of the parties

A separate, changed mindset of the people representing union and the employer is a pre-requisite for successful collective bargaining. Both the parties should have positive mindset to accept that each party needs to sacrifice something in exchange for something else. That means, collective agreement must be based on 'win-win' perception not 'win-lose' perception—a thought process reflected on integrative bargaining.

4. Recognition of trade union

For successful collective bargaining trade union should be recognized as a bargaining agent. If the union is not recognized, it is difficult for the management to negotiate with it for settlement of issues. The employer recognizes a union when it is stable, strong and has a larg number of members. It happens that the unrecognized union does not have adequate number of members and it becomes weak and unstable. So it is a risky decision for the management to give recognition to such a union. The employer, in his own interest gives recognition to a union that has a control over most of the employees and can influence them to implement a decision taken through collective bargaining process.

5. Unfair labour practice

It occurs that both the parties—management and union resort to unfair labour practices. Under such situation climate of mistrust, suspicion is generated and it happens that successful collective bargaining is a rare possibility. So, to make the collective bargaining effective, both parties should avoid such practice.

6. Comfortable and congenial political climate

A congenial and comfortable political climate is a necessity for effective collective bargaining in an organization If the government is facilitative, and supportive, it encourages collective bargaining as a means for settlement of issues, takes necessary measures to remove any provisions of law that affects collective bargaining and incorporates any new provision to it that strengthens the collective bargaining.

7. Attitudes, thought process and desire of the parties

One of the pre-requisites for successful collective bargaining is the attitudes, thought pattern and desire of the parties. Both the parties—employer and employees should have positive and constructive attitudes, thought process and desire for settlement of issues through collective bargaining. During collective bargaining both the parties need to sacrifice some share to arrive at an agreement. The parties should consider the whole bargaining process as 'win-win' activity not 'win-lose' activity; that means both parties win.

Issues of Collective Bargaining

Collective bargaining is a mechanism to settle disputes/issues through discussion, negotiation by the representatives of union and management in a group.

In earlier period issues like wages, hours of work, working condition were the subject matter of the collective bargaining. In times of unionization, issues relating to recognition of unions, unions security were the main issues of collective bargaining. During times of recession, lay off, retrenchment, job sharing were the subject matter of the collective bargaining.

In the USA the National Labour Relations Act, 1947 has classified the issues for bargaining purpose into three categories:

- Mandatory issues are those issues which the parties must bargain if they are placed at the bargaining table by any party to the bargaining exercise.
- Voluntary issues are those issues which are neither mandatory nor illegal. The parties may bargain on those issues in good faith

and the issues may be incorporated in the final document of the agreement if both the parties agree.

- Illegal issues are those issues which are prohibited by law.

Ghosh and Nath (1973) have expressed the following issues being the subject matter of the bargaining;

- Recognition of union
- Wages and allowances
- Hours of work
- Leave and festival holidays
- Bonus and profit sharing schemes
- Seniority
- Nationalization
- Fixation of work loads
- Standard labour force
- Programmes of planning and development
- Lay off and retrenchment
- Victimization for trade union activities
- Provident fund, gratuity and other retiral benefits
- Incentives
- Housing and transport facilities
- Discipline, safety, accident prevention
- Occupational diseases, protective clothing
- Canteen, rest rooms, medical and health services, crèches
- Administration of welfare fund, cooperative thrift and credit societies
- Educational, recreational and training schemes[5]

So, the issues of collective bargaining may be economic issues and also non-economic issues relating to welfare, social security, developmental and industrial relations.

Growth of Collective Bargaining in India

The growth and development of collective bargaining in India can be divided into the following periods:

5 Ghosh, P and Nath S, *Labour Relations in India* (Sandha Publications, New Delhi, 1973)

- Early period of collective bargaining (The period up to 1920)
- Infancy period of collective bargaining (The period from 1921 to 1947)
- Post-Independence period of collective bargaining (The period after 1947)

Early period of Collective Bargaining (The period up to 1920)

During this period, settlement of issues, demands through collective bargaining process were not popular. Instances of joint negotiation, discussion at the plant level were not uncommon. Settlements at the industry level were very few. Attempts were made to settle disputes in textile mills in Ahmedabad through joint negotiation in 1918. Parties to the dispute were made to understand that in case of failure to reach an agreement through mutual discussion and negotiation, the matter would be resolved through conciliation, and in the event of its failure, decision would be taken by agreed arbitrator or board of arbitration consisting of representatives of workers and employer. Ultimately board of arbitration resolved the issues.

In 1920, Textile Labour Association (TLA) and Ahmedabad Mill Owners' Association made an agreement in the matter that issues/disputes would be discussed first between the workers and the management of the mills. If no settlement could be arrived at, the matter would be reported by the TLA to the Mills Owners' Association for amicable settlement through negotiation and discussion. In case of not having reached a settlement, the matter was required to be referred to permanent arbitration board. A number of industrial disputes were resolved through mutual negotiations.

In fact during this period collective bargaining in the real sense did not occur except collective bargaining agreement made in 1920.

Infancy period of collective bargaining (The period from 1921 to 1947)

The revolutionary waves generated by the Russian Revolution united the working class to play meaningful role in trade union activities. In 1925 check-off system was introduced in TISCO through the efforts of the trade union. The Trade Unions Act, 1926 and the Trade Disputes Act, 1929 encouraged the working community to strengthen the trade unions. The appointment of the Royal Commission on Labour in 1929 was an indication of giving importance to the labour related problems. The Report of the Commission placed in 1931 gave emphasis on industrial peace and harmony through settlement of issues.

The Bombay Trade Disputes Conciliation Act, 1934 gave much emphasis on the settlement of industrial disputes and bringing peace and harmony in industry through making provisions for appointment of Labour Officers, Special Conciliators. Subsequently this Act was replaced by the Bombay Industrial Disputes Act, 1938 that provided for an elaborate machinery to promote peaceful and amicable settlement of industrial disputes.

Prior to Independence not much headway was noticed in the collective bargaining process. The Defence of India Rules was amended and in 1942, Rule 81(A) was added to it. Such rules empowered the government to refer any dispute to conciliation or adjudication and to prohibit any strike and lock-out if resorted to without notice. All this hindered the growth of collective bargaining. However, one positive sign was noticed when tripartite Indian Labour Conference and Standing Labour Committee were set up in 1942 with objectives of discussing all matters of national importance as between employer and employees and laying down of procedure for the settlement of industrial disputes. The unanimous decision taken in this tripartite committee on vital issues relating to labour greatly influenced the government's labour policy and also the industrial relations pattern of Indian industries. All this made an impact on the mode of settlement of issues through joint discussion, deliberation, negotiation and ultimately through the system of collective bargaining.

This period saw an emergence of new climate of mutuality in industrial settings in 1946 by enacting the labour law—Industrial Employment (Standing Orders) Act, 1946 that makes it compulsory for the establishments having 100 or more employees to get the standing orders certified by the appropriate government official. The Standing Orders contain the issues relating to employment, terms of employment, condition of labour and discipline and before orders are certified, trade union/employees are given chance to present their suggestions/ comments in the matter.

The Bombay Industrial Relations Act, 1946 was promulgated replacing the Bombay Industrial Disputes Act, 1938 with the objectives of generating a climate of peace and harmony in industry through settlement of issues by the parties.

The Industrial Disputes Act, 1947 came into force from April, 1947 to provide for constitution of works committees in industrial undertakings to promote measures for securing and preserving amity and good relations between employer and the workers and to that end, to comment upon matters of common interest or concern and to endeavour to compose any material difference of opinion in respect of such matter. The Act provides for conciliation services through appointment of conciliation authorities, viz., conciliation officers, Board of Conciliation, and also adjudication services through Labour Court, Tribunal and National Tribunal.

The Indian National Trade Union Congress formed in 1947 helped to promote sound industrial relations in undertakings through participation in bipartite and tripartite level committee meeting, discussion and negotiation.

Post-Independence period of collective bargaining (The period after 1947)

After independence the activities for collective agreement have increased. Trade unions have been growing and have made an important position in industrial settings to make the collective bargaining process effective and desirable. It has been very common for the organizations to make collective agreements with unions after independence. The factors necessitate the growth of collective bargaining include

- significant increase in the level of education of the employees
- change of attitudes of employees
- growing needs for satisfaction of higher order needs of employees
- recognition of human values by the management
- considering employees as the assets by the management
- contribution of employees in the hyper-competitive market
- New Economic Policy that shifts CRP (Controlled, Regulated and Protected) economy to LPG (Liberalized, Privatized and Global) economy.

A brief idea on the growth of collective bargaining in India after independence can be obtained from the following:

1. In India collective bargaining agreements are made at the plant level, industry level and national level.

At the plant level

Some of the plant level agreements include

- The TISCO agreement 1956, 1959
- The Bata Shoe Company Agreement, 1955, 1958 and 1962
- The Belur Agreement (between the Aluminium Company and its employees' union) 1956
- The Modi Spinning and Weaving Mills Company's Agreement, 1956

- The National Newsprint Nepanagar Agreement, 1956
- The Indian Tea Association and Indian Tea Planters' Association, 1956

At the industry level

Some of the industry level agreements are:

- The Ahmedabad Millowners' Association and the Ahmedabad Textile Labour Association, 1955
- Agreement reached after independence in industries viz., Plantation in South and in Assam; Coal, Iron and Steel, Chemicals, Petroleum, etc.
- Agreement made in 1992 between Cement Manufacturers' Association and major central federation of trade unions namely, BMS, INTUC, HMS, CITU and AITUC.

At the national level

Some important Collective Agreements made at the national level are:

- The Bonus Agreement for Plantation Workers, 1956
- Agreement reached in Ports and Docks, 1977, 1981, 1994

2. Both union and management are in favour of contract agreements in the form of settlement that may have binding on the parties.
3. Growth of trade unions is prevalent during post-independence period as is witnessed from the formation of central federations of trade unions namely, INTUC (1947), HMS (1948), UTUC (1948), BMS (1955), CITU (1970), NLO (1972), UTUC-LS and TUCC. Formation of central federations of trade unions encouraged employers to strengthen their associations. All this enhanced the importance of bipartite settlements at different levels, viz., plant level, industry level and national level.
4. A great deal of importance has been given on collective bargaining as a mechanism to settle disputes and to this effect the issues like recognition of trade unions, unfair labour practice, and grievance redressal procedure have been discussed thread barely in 16th session of Labour Conference in 1958 and Code of Discipline provided guidelines in the matter.
5. Five-year plans have stressed upon the necessity of bringing peace and harmony in industries to promote sound industrial relations in organization. All this is possible through collective bargaining and mutual settlement of disputes.

6. Most management people have accepted collective bargaining as an effective tool for disposal of employee issues. So, the trade unions submit their charter of demands to the management and the management in turn, submit counter demands to the trade union.
7. During post-independence period the scope for collective bargaining has increased. It now covers a lot of issues for discussion, negotiation and reaching an agreement.
8. To develop mutual understanding between labour and management some companies have introduced schemes like workers' participation in management, employee involvement and employee empowerment, quality circles and much more. All this indicates a positive approach of management and unions to the solutions of industrial disputes through bipartite settlements.

Hindrances of Collective Bargaining in India

Collective bargaining brings the parties—management and union closer and helps promote sound relationship between them. In a state of mutuality it is possible for the management to negotiate with the union and arrive at a collective agreement. So, for settlement of issues collective bargaining should be effective, but in reality collective bargaining has not developed as is needed. There are a lot of hindrances/obstacles to the growth of collective bargaining. They are:

1. Outsiders controlling trade unions

It happens that Indian trade unions are controlled largely by outsiders. So growth of trade unions affecting collective bargaining suffers from the following

- Outside trade union leaders are not well aware of various processes of industrial activities that hinder them to make bargain effectively with employers.
- Outside leaders are much more self-centered than union-centered ones. So, they look towards their interest more than the union interest. Casual approach of outside leaders towards problems of workers makes the union weak.

2. Non-recognition of trade unions

If the trade union is recognized by the employer, it may have the rights to bargain with the employer as a bargaining agent. The recognized union can, therefore, take up employee issues with the employer for negotiation and agreement and make the collective bargaining effective. In our country recognition of union has been a voluntary activity; there is no statutory compulsion or obligation on the part of the employer to recognize representative union. It is exclusively management prerogative to decide whether it intends to confer recognition upon a union or not. In such a situation possibility of settling workers' demands by union through collective bargaining process is remote. All this makes the union ineffective and inhibits the growth of collective bargaining.

3. Multiplicity of unions

In India unions are formed on the basis of religion, caste, creed, language, place, etc., that results in mushroom growth of unions in the organization. Multiplicity of unions creates a lot of problems for the unions for their survival, growth and development.

The problems are

- It crushes the solidarity of workers
- Employers ignore unions as they know the strength of unions
- It weakens the pecuniary support of unions

Multiplicity of unions makes the unions weak; financially unsound that inhibits the growth of collective bargaining. Size of the union determines the bargaining strength. Bigger the size of a union, higher is the bargaining strength and reverse is the case when the size of a union is small.

4. Use of adjudication machineries

The government machineries like Labour Courts, Tribunals, Industrial Tribunals and National Tribunals have been set up under the Industrial Disputes Act, 1947 to settle the industrial disputes referred to them. Settlement of disputes through adjudication machineries gives an indication that much more emphasis has been laid up on such machineries than the machinery (collective bargaining) used to settle disputes by the parties through discussion, negotiation.

It also occurs that the workers cannot go on strikes when the management does not concede to their demands, (i) during the conciliation proceedings are pending (ii) during the pendency of proceeding before a Labour Court, Tribunal or National Tribunal and within two months after the conclusion of such proceeding (iii) during any period in which a settlement or award is in operation in respect of any of the matters covered by this settlement or award. In such a situation collective bargaining as a method of disputes settlement through discussion and negotiation cannot work effectively and its growth is handicapped obviously.

5. Degree of unionization

For effective collective bargaining union should be strong and it is possible if the workers feel the necessity of organizing union and become the members of the union. In reality it happens that in India an insignificant percentage of workers is organized. The strength of union comes from the workers who give their all out efforts to make union programmes a success. Degree of unionization in India is much lower in comparison to countries like the USA, Great Britain, France and many other European countries.

6. Other factors

The following factors create hurdles in the growth process of collective bargaining.

a. **Employers' attitudes**

Employers' negative values, beliefs, attitudes and autocratic leadership style create a great hurdle in the development of trade union. Such employers show their apathetic and unwilling attitudes to discuss and negotiate concerning the workers' issues with unions. They think it is their prerogative to decide the issues like promotion, transfer, wages, allowances, reward, etc. Union has got nothing to interfere. All this inhibits the growth of collective bargaining.

b. **Absence of statutory compulsion**

There is no appropriate legislative provision for settlement of industrial disputes through collective bargaining. The employers, therefore, treat this matter casually and think it is their absolute jurisdiction to decide whether they will accept collective bargaining or not, as a method of dispute settlement.

c. **Determination of bargaining agent**

To determine the bargaining agent is a necessity for holding discussion and negotiation on the issues for reaching a collective agreement. In India there is no provision under any legislation regarding determination of representative union. There are different methods for ascertaining majority union like secret ballot, verification of membership through 'check-off' or other system, but no method has been provided under law. This creates hurdles in the development of collective bargaining.

Suggestions to Make the Collective Bargaining Effective in India

Collective bargaining plays a pivotal role in establishing sound industrial relations in organizations. Collective bargaining in India has not made much headway because of some hurdles. The following suggestion, if implemented, can make collective bargaining effective in India.

1. Trade union activities—management and administration should be controlled through internal leaders. Outside membership in the union should be restricted to a certain percentage, not above 10% of the total strength. The Trade Unions Act, 1926 needs to be amended accordingly.
2. Trade union should be strong and stable so that it can place the workers' demands with confidence, strength and assertiveness and can make the collective bargaining effective.
3. Workers should be given proper training, education to make them feel the necessity of organizing unions.
4. Political interference in trade union activities should be discouraged. Internal leaders need to be educated and trained so that they can replace political leaders.
5. To check multiplicity of unions, Trade Unions Act 1926 should be appropriately amended and the minimum number of persons required for registration of union should be increased from 7 to 20% of the total employees' strength with a minimum of 20.
6. The majority union should be recognized. There should be provision in the Trade Unions Act 1926 that every employer shall recognise the majority union to work as bargaining agent.
7. There should be appropriate provision in the Trade Unions Act, 1926 to determine the representative union through secret ballot system.
8. The Industrial Disputes Act 1947 should be amended appropriately to make the collective bargaining agreement binding all workers irrespective of their associations with unions.
9. Grievance Redressal Procedure (GRP) should be strengthened so that a large number of issues can be disposed off through GRP and the issues concerning general interest should be taken up for settlement through collective bargaining process.
10. A climate of OCMA (Openness, Cooperation, Mutuality and Acceptance) needs to be established in the organizations to generate a 'feeling of we-ness' 'togetherness' amongst the management and

employees. The climate will facilitate collective bargaining to reach an agreement.

The National Commission on Labour has made the following recommendations to make the collective bargaining more effective.

1. The employers' organization should be held greatly responsible to make collective bargaining widely accepted. It should undertake promotion of collective bargaining at various level.
2. The employers' association should work towards elimination of unfair labour practice by employers.
3. Compulsory adjudication of dispute should be made when all measures yield no result.
4. Trade unions should be strengthened both organizationally and financially by amending the Trade Unions Act, 1926 to make registration of union compulsory, enhance the union membership fee, reduce the presence of outsiders in the union executive and among the office-bearers and increase the minimum number of members in respect of the union applying for registration.
5. Legal provision may be made either by a separate legislation or by amending the existing enactment for
   - compulsory recognition of trade unions and certification of unions as bargaining agents
   - prohibition and penalization of unfair labour practices
   - bargaining in good faith by both employer and unions
   - conferring legal validity and legitimacy on collective agreements
6. Workers' education should be intensified for building up internal union leadership and making workers more knowledgeable and conscious about rights and obligations.
7. The idea of union for one plant or one industry should be popularized and made a reality.
8. The government should declare its policy to allow and encourage the parties to settle their conflicts by bipartite consultation and negotiation consistent with public safety and interest of the society in general.

Collective Bargaining Process

Collective bargaining process starts generally after the charter of demands is submitted to the management by the union. If there is already an agreement existing in the organization, it remains in operation till the date of expiry of the agreement or the date on which fresh agreement is signed whichever is latter. So for holding collective bargaining and reaching an agreement it needs to pass through different steps. The steps and sequencing of collective bargaining may vary from company to company depending on the nature of involvement of the parties in the collective bargaining process. The probable involvement of the parties may be like

1. One company and one union
2. One company and more than one unions
3. More than one companies and one union
4. More than one companies and more than one unions

If the company is involved with single union the collective bargaining process becomes very easy and simple but in other cases it becomes very complicated. The steps involved in collective bargaining process are grouped into the following 3 phases as shown in Figure-4. 1

1. Pre-negotiation phase
2. Negotiation phase
3. Post-negotiation phases

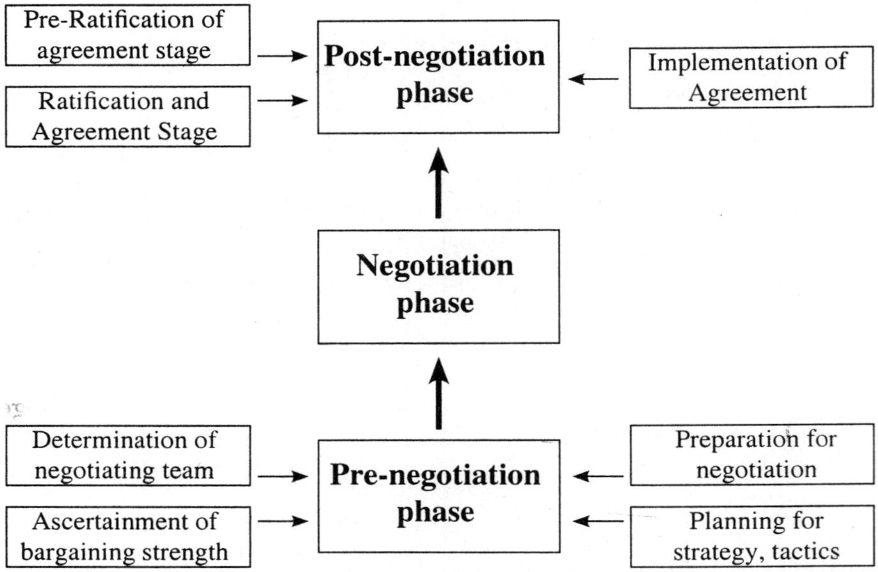

Figure 4. 1: Diagrammatic Presentation of Collective Bargaining Process

1. Pre-negotiation phase

This is a phase prior to negotiation. This phase includes the following steps/activities

a. Determination of negotiating team

b. Ascertainment of bargaining strength

c. Preparation for negotiation

d. Planning for strategy, tactics

a. Determination of negotiating team

This is very important to select a team that will participate in bargaining process. From the management side negotiating team may consist of one spokesman or chief negotiator who is generally the senior executive of the company. Generally the Chairman of the company remains outside the purview of the negotiating committee. Some executives who have vast knowledge and experience in work activities as also have expertise in negotiation are taken as members in the committee. Generally executives in senior positions like Personnel/HR Head, Production Head, Marketing Head, Financial Advisor/Chief Accounts Officer, Factory/Plant Head, who are considered to be resource persons are included in the negotiating team. There is no hard and fast rule regarding number of members to be included in the team. It happens that mostly team consists of 3 to 6 members depending upon the size of the company.

On the workers' side negotiating team consists of office-bearers of the union. When there is only one union in the organization, there no problem in the formation of negotiating committee. It creates a problem for the management to take decision regarding bargaining agent when there are more than one unions in the company. It occurs that each union claims that it has maximum number of members in its fold. Under such eventuality the management can

i. select the representative union through secret ballot or

ii. select the union through verification of membership by government agency or

iii. bargain with united forum of unions constituted with representatives of all unions in proportion to their verified membership, for the purpose of negotiation in bargaining.

b. Ascertaining the bargaining strength

It is very important for both the parties to ascertain its strength to carry on bargaining with its desired objectives and also the strength of other party that may create obstacles to the success of bargaining. To understand strength each party makes thorough study and analysis of the following.

- *Market situation:* Whether work stoppage will affect the company's image, whether company's product has made a significant place in the market, whether the market passes through recession stage and the demand for the product falls down?
- *Competition:* Whether discontinuity in service, production will affect the competition, if so, to what extent? Under such situation how and to what extent it will affect the company in obtaining competitive advantages?
- *Labour availability:* Whether labour is abundantly available at cheap rate or supply is uncertain and labour cost is expensive?
- *Technology implication:* Whether technology installed with the company will be affected if its operation is disturbed, if so, to what extent?
- *Financial strength:* Whether financial strength of the company is sound and has the capacity to pay if the union's demand is accepted or otherwise? Financial strength of the union to which employees belong is studied to make an idea whether it can be able to assist them during the period of work stoppage?
- *Legal compulsion:* Whether laws of the country are against the situation that restricts production, service and impose penalties, stringent measures against violation, non-compliance of rules; or otherwise?
- *Government attitudes:* Whether the government attitude is tough, strict and immediate action is taken to ensure compliance, adherence to rules, or the situation arises out of political instability creating a state of chaos, uncertainty and misrule?
- *Public sympathy and inconvenience:* Whether disturbance in work activities will cause hardship, inconvenience to the public resulting in loosing public support, sympathy, or otherwise?
- *Reaction of shareholders and directors:* Whether shareholders and directors will take otherwise if a situation of uncertainty, disturbance in work activities is created. It happens that shareholders, directors intend for maximum profit of the company yielding high amount of dividend?

Both the parties (union and employer) generally give a serious thought in the above matter to decide each other's strength in the bargaining activities. On the basis of information, data, reports, records, material facts gathered from different sources in respect of the areas mentioned above, total cost (monetary and non-monetary) of work stoppage is ascertained. If the cost is much more than usual management may agree to give higher concession to reach a settlement and reverse may be the case if the cost is less than expected.

c. Preparation for negotiation

Before negotiation starts both union and management prepare themselves to make the bargaining successful. Each party strives its best to negotiate the issues in a manner that agreement is made in his favour. So, the parties do a lot of homework to keep everything in their grips. To substantiate facts each party prepares its arguments, counter-arguments with necessary data, information with the intention to make the other party compelled to agree.

Some of the activities which the parties generally follow to prepare them for negotiations are mentioned below:

i. Collection of data, information and preparation of note for discussion

HR department/Personnel Department of the company collects data, information issue-wise from own records, records of zonal office, corporate office also records from office of the employers' association and other sources. A note is prepared by the department for all issues mentioned in the charter of demands giving emphasis on the following areas:

- details of facts
- present position of the issue
- action taken, if any
- resultant effect, if agreed
- estimated financial obligations, if any
- settlement made by other companies, on such issues
- statutory obligations
- suggestions of the department vis-à-vis the company

ii. Making confidential conferences with the members of the negotiating team on the charter of demands

The objective of such conference is to make the members aware of the issues, to get new ideas, thought, suggestion from the members through in depth study, discussion, interaction, analysis of the issues, etc., and also to generate a feeling of 'we-ness' 'togetherness' and a sense of belonging to the group.

iii. Inclusion or deletion of some clauses in the existing agreement:

It happens that some issues mentioned in clauses for the existing agreement are not effectively workable and the need for deletion of such clauses is felt. A detailed note is required to be prepared for discussion on the negotiation table to ensure that deletion of such clauses is made.

iv. Incorporating new clauses in the agreement

It occurs that some companies doing the similar operations in the locality have introduced some clauses in their agreement that work effectively in the companies. A list of such clauses can be prepared along with its details and be presented on the negotiation table for incorporation in the agreement.

v. Preparation of note for discussion on wage issue

Wage issue is most vital and complicated for settlement through collective bargaining. For effective discussion and negotiation on such issue a detailed and complete wage picture of the concerned work community needs to be presented during discussion. It may be required to place wage data, production and productivity figure and also reward package including various benefits and perquisites provided by different companies in the locality to make a comparison of wages given to the employees working with various organizations. So preparation of a detailed note on such issues is a necessity to make effective deliberation/presentation of the case by negotiating team in its favour.

From union side

i. Collection of data, information and preparation of note for discussion

The union is required to collect data from central organization, government reports, survey records, etc., and make the team members aware of the facts on various issues prepared on the basis of such data, records, etc., for presentation in the bargaining table.

ii. Making comparative study and analysis on various issues

The union needs to collect information from various similar organizations situated in the region/locality regarding wages, compensation packages, well-fare and social security benefits provided to their employees; and makes the comparative study and analysis to present in the bargaining table to make its stand strong and convincing.

iii. Assessing management stand on issues submitted by them

It may be a difficult task for the union to get to know the stand management will take on various issues at the bargaining table. Union needs to give its best to procure idea about what management/ negotiating team thinks to take stand on issues under negotiation. If prior assessment can be made, union can decide its stand to get the best out of it.

iv. Understanding rank and file expectations on issues and their desire to use methods to fulfil their expectations

The union needs to know what rank and file workers do expect from the negotiation and what do they want if negotiation fails. Do they want to go for a strike? If so, for how many days? These are the areas the union should get to know. Generally through survey or attitudinal administration the union can have information on the issues. On receipt of such information union decides its stand.

d. Planning for strategy and tactics

Bargaining process involves strategic activities that are pre-requisites for effective bargaining. Strategy is concerned with mapping out the plan and basic policies to be followed in the bargaining process. So, it is decided to make overall plan to proceed at the bargaining table to achieve its objectives and for such purpose some strategies are taken.

i. Different types of bargaining strategies are adopted to arrive at an agreement looking at bargaining strength, issues of bargaining and other factors. Some of them are discussed below in short:

a. Distributive bargaining/conjunctive bargaining/competitive bargaining

Under this bargaining strategy both parties try to get the maximum from the deal. The intention of each party is to maximize gain through 'zero-sum' game that indicates 'my gain is your loss, and your gain is my loss'. It is basically a strategy based on 'win-loss' approach. The focus is on self and one's narrow interest; and the strategy is to grab the bigger size of the cake.

b. Integrated bargaining

The strategy under this bargaining is to make the size of the cake bigger to give a large share to both the parties. The main idea behind this strategy is to produce more, earn more and give the workers more from the earnings. This is a unique strategy which is based on 'win-win' that means both parties win.

c. Haggling bargaining

It is an old strategy practised for a long period. It is based on two approaches—piece meal approach and total approach. Under peace meal approach issues are taken for discussion, negotiation and settlement one by one in some order, viz., easiest issues are taken first or issues as mentioned in the charter of demands are settled in seriatim.

In total approach issues are considered to be interrelated and interwoven with each other. So, no issue is settled separately. Each issue is kept open until the whole negotiating process is ready to crystallize into a total agreement.

d. Boulwarism

It is totally a different type of strategy taken by the company to deal with negotiation. This negotiating procedure is known after its originator, Lemuel Boulware, formerly head of employee relation department of GEC. In this method company makes a thorough survey to get to know the employees' desire, needs, expectation; and on the basis of survey finding and also the issues of bargaining mentioned in the unions' charter of demands company design its own package. As a strategy the company does not make any change in the offer at the bargaining table unless new facts are brought to the knowledge of the management.

e. Attitudinal structuring

It is a shaping and reshaping of attitudes to attain desired level of relationship between parties in the bargaining. Dale Yoder and Paul Staudohar (1984) expressed attitudinal structuring as a process that creates attitudes conducive to compromise and settlement. They argue that strategy and tactics need to be planned keeping these attitudes in mind[6]. So, the strategy focuses on trust and confidence in the other party. It means a shift from the mere settlement of issues to establishment of sound human relations.

f. Intra-organizational bargaining

Intra-organizational bargaining is one of the strategies that the parties may adopt before the negotiation starts. It takes place within one's own group. It may happen that the agreement arrived at between management and union is not welcomed by local unions or by some management executives. So the chief negotiator of the union may feel that it is necessary to negotiate with various local union officials so that if certain proposals are later agreed to with management the local officials will recommend ratification to the overall union membership. Similarly, the chief negotiator for

6 Yoder, Dale and Staudohar, Paul. D: *Personnel Management and Industrial Relations* (Prentice Hall, India, New Delhi, 7th Edn 1984, P 479)

management may have to coordinate closely with top management if he feels it necessary to modify bargaining strategy[7].

g. Continuous bargaining

It is a strategic bargaining that calls for the exploration of the difficult issues under negotiation by the parties through joint meeting over a period of time, sometimes throughout the life of each agreement. The objective of such bargaining is to generate a healthy climate of negotiation by ensuring that no issue is kept unattained and for solution of the difficult issues a joint committee is set up.

ii. It may be decided beforehand by the management concerning the maximum amount of concession they can grant to the union. Likewise, the union may decide the minimum offer of management they can accept to reach an agreement. Both parties should know how far they can go without creating a situation where the work may be stopped.

iii. As a strategic planning in the bargaining each party should have thorough understanding about the strength, weakness, level of expectation, reputation, standing in the market of other party.

iv. Each party should keep its eyes on the entire package. It can avoid immediate gain to achieve.

Tactics of Bargaining

Tactics are used by negotiating team members at the time of bargaining. The objective of using tactics by the parties is to present their case in their favour and to win; may be, through bluffing, misrepresenting the whole matter in a way that the other party may be compelled to agree. Some of the tactics adopted by the negotiating team members are given below:

- table pounding
- getting up from the negotiating table in a huff
- anticipating objections to a proposal and answering them before they are voiced
- acting irrationally by attaching great emotional importance to little things
- shouting
- requesting a recess

7 ibid P 469

- tabling a difficult clause
- decoy
- acting very pleased or very upset about something
- behaving friendly towards one member of the opposite team while other members of the same team behave very badly
- counter proposal, trade offs and the like

So, the tactics are the methods used by individual team members to implement strategy of the team. The negotiating team decides beforehand what tactics will be employed at the time of bargaining.

2. Negotiation phase

Negotiation is essentially a process of advancing proposals, discussing and criticizing them, explaining and exploring their meaning and effects; seeking to secure their acceptance, and making counter-proposals or modifications for similar evaluation[8].

In the negotiation phase the following activities are usually performed

- Formal talks begin with a meeting which needs to be presided over by a member of the negotiating teams. The selection of chairman is made by the parties. In some cases it is observed that the parties decide that one member from the employer's side will act as chairman. In some situations it also happens that each side in turn will select chairman.
- At the first meeting normally from union side initiative is taken to start discussion and leader of the union's negotiating team submits a claim.
- Team leaders of both teams deliver opening statements before discussion on issues starts.
- Issues may be taken for discussion in seriatim or easiest/less significant issues are taken for discussion to arrive at a decision. It also occurs that all issues are taken for discussion and agreement is made on its entirety. From union's side spokesperson tries his best to justify the demands and for that he presents the case with supportive figures, data, information. From management side the spokesperson highlights the total case in its reality giving a clear idea to the members concerning the financial position of the company, capacity to pay of the company and also production,

8 Yoder, Dale, Et al: *Handbook of Personnel Management and Labour Relations* (McGraw Hill, New York,1958 Pp 20)

productivity trend, sales, market share, profits, etc. He also makes a comparison with other companies operating in this locality, region and in other places in respect of compensation package, benefits, perquisites provided to their employees and also the production, sale, profit of the concerned companies. With this company spokesperson expresses the offer if they can go for a settlement.

- Spokesperson of union's negotiating team may demand for something which may be much more than the offer management's spokesperson makes. So, interaction takes place between teams and obviously exercise of giving, proposals, and counter-proposals is made. In such situation the following activities can occur:
  - management may consider the union's demands in exchange for agreeing to its counter-demands by union
  - management may agree to some union's demands and for the rest demands management may offer up to some level to which union may agree or may not agree creating a temporary blockade in the bargaining process to restart with later on.
  - rejection of all demands as irrational, unjust and unreasonable creating a situation of deadlock.
- At the bargaining table both the parties try to identify the strong points and also the weak points in other defences to get the maximum from the negotiation.
- Both the parties endeavour to adopt appropriate strategy and tactics to make the other party lose. In the process each party tries to find out the 'negotiating point' of the other party below which it cannot argue. Pigou[9] refers to this 'negotiating point' as 'sticking point'. According to it, management has an upper limit of what it will concede in terms of money, etc., and the union has a lower limit, below which it will not accept a settlement. For reaching an agreement this is very important to identify the 'sticking point' or 'negotiating point' and operate within them. It may be very easy to find out the 'sticking point'/'negotiating point' and reach an agreement if the negotiator is experienced and has a thorough exposure to dynamics of negotiation. It happens after discussion for a long period the veteran, experienced spokesperson can dig out factors causing differences, measure acceptable terms through cost benefit analysis, make some alternatives and manovour them. Subsequently, an agreement is reached.

9 Pigou, AC as in NW Chamberlin and JW Kuhn, *Collective Bargaining*, (New York, McGraw-Hill, 2nd Edn, 1965)

It may take a lot of time to reach an agreement if there is a deadlock/ breakdown in the bargaining. In such situation a series of meetings and discussions need to take place to find out causes of differences, sort out differences and reach an amicable settlement.

To make an effective bargaining resulting in reaching an agreement the following points need to be adhered to.

i. No breakdown, deadlock in the bargaining

Both negotiating teams should carry on their talks to sort out differences. They should make all efforts to ensure that the situation making the bargaining breakdown, deadlock is avoided.

ii. Creating a congenial and conducive climate of bargaining

A climate of congeniality, conducivity in the bargaining place as also in the organization should exist. This may help the bargainers to keep cool and soft on the issues.

iii. Developing the attitudes of helping the organization to grow

While bargaining, negotiators should always look at the growth and development of the organization. Union should not make unreasonable demands which management cannot agree with considering its financial health, capacity to pay and other aspects. Similarly the management should not show its unwillingness, uncompromising and stubborn attitudes to stick to one point. Both parties need to be flexible.

iv. Generating a state of mutuality

The parties should prepare their minds to develop a state of mutuality, i.e., mutual understanding, mutual faith, mutual trust and mutual responsibility between union and management team members negotiating for settlement.

v. Effective listening

Each party must listen to other party's views attentively. No party should interrupt the other party's views, deliberation when made. They must be good listeners.

vi. Following strategies, objectives

Bargainers should take steps to proceed further measuring each other's objectives/strategies.

vii. Face saving

Each party must respect the other party. It happens that one party sticks to the position in the bargaining from where it wants to come back, that means it intends to make a face saving. The other party must respect the importance of face saving.

viii. Fair, firm and unbiased

Bargainers must develop a reputation of being firm, unbiased and fair.

ix. Fire-fighting approach:

Negotiators should consider the issues as serious that need immediate solution. The solution should be made without looking at who will win and who will lose. So the approach should be problem-solving not being based on the attitudes of the parties of winning an agreement resulting in a loss to another.

3. Post Negotiation Phase

After negotiation process is completed it needs to prepare agreement, to ratify and approve it and implement it. So, this post--negotiation phase consists of three phases/stages. They are

a. Pre-ratification of agreement stage
b. Ratification and Agreement Stage
c. Implementation of Agreement

a. Pre-ratification of agreement stage

In the process of negotiation both the parties arrive at an agreement. This agreement remains informal till it is signed and approved by the union and management who are authorized to do so. In this phase the informal agreement is written down. This written form of agreement consists of

i. a preamble
ii. clauses and appendices mentioning details of item
iii. date of operation
iv. period of operation
v. mechanism to sort differences over interpretation of clauses
vi. names of signatories to the agreement

After preparation of the agreement it is sent to union and management for ratification and approval.

b. Ratification and Agreement Stage

On receipt of un-ratified agreement both union and management who are authorized go through it, ratify, sign and approve it. The ratification of the negotiated agreement is a necessity because the negotiating team members may not have authority to decide some issues referred to for bargaining and incorporated in the agreement. The agreement is also called labour contract/union contract or labour management agreement.

The ratification of agreement is also required for legal provisions. Section 18 (i) of the Industrial Disputes Act 1947 deals with this matter. In terms of this section 'an agreement shall be binding only on the parties to the agreement'. That means any collective bargaining agreement is not automatically applicable to all workers in the organization. So, the agreement only after having duly ratified, signed and approved by union and management representatives becomes officials. However, collective agreement has a strong moral force: the parties to the agreement will not breach their terms except in case of real pressure. The unions want collective agreements because they formalize improvements to terms and conditions that they have negotiated and because they restrict managerial prerogatives. The managements want collective agreements because they commit to the unions and the employees they represent to the terms of agreement. Agreements are two-way processes; management and unions both gain from them[10].

c. Implementation of agreement

The implementation of agreement is most vital because agreement becomes insignificant if it is not implemented. In the process of implementation it is experienced that a lot of disputes arise over

- interpretation of some ambiguous clauses of the agreement
- the procedure/mechanism to be followed for resolving disputes
- its applicability to the workers not belonging to union that makes agreement

It is the duty of the management particularly Human Resource Department/Personnel Department of the organization to ensure that the agreed issues are implemented at shortest possible time.

Books Recommended

1. Sidney Webb and Beatrice Webb : *Industrial Democracy* (Seaham Divisional Labour Party, London, 1920)
2. Dale Yoder, *Personnel Management: Principles and Policies* (Prentice-hall, New York, 1959)

---

10 Brewster, Chris, *Collective Agreements in Brain Towers(ed) A Handbook of Industrial Relations Practice* (Kogan Page, London, 1987 P 117)

3. P Ghosh and S Nath, *Labour Relations in India* (Sudha Publication, New Delhi, 1973)

4. TN Chhabra and RK Suri, *Industrial Relations: Concepts and Issues* (Dhanpat Rai & Co (P) Ltd, Delhi, 2003)

5. BR Patil, *Collective Bargaining : Perspectives and Practices* (Universities Press, Hyderabad, 1993)

6. CS Venkata Ratnam, *Industrial Relations* (Oxford University Press, New Delhi, 2006)

7. BD Singh, *Industrial Relations Emerging Paradigms* (Excel Books, New Delhi, 2004)

8. Arun Manappa, *Industrial Relations* (Tata McGraw Hill Publishing Company Limited, New Delhi, 1985)

Questions

1. What is collective bargaining? State and explain the salient features of collective bargaining.
2. Discuss in brief the objectives of collective bargaining.
3. "Collective bargaining plays an important role to improve labour-management relation and to ensure peace and harmony in industry" Justify this.
4. What are the pre-requisites for successful collective bargaining? Explain them.
5. Explain the growth and development of collective bargaining in India.
6. There are a lot of hindrances to the growth of collective bargaining in India— What are those hindrances? Discuss.
7. Suggest measure to make the collective bargaining effective in India.
8. Explain in brief the collective bargaining procedures in an enterprise with which you are familiar.
9. State the points which should be remembered in a negotiation process that may result in reaching an agreement.
10. write short notes on:
    a. Strategies and tactics of bargaining
    b. Issues of collective bargaining
    c. Benefits of collective bargaining
    d. Contents of a collective bargaining agreement

Case study

Arogya Pharmaceuticals Private Ltd was set up by Dr SR Purohit, a scientist in 2000 at Rishra, West Bengal. The company was a small scale unit manufacturing anti-malarial medicines.

It had 6 days working per week making 26 working days per month and was running smoothly without any disturbance. There was no workers' union till 2004. In July 2005 some workers formed union with an outsider Mr J Paul who was made General Secretary of the union. The attitudes of office bearers were rough, indecent, violent and aggressive. The industrial relations started deteriorating making it difficult for the company to survive. Mr Purohit and other partners held informal discussion amongst themselves on the issue of company's problems and prospects and lastly they decided to sell their shares. In August 2009 they sold their shares to XYZ Pharmaceuticals Limited. XYZ Pharmaceuticals had 250 workers, 70 executives including scientists, 25 clerks, 10 peons and 20 watch and ward staff.

The pay scales of clerks, peons and watch & ward staff members are determined on the basis of agreement made between management and the recognized trade union under collective bargaining process. The scales are revised once in 4 years and the recent agreement came into force with effect from July, 2009.

The pay scales of workers, clerks, peons and watch & ward staff are enhanced with effect from July 2009 in consequence to the latest agreement, as per the following:

	Existing scale (Rs)	Enhanced scale (Rs)
Clerks	2500 — 4000	4000 — 6000
Workers	1400 — 2500	2000 — 3000
Peons	1800 --- 3000	2700 — 4500
Watch & ward staff	2200 — 3500	3500 — 5000

The agreement further says that the pay scales of the clerks, workers, peons watch & ward staff drawing pay in the respective scales as aforementioned will be fixed in the corresponding enhanced scale.

At the time of taking over of the company by XYZ Pharmaceuticals Ltd the manpower strength of the plant was 80 in which 25 were workers, 33 were executives including scientists, clerks 5, peons 5, watch & ward staff 12.

After taking over, XYZ Pharmaceuticals made many changes and the major ones were:

- They shifted from 6 days' working per week to 7 days working per week to improve the productivity and enhance cost effectiveness of the unit.
- All the non-executive staff members were fixed in the pay scale prevalent prior to July 2009.

The shift from 6 days to 7 days working without any financial gains and not fixing the pay in the enhanced scale (new scale) made non-executive staff members unhappy, dissatisfied and they revolted against management.

In the matter of fixing non-executives in the pay scale the HR Department of the company made it clear that only the staff members who are drawing the scale prevalent prior to the enhanced scale (i.e., scale as per agreement) are now eligible to draw the enhanced (new) scale.

Mentionably, the company has introduced grievance redressal procedure through which individual grievances are dealt with for redressal. 12 watch & ward staff members were not happy with the fixation of their pay in the scale of Rs 2200---3500 as made by the HR Department of the company. They appealed before the management for their fixation in the pay scale of Rs 3500---5000 but their appeal was rejected by the HR Department on the ground that the concerned watch & ward staff members were not drawing the scale of pay of Rs 2200 — 3500 prior to July 2009 (i.e., the date of effect of agreement), as only the non-executive staff members drawing the pay scale fixed by the company prior to the effective date of agreement are eligible to draw the new scale of pay.

Read the above case thoroughly and answer the following questions.

i. If you are Head of HR Department of the above company, how would you redress this grievance of the 12 watch & ward staff?

ii. As HR Head of the company do you endorse the company's decision of shifting the working days from 6 to 7 days per week? If yes, why? If not, why not?

iii. Is there any scope for settlement of the two issues mentioned in question no (i) and (ii) above through collective bargaining? If so, how these issues can be raised? Also discuss the procedure to be followed for settlement of issues through collective bargaining.

iv. Do you think the decision given by the HR Department of the company is correct? If yes, why? If not, why not?

V

Management of Grievance

Meaning of Grievance

Grievance is the discontent or dissatisfaction created by anything which a person may feel, think or perceive to be irrational, unjust or inequitable. This grievance an individual may have while living in a family, society or working with an organization. The dictionary meaning of grievance is a real or imaginary wrong regarded as cause for complaint or resentment. In the context of industrial setting it becomes obvious that people work with peers, boss in the organizations having different objectives, values, beliefs, culture, environment that may or may not be comfortable, convenient, adaptable to them. Some may feel, think or perceive that all these are not proper, conducive, congenial to working. In the process they develop discontent, dissatisfaction and unhappiness that results in grievance. People may express or may not express their grievances but they manifest them through their behavioural activities. It may happen that some grievances are not legitimate, reasonable or true but the people do have grievances.

The term 'grievance' has been defined in various ways by different authorities and experts. Michael J Jucius, (1971) for example, defines 'grievance' as "any discontent or dissatisfaction, whether expressed or not, arising out of anything connected with the company that an employee thinks, believes or even feels, is unfair, unjust or inequitable".[1]

1 Michael J Jucius, *Personnel Management* (Richard D Irwin, Illinois, 1971, P 108)

In the opinion of the National Commission on Labour (1969) "complaints affecting one or more individual workers in respect of wage, payments, overtime, leave, transfer, promotion, seniority, work assignment and discharges constitute grievance".[2]

According to the International Labour Organization, grievance is a complaint of one or more workers in respect of wages, allowances, conditions of work and interpretation of service stipulations covering such area as overtime, leave, transfer, promotion, seniority, job assignment and termination of service.

Keith Davis (1971) defines grievance as "any real or imagined feeling of personal injustice that an employee has about employment relationship".[3] Dale Yoder (1972) on the other hand, defines it as "a written complaint filed by an employee and claiming unfair treatment".[4]

Now, the term grievance may be defined as a complaint of one or more employees against an employer in respect of employment, non-employment, terms of employment and condition of labour.

Features of Grievance

The grievance of the employee has many characteristics or features. Some of the important features are mentioned below:

- Grievance generates discontent, dissatisfaction.
- Grievance may be expressed or unvoiced.
- It may be legitimate and valid or may be false, spurious, based on imaginary perception.
- It may be written or oral.
- It may arise out of situation which may be connected with employment or non-employment or terms of employment or condition of labour.
- The employee develops a feeling, thought pattern, perception in the matter that injustice has been done to him.
- Grievance is of individual nature. When the grievance is transformed into a general issue/dispute it comes under the purview of collective bargaining for its settlement.

---

2 *Report of the National Commission on Labour*, Government of India; Ministry of Labour, Employment and Rehabilitation, New Delhi, 1969.

3 Keith Davis, *Human Behaviour at Work: Organizational Behaviour* (Tata McGraw-Hill Publishing Company Limited, New Delhi, 1981, P 361)

4 Dale Yoder, *Personnel Management and Industrial Relations* (Prentice-Hall of India Private Ltd, New Delhi, 1972)

- Grievance may give rise to frustration, low morale that may lead to fall in productivity, increase in rate of absenteeism, turnover, accident, etc.

Causes of Grievances

It is quite natural that the people do have some grievances. But the management should ensure that the grievances are not piled up and are disposed off as and when they crop up. Immediate settlement of grievances is a necessity for the establishment of human relations vis-à-vis industrial relations in the context of attainment of organizational excellence. So, for disposal of grievances it is the primary task of management to find the causes of grievances. If the root or genesis of grievances is detected, it is easier for the management to take curative and prophylactic measures to eradicate the grievances in the organization. The causes of employee grievances are mentioned below under different categories:

1. Wages

- Less payment or irregular payment of wages
- Mistake in calculation of wages
- Low rate of incentive
- Non-payment or less payment of officiating allowance
- Low piece rate

2. Working conditions

- Unsafe working conditions
- Dirty, unclean toilets
- Inadequate toilet facilities
- Inadequate light, air in the workplace
- Dirty, unclean canteen
- Inadequate supply of store materials, tools, equipment
- Dampness, noise in the work place
- Safety and health
- Production standard fixed not as per capabilities and competencies of employees

3. Supervision

- Poor dyadic relationship
- Indifferent attitudes of supervisors

- Poor technical skill of supervisors
- Improper instructions given by foreman
- Biased, accentric supervisor
- Not paying heed to the problems of workers by supervisor
- Indulgence in unlawful activities by supervisor
- Failure to maintain discipline in work place
- Unacceptable supervisor
- Style of leadership

4. Company Policies

- Unfavourable, unsuitable promotion policy
- Frequent transfer
- No clear cut policy on transfer
- Denial of transfer
- Seniority in service not considered for promotion
- Transfer policy not practised
- No promotion policy, promotion on the basis of pick and choose
- No policy on career planning and development
- No leave rules
- Mistake in interpretation of various leave rules
- Leave not sanctioned as and when required
- Rejection of leave on flimsy ground
- Double standard maintained in sanctioning leave
- Overtime payment not made as per statute/rules
- Incorrect calculation of overtime
- Hostility toward a labour union

5. Alleged violation of rules, agreement, etc.

- Violation of settlement/collective bargaining agreement
- Past practice
- Understanding reached between management and recognized union
- State or central laws
- Company manual, rules, procedures, instructions

6. Benefits, services

- Retrial benefits
- Unsatisfactory welfare measures
- Inadequate medical benefits
- Hospitalization benefits
- Wrongful calculation of gratuity

7. Grievant related

- High expectation, desire
- Incompetence, not capable to reach the desired goals
- Over-ambition
- Imbalanced ego-state influencing/contaminating decision
- Excessive self-esteem
- Attitudinal problems

The important causes of employee grievances as generally occurred in Indian organization are mentioned above. S Chandra (1968) has mentioned the following areas as causes of employee grievance. [5]

- Promotions
- amenities
- Continuity of service
- Compensation
- Disciplinary action
- Fines
- Increments
- Leave
- Medical benefits
- Nature of job
- Payment
- Acting promotion
- Recovery of dues
- Safety appliances
- Superannuation

---

5 S Chandra, *Grievance Procedure: A Survey of Practices in Industries in India* (Hyderabad, Administrative Staff College of India, 1968)

- Supercession
- Transfer
- Victimization
- Condition of work

JJ Cruden and AW Sherman (1963) have classified the causes of employee grievance into following three categories. [6]

i. Management policies and practices that include company policies relating to HR and IRs, style of functioning, approaches to deal with individual problems, grievances, attitude and the practices exercised for redressal of grievances.

ii. Trade union practices including values, beliefs, attitudes of union leaders to increase union strength, to manipulate/make grievance on false or imaginary pretext.

iii. Personality traits that include impractical attitude, biased ego-state, over-ambition, excessive self-esteem, personal maladjustment, etc.

Forms/Types of Grievances

Grievances are of different forms. Some grievances may be factual, real while other may be imaginary. Some grievances remain in disguised or hidden form. When the people feel that injustice is done to them, the grievance may take any one of the following forms

- Factual or informative
- Imaginary or unreal
- Hidden or concealed

Factual

It is based on fact, data, information which makes the employee believe that injustice has been done to him. It occurs that management has agreed to pay some allowance to an employee but does not implement and keeps pending. If such form of grievance is not redressed and allowed to linger for a long period, it may be transformed into an industrial dispute.

Imaginary or Unreal

This sort of grievance is not based on any material fact, data. Under such form of grievance the employee's feeling is based on imagination or incorrect reasoning. It is considered to be a grievance when the concerned employee develops a feeling of injustice. It happens that some employees

---

6 JJ Cruden and AW Sherman, *Personnel Management* (South Western Publishing Co, Cincinnati, Ohio, 1963 Pp 433-435)

perceive something which is not real but on the basis of such perception they develop a feeling that they are ignored, neglected and injustice is done to them.

Hidden or Concealed

This form of grievance remains hidden, concealed. It needs a deep analysis to find out the cause of such grievance. It happens in organization that some employees do not have any real grievance but they remain unhappy, dissatisfied. In such case it is the task of the management to detect the real cause and solve it. It occurs when an employee is appreciated for his excellent performances other employees who have not been treated likewise for the similar performance in the past, show their displeasure, dissatisfaction. Such employees feel that injustice is done to them.

Grievance Identification Methods

It is difficult for the organization to achieve its goals if the employees are dissatisfied, unhappy. Employees feel dissatisfied, remain unhappy if they have a lot of grievances. So it is the primary task of the management to introduce suitable methods for discovery of the employee grievances as and when cropped up. It will be possible for the management to redress grievances only when identification of grievances is made. The following methods may be used by the management in the organization to identify employee's grievances.

1. Attitudinal survey

Employees' attitudes, feeling, expectation can be understood through attitudinal survey. This sort of survey gives an idea about the problems, grievances and the suffering the people have. Organization can get to know about employee grievances in a regular way if periodic survey is conducted.

2. Open-door policy

Organization can introduce a system of inviting employees to meet the respective head of the department/designated manager on stipulated date and time to make him aware of their grievances if any. It will make the employees come close to the management and tell him about the grievances they have. The use of this method may not be workable in big organizations because higher management may not have sufficient time to attend to the employee grievances

3. Exit interview

Some organizations have developed a practice to gather information on different aspects of organizational activities from the employees leaving organizations. It happens that the employees who quit organizations feel free to let the management know the shortcomings, problems, grievances where remedial measures are required to be taken This method if conducted properly can generate very useful information to redress grievances.

4. Gripe box

Under this method employees are required to drop their anonymous complaints in the box. It is different from the suggestion box in which suggestions are given with names and address of the applicants to obtain reward if selected. The gripe box system makes the management aware of the complaints/grievances of employees in the organization so that management can take appropriate measures to redress the grievances.

5. Incidents analysis

Employee grievances can be discovered, complainants can be identified through close observation, watch, careful analysis of the following incidents by supervisors, higher management.

- Productivity rate of employees when it is below the normal standard or unusually low rate
- Accident rate when it is higher than normal and it is due to employees' negligent, carelessness and lack of seriousness
- Wastes/scraps, defects when percentage/quantum of waste, scraps, defects is considerably higher than normal
- Labour turnover rate when it is much more than standard rate
- Indisciplined activities of employees

The above incidents/occurrences help management discover grievances of employees in the organization.

Impacts of Grievance

Employee grievances need to be redressed immediately after its occurrence. It happens that delay in disposal of grievances makes the grievants much more dissatisfied, intolerant that affects labour management relations in the organization. The employee grievances if not redressed may make an impact on the concerned employees, management and the organization. The effects or impacts of grievances are discussed in brief.

Impacts on Employees

- **Decrease in production**

Employees may not be able to give their best to produce the standard level of production. Since the production decreases, the employees earn less.

- **Absenteeism**

Employees feel unhappy, dissatisfied. They may not like to attend to the task assigned to them. They remain absent frequently that results in increase in rate of absenteeism.

- **Turnover**

Dissatisfied group of workers prefer to leave the organization if their grievances are not redressed to their satisfaction. This may increase the rate of labour turnover.

- **Morale**

Accumulation of grievances affects the morale of the grievants. The concerned employees may feel that they are neglected, deprived of their legitimate and reasonable benefits. All these may reduce the degree of employee morale.

- **Feeling of insecurity**

If the grievances are not redressed by the management, the employees may develop a feeling of insecurity in the organization.

- **A state of casualism**

If the management does not take any initiative to sort out the grievances and keeps them pending for months together, the employees may feel that they are neglected, they are unimportant elements of the organization. All this may generate a state of casualism and insincerity among the employees.

- **Accident**

The rate of accident may go high if the employees become insincere, casual and work reluctantly.

- **Agony, anxiety and worries**

If the organization does not have grievance redressal system the degree of anxiety, worries, agony of the complainants gets increased as they do not find any outlet to release their emotions.

Impact on Management

- **Dyadic relation**

Dyadic relationship between supervisor and the grievant employee is affected in a situation when the employee grievance is not redressed and is piled up for long.

• **Work activity**

When the employees remain unhappy because of their grievances not being disposed off, it is difficult for the supervisor to effectively run the department and make the production system smooth.

• **Indisciplined activities**

Supervisor may be required to work with a lot of employees who have filed written complaints for solution. If such grievances remain pending for a long period there is every possibility that issues may flare up. So, the supervisor may need much more time to handle such acts of indiscipline that may affect administration of the department.

• **Absence of a climate of mutuality**

In a situation when employees are unhappy, dissatisfied a climate of mutuality (i.e., mutual understanding, mutual trust, and mutual confidence) which is a pre-requisite for sound industrial relations cannot be generated in the organization.

• **More disciplinary cases**

It may increase the number of disciplinary action cases. The activities like issuing show cause notices, chargesheet, warning, caution letters may take the form of a regular phenomenon.

• **Incompetency, inefficacy**

Accumulation of grievances indicates the ineffectiveness and incompetencies of the management that may affect the career growth of the management vis-à-vis overall functioning of the organization.

Impact on Organization

Employee grievances affect the organization. The effects includes:

• **Production**

Employees may not give optimum production. So, production may decrease.

• **Quality product**

The unhappy employees may not work sincerely, and attentively that may result in deterioration in quality of products.

• **Wastes, scrap and defects**

The company may witness unusual increase in wastages, scraps and defects that appear in the process of working by the employees.

- **Production cost**

In a situation where production decreases, quality of products deteriorates, rate of wastes, scraps increases, there is the possibility that cost of production per unit decreases.

- **Customers' delightment**

It may be difficult for the company to supply quality goods and services to the customers at lesser price. So, providing customers' delightment is wellnigh impossible.

- **Organizational goals**

In a situation where grievances are accumulated for days together, it may not be possible to achieve individual goals, group goals and corporate goals.

Concept of Grievance Procedure

The organization cannot function smoothly, effectively if employee grievances are allowed to accumulate and no systematic procedure is introduced to redress the grievances. The employee grievances affect directly and indirectly on production, productivity, sales, profit vis-a- vis goals of the organization. So, the organization needs to have a formal process to resolve grievances within a given timeframe. This process is called grievance procedure or grievance redressal procedure.

According to Walter E Bear (1970) the grievance procedure is a problem-solving, dispute-settling machinery which is set up following an agreement to that effect between labour and management. It is the means by which a trade union or an employee makes and processes his claim that there has been a violation of the labour agreement by the company.[7] Keith Davis (1981) defines grievance procedure as a method by which a grievance is filed and carried through different steps (decision level) to an ultimate decision. [8]

The grievance procedure may, therefore, be defined as a planned, systematic and formal process to redress grievance of the people at work, within a stipulated period of time.

Essential Features of a Sound Grievance Procedure

It is the method of disposal of grievances of employees in the organization. It is natural that the employees want to get their grievances redressed by the management at the shortest possible time. They do not

---

7 Walter E Bear, *Grievance Handling: 101 Guides for Supervisors* (American Management Association, New York, 1970 P3)

8 Keith Davis. op. cit p365

like to keep pending their day-to-day issues/grievances like employment conditions, welfare, social security, fringe benefits for days together. They manifest their feeling of dissatisfaction/resentment in their behavioural activities which make their relations with the management unhealthy, bitter and unpleasant. This sort of relations stand in the way of achieving individual goals, team goals and organizational goals and deters growth and development of the people at work and the organization as well. So, there is a need for introduction of a system for redressal of grievances within a reasonable period of time.

Grievance procedure is a necessity for effective functioning of the organizational activities. So, there is a need for formulating sound, effective, meaningful grievance procedure that can serve the objectives of the organization. The essential features of sound grievance procedure include:

- **Steps**

It may not happen that grievances are settled at the first level i.e., supervisory or foreman level. So, for redressal of grievance some steps must be there through which grievances should be routed for solution. However, the procedure should have limited number of steps.

- **Speedy**

Speedy disposal of grievances is one of the important characteristics of grievance procedure. If the settlement of grievances takes a lot of time, the concerned employee may turn out to be violent, and aggressive. It may create a problematic situation of labour–management relations in the company. So, the procedure should aim at prompt settlement of grievances.

- **Simplicity**

The grievance handling procedure should be simple so that employees can understand and make proper use of it.

- **Unambiguity**

Each and every aspect of the grievance procedure should be clear and unambiguous. Employees must have a clear idea about the procedure to be followed for handling grievances.

- **Legislative provision**

While framing the procedure it must be taken into consideration that violation of any statute, rule is not made.

- **Participation**

The grievance handling procedure should be designed with the participation of employees in order to make it acceptable to all.

• **Applicability**

The grievance procedure should be made applicable to all employees in the organization

• **Training on grievance handling**

It occurs that both supervisor and the employees/trade union representative are not aware of various aspects of grievance handling. So, the procedure may turn out to be ineffective. It is, therefore, a necessity to impart training to supervisors and union leaders in grievance handling activation.

• **Fairness**

The grievance procedure needs to be acceptable to the employees and it is possible if the procedure ensures a sense of fair play and justice to the workers.

• **Follow up**

Periodic follow up with modification/change, if required, should be made by the HR/personnel department to ensure that the procedure works well.

Importance of Grievance Procedure

Grievance procedure is a necessity for the organization for redressal of grievances of the employees. It is known to everybody that accumulated employee grievances create a situation that disturbs peace and harmony in the organization.

The importance of grievance can be ascertained from the following.

1. The management can come to know the nature and type of grievances the people do have and on looking at it they can take preventive measure.
2. The higher management can have a thorough idea about strengths and weaknesses of the lower and middle level management as grievances are referred to them stepwide for redressal.
3. The company can get to know about the climate of industrial relations through analysis of grievance rate (i.e., the written complaints/grievance per 100) and can take appropriate steps for promoting sound industrial relations if need arises.
4. The grievance procedure acts as safety valve to release the emotion, angers, discontents of the employees and to maintain a cool, calm and normal situation thereafter in the organization.
5. The grievance procedure system makes the employees feel that

their problems/grievances do not remain unnoticed, unattended; and management gives all efforts to solve their grievances. This feeling changes their attitudes and makes them committed to work and to the organization.

6. It encourages employees to raise their problems without fear of victimization, retaliation.
7. It reduces whimsical and arbitrary activities of supervisor in the matter of dealing with problems of employees because the supervisors know that aggrieved employees can approach to the higher management for intervention and disposal of such behavioural activities.
8. This grievance system promotes confidence of employees towards management that improves employee morale.
9. It helps in promoting work culture. As interpretation of various problems, grievances, handling of such issues through grievance procedure are made in terms of company rules, policies it make the people learn to develop work-oriented approach to the work place.
10. The grievance system integrates the various levels in the organization into a team that works together to resolve issues which concerns both worker and the manager.

Michael Armstrong (1990) has expressed his views about the importance of a formal grievance procedure. According to him the formal grievance procedure provides

- a channel for an aggrieved employee to express and present his grievance.
- an assurance for dispassionate handling of one's grievance.
- an assurance about the availability of some machinery for prompt handling of grievance.
- a means by which an aggrieved employee can release his feeling of discontent or dissatisfaction. [9]

Grievance Redressal Practices in some Companies in India

It is true that organizations without employee grievances are rare. Grievances are there but all grievances are not invariably legitimate, reasonable and true. Some are imaginary based on wrong perception about grievances, some are unreasonable or false. But, all these grievances need to be redressed in the interest of employees and the organization as well.

9 Michael Armstrong : *A Handbook of Human Resource Management* (Aditya Books Private Ltd, New Delhi, 1990, P222)

The employee grievances may be resolved through proper counselling with supportive and convincing facts and data. A threadbare discussion with grievants may sometimes yield results in disposal of grievances. But, for all this establishing a climate of mutuality is a must. It occurs that counselling and discussion methods act as effective tools to redress grievances which are whimsical, imaginary, illegitimate and unreasonable.

For redressal of grievances different companies have developed different policies. Some companies resolve employee grievances through grievance procedure set up jointly by management and union under mutual understanding.

Some companies do not have grievance procedure but they practice a system for some period to solve grievances. In some companies open-door policy has been introduced to deal with the employee grievances.

So, redressal of employee grievances in Indian companies is made generally through

- Open-door policy, or
- System developed for redressal, or
- Step-by-Step Grievance Procedure/Step-Ladder Grievance Procedure.

Open-door Policy

Under this policy a specific culture is created for discussion and disposal of grievance. The higher management makes a policy for entertaining employee grievances. In terms of the policy the person who has any grievance may meet the manager and talk over his grievance. This policy for redressal of grievance may be considered by grievants as effective device if they become happy with the redressal process the management of the company adopts. But, in reality it is seen that this policy cannot yield results in disposal of grievances because of the following:

- Dealing with employees' grievances by top management, bypassing the supervisor creates a problem of misunderstanding, mistrust between a frontline management (supervisor) and the higher management. All this results in unhealthy human relations that affect industrial relations of the company.
- It is not possible for the higher management to get to know the details of the case, the historical issues involved in the case, the effect on other cases/past cases and other allied issues.
- The higher management cannot afford much time on redressal of grievances because of his preoccupation on other business activities.

- The higher management may think it as burdensome, additional or secondary task. He may take it casually.
- The employees may feel uncomfortable, uneasy generating an internal resistance (social and psychological resistance) to drop in manager's room with their grievances.

System Developed for Redressal

Some companies practice a system for some period for redressal of employee grievances. Under such system when an employee feels that injustice has been done to him, he talks to his supervisor or departmental head first. If he is happy with the handling of his grievance by the supervisor or departmental head the matter stops there. But, if the concerned employee is not satisfied with the dealing of his complaint by the supervisor or departmental head he meets Personnel Officer/Manager or HR Officer/Manager and talks to him. After this, the employee submits complaint in writing to the Personnel Officer/Manager or HR Officer/Manager. Then within three to five days the grievant gets to know the decision. If the decision does not make him happy, he may appeal to the manager for revision of decision If the complainant is not satisfied with the manager's decision, he may submit his complaint to the Assistant Labour Commissioner/Deputy Labour Commissioner of the area for conciliation.

Under this system no formal procedure is developed. But grievances are being dealt with for a long period as per the practice followed in the company.

This method may not be effective in big organizations where possibility of accumulation of complaints with Personnel/Human Resource Department is high. It happens that most cases are referred to Personnel Department/Human Resource Department by the concerned departments from where grievances originate as they think it is not their responsibility to dispose off grievances and in the process the Personnel/HR Department gets over burdened.

It may generate a conflicting climate arising out of line and staff relationship in a situation where more power/authority is given to Personnel/HR Department to deal with the issues particularly the complicated issues concerning policy aspects of the company.

This grievance redressal system may not yield results if Personnel/HR Department is not manned by dynamic, competent, matured Personnel/HR executives who can have greater acceptability in the organization and have had a good standing in the company.

Step-by-Step Grievance Procedure/Step-Ladder Grievance Procedure

Some companies have set up grievance procedure in consultation with union for redressal of employee grievances/complaints. This redressal procedure is called Step-by-Step grievance procedure or Step-Ladder grievance procedure because redressal of grievance needs to move (or take step) forward for the next step if the redressal at the existing step fails. A five-step grievance is shown in Fig 5. 1

Under this procedure the five steps as followed in the organization are briefly discussed below:

1st step : The grievant employee needs to submit written complaint/grievance to supervisor or foreman of the concerned department. The supervisor/foreman is required to redress the grievance.

2nd step : If the supervisor/foreman fails to resolve grievance/ satisfy grievant, the complainant may refer the grievance to the Head of the Department.

3rd step : If the Head of the Department fails to satisfy the employee, the grievance may be referred to Joint Grievance Committee constituted with equal representation of management and union for redressal of grievance.

4th step : If the grievance remains unresolved the grievant employee may approach the Factory Head for redressal.

5th step : If the decision of the Factory Head cannot satisfy the complainant, the matter may be referred to Arbitrator for voluntary arbitration whose decision remains binding to both the parties.

It is now apparent that different companies resolve workers' grievances either through open-door policy or through a system developed on its own or through step-ladder grievance procedure set up mutually by union and management of the organization.

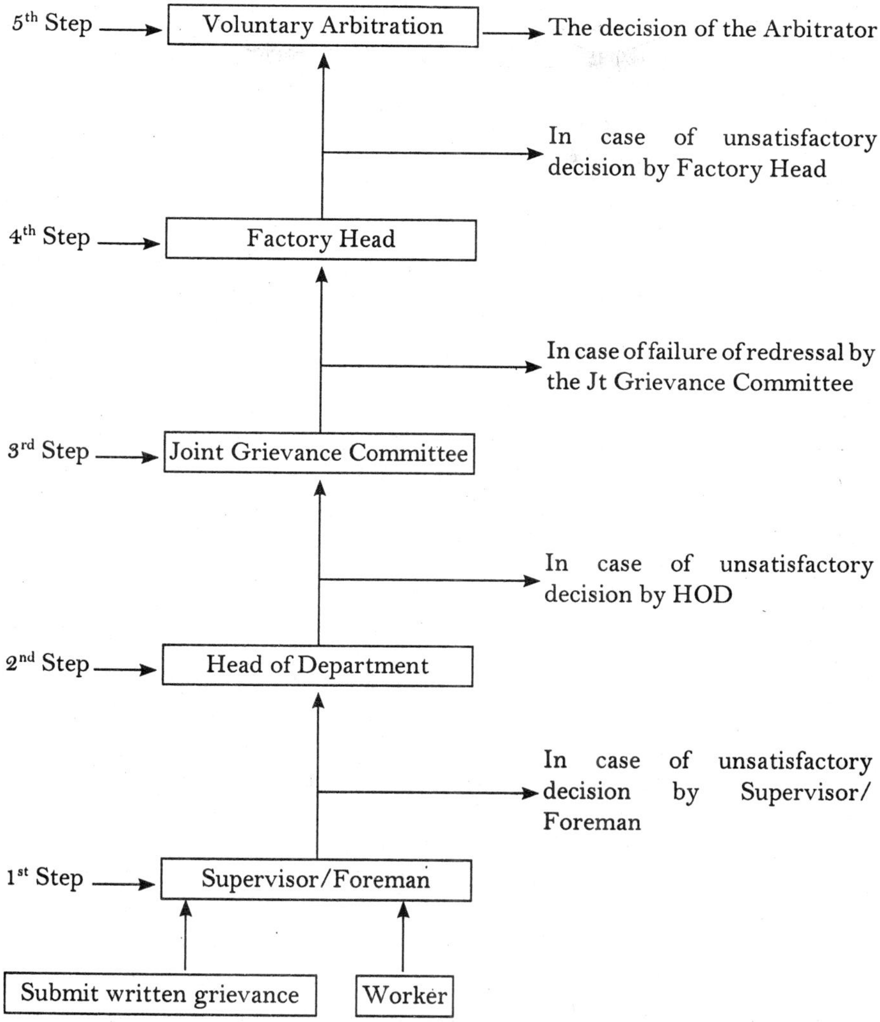

Figure 5. 1: Showing 5 step-ladder grievance procedure/ step-by-step grievance procedure

A clear idea can be obtained with regard to the grievance redressal procedure practised in a bank and also TISCO (works).

Grievance Redressal Procedure

Practised in a Bank: An Example

In a bank's branches employees' grievances are redressed in a systematic way. The following procedures are taken to resolve employee grievances/complaints.

1st step : If an employee does have any grievance he may approach the concerned departmental officer/departmental head in writing for redressal of his grievance. In most cases the trifling issues are disposed off by the departmental head/officer in consultation with Joint Manager (Accountant).

2nd step : If the grievance is not resolved in step 1, it is referred to the Branch Head who in consultation/discussion with Joint Manager, concerned Departmental Head/Officer and also with the grievant redresses the grievance.

3rd step : If at the branch level the grievance is not redressed it is referred to the Regional office. The Personnel/HR Department takes up the matter and discusses with the Regional Manager. The Senior Manager (Personnel/HR) gives his views, suggestions to the Regional Manager for its disposal. The decision is taken on the matter and communicated to the concerned Branch Manager who informs the grievant accordingly.

4th step : If the concerned employee is not satisfied with Regional Manager's decision, the matter is taken up by the union for discussion and settlement at the regional structured meeting which is held regularly at periodical interval and presided over by the Regional Manager. In the structured meeting fresh grievances, unresolved grievances, the grievances on which decisions were taken by the Branch Manager/Regional Manager along with other issues are discussed and decisions are taken. The structured meeting is attended and represented by union and management people. Both the parties agree to implement the decision taken at the structured meeting.

5th step : If any grievance remains unresolved in the structured meeting or the decision taken by the Regional Manager cannot make the grievant happy, the matter is referred to Zonal Office by the concerned employee/union, for decision.

6th step : In the Zonal Office a system is developed to hold Zonal Structured meeting at a regular interval with the representatives of union and the management of the regions and the zone. The meeting is presided over by the Zonal Head. In this structured meeting fresh individual grievances, unresolved issues pending with regional offices and zonal office, grievances against which decisions were taken by the Regional Manager and the

Zonal Manager along with some other grievances are discussed threadbare and decisions on some grievances are taken by the management.

7th step : The unresolved issues lying with regional offices and zonal office, some decisions of Regional Managers, Zonal Manager, along with fresh issues are taken up by the union with corporate office for discussion and settlement in the Corporate Structured meeting.

It happens that the issues/grievances not resolved by the higher authorities or decisions of the higher authorities not acceptable to the complainants are sometimes referred to conciliation by the union.

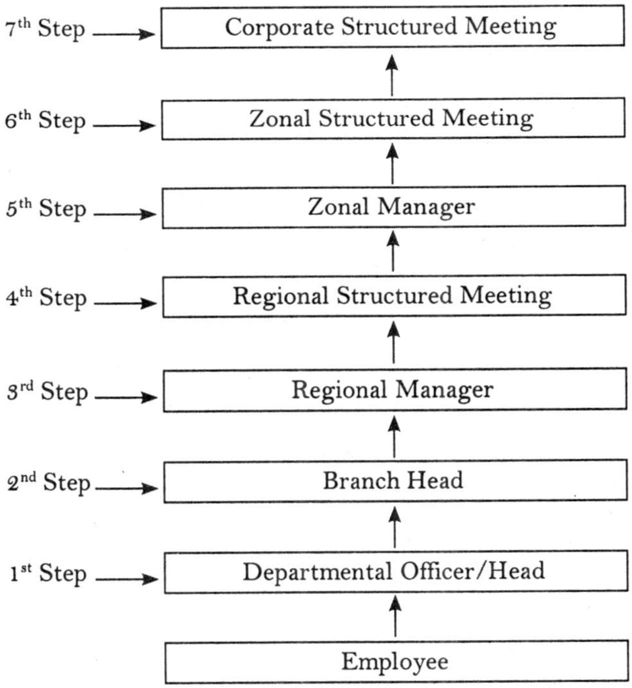

Figure 5. 2: Showing the grievance redressal procedure practised in Bank

Grievance Redressal Procedure Practised In TISCO (works): An Example

Another example of grievance redressal procedure followed at the unit level in TISCO (works)[10] is given below;

1st step : The grievant worker fills in a form and submits it to the shift-in-charge for consideration.

10 Arun Monappa and Mirza S Saiyadain, *Personnel Management* (Tata McGraw Hill Publishing Company Limited, New Delhi P241)

2nd step : If the worker is not satisfied with the decision of the shift-in-charge he approaches the department head for consideration

3rd step : If the worker is still dissatisfied he forwards it to the appropriate chairman of the Zonal Works Committee (ZWC) of which there are six for works and one for the non-factory staff (departments are clustered together and are covered by one committee). Each Zonal Works Committee consists of five management and five union representatives and they work on the basis of a unanimous decision which is final and binding on both parties. The Zonal Works Committee considers individual grievances pertaining to promotion, suspension, discharge, dismissal and disciplinary matters.

If the Zonal Works Committee cannot reach a unanimous decision, the grievance is referred to the Central Works Committee. If no unanimous decision is reached in this committee, the matter is referred to the Chairman of the company for the final decision.

Legal Aspects of Grievance Management in Indian Industry

There was no statutory provisions for settlement of employee grievances prior to enactment of Industrial Employment (Standing Orders) Act, 1946. So there was a great possibility to keep the grievances pending or not to redress grievances by the management of some companies during that period. That means, the disposal of employee grievances did not receive much attention. Today the companies are required to redress the grievances of their workers in a systematic way in terms of provisions of some laws. The following legislations deal with the grievances of employees working in various industries in India.

1. The Industrial Employment (Standing Orders) Act, 1946
2. The Industrial Disputes Act, 1947
3. The Factories Act, 1948

The Industrial Employment (Standing Orders) Act, 1946

In terms of clause 15 of the Model Standing Orders in the Schedule of the Industrial Employment (Standing Orders) Act, 1946 that in every establishment employing 100 or more workers all complaints arising out of the employment including those relating to unfair treatment or wrongful action on the part of the employer or his agent shall be submitted to the manager or to another person specified on his behalf with the right of appeal to the employer.

The Industrial Disputes Act 1947

The Industrial Disputes Act 1947 deals with employee grievances and also grievance settlement authorities.

- Under section 2A of the Industrial Disputes Act 1947 amended in 1965 any dispute or difference between an individual workman and his employer connected with or arising out of discharge, dismissal, retrenchment or termination is deemed to be an industrial dispute.
- The Industrial Disputes Act 1947 amended in 1982 provides for setting up of Grievance Settlement Authorities and reference of certain individual disputes to such authorities. Section 9C of the amended Act provides the following:

i. Every industrial establishment having 50 or more workmen shall have Grievance Settlement Authority for the settlement of industrial disputes connected with an individual workman employed in the establishment.

ii. A workman or any trade union to which he is a member may refer any dispute to the Grievance Settlement Authority.

iii. The Grievance Settlement Authority will follow procedure and complete proceeding during such time that will be prescribed.

iv. Any dispute can be referred to Boards, Courts or Tribunals only when the concerned dispute is referred to the Grievance Settlement Authority and the decision of such authority is not acceptable to any of the parties to the dispute.

The Factories Act 1948

To deal with employee problems and grievances in factories a provision has been made in the Factories Act 1948. Section 49 of the said Act provides for appointment of welfare officers in every factory wherein 500 or more workers are ordinarily employed. These Welfare Officers are entrusted with the task of looking to problems, complaints and grievances of the workers and to redress them, in addition to other duties they are required to perform. It happens that welfare officers cannot discharge their activities effectively, particularly in the area of redressal of employee grievances, because of the dual role they are required to play.

Model Grievance Procedure

Model grievance procedure is a voluntary method for disposal of grievances of employees in an organization. The issue of introducing model grievance procedure was taken up for discussion in the 15th session of the Indian Labour Conference in July 1957 and both the parties, management and union, agreed in principle concerning the establishment of model grievance procedure in industrial units. For this purpose a sub-committee was formed that considered the principles of discipline in industry. The 16th session of Indian Labour Conference approved the Code of Discipline in 1958. The Model Grievance Procedure which is a part of Code of Discipline was formulated. The National Commission on Labour has suggested a model grievance procedure involving six successive time-bound steps each leading to the next in case of dissatisfaction. These steps are mentioned below.

1st step : The complainant will verbally approach the designated officer/immediate boss for disposal of his grievance.

2nd step : If no solution is arrived at within 48 hours or the concerned worker is unhappy with the decision he will represent his case personally or with the help of co-worker, to the Head of the Department.

3rd step : If the aggrieved worker does not get reply within 3 days from the date of submission/representation of his case or is dissatisfied with the decision, he or his representative will submit a plea before the grievance committee constituted with the nominees of workers and management of the organization for redressal of the grievance.

4th step : If the grievance committee fails to send its recommendation within 7 days to the manager, the reason for failure of submission of recommendation is recorded. If the committee cannot have unanimity in decision, the matter will be referred to the manager who will give his decision within 3 days.

5th step : If the worker is not happy with the manager's decision, he may appeal before the higher authority who will work as appellate authority for this purpose. The aggrieved worker may take the help of his union representative on the day of hearing of his appeal. The disposal of appeal is expected to make within 7 days from the date of receipt of the appeal.

6th step : If the appellate authority's decision is not acceptable to the concerned worker, the management and the union may refer the matter to voluntary arbitration within 7 days from the date of receipt of the order of the appellate authority.

In case of issues relating to discharge, dismissal, the aggrieved worker may prefer appeal before the dismissing authority or any senior officer specified for the purpose, within 7 days from the date of dismissal/ discharge.

However, if the organization grievance procedure is established mutually by the union and management, and successful implementation of grievance procedure as a method for settlement of grievances depends mostly on the degree and extent of relationship the management and workers/union develop between them. Steps for settlement of grievances under Model Grievance Procedure are shown in Figure 5. 3.

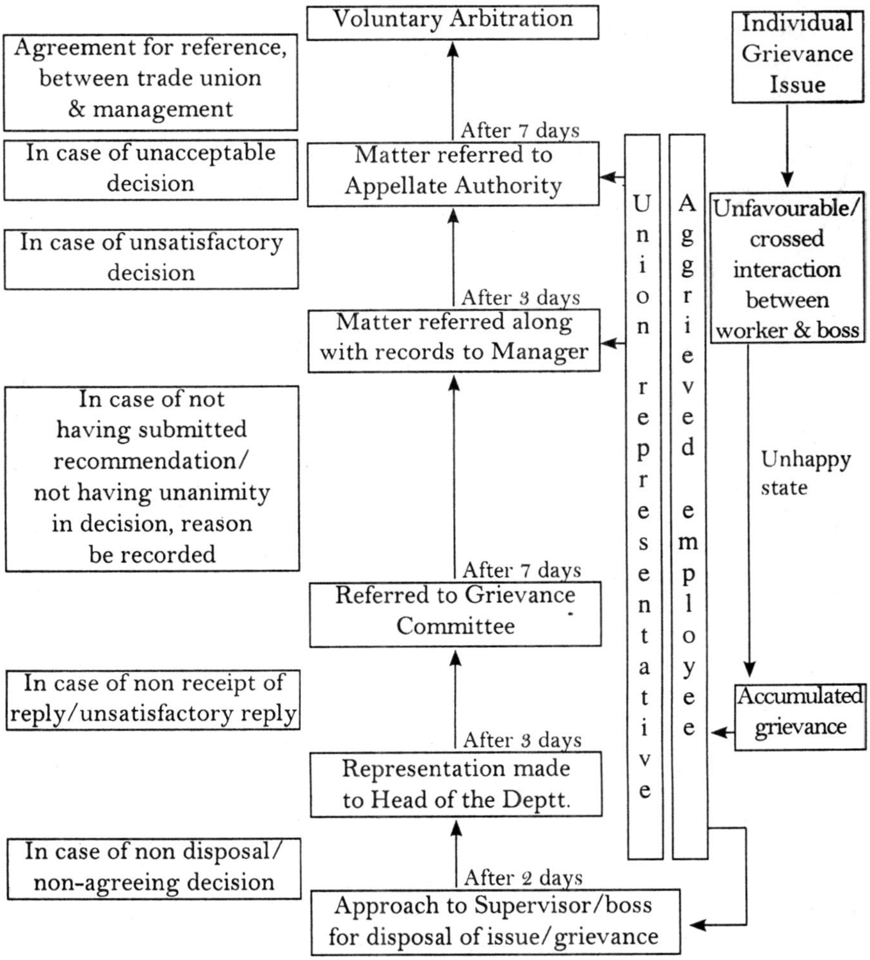

Figure 5. 3: Steps for settlement of grievances under Model Grievance Procedure

Effective Ways to Deal with Employee Grievances

Employees may have problems, complaints, grievances while working in the organization and they expect that their grievances should be disposed off expeditiously. But, in reality it may not happen all the time. Generally it occurs that grievances are piled up. They are not redressed properly, people remain dissatisfied, aggrieved. All this affects production, productivity and the organizational activities that make it difficult to achieve organizational goals. So, for smooth and effective running of the organization, management should follow some guidelines, norms, principles to deal with employee grievances.

1. Importance of grievance

The supervisors/managers should give equal importance to the employee grievances. It is not that small or trifling grievances should be ignored and the grievance that may have wider impact be given due consideration for redressal. It happens that today's small grievance may take the shape of an issue in future if they are accumulated for a long period.

2. Receiving grievance and recording of grievance

The complainant should be encouraged to submit his grievance in writing. Written grievance may give a clear picture of the complaint to the supervisor or manager who can record the grievance accordingly in the grievance register. So there may not be any chance of recording vague, ambiguous grievance. In respect of writing about ambiguous nature of grievances Michael J Jucius (1979)[11] expresses that grievances of today often have their roots in the acts of yesterday and their branches in the effects of tomorrow. The roots are sometimes difficult to locate, and how the branches will grow, is difficult to forecast. But, difficult though the task is, it must be tackled as best as one can, else grievance handling becomes grievance fighting.

3. Concern about the grievance

The managers/supervisors should show their sincerity in dealing with the employee grievances. There should not be any casualism in their behavioural manifestation/approach to the solution of employee problems. Managers/Supervisors must create a situation through interaction, discussion, active listening and various behavioural activities that can make the grievants develop a sense of reliance, confidence upon their boss/managers about handling of grievances.

4. Discovery of problem/grievance

It becomes easier for the managers/supervisors to discover the grievance of the concerned employee when he develops a feeling that he

11 Michael J Jucius, op cit

is concerned about the latter and his problem. It is highly important to get to know whether it is really a problem/grievance or it is an imaginary manifestation of ego-contamination of the complainant.

5. Gathering data, information

If the grievance is found to be imaginary, spurious, the grievant needs to be counselled. But, if it is observed through problem discovery analysis that the complaint is logical it should be the task of the supervisor/ manager to gather data information, facts, proof relating to the grievance. With regard to collecting information Walter E Bear (1970)[12] suggests "to get all relevant facts about the grievance. Examine the personal record of the aggrieved worker. See whether any witnesses are available. Visit the work area". All this needs to be recorded in a proper and systematic way so that the same can be used for further reference. This will also generate a faith and trust into the minds of grievants about managers'/ supervisors' sincerity and honesty of purpose.

6. Finding the genesis of the problem

After collecting information through various sources it is utmost important for the manager, supervisor to find the genesis, root cause of the problem, and for such purpose it needs to make analytical interpretation, in-depth study, overhauling and examining of various records, reports, settlement, practices, laws, rules, regulations relating to the problem and also to make an explorative attempt to dig out the real cause of the grievance from various perspective by putting question like 'why', 'when', 'what', 'where' and 'how'.

7. Making Solution

After getting to know the root cause of the grievance the management should find ways and means to solve the problem and take decision. In the process of decision making the management should make a list of alternative solutions and should see whether a particular decision can have

- an adverse impact on peers, other departments, organization as a whole
- an effect on labour-management relations
- a possibility of affecting union interest
- chances of creating inter-union rivalry
- chances to make the working situation worse
- an impact on industrial relations pattern

---

12 Walter E Bear, op cit

- an effect on production, cost, customers' service and overall functioning of the departments/organization

Looking these conditions mentioned above a decision is taken to solve the problem/grievance. The completion of this process should not take much time as prompt and speedy redressal of grievance is a necessity from organization's industrial relations point of view.

8. Communication of the decision

The management should not delay to communicate the decision to the grievant. It may happen that the decision of the management cannot make the aggrieved person happy. However, under such situation the management should make an attempt to convince the complainant by explaining elaborately from various perspectives to justify the decision.

9. Implementation of the decision

It is very much important to ensure that the decision taken is implemented because non-implementation of the decision may make the employee unhappy that generates grievance.

10. Follow up

The Personnel/HR Department of the company should take necessary follow up measures so that decision order is effected. Sometimes some department may need clarification/interpretation of the decision order for its implementation. The HR/Personnel Department should come forward and immediately help the concerned department.

Books Recommended

1. Michael J Jucius, *Personnel Management* (Richard D Irwen, lllinois, 1971)
2. Keith Davis, *Human Behaviour at Work: Organizational Behaviour* (Tata McGraw-Hill Publishing Company Limited, New Delhi, 1972)
3. S Chandra, *Grievance Procedure: A Survey of Practices in Industries in India* (Hyderabad, Administrative Staff College of India, 1968)
4. JJ Cruden and AW Sherman, *Personnel Management* (South Westren Publishing Company, Cincinnati, Ohio, 1963)
5. Walter E Bear, *Grievance Handling ; 101 Guides for Supervisor* (american Management Association, New York, 1970)
6. Arun Monappa and Mirza S. Saiyadain, *Personnel Management* (Tata McGraw-Hill Publishing Company Limited, New Delhi)

Questions

1. What is grievance? State and explain salient characteristics of grievance.
2. Discuss the factors responsible for employee grievances.
3. Explain the forms of employee grievances.
4. Different methods are used by the management to identify employee grievances. What are these methods? Explain.
5. The employee grievances if not redressed may make an impact on the employees, management and the organization. Do you justify this statement? Submit your views.
6. What is grievance management procedure? Discuss in brief the essential characteristics of a sound grievance procedure.
7. Grievance management procedure is a necessity for redressal of employee grievances in the organization. Justify this statement.
8. For redressal of grievance, different companies have developed different practices. Explain, in brief, the grievance redressal methods used by any reputed organization.
9. Explain, in brief, the legal aspects of grievance management in Indian industries.
10. The National Commission on Labour has suggested a model grievance procedure. Discuss the model grievance procedure in this context.
11. For smooth and effective running of the organization the management should follow some guidelines, principles, norms to deal with employee grievance. Do you endorse this view? If yes, why? If not, why not?

Case Study

Mr AP Baisnab is the Chief Manager (HR) of ABC Steel Pvt Ltd. The factory is situated at Rishra, West Bengal and its first production activities started in the year 2002. The total number of employees including supervisors and Officers comes around 1700 of which 85 employees work with company's Head office in Kolkata. The factory is headed by Mr SK Goswami, Factory Manager who is assisted by Mr J Malhotra, Dy Factory Manager, Mr LN Banerjee, Marketing Manager, Mr SN Murarka, Chief Engineer and Mr AP Baisnab, Chief Manager (HR)

Mr AK Kumar, the Chairman and Managing Director (CMD) of the company remains in the Head office 4 to 5 days a week and pays visit to factory at least once in a week. He is a dynamic personality and believes in 'direct and open discussion' mechanism for sorting individual problems. He is accessible to rank and file of the people at work of the company. He subsequently introduces 'open-door policy'.

It is due to persistent efforts of Mr Kumar the company has been able to introduce HRD system to look at the following activities.

- Training and development
- Performance appraisal
- Creativity reward
- Career planning and development
- TQM
- Counselling Programme
- Employee participation, involvement and empowerment
- Quality Circle

Achievements

- The company secured ISO 9000 certificate in 2004 for quality production and marketing activities.
- It received Award for Excellent Performance and Quality Product from the Ministry of HRD in 2005.
- The market share of the company increased considerably from 15% in 2003 to 70% in 2006.

Mr SK Goswami

Mr Goswami is a cool, soft spoken and well mannered person. He is a workaholic, busy and hard working personality. He keeps every aspect of the entire factory activities under his grip. He works 14 to 15 hours daily in the factory. On Sunday he works 4 to 5 hours in the factory. He keeps his managers and officers busy on Sundays.

The job profile of Mr Goswami includes

- Overall administration of the factory
- Supervision of the activities of functional heads
- Smooth and effective running of the factory
- Developing liaison with Factory Inspectors, Government Labour Department officials, Inspectors, Tax official
- Ensuring growth and development of the company

In March 2007 the Chairman and Managing Director received an anonymous complaint against Mr Goswami with regard to his behavioural activities. In the said complaint it was alleged that his whimsical, autocratic and stubborn activities have demoralized the whole working community of the company. Earlier CMD got to know from some line managers about the style of functioning and undesirable act of behaviour of Mr Goswami in some specific cases. Then Mr Goswami was directed to rectify and improve his behaviour.

In May 2007 the company engaged PQR consultants of Kolkata to study factory working and employee problems and morale.

The consultancy team had a detailed study/observations of factory operations for 3 months made attitudinal survey and held discussions/ interactions with some employees of different cadres of the company.

Some of the findings of the study are given below:

i. 80% of the experimental group are unhappy on the activities of Mr Goswami.

ii. Mr Goswami does not believe on delegation of authority to the subordinates.

iii. Need based training is not given.

iv. The department supervisors are not authorized for sanctioning leave of workers.

v. Rank and file of workers do not like to present their problem/ grievance to the CMD. They do not feel comfortable to talk to the CMD or Factory Manager about their grievances.

vi. Workers have lot of problems, grievances which are accumulated.

Read the above case thoroughly and answer the following questions

a. Point out the strengths and weaknesses of Mr SK Goswami.

b. Is 'open-door policy' a good means to redress grievance? If yes, why? If not, why not?

c. Prepare a detailed procedure for settlement of grievances.

d. How will you differentiate between collective bargaining and grievance management procedure?

e. What do you think could be the feeling of employees about the style of functioning of Mr Goswami?

VI

Employee Discipline

The Concept, Meaning and Features of Discipline

Discipline means regulation of human activities for a desired performance. That means controlling human behaviour by enforcing rules, adjustment for a certain activity. Discipline is a necessity in every field of activity, be it a social, political, economic or any other field of activity. People need to obey rules, regulations, procedures framed for a desired purpose or goals.

The word 'discipline' according to Webster's Dictionary means (a) training that corrects, moulds, strengthens or perfects or (b) control gained by enforcing obedience or (c) punishment or chastisement.

Ordway Tead (1933) defines discipline as the orderly conduct of affairs by the members of an organization who adhere to its necessary regulations because they desire to cooperate harmoniously in forwarding the end which the group has in view and willingly recognize that, to do this, their wishes must be brought into a reasonable unison with the requirements of the group in action. [1]

1 Ordway Tead, *"The New Discipline" in Human Nature and Management,* 1933

In the opinion of Leon C Megginson (1977)[2] the word 'discipline' means

- self-discipline
- the necessary condition of orderly behaviour and
- the act of training and punishing

William R. Spreigel and Edward Schultz define discipline as "the force that prompts an individual or group to observe the rules, regulations and procedures which are deemed to be necessary to the attainment of an objective; it is force or fear of force which restrains an individual or a group from doing things which are deemed to be destructive of group objectives. It is also the exercise of restraint or the enforcement of penalties for the violation of group regulations". [3]

From the above definitions the following salient features of discipline are observed:

1. It is observance of rules, regulation and procedures. The company frames rules, regulation, procedures for its effective functioning, and the people at work are required to observe such rules, regulations to make the company run smoothly and effectively.
2. It is self-discipline. People follow rules, regulations and behave orderly spontaneously from the core of their heart. They do not require external control for observance of rules. They put in efforts to adjust to system of activity the company demands.
3. It is a negative approach. Discipline makes the people aware of the desired activity, encourages them to perform and restrains them from undertaking others activities.
4. It is an influencing factor of industrial relations. It has a close relation with industrial relations scenario of the company. Positive, well disciplined working force help develop sound industrial relations in the organization.
4. It is a behaviour moulding activity through punitive process. All people do not behave equally as per prescribed norms. Some behave properly on their own as per demand of the company; some do not behave as per requirement, they violate company's norms, rules. In such case their behaviour is set right through punitive action.
5. It is an orderly behaviour. It is obeying rules framed by the company to regulate human conduct. That means behaving properly by the

2 Leon C Megginson, *Personnel and Human Administration*, Richared D Irwin, Homeword, 1977

3 William R Spreigrel and Edward Schultz, *Industrial Management*, 1957

employees as per demand of the company. Orderly behaviour is a group desire that helps attainment of business excellence and achievement of organization goals.

Types of Discipline

Generally, discipline is of two types- positive discipline and negative discipline. A brief idea about them is given below:

1. Positive discipline

It refers to observance of prescribed rules/norms of the company by the individuals willingly through their own efforts. It does not require external pressure or punitive exercise to make the employees obey rules. Employees spontaneously obey rules, norms, behave orderly, put in efforts to control themselves for adjustment to the desired needs and demands of the company. The elements of determinative or cooperative willingness to conform to rules do always exists in the minds of the employees. That is why this discipline is called determinative discipline or cooperative discipline.

Positive discipline is called self-discipline as discipline is developed from within. The effects of positive discipline include:

- increased production and productivity
- increase in quality of goods and services
- high morale
- high degree of job satisfaction
- low rate of employee turnover, absenteeism, accident, wastes, defects
- high degree of QWL
- healthy dyadic relationship
- sound industrial relations
- increased capability to face competition, to obtain competitive advantage
- less industrial conflicts
- customer delightment

It becomes obvious from the above discussion that positive discipline is warranted, desired for the growth and development of the people and the organization as well.

Essential conditions or prerequisites of positive discipline

The important conditions or prerequisites of positive discipline include:

- **Employee attitude**

Positive values, beliefs, attitudes of the employees help promote positive discipline. Such employees willingly conform to rules, regulations, procedures of the company that are framed for achievement of goals.

- **Ego-state/Ego pattern of employees**

Employees should have unbiased, contamination-free ego pattern because such ego state can make the employees adjust to the environment/ system made for smooth and effective functioning of organizational activities.

- **Objective of industrial discipline**

Objective of industrial disciplines should be very clear; and there cannot be any ambiguity with regard to the standard expected from the employees and the management people.

- **Company policies, practices**

Positive employee cum task oriented policies based on reward and employee development and also its timely and effective practices help promote positive discipline. Such policies and its proper implementation can make the employee satisfied, contented and committed to work and to the organization.

- **Handling of grievances**

There should be a system to dispose off employees' grievances through grievance procedure, promptly and within time limit prescribed for the purpose.

- **A prevailing state of mutuality**

Existence of a state of mutual understanding, mutual trust, mutual respect, mutual faith and confidence between employees and management in the organization can bring a change in the thought process, mind frame of the employees. All this can generate a sense of belonging, "we-ness"and a feeling to deliver the best according to the need and requirement of the company.

- **Sound industrial relations climate**

A healthy industrial relations climate of the organization helps the people change themselves from within. In such situation people feel a congenial and conducive working atmosphere where dyadic relationship becomes strong, incidence of industrial conflict is less and people make efforts for the betterment of working community and the organization as well.

- Use of HRD mechanisms and motivational technique in the organization

- Various HRD mechanisms and positive motivational techniques like participation, empowerment, incentive pay, used by the company may change behavioural pattern of the employees. So, this may work as one of the prerequisites for positive discipline.
- Efforts to create a reservoir of competent, contented and committed work force

If the objective of the company is to create a reservoir of competent, contented and committed workforce it needs to put in persistent efforts to attain the objective through identification of the areas requiring reinforcement/change to make the people happy, contented and committed, modification/introduction of schemes, measures and proper, effective implementation of such schemes, measures. Such activities of the company facilitate a change in the organizational culture which may help the employee to change themselves.

2. Negative discipline

It refers to discipline arising out of external pressure exerted by the management for observance of rules by the employee. It is an imposed/ enforced discipline. Employees are compelled to obey orders, instructions of the superior and to perform their task in terms of rules, regulations and procedure of the company as they know the consequences, effects if they do not conform to such rules. Punishment is inflicted upon the wrongdoers, delinquent and erring employees to correct/rectify their behaviour, improve their conduct and to make them disciplined. That is why it is called punitive or corrective discipline.

It happens that the management needs to impose a series of punitive actions against an employee for his reported acts of misconduct during a certain period of time. It may be like that for the first time offence he is orally reprimanded and then for subsequent offences at different times he is punished through issuing caution order, warning order, order for temporary suspension and discharge or dismissal. This way the concerned employee is disciplined, and this discipline is called progressive discipline. So, it progresses sequentially, chronologically and systematically through a prescribed series of events or steps.

Objectives of Discipline

Discipline is a necessity for smooth and effective functioning of organizational activities. Organisation has its goals and objectives and it cannot attain its goals if its people are not disciplined. So, discipline makes the organization function and achieve goals. The important objectives of discipline include:

1. **To make people aware of rules and develop a sense of responsibility**

   One of the objectives of discipline is to let the people know the rules framed in the company that are required to be followed by them for their performance. In the process of acquainting rules, procedure they develop a sense of responsibility as members of the workteam.

2. **To develop among people a feeling of adjustment and adaptation to new method, environment, process**

   People come from different families, societies having different values, beliefs, attitudes and it is obvious that they may face inconveniences, difficulties to perform their jobs if no clear cut standard, rules are framed. Prescribed rules help the people make suitable adjustment, adaptation as and where required.

3. **To generate a congenial and conducive climate of work**

   One important objective of discipline is to create a congenial and conducive climate of work in a team through adherence of rule, procedures of the company framed for smooth and effective functioning of team activities.

4. **To establish a state of mutuality**

   Through observance of rules, regulations, procedures employees come close to supervisors, managers and develop a state of mutuality, that means mutual understanding, mutual obligation, mutual faith and mutual confidence among them.

5. **To develop a sense of cooperation among the people at work**

   When the employees accept rules, regulations, procedures they spontaneously develop a feeling to cooperate, help and assist the company.

6. **To increase the level of morale of employees**

   One of the objectives of the discipline is to ensure that degree of morale of employees is increased. It may happen that the employees feel a high degree of morale when positive discipline exists in the organization.

7. **To face challenges and obtain competitive advantages**

   Today, in the changing situation every organization needs to face challenges and obtain competitive advantages for its survival, growth and development. This may be possible if the organization has well disciplined workforce.

8. **To improve peace and harmony**

   It may be possible for the company to improve peace and harmony if the people feel happy, contented, satisfied and develop a climate of self-discipline and self-control. All this results in promoting dyadic relation and also sound industrial relations. In a situation of better industrial relations it may generally occur that a peaceful and harmonious climate prevails in the organization.

9. **To generate an environment of respect for the human personality**

10. **To increase production, productivity and other activities in the organization performed by the employees**

11. **To develop among employees a spirit of tolerance and create a sense of involvement in the organization**

12. **To make a significant place in industry through attainment of business excellence**

Code of Discipline: Its Evaluative Perspectives

It is a method used to bring harmony and peace in the industry through prevention of industrial disputes. Simply, code of discipline means a set of regulations or principles that control and promote discipline. This code of discipline is exercised to regulate and promote the conduct of both workers and management. The norms and rules are framed and followed by management and workers to restrict and improve their behaviour in order to develop mutual understanding, mutual confidence and faith between themselves. It is felt that through enactment of labour legislations, labour-management relations cannot be improved. The most essential requirement is, therefore, to frame some mutually agreed norms/ rules of conduct which both management and workers should follow.

The importance of mutually agreed code was discussed in the Second Five-Year Plan and it suggested that voluntary code of discipline be framed and followed by the management and labour in the industry. The Second Five-Year plan stated, "While the observance of stricter discipline, both on the part of labour and management, is a matter which cannot be imposed by legislation, it has to be achieved by organizations of employers and workers by evolving suitable sanctions on their own". [4] The matter was raised in the Fifteenth Indian Labour Conference in 1957 to follow the principles by employees and employers for maintaining and improving discipline in industry and so code of discipline was evolved. The central trade union organizations i.e., Indian National Trade Union Congress (INTUC), All India Trade Union Congress (AITUC), Hind Mazdoor

4 The Second Five-Year Plan

Sabha (HMS), United Trade Union Congress (UTUC) on behalf of workers and the employers' associations i.e., Employers' Federation of India (EFI), All India Organization of Industrial Employers (AIOIE) and All India Manufacturers' Organization (AIMO) on behalf of employers accepted the code. The code of discipline came into effect from 1st June 1958.

Principles of the Code of Discipline

The Fifteenth Indian Labour Conference had a detailed and threadbare discussion in July 1957 on the question of maintaining discipline and also ensuring better discipline in industries and suggested to evolve a code of discipline. The code is based on the following general principles

i. There should be no strike or lockout without notice.

ii. There should not be any unilateral action in connection with any industrial matter.

iii. There should be no recourse to go slow tactics.

iv. No deliberate damage should be caused to plant or property.

v. Acts of violence, intimidation, coercion or instigation should not be resorted to.

vi. The existing machinery for settlement of disputes should be utilized.

vii. Awards and agreements should be speedily implemented.

viii. Any agreement which disturbs cordial industrial relations should be avoided.

Importance of the Code of Discipline

The importance of the code of discipline cannot be denied. It helps to avoid work stoppage, promote constructive criticism at the management and trade union level, settle industrial disputes mutually.

The code of discipline helps prevent industrial disputes and bring harmony in industry. This is clear and justified from the following.

- Since the necessity to frame rules/norms to improve behaviour, discipline is felt spontaneously both by employers and employees and code of discipline is accepted by them; they honour the code. This prevents the industrial disputes to crop up.
- The code of discipline is based on mutuality of principles that results in development of mutual understanding, mutual trust and mutual confidence amongst management and workers in the industry.
- Attitudinal changes amongst workers and management occur. Both the parties feel the importance of continuing uninterrupted

production and services. So, industrial unrest and conflict do not crop up.

- Code of discipline facilitates creation of conducive, congenial environment in the organization. This brings harmony and peace in the industry.
- A state of co-operation, 'we-feeling' and 'togetherness' exists which unites the workers and management to work as members of one family/unit. This situation avoids conflict, disputes, disagreement, and differences.
- Since both the parties agree to abide by the rules, norms of discipline, they honour the code and ensure that the number of work stoppages, cases of go-slow/work to rule, lockouts and other forms of industrial disputes are reduced.
- Cases of intimidation, coercion, threat, gherao, physical assault, unfair labour practice, victimization do not occur.
- Disputes are settled at the earliest. Collective bargaining and grievance procedure mechanism are used to ventilate grievances/ issues.

Contents of the Code of Discipline

In Fifteenth Indian Labour Conference a lot of discussions were held between the parties for maintaining discipline in both public and private sectors and for ensuring better discipline in industries. With regard to maintaining discipline it was felt that there has to be

i. A just recognition by employers and workers of the rights and responsibilities of either party as defined by the laws and agreements (including bipartite and tripartite agreement arrived at all level from time to time) and

ii. A proper and willing discharge by either party of its obligations consequent on such recognition. The Central and State Governments, on their parts, will arrange to examine and set right any shortcomings in the machinery they constitute for the administration of labour laws.

For ensuring better discipline in industry it was agreed by the management and the union that in some areas of activities there has to be joint obligation to comply with and in other areas of activities individual party has the sole responsibility to discharge. That means the code of discipline has three sets of principles. A brief idea is given on these sets of principles.

The first set of principles is meant for both the parties, that is management and union. In terms of the principle both management and union need to settle disputes and grievances promptly through negotiation, conciliation and voluntary arbitration; and grievance procedures need to be established mutually. The parties should not resort to activities like coercion, intimidation, victimization, go-slow, stay in and sit-down strike and lockout.

The second set is applicable to the management. It makes it obligatory on the part of management to ensure that workload is not increased arbitrarily; unfair labour practice like interference with the right of employees for union membership, discrimination, restraint, coercion, victimization of employees and abuse of authority is not resorted to. It lays down that the management must take prompt action for settlement of grievances, implementation of settlements, awards, decisions and orders and for affording opportunity to employees to appeal in all cases. It is management's obligation to take disciplinary action against its officers if they are held responsible for the indisciplined activities of workers. The management is to recognize union in terms of criteria laid down in the code. In this context the code specifies that to qualify for recognition a union must observe the code and must have membership in good standing atleast 15% of the workers concerned. Where there is more than one union the largest should be recognized only if it has been functioning for atleast one year. A union may claim recognition as the representative union for workers in all establishments in an industry in local area if atleast 25% of the workers are its members. But, if a union has 50% or more workers as its members in any one of those establishments it may represent its members in purely local matter such as grievances, working hours, etc.

The third set of principles deals with the obligations of union. It lays down that union must not engage in physical duress, must not allow unpeaceful demonstration, rowdism in demonstration, must not make their members engage, cause other employees engage in union activity during working hours. Unions must discourage unfair labour practices like negligence of duty, careless operation, damage to property, disturbance to work, interference with work, insubordination. The unions are to take prompt action to implement awards, agreements, settlements and decisions to take disciplinary action against office bearers and members who violate the spirit of the code.

The contents of the code are given in the table 6.1

Table 6.1: Contents of Code of Discipline

Management and union agree

i. that no unilateral action should be taken in connection with any industrial matter and that disputes should be settled at appropriate level.

ii. that the existing machinery for settlement of disputes should be utilized with the utmost expedition.

iii. that there should be no strike or lockout without notice.

iv. that affirming their faith in democratic principles, they bind themselves to settle all future differences, disputes and grievances by mutual negotiations, conciliation and voluntary arbitration, provided that the provision regarding voluntary arbitration as aforesaid shall not apply to cases involving security consideration.

v. that neither party will have recourse to (a) coercion (b) intimidation (c) victimization or (d) go-slow.

vi. that they will avoid (a) litigation (b) sit-down and stay-in strikes and (c) lockouts.

vii. that they will promote constructive co-operation between their representatives at all levels.

viii. that they will establish, upon a mutually agreed basis, a grievance procedure which will ensure a speedy and full investigation leading to settlement.

ix. that they will abide by various stages in the grievance procedure and take up no arbitrary action which would by pass this procedure and

x. that they will educate the management personnel and workers regarding their obligations to each other

Management agrees

i. not to increase work-load unless agreed upon or settled otherwise

ii. not to support or encourage any unfair labour practices such as (a) interference with the right of employees to enrol or continue as union members (b) discrimination, restraint or coercion against any employee because of recognized activity of trade unions and (c) victimization of any employee and abuse of authority in any form

iii. to take prompt action for (a) settlement of grievances, and (b) implementation of settlements, awards, decisions and orders

iv. to display in conspicuous places in the undertaking the provision of this code in the local language

v. to distinguish between action justifying immediate discharge and those where discharge must be proceeded by a warning, reprimand, suspension or some other form of disciplinary action should be subject to an appeal through normal grievance procedure

vi. to take appropriate disciplinary action against its officers and members in cases where enquiries reveal that they were responsible to precipitate action by workers leading to discipline and

vii. to recongnise the union in accordance with the criteria evolved at the 16th session of the Indian Labour conference held in May 1958.

Unions agree

i. not to engage in any form of physical duress

ii. not to permit demonstrations which are not peaceful and not to permit rowdism in demonstration

iii. that their members will not engage or cause other employees to engage in any union activity during working hours, unless as provided for by law agreement or practice

iv. to discourage unfair labour practices such as (a) negligence of duty (b) careless operation (c) damage to property (d) interference with or disturbance to normal work and (e) insubordination

v. to take prompt action to implement awards, agreement, settlements and decisions

vi. to display in conspicuous places in the union offices, the provisions of this code in the local language and

vii. to express disapproval and to take appropriate action against office bearers and members for indulging in action against the spirit of the code

The Code does not have any legal sanction but the central employers' and workers' organizations take steps against their members who breach the Code. Such steps include:

- asking the members to explain infringement of the provisions of the Code.
- giving notices to set right the infringement.
- warning or censuring the erring members.
- disaffiliating the member organization.
- derecognising the member organization.
- wide publicity for breach of the Code by any member.
- imposing on the unit any other penalties open to the organization.

The National Commission on Labour in its Report (1969) expressed displeasure on the effect of the code towards mitigating industrial unrest and establishing peace and harmony in industries because of the following reasons

- lack of spirit to accept and comply with the Code by the parties.
- absence of whole hearted support to the Code by the parties.
- conflict of Code with the law.
- appealingly low economic conditions of workers.
- inability of some employers to honour the Code.

The Commission suggested that some provisions of the Code should be given legal shape. Such provisions include

- recognition of union for the purpose of bargaining.
- penalties for unfair labour practice.
- formation of a grievance procedure.
- prohibition of strikes and lockouts without proper notices
- voluntary arbitration.

Meaning of Indiscipline

In the narrow sense 'indiscipline' means non-conforming to rules and regulations. Every company has its rules and regulations. Some of them are formal, some are informal. The people at work in the organization need to comply with such rules and regulations. But, all people do not adhere to rules, regulations and standard of behaviours. Some of them comply with and some others depart from the rules, regulations and prescribed disciplined behaviours. Such departure from rules, regulations and standard behavioural activity is 'indiscipline'.

The indisciplined behavioural activity is unwarranted in organizational setting. It disturbs the smooth functioning of organizational activities and makes it difficult for the organization to achieve its goals. It is, therefore, a necessity for the company to find the factors that cause indiscipline and to take necessary steps to promote discipline.

Factors Causing Indiscipline

Various factors are responsible for making people indisciplined. Such factors may be grouped in following categories:

i. economic factors
ii. work related factors
iii. management related factors
iv. employment related factors
v. socio-political factors
vi. individual factors
vii. other factors

i. Economic factors

People work in the organizations to satisfy their physiological needs first. So, they expect better wages/salaries from the company to maintain their livelihood. But, it happens that some employees do not get wages/ salaries as per their expectation, needs. Such employees, then express their grievances, unhappiness and resort to act of indiscipline.

The economic factors that cause indiscipline include:

- low wages/salaries, allowances
- wages differentials
- irregular payment of wages, non-payments of wages, allowances
- price spiralling leading to fall in real wages
- recession effecting economic health of the people
- downsizing of company with consequential effect

ii. Work related factors

It happens that the work itself is the cause of indiscipline. If the people do not get interest in work, if they find that the work itself is boring, monotonous they develop a feeling of non-cooperation, avoidance, aloofness and non-complying to rules, regulations of the organization. Work related factors lead to indiscipline that may arise due to

- faulty and improper work design/job design
- irrational and unreasonable work load

- absence of a system for job redesign
- uninteresting job
- discrimination in work allocation

iii. Management related factors

Management personnel may be responsible for indiscipline activities of employees. People work with boss and peers. So, in the process of working if the people develop a healthy dyadic relation with boss/ management the chances of resorting to indiscipline activities may be remote. The management related factors causing indiscipline may include the following:

- unfair management practice like non-compliance of promotion policies, reward/incentive scheme
- application/use of double standard methods by the management in settling disputes, grievances of the employees looking to religion, caste, union affiliation, etc.
- not paying heed to the problem, grievance of employees leading to accumulation of grievances
- delay in disposing off individual grievances
- discrimination in imposition of punishment to employees in disciplinary cases
- biased decision of the management
- non-implementation, delay in implementation of awards, settlement
- attitude, philosophy, style of functioning of management
- faulty stroking pattern like abusing erring employees in presence of peers
- unwillingness of the management to talk on individual grievances
- undesirable behaviour of management personnel
- defective communication system

iv. Employment related factors

Employees may feel unhappy if the employment conditions do not suit them. They manifest their unhappiness by resorting to acts of indiscipline. The employment related factors that cause indiscipline are as follows:

- non-placement of the right persons at the right job without looking to experience, qualification, attitude and competency
- unhealthy and incongenial working condition
- lack of job security, absence of peaceful work environment
- no clear cut policy, scheme for promotion, transfer, posting
- unsound and unhealthy dyadic relationship
- victimization of workers by management
- rigid, multiple rules and improper interpretation affecting workers' reaction
- unsatisfactory employment rules, policies and practices
- errors of judgement by management on matter relating to condition of employment, terms of employment e.g., favouritism in granting benefits, perquisites, posting, special increment, hire and fire of employees.

v. Socio-political factors

It happens that employees express their displeasure, unhappiness when social and political activities affect them. In such a situation they resort to various acts of indiscipline.

Some of the socio-political factors leading to acts of indiscipline include

- discrimination based on caste, creed, religion, language, place in matter of promotion, transfer, posting, reward, etc.
- maltreatment, illtreatment made by management personnel on the ground of being hailed from the specific class of society
- granting benefit, facility, privilege on the basis of power structure, not on the basis of objective consideration
- political influence
- social background creating an apparent division amongst peers

vi. Individual factors

All individuals are not same in respect of values, beliefs, attitude, thought process they have acquired, gained in family, society under various nurturing systems. So, some may have positive qualities, some may not have. All such individuals when they join organization may not manifest the same behavioural activities. The individuals who possess positive values, beliefs may conform to company's rules, regulations, procedures and those individuals who possess negative values, beliefs may not observe rules, may perhaps violate rules and resort to acts of indiscipline.

Some of the individual factors responsible for acts of indiscipline are given below:

- tendency to violate rules
- imbalance ego-state pattern creating a problem of discipline
- illiteracy, drunkenness, indebtedness and family problems making the employee indisciplined
- low degree of work ethic creating a state of aloofness from the job that makes the people indisciplined
- difference in perception to work, reward and motivation techniques
- lack of understanding of management policy
- faulty evaluation of performance
- dishonesty

vii. Other factors

Some other factors may result in acts of indiscipline. The important factors that cause indisciplined behaviour are as follows:

- lack of co-ordination between individuals, absence of a system of fixing responsibility
- ineffective, weak leadership
- autocratic style of leadership
- attitude of supervisory personnel that may result in resentment among employees
- inter-union, intra-union rivalry
- harassment of workers with a view to creating a fear complex among them
- workers' reaction to static and multiplicity of rules, improper interpretation of rules
- internal fighting and indiscipline

Maintaining and Promoting Discipline

It is a great necessity to maintain and promote discipline in organizations in order to achieve organizational goals through performance of work activities by the people. If the people themselves generate discipline and develop a sense of self-control then it becomes easy for the management to run the organizational activities smoothly and effectively and attain business excellence; but such situation does not happen always. It occurs that some people violate company's rules, regulations and resort to act of indiscipline resulting in creation of interruptions in day-to-day work activities. In such case erring people need to be disciplined for achievement of organizational goals. So, maintaining and promoting discipline in organization is very much essential for its survival, growth and development.

Now, the question arises as to how organization can maintain and promote discipline. That means what steps/measures are required to be taken for such purpose. A brief discussion is made below to highlight the measures to be adopted for maintenance and promoting of discipline in organization.

1. A climate of self-discipline

If the climate of self- discipline prevails in an organization there cannot be any possibility for the people to resort to any act of indiscipline. So, the management should ensure that a climate of self-discipline is generated; and it is possible to establish such climate if the people feel contented, happy, satisfied and are committed to work and to the organization as well.

2. Dyadic relationship

The attitudes of management personnel, their behaviour, style of functioning, manner of settling grievances contribute a lot to the establishment of dyadic relationship between boss and subordinates. If the dyadic relationship in the company is positive there can be an indication of healthy industrial relations in organization. So, the company needs to ensure that management people with positive values, beliefs and with elements of dynamisms are recruited and are given training to develop their competence under a continuous learning system in the organization.

3. Use of 'hot-stove' rule in the organization

The 'hot-stove' rule of Douglas Mc Gregor can be used to maintain and promote discipline in the organization. The important elements of the rule include

- Warning
- Immediacy
- Impartiality
- Impersonality

According to the rules the hot stove gives warning to keep safe distance from the stove when it emits glow sign. If someone does not conform to the rule and touches the stove he is burnt immediately. The stove does not consider the person's age, sex, status, position, etc. when it burns the concerned part of the person. For the stove, all are same, whoever touches the hot stove gets burnt proportionately. The stove does not have personal feeling of pleasure or displeasure in inflicting pain on the person who touches it. So, in organizational setting the following steps can be taken for maintaining and promoting discipline:

- People should be made aware of the rules in respect of misconducts for observance. It warns the people in advance in case they violate the rules or resort to misconduct.
- If someone violates the rules the company should have the system to start disciplinary procedure immediately against the delinquent person for imposing punishment.
- When punishment is imposed the management should not consider who is the erring person? What is his status, linking channel? The disciplinary authority should not be influenced by all these. He should be impartial when he takes the decision to punish.
- The management people should not express the feeling of elation or displeasure when punishment is imposed upon the delinquent employee. They should behave normally. They should think that objective of punishment is to correct the person's beheviour, not to attack him personally.

4. Culture of Participation

The management needs to establish a culture of participation through introduction of schemes like participation, involvement and empowerment of employees. All this generates a feeling of, 'we-ness', togetherness 'belonging to the company' that makes them loyal, obedient and conform to rules of the company. So an atmosphere of developing organization willingly and spontaneously by the employees is established.

5. Counselling

Employee's behaviour can be rectified if he is counselled before decision for imposing punishment is taken. The focus of the counselling approach should be on fact finding and guiding to encourage desirable behaviour instead of using penalties to discourage undesirable behaviours. The emphasis should be on 'do this' rather than don't do that. In the process employee's self-image and dignity are retained and dyadic relationship gets strengthened.[5]

6. Extinction approach

The management can introduce extinction approach to deal with indiscipline activities. It happens that for some indiscipline activities the erring employee gets support, encouragement and praise from his peers. This approach suggests that when a person resorts to an act of indiscipline, the management needs to find the persons who instigate, encourage him to do it. After identification, the persons should be asked not to support the unruly behaviour and to cooperate with the management. When the erring person does not get reinforcement, support from peers, such undesirable bahaviours stop.

7. Preventing recurrence of indiscipline activities

It is always desirable to establish a climate in the organization that can prevent recurrence of indiscipline activities in future. This sort of climate generates a feeling among employees to conform to rules, discharge performance as per requirement, give their best to attain excellence in organizational activities. The chances of violating rules, manifestation of indiscipline behaviour by the employees in such situation are remote. So, in order to maintain and promote discipline the management needs to give much emphasis on preventing recurrence of indiscipline behaviour through establishing a congenial and conducive climate in the organization.

8. Creating a friendly, facilitative and supportive environment

It is very easy to maintain and promote discipline if the people obey rules, instructions, orders willingly on their own; and it is possible if a friendly, facilitation and supportive environment is created in the organization. For establishing such environment the organization needs to take proper steps to ensure that

- a reservoir of committed, competent and dynamic workforce is made to face challenges, to accept changes and to achieve excellence.
- management personnel scrupulously observe rules and regulations and behave in an orderly and disciplined way to set examples before their team members.
- employee morale is enhanced to reset the mind frame for performance in group/team to achieve goals.

5 Keith Davis, *Human Behaviour at work: Organizational behaviour* (Tata Mc-Graw-Hill Publishing Co Ltd, New Delhi, 1981, Pp-321)

- decisions in economic and non-economic issues are taken on the basis of just, equity, reasons, rationality and objectivity.
- employee grievances are not accumulated, they are settled promptly through grievances redressal procedure, to the fullest satisfaction of the employees.
- a systematic training process works in the organization to develop competencies of the people and also to make them aware of their rights, duties, responsibilities.
- employees develop a feeling that they are given due respect as human beings, treated as essential members of the company.
- communication system in the organization works smoothly and effectively under top-down and bottom-up approach.
- a spirit of compliance is generated amongst the employees through developing a desire to perform, cooperate, achieve and win.

Some Suggestive Guidelines for Maintaining and Promoting Discipline

The following suggestions may work as effective to maintain and promote discipline in work situations:

- Generating an atmosphere of cooperation, assertion and mutuality
- Appreciating an employee for his excellent performance in the presence of others and criticizing/reprimanding a non-performer/wrongdoer privately without hurting him
- Manifesting empathetic behaviour/activities to the problems of the employee and ensuring speedy disposal of problems
- Exercising power/authority that suits in specific situation
- Introducing a system of open discussion, consultation, exchanging views on matter of interests
- Creating a culture of participation, involvement and accountability
- Inculcating a spirit amongst the employees to perform better, to excel and to make a place in the competitive situation
- Changing mindset of the people for a desired target
- Introducing a training and counselling system to make the employees able to accept the necessity of positive behaviour
- Making both management and employees realize the necessity of code of conduct and introducing it in the organization under amicably settled mutual programme.

Approaches to deal with Indiscipline Activities

Company frames rules, regulations for smooth and effective functioning of the organizational activities. It is expected that all employees will conform to rules, but in reality it does not happen. Some employees do not obey and they violate such rules. Obeying or not obeying rules, norms, orders depends on

- Person's attitudes shaped by heredity, education and economic conditions, values, beliefs
- Environment under which person is nurtured, brought up
- Perception level of person about boss
- Expectation of boss with regard to behaviour of subordinate
- Boss's attitudes, values, beliefs

So, when the employee's attitudes, beliefs, expectation fit in with the boss's expectation, attitudes, there is no problem. In such a case subordinate conforms, adheres to rules regulations of the company. But, when the two do not agree the problem or crisis arises. This problem/ crisis needs to be tackled by the management. In such situation the boss may be required to use legal measure/procedure or informal method to correct the behaviour of the subordinate. It means the boss may make the subordinate disciplined through the use of disciplinary action/punitive measure or through other methods.

Various approaches have been in use to tackle indisciplinary activities in organization. They are

i. Douglas McGregor's Hot Stove Rule
ii. Traditional/Legalistic Approach
iii. Judicial Approach
iv. Humanitarian/Human Relations Approach
v. Behavioural Approach
vi. Human Resource Approach

Douglas McGregor's Hot Stove Rule

The hot stove rule is applied to tackle indisciplinary activities resorted to by the employees of the organization. It is an effective guide for corrective discipline.

Origin/Concept

This concept originated from the use of hot stove in the cold countries. The hot stove was used to heat rooms in winter in those days when central heating or air conditioning system was not introduced.

In India particularly in the Kashmir Valley the hot stove known as 'Bhukhari' is used during winter. People sit around it and enjoy the warmth.

Some Significant Perspectives

1. Advance warning

- Hot stove emits heat and displays a glow sign that gives advance warning so that no one touches the stove

2. Impartiality

- The person who touches the hot stove gets his finger(s) burnt. The hot stove does not consider whether he is an adult or a child or he is an influential person. It burns whoever touches it.

3. Immediacy

- The hot stove burns immediately, automatically

4. Proportion

- The nature and extent of burning depends on the nature and extent of the touch.

5. Impersonality

- The hot stove does not have a sense of elation or pleasure when it burns the finger(s) of the person.

Application of Hot Stove Rule in Industrial Setting

Hot stove rule is applied in the context of discipline and disciplinary action in the industrial setting in the following manner:

- The organization should have clear rules of discipline and disciplinary action viz., acts of misconduct, punishment, etc. The people should be made aware that violation of rules produces/imposes punishment like burning of fingers for touching the hot stove.
- The initiative for imposing penalty for the violation of rules should be immediate, almost automatic.
- There should not be marked difference in action taken just as the hot stove burns all fingers or all limbs that touch it in the same manner without considering whether it is a child or an old man.
- The disciplinary authority should not experience pleasure or excitment feeling when an erring employee is punished just like the hot stove that does not have any feeling in burning fingers or limbs.

- The punishment of the delinquent employee should be proportionate to the nature and extent of misconduct just as the penalty for touching the hot stove is proportionate with the nature and extent of touch.

Traditional/Legalistic Approach

This approach to discipline management emerges from compliance with legal/formal rules, regulations, procedures framed for specific porposes. This is based on legalistic consideration.

Salient Features

1. Strict compliance with/adherence to rules, contract of employment, obedience to instructions, orders of superiors is a necessity in terms of standing orders, service rules, settlement, etc.
2. It makes legalistic consideration a basis for ascertaining discipline activities.
3. Discipline is nothing more than obediency and orderly behaviour.
4. Acts of misconducts, penalties, appeal, etc., are mentioned in the standing orders, service rules for compliance.
5. Any deviation from the standard or violation of rules is considered as an act of indiscipline.
6. Action is taken against an employee who violates rules.

Limitations

1. It gives emphasis on McGregor's Theory 'X', 'Carrot and Stick Approach' for obtaining performance from the people which may not yield results always.
2. Mere observance of rules and regulation may not be accepted as the end-objective of discipline.
3. The concept of people as valued assets has been ignored.
4. It completely ignores positive discipline.
5. Punitive action may not be considered as an effective measure to correct the behaviour of erring employee.
6. Disciplinary action may not act as the only tool to punish a person.
7. No chance is given to the delinquent employee to improve his conduct.

8. It creates a group of discontented employees that may outburst to unrest and disharmony in the organization.
9. It looks to the past activities of the employees who violate rules, regulations, and does not look for the future effectively.
10. It creates hindrance in the process of establishing a state of mutuality between boss and subordinates.
11. It encourages retaliation, resistance from the people.
12. The process of imposing punishment is time consuming, costly.

Judicial Approach

Judicial approach is one of the approaches that deals with indisciplinary activities. It is based on the procedures followed by a court of law for giving judgment in a case. The use of the approach is much more than any other approach in our country.

Salient Features

1. Degree and nature of offence is determined through a series of activities like measuring evidence, following step prescribed for disciplinary procedures.
2. Emphasis is given to follow the principles of natural justice as non-observance of norms of natural justice makes the disciplinary action exercise ineffective, invalid.
3. Every opportunity is given to the delinquent employee to defend his case, to correct the mistakes in the facts and allegations levelled against him, to cite mitigating factors like provocations, etc.
4. Extenuating factors, aggravating factors and the service records of the erring employee are given due importance while decision for imposing punishment is made.
5. The Labour Court, Industrial Tribunal or National Tribunal have the power to set aside an order of discharge or dismissal and direct reinstatement or to award lesser punishment. So, the tribunal can intervene in order to review cases of dismissal of workers after domestic enquiry. The tribunals rely only on the materials on records and do not take fresh evidence in relation to the matter.

Limitation

1. It gives a lot of stress, emphasis on the procedural aspects of the application of law, rules, judgment, etc.

2. Human values, qualities are not given due weightage.
3. No effort is given to ascertain the genesis or root cause of indiscipline. Proper remedial measures are not prescribed for improving the conduct, behaviour of erring employees.
4. It does not generate a feeling amongst the delinquent employees to perform, to achieve and excel as they think it is not more than taking disciplinary action under some procedural system.
5. There is less or no possibility of developing self-discipline or self-control and all this arises out of positive discipline.
6. It looks to a small part of activities of the offender that can make him liable for disciplinary action, but the other remaining part that may contain a huge qualitative attribute is entirely ignored. So, it fails to make proper judgement of a person's conduct or behaviour.

Humanitarian or Human Relations Approach

This approach is based on the humanitarian aspect of people activities that avoid the mechanical application of rules and regulation to deal with indiscipline activities. It is one of the approaches to discipline management that pays much emphasis on human dignity, respect.

The salient characteristics of humanitarian approach are mentioned.

Salient Characteristics

1. The employee is treated as human being who is honest, sincere and loyal, and he loves to work if he is properly motivated.
2. A person has a lot of activities. He manifests such activities in different ways. Indiscipline pattern of activities is one way of manifestation that may not be a normal pattern of activity.
3. The totality of personality/behaviour is taken into consideration for ascertaining an offence.
4. For any violation, queries are used to find the factors that make the person defy the authority, question or challenge the rules, regulations, orders and instructions.
5. If after enquiry or investigation, it is found that the reason for violation of rules, regulations is such that it is beyond the control of the person (may be, it is due to the effect of fatigue, ill health and the like) an attempt is made to help the person to get over such a personal difficulty.
6. Extenuating factor is given much more weightage before decision for imposing punishment is taken.

Limitation

Some of the limitations include

- More emphasis is given on human aspect. It is more human oriented than performance oriented.
- In absence of penal action people may not like to improve, and they may repeat the same indisciplinary activity several times.
- It is not accepted by the organization magnet to use it as a tool to correct the indisciplinary behaviour of the employees. So, its use in the organizational setting is limited.
- This approach may make the organizational system of activities slow as this needs a lot of time to complete the process.
- Some industry experts think that application of this approach may not be advantageous for the organization as they need to take quick and corrective steps including punitive action against the erring employee which this approach cannot make.

Behavioural Approach

Behavioural approach is based on the behavioural activities of the boss. The main emphasis is given on the orderly behaviour of the management personnel in the organization.

Salient Features

The salient features of the behavioural approach include.

1. Observance of rules by boss

Under this approach the management personnel while working with the subordinates manifest their behavioural activities in an orderly and/disciplined way and then expect the same behaviour from their subordinates.

2. Setting example

The boss himself needs to set example of disciplined activities by observing rules, regulation in the organization. It may be like that if boss pays respect to his boss he can expect respect from his subordinates or if boss is punctual he can expect that his subordinate is also punctual.

3. Role model

There may be the possibility of establishing a disciplined culture in the organization through exercising role model activities by the management personnel.

4. Dyadic relationship

Promoting relation between boss and subordinate depends on the behaviour of subordinate expected by the boss and the behaviour of boss manifested in the organization. That means, if the boss is well disciplined, well behaved, he can obviously expect that his subordinate will be well disciplined and better dyadic relationship can be expected. But, an indisciplined boss cannot expect disciplined activities from subordinate but if he expects so, it severely affects the dyadic relationship.

Limitations

This approach is not free from limitations. It has some limitations. They are

1. It may give the idea in the matter that if the boss has negative activity in one area out of so many positive activities, the subordinate may follow the negative one. This may develop an error in the process of observing boss's activities.
2. Some qualitative attributes the boss possesses remain hidden and are not exposed to the subordinates or team members. So, the subordinates' judgement, perception about the boss makes misleading consequences.
3. Some areas of a person which get fixed during formative childhood under a constant and vigorous nurturing process may not be changed through the influencial exercise of the boss.
4. If a person's adult ego is contaminated greatly by critical parent, it becomes a difficult task for the boss having balanced ego-state, to influence the person's activities.

Human Resource Approach or Human Resource Development Approach

Under this approach people are considered to be valued assets, human resource that needs to be managed and developed for attainment of organizational excellence.

Salient Characteristics

The important characteristics of HR approach/HRD approach are

1. Every employee is an asset/resource to the employer that helps the organization to achieve its goals.
2. People need to be trained, motivated and nurtured to increase the level of efficiency as required by the company. A huge amount of money and energy is spent in training and developing the human

resources so that they can improve their competency to excel their performance.

3. It is the responsibility of the management to identify the areas where the people need training for reinforcement and strengthen those areas through training and development measures. If there is an indiscipline activity it may occur that it is due to
   - failure of training or
   - ineffective motivating system or
   - individual's failure/aberration

For any indiscipline activity people alone cannot be held responsible, the management is equally responsible.

4. Most of the management people's assumption about the people at work is based on Theory Y. Their assumptions about people include
   - People like work as natural as play or rest
   - They are not indolent, lazy
   - They exercise self-direction and self-control for performance of activities
   - They have potential, imagination, creativity
   - They want challenging job, responsibility; want to lead

All these mean that people have capability to excel, willingness to obey, conform to rules and to face challenges. So, handling people's problems need tricks, experience and use of appropriate stroking/motivation tools to ensure that competency and willingness of the people are not affected, destroyed. It may occur that punitive action may demotivate, demoralize and damage the human resource. So, this approach does not call for application of punitive discipline.

This approach gives stress on corrective aspect of people's behaviour, conduct. It looks at the needs of the organization first, the human resource has only a value relative to it to meet the objectives of the organization. This approach does not have sympathy for the people who are non-performers, deadwoods. Disciplinary action is taken against an erring employee as the last resort to correct, promote and develop the behavioural area that needs reinforcement to sustain, perform, excel.

It makes a departure in the management perception about discipline from enforcing obediency to natural, spontaneous and willing acceptance of rules, regulations of the organization. That means it looks for winning cooperation and for enforcing and extracting compliance.

Limitations

1. It gives a blind support accepting all people are performers, achievers which may not be correct all the time.
2. It is very difficult to generate a climate of positive discipline. It is possible only when people in the organization are happy, contented, satisfied, committed to work and to the organization.
3. Some people are incorrigible. They need punishment through disciplinary procedure. Counselling in such cases may not help to prevent recurrence of indiscipline activities.
4. It happens in the organization that some people resort to such acts of misconducts which according to service rules or standing orders are major misconducts warranting capital punishment.

Books Recommended

1. Leon C Megginson, *Personnel and Human Administration* (Richard D lrwin, Homewood, 1977)
2. SK Dutta, *Guide to Disciplinary Action* (Tata McGraw-Hill Publishing Company Limited, New Delhi, 1994)
3. NN Chatterjee, *Management of Personnel in Indian Enterprises* (Allied Book Agency, Delhi, 1978)
4. YB Bhonsle, *Disciplinary Action; A Handbook for Managers* (S Chand, New Delhi, 1972)
5. Henry Fayol, *General and Industrial Management* (Pitman Publishing Co, New York, 1951)
6. CB Mamoria and SV Gankar, *Personnel Management: Text and Cases* (Himalaya Publishing House, Delhi, 2001)
7. AK Ghosh, *Human Resource Management* (With cases) (Manas Publications, New Delhi, 2006)

Questions

1. Some say discipline means self-discipline. As a student of Management do you endorse this? If yes, why? If not, why not?
2. What is discipline? State and explain the important characteristics of discipline?
3. 'Discipline is an orderly behaviour'. How will you justify this?
4. Explain in brief the prerequisites of positive discipline. Also state the effect of positive discipline.

5. 'Discipline makes the organization function and achieve goals'. Discuss in this context the objectives of discipline.
6. What is code of discipline? Why code of discipline is important?
7. Explain in brief the content of code of discipline.
8. Define code of discipline. What steps the central employers' organizations and workers' organizations can take against their members for violation of the code?
9. What is indiscipline? State the factors responsible for indiscipline activities.
10. Do you think economic factor is the only factor that makes the employee indisciplined? Discuss.
11. State and explain the measures to be adopted for maintenance and promoting discipline.
12. What are the approaches to disciplinary action? Can hot stove rule be applied in industrial settings?
13. Point the difference between Hot Stove Rule and Traditional Approach.
14. Explain Judicial Approach. State its salient features and also its limitations.
15. State the differences between Humanitarian Approach and Human Resource Development Approach.

Case Study

On 9th December 2006 Mr Naren Biswas was recruited as a mechanic for a medium sized automobile service station in Kota. Mr Biswas was to do routine maintenance on the cars that were leased out to various local firms from time to time. When he first started his job he was assigned the duty to check on the time clock at 7am. On 30th July 2008 Mr RP Dutta, Supervisor called Mr Biswas to his office and told Mr Biswas that he noticed during July that he was late for work several times. The Supervisor also told that after confirmation in service he had not been reporting for work on time. Mr Dutta expressed his empathetic attitude to help Mr Biswas so that he could come on time.

Mr Biswas replied, "It would be nice if you permit me to come at 8am instead of 7am, since I have to travel a lot daily". Then Mr Dutta told him that he was satisfied with his overall work activities and it did not matter if his workday began at 8am. During the month of August, 2008 Mr Biswas was late 10 times. On 10th September 2008 Mr Dutta posted the following notice on the display board:

"Any employee late for work more than thrice in any particular month is subject to disciplinary action".

On November 12, 2008 Mr Dutta called Mr Biswas into his cabin and gave him a letter that read:

"During October 2008 you were late for work 6 times. If this behaviour continues, you are subject to disciplinary action".

Mr Biswas acknowledged receipt of this letter. Mr Biswas was again late 8 times in November 2008. On December 8, 2008 Mr Dutta again called Mr Biswas into his cabin and gave him a letter mentioning that "During November 2008 you were late for work 8 times which were more than permissible time. You are directed to be punctual at your attendance. If such behaviour continues, disciplinary action will be taken against you. "Mr Biswas received the letter against acknowledgement.

On December 10,2008 at about 2.30pm Mr Biswas along with the General Secretary of the Union entered the cabin of Mr Dutta when Mr Dutta was doing some paper work. Then Mr Biswas shouted at Mr Dutta, threw away visiting chairs from the cabin, broke the table glass, threatened him with dire consequences if disciplinary action was taken against him. After this, both the General Secretary of the union and Mr Biswas left the office premises.

On the basis of what has been stated above answer the following questions:

1. Give an outline of the steps to be taken to deal with indisciplinary activities under

- Hot Stove Rule
- Traditional Approach
- Behavioural Approach
- Humanitarian Approach and
- HRD Approach
- Judicial Approach

2. What are the steps you will suggest to generate positive discipline in the company?

3. Differentiate between

a. Hot Stove Rule and Judicial Approach

b. Behavioural Approach and HRD Approach

4. **State the steps to be taken for disciplinary action against Mr Biswas.**

5. **Can Mr Biswas be punished without holding domestic enquiry? Give reasons for your answer.**

VII

Disciplinary Action

Concept of Disciplinary Action

Disciplinary action means the action taken against an employee who resorts to an act of misconduct concerning the standing orders, service rules, bipartite settlement, agreements of the company. It happens when an employee violates rules, regulations, resorts to indiscipline activities management takes constructive, preventive and motivating measures to correct his behaviour, improve his conduct so that he does not make the same mistakes in future; but when the employee does not improve his conduct and again resorts to act of misconducts the disciplinary action is taken against him.

The employer has a right to impose punishment on the erring employee for a misconduct but normally he cannot do so without holding departmental/domestic enquiry according to the rules of imparting justice. However, all this is mentioned in the standing orders, rules, regulations of the company.

Meaning of Misconduct

There is no clear definition of misconduct in any legislation in our country. The Industrial Disputes Act 1947 is completely silent about 'misconduct'. The Industrial Employment (Standing Orders) Act 1946 that deals with the condition of employee does not provide definition or a clear concept about 'misconduct'. This Act only gives a list of acts of misconduct. The dictionary meaning of misconduct is improper behaviour or deliberate violation of a rule or standard of behaviour.

In the work situation the misconduct means malfeasance or culpable neglect of an official in regard to his office. It is an act or omission on the part of an employee which is breach of any duty, obligation or assignment under contract of employment.

The staff regulations, standing orders, service rules, bipartite settlement governing service condition of employees have not defined the term 'misconduct', all these have enumerated the acts or omission which constitute misconduct.

From the above, it is clear that 'misconduct' means indiscipline activity. Every act of indisciplinary is called misconduct.

What are the Acts of Misconduct?

The acts of misconducts are enumerated in standing orders, service rules, staff regulations, Settlements governing service conditions of employees, but all these acts of misconduct are merely illustrative in nature, not exhaustive and it needs to be mentioned specifically in the standing orders in view of the judgement of the Supreme Court[1]. It is difficult to prepare an exhaustive lists of acts of misconduct because it is not possible to foresee and enumerate all possible and imaginable acts of misconduct within the ambit of service rules and staff regulations.

It is observed that some service rules, settlements mention the misconducts separately under two heads – gross misconduct and minor misconduct. In banking industry such distinction has been made in respect of misconducts of non-officers. The acts of misconducts – gross and minor misconduct – laid down in the Bipartite Settlement applicable for non-officers (i.e., clerks and subordinate staff) working with banking industry in India, are mentioned herein.[2]

1 Glaxo Ltd vs Presiding Officer, Meerut, 1989, Lab , I.C.P 1909

2 Clause 5 of the Memoranda of Settlement dated 10th April 2002 and 27th May 2002 between the Management of 52 'A' class Banks as represented by the Indian Banks Association and their workmen as represented by the All India Bank Employee's Association, National Confederation of Bank Employees, India National Bank Employees' Federation and also Bank Karmachari Sena Mahasangh, Pp 135-137

By the expression 'gross misconduct' shall be meant any of the following acts and omissions on the part of an employee:

a) engaging any trade or business outside the scope of his duties except with the written permission of the bank;

b) unauthorised disclosure of information regarding the affairs of the bank or any of its customers or any other person connected with the business of the bank which is confidential or the disclosure of which is likely to be prejudicial to the interests of the bank;

c) drunkenness or riotous or disorderly or indecent behaviour on the premises of the bank;

d) wilful damage or attempt to cause damage to the property of the bank or any of its customers;

e) wilful insubordination or disobedience of any lawful and reasonable order of the management or of a superior;

f) habitual doing of any act which amounts to "minor misconduct" as defined below, "habitual" meaning a course of action taken or persisted in, notwithstanding that at least on three previous occasions censure or warnings have been administered or an adverse remark has been entered against him;

g) wilful slowing down in performance of work;

h) gambling or betting on the premises of the bank;

i) speculation in stocks, shares, securities or any commodity whether on his account or that of any other persons;

j) any act prejudicial to the interest of the bank or gross negligence or negligence involving or likely to involve the bank in serious loss;

k) giving or taking a bribe or illegal gratification from a customer or an employee of the bank;

l) abetment or instigation of any of the acts or omissions above mentioned;

m) knowingly making a false statement in any document pertaining to or in connection with his employment in the bank;

n) resorting to unfair practice of any nature whatsoever in any examination conducted by the Indian Institute of Bankers or by or on behalf of the bank and where the employee is caught in the act of resorting to such unfair practice and a report to that effect has been received by the bank from the concerned authority;

o) resorting to unfair practice of any nature whatsoever in any examination conducted by the Indian Institute of Bankers or by or on behalf of the bank in cases not covered by the above Sub-Clause(s) and where a report to that effect has been received by the bank from the concerned authority and the employee does not accept the charge;

p) remaining unauthorisedly absent without intimation continuously for a period exceeding 30 days;

q) misbehaviour towards customers arising out of bank's business.

r) contesting election for parliament/legislative assembly/legislative council/local bodies/municipal corporation/panchayat, without explicit written permission of the bank;

s) conviction by a criminal Court of Law for an offence involving moral turpitude;

t) indulging in any act of 'sexual harassment' of any woman at her workplace;

Note; Sexual harassment shall include such unwelcome sexually determined behaviour (whether directly or otherwise) as

a. physical contact and advances;

b. demand or request for sexual favours;

c. sexually coloured remarks;

d. showing pornography; or

e. any other unwelcome physical, verbal or non-verbal conduct of a sexual nature.

u) (for State Bank of India)

the giving or taking or abetting the giving or taking of dowry or demanding directly or indirectly from the parents or guardians of a bride or bridegroom, as the case may be, any dowry.

Explanation - For the purpose of sub-clause (u) the word 'dowry' has the same meaning as in the "Dowry Prohibition Act, 1961".

By the expression 'minor misconduct' shall be meant any of the following acts and omissions on the part of an employee:

a) absence without leave or overstaying sanctioned leave without sufficient grounds;

b) unpunctual or irregular attendance;

c) neglect of work, negligence in performing duties;

d) breach of any rule of business of the bank or instruction for the running of any department;

e) committing nuisance on the premises of the bank;

f) entering or leaving the premises of the bank except by an entrance provided for the purpose;

g) attempt to collect or collecting moneys within the premises of the bank without the previous permission of the management or except as allowed by any rule or law in force at the time;

h) holding or attempting to hold or attending any meeting on the premises of the bank without the previous permission of the management or except in accordance with the provisions of any rule or law in force at the time;

i) canvassing for union membership or collection of union dues or subscriptions within the premises of the bank without the previous permission of the management or except in accordance with the provisions of any rule or law in force at the time;

j) failing to show proper consideration, courtesy or attention towards officers, customers or other employees of the bank, unseemly or unsatisfactory behaviour while on duty;

k) marked disregard of ordinary requirements of decency and cleanliness in person or dress;

l) incurring debts to an extent considered by the management as excessive;

m) resorting to unfair practice of any nature whatsoever in any examination conducted by the Indian Institute of Bankers or by or on behalf of the bank in cases not covered by sub-clause;

n) under 'Gross Misconduct' and where a report to that effect has been received by the bank from the concerned authority and the employee accepts the charge;

o) refusal to attend training programmes without assigning sufficient and valid reasons;

p) not wearing, while on duty, identity card issued by the bank;

q) not wearing, while on duty, the uniforms supplied by the bank, in clean condition[3].

The Model Standing Orders in respect of industrial establishment other than coal mines lay down the following acts and omissions as misconduct:

3 Ibid, Pp 138-139

a) wilful insubordination or disobedience, whether alone or in combination with others, to any lawful and reasonable order of a superior;

b) theft, fraud, or dishonesty in connection with the employers' business or property;

c) wilful damage to or loss of employers' goods or property;

d) taking or giving bribes or any illegal gratification;

e) habitual absence without leave or absence without leave for more than 10 days;

f) habitual late attendance;

g) habitual breach of any law applicable to the establishment;

h) riotous or disorderly behaviour during working hours at the establishment or any act subversive of discipline;

i) habitual negligence or neglect of act;

j) frequent repetition of any act or omission for which a fine may be imposed to a maximum of two percent of the wages in a month;

k) striking at work or inciting other to strike at work in contravention of the provisions of any law or rule having the force of law[4].

Misconducts under Model Conduct, Discipline and Appeal Rules for Public Sector Undertakings

The officers and employees engaged in public undertaking but not governed by the statutory standing orders are covered under the purview of Model Conduct, Discipline and Appeal Rules. So, the workmen engaged in such undertaking but governed by the statutory standing orders are excluded. It means these rules are applicable to officers and employees not covered as 'workmen' in terms of Industrial Disputes Act, 1947 and Industrial Employment (Standing Orders) Act, 1946.

The following acts of omission and commission shall be treated as misconduct:

1. Theft, fraud or dishonesty in connection with the business or property of the corporation/company or of property of another person within the premises of the corporation/company;
2. Taking or giving bribes or any illegal gratification;
3. Possession of pecuniary resources or property disproportionate to the known source of income by the employee or on his behalf by another, which the employee cannot satisfactorily account for;

4 Rule 3(1) of the Industrial Employment (Standing Orders) Central Rules, 1946

4. Furnishing false information regarding name, age, father's name, qualifications, ability or previous service or any other matter germane to the employment at the time of employment or during the course of employment;
5. Acting in a manner prejudicial to the interest of the corporation/ company;
6. Wilful insubordination or disobedience, whether or not in combination with others, of any lawful and reasonable order of superior;
7. Absence without leave or overstaying the sanctioned leave for more than four consecutive days without sufficient ground or proper or satisfactory explanation;
8. Habitual late or irregular attendance;
9. Neglect of work or negligence in the performance of duty including malingering or slowing down of work;
10. Damage to any property of the corporation/company;
11. Interference or tampering with any safety devices installed in or about the premises of the corporation/company;
12. Drunkenness or riotous or disorderly or indecent behaviour in the premises of the corporation/company or outside such premises where such behaviour is related to or connected with the employment;
13. Gambling within the premises of the establishment;
14. Smoking within the premises of the establishment where it is prohibited;
15. Collection without the permission of the competent authority of any money within the premises of the corporation/company except as sanctioned by any law of the land being in force or rules of the corporation/company;
16. Sleeping while on duty;
17. Commission of any acts which amount to a criminal offence involving moral turpitude;
18. Absence from the employee's appointed place of work without permission or sufficient cause;
19. Purchasing properties, machinery, stores, etc., from or selling properties, machinery, stores, etc., to the corporation/company without express permission in writing from the competent authority;

20. Commission of any act subversive of discipline or of good behaviour;
21. Abetment of or attempt at abetment of any act which amounts to misconduct.

Vigilance and Non-Vigilance Disciplinary Cases

It is apparent that some misconducts of employees mentioned in the service rules/standing orders or agreements directly or indirectly relate to corruption and malpractice. The conduct of employees indulging such activities creates a bad image about the organization/institution and pollutes the societal climate. Looking to the ill-effect this sort of activities may make in the mindset of the people in the society it is a great necessity to develop the conduct and behaviour of the employees through close and constant scrutiny of misconduct dealing with cases separately and ensuring just and fair exercise of administrative powers vested in various authorities by statutory rules or by non-statutory orders. For such purpose Central Vigilance Commission has been set up by the Government of India in February, 1964. The Commission's main function is to supervise and to advise them in such matters.

The following acts of misconduct which a public servant is likely to resort to in the discharge of his official duty come under the purview of vigilance cases:

- Abuse of power;
- Acquiring assets disproportionate to one's known sources of income;
- Maintaining a style of living beyond one's means;
- Cheating;
- Falsification of records;
- Showing favours to private parties in dealing with them and/or accepting favours from them;
- Misappropriation of Government property;
- Negligence in the discharge of one's official duties;
- Trying to wreak vengeance on others;
- Indulging in private business;
- Misfeasance and other lapses of character like getting intoxicated in public places;
- Indebtedness; and

- Other miscellaneous acts which are likely to bring Government or the employer into disrepute.

The aforenoted acts of misconduct involve

- dereliction of duty if made unintentionally through carelessness and negligence
- an element of integrity if committed with an intention or motion
- an element of corruption if committed with an intention or motion and also in consideration of some gratification in the form of money, goods or services.

Since all disciplinary cases do not have vigilance angle (some belong to vigilance cases, some others belong to non-vigilance cases) Government organizations have laid down clear guidelines for monitoring and disposal of these categories of disciplinary cases. Disciplinary procedures and conducting of enquiry more or less are same in both cases except in some area of vigilance cases where approval is taken from some specified authority at some stages (maybe, prior to the stage of issuing chargesheet, placing an employee under suspension, imposing punishment or revocation of suspension). That means, reference to the appropritate authority at different stages (like first stage reference, second stage reference) is required.

An illustrative list of vigilance cases and non-vigilance for non-officers and officers upto MMG/s III of a bank is given below:

Vigilance Cases

- Misappropriation of cash
- Irregularities in advance, large excesses/temporary overdraft (TODS), etc.
- Fraud
- Bribe/illegal gratification/corruption
- Possession of disproportionate assets
- Misuse of official position for personal gains
- Unauthorized disclosure of information regarding affairs of the Bank/Customers/or any person connected with the business of the Bank which is confidential or disclosure of which is likely to be prejudicial to the interest of the Bank

5 SK Datta, *Guide to Disciplinary Action* (Tata McGraw Hill Publishing Company Ltd, New Delhi 2000, p181)

- Investment made by employees under Promoters'/Employees' Quota
- Credit card/TODs

Non-Vigilance Cases

- Any violation of Service Rules/Regulations
- Copying in CAIIB Examination
- Misconduct involving moral turpitude
- Misuse of staff quarters
- Non- Submission of Assets and Liabilities statement
- Misuse of Bank's loan including housing loan
- False claims of TA/DA/LFC/LTC
- Cash shortage (not misappropriation of cash)
- False caste certificate/education certificate/concealment of birth certificate
- Suppression of educational qualification.

Types of Indiscipline Cases

Discipline is a necessity for smooth and effective functioning of the organizational activities. All people should conform to rules, regulations of the organization. All people do not obey the norms and resort to indisciplinary activities. It occurs that an employee violates rules, behaves disorderly and indulges in indisciplinary activity. It also occurs that some employees collectively resort to indisciplinary activities. In both cases disciplinary action needs to be taken.

From the context of indisciplinary activities of employees disciplinary action needs to be taken against an individual employee and also against employees for collective acts of indiscipline. Such cases can be of two types

- Individual cases
- Collective cases

Individual Cases

In this case individual employee manifests his anger, unhappiness, displeasure by violating norms, rules and resorting to indisciplinary activities like coming late, remaining absent unauthorisedly, coming to workplace/premises under the influence of alcohol, etc. This is an attitudinal problem of the concerned employee and this can be tackled, in case of minor misconduct:

- through a fair, timely and consistent counselling
- by making the person feel that management is sympathetic to his problem and the intention of the management is to correct behaviours
- by taking disciplinary action in terms of service rules, settlements, etc.

But, in case of gross misconduct of an employee affecting organizational activities and also working climate of the organization, the management can take drastic disciplinary action against that employee.

Collective Cases

In this case some employees in group violate norms, rules of the company. They manifest their indisciplinary activities by gheraoing executives, slowing down performance, availing en masse casual leave and others. They do all this in a preplanned and calculated way under the direction/instigation of a formal or informal group. Their intention, to resort to such act of misconduct is to put pressure on the management so that they agree with their demands. This is a very sensitive issue that affects industrial relations of the company. It needs to be tackled cautiously. The following measures may be taken to deal with such issues/problems.

1. Collection and analysis of information, data

- To study the strength, support of the group to carry on their activities
- To get an idea about general impression of workers' community on the action, steps taken by the group
- To analyse the nature of problems, issues; ascertain the hurdles, difficulties to overcome
- To find out the real reasons/inherent causes that make the worker indisciplined
- To ascertain the loss of the company due to collective acts of indiscipline
- To collect the information whether the union to which the group members belong really want such indisciplinary activities
- To get to know whether the group members resort to act of indiscipline as a protest against management inaction, activities that deviate from the standard norms, rules, agreement, practices

- To have a complete idea about the statutory binding of the management in respect of the issue/dispute

2. Discussion and negotiation with group members/union

The management may start discussion, negotiation for amicable settlement with the group members/union. Sometimes it happens that problem crops up due to misunderstanding on the issue occurred between employees and the management. In such a case open and threadbare discussion may help to bring the parties closer and develop understanding.

3. Counter action, discussion and settlement

In some cases when the management find that on their part they are on the right track, they are very strong on the issue from legal perspective and also in the context of agreement, they may go for counter action. The management's tough stand may make the group members compelled to surrender; and sometime it happens the group member union, for its face saving go for discussion and settlement.

4. Disciplinary action

The management may also take disciplinary measures against the erring group of employees. So, bulk chargesheet, suspension orders may be issued to tackle the indisciplined activities. Before taking disciplinary action the management should ensure that such step will not affect industrial relations climate of the company and their stand is perfectly on the right path.

Natural Justice

The term 'natural justice' means the justice according to conscience. It makes it clear that before the decision of an issue is taken one should be guided by his own conscience. It is derived from the Roman concept of 'Jus Naturale' that means principles of natural law, natural justice, equity or good conscience. It is the natural sense of what is justice according to good conscience.

Natural justice are those principles of natural law which have not yet been enacted into positive law governing the people. These principles still exist and are followed. Natural justice is implied where the law itself is silent and is not inconsistent with what it provides.

Some of the principles of natural justice are given below:

1. No person should be judged in his own case or in a case in which he has some interest.
2. No person should be tried in absentia and without giving reasonable time and opportunity to defend himself.

3. The chargesheeted employee should know what is alleged against him.
4. All documents and evidence against the chargesheeted employee should be recorded in his presence and no material evidence should be relied on against him without giving him an opportunity to explain it.
5. The chargesheeted employee should be given an opportunity to bring his evidence in his defence.
6. He should have an opportunity to cross examine witnesses brought against him.
7. He should be informed through issuance of notice about holding the enquiry.
8. There should be a fair and impartial enquiry.
9. The punishment should not be grossly disproportionate with the nature of the offence or misconduct.

Importance of the Principle of Natural Justice

It is very important to follow the principles of natural justice in the departmental proceedings. The departmental enquiry is not a mere formality and, therefore, it should be conducted with all the seriousness. The non-compliance of the rules that result in the denial of reasonable opportunity to the erring employee and violation of the principle of natural justice will vitiate the enquiry.

The importance of the principles of natural justice can be ascertained from the following:

1. Providing guidelines

The proceedings before the Civil Court and Criminal Court are governed by the Codes (that means Code of Civil Procedure and Criminal Procedure Code) that give the guideline how a Civil or Criminal Court should act in different contingencies, but no such detailed guidelines are usually available for holding departmental enquiry. So, in the departmental proceeding the enquiry officer is required to fall back upon the principles of natural justice and to speculate upon the applicability of such principle in varying conditions and circumstances. It becomes easier and proper for the enquiry officer to conduct enquiry as he develops understanding from the principles of natural justice.

2. Removing the elements of defective enquiry

Since principles of natural justice are not codified and they differ in varying circumstances, the enquiry officer needs to have a thorough understanding and knowledge on the principles of natural justice. He should have mastery over the subject so that he can conduct enquiry in fair and rational way, consider and assess evidences, arguments, find and prepare a just and proper report. This can help him remove the elements of defective enquiry as it occurs that lack of such knowledge, skill and expertise can make the enquiry defective.

3. Helping to perform the function of holding enquiry smoothly and effectively

If the departmental enquiry is conducted by the enquiry officer without looking at the principles of natural justice, it may happen that the report suffers from its qualitative perspectives. The consequence of such enquiry becomes very serious for the management as the function of holding enquiry goes out of control of the management. So, conducting enquiry in terms of rules of natural justice may help perform the function of holding enquiry smoothly and effectively.

4. To obtain justice when interfered by the Labour Court/ Tribunal

The Labour Court/Tribunal can interfere with the order of discharge or dismissal of the management and can give the order of reinstatement of the dismissed employee if it finds that

i. there is want of good faith or
ii. there is victimization or unfair labour practices or
iii. the management is guilty of a basic error or violation of the principles of natural justice or
iv. on the material on record the findings are completely baseless or perverse[6].

So, following principles of natural justice by enquiry officer is a prerequisite for conducting departmental enquiry. And in such case there may be the least possibility to consider the enquiry proceeding as defective, by the labour court/Tribunal.

5. Improving morale of the workers

Effective departmental enquiry which is conducted by enquiry officer in terms of principles of natural justice generates a faith, confidence among the workers over the enquiry process. This helps improve morale of the workers.

---

6 Supreme Court, *Indian Iron and Steel Company Ltd. and another vs their workmen*, 1958 IL LKJ 260

6. Helping to establish healthy human relations

Since the principles of natural justice are based on justice, equity and good conscience, there is a possibility of developing healthy human relations in the organization.

7. Helping to make a solid foundation of discipline management system

Departmental enquiry is a vital activity in discipline management. Justification of disciplinary action taken by management depends on how departmental enquiry is conducted, whether enquiry officer is biased or unbiased, whether principles of natural justices are followed or not. Enquiry officer's activities reflected in his report may or may not justify the actions of the disciplinary authority. So, an effective, proper and transparent enquiry process helps make a solid foundation of discipline management.

Requirements of an Effective Disciplinary System

One of the principal objectives of discipline management is to improve the conduct of those employees who knowingly or unknowingly violate the norms of conduct. For improvement of the conducts of such employees management takes various steps/measures like

- ascertaining the reasons for violating norms; and discussing, interacting and counselling
- providing support/help to overcome situations that create violation
- advising verbally/orally to improve conduct
- issuing advisory note to improve behaviour
- changing behaviour through training and development activities
- issuing show cause notice, chargesheet and imposing punishment, and other measures.

So, the management needs to impose punishment on the erring employees when all persuasive/motivation techniques fail to improve their behaviour/conduct. Since punishment issue is very sensitive to discipline management, the management should ensure that an effective disciplinary system exists in the organization.

For an effective disciplinary system the organization should adopt the following guidelines/procedures:

1. Thorough knowledge and understanding of the rules of discipline

The employees including management personnel should have thorough knowledge and understanding of the rules of discipline in the company so that they can generate self discipline.

The organization should take proper steps to make the people know

- the acts of misconduct – minor misconduct, major misconduct
- the procedures followed to take disciplinary action
- the punishment under minor misconduct and major misconduct
- the procedures for appeal

The company can make the employees aware of disciplinary issues/ actions through training, discussion and deliberations by supervisor or/boss.

2. Disciplinary actions taken as per rules

Disciplinary actions should be taken in terms of Standing Orders or Settlements/Services Rules, awards, Shops and Establishment Act, etc.

Before taking disciplinary action the management should ensure

- that the reported complaint has been verified
- that the fact has been ascertained.
- that there is a prima-facie case and the concerned employee is at fault
- that there is a violation of rules.

The management should decide whether show cause notice can be issued to the delinquent to give him a chance to explain the reason of his conduct, or chargesheet be issued. If the decision to issue show cause notice is taken, the delinquent employee needs to submit reply within stipulated period. On receipt of the reply to the show cause notice if the management observes that the explanation of the employee is satisfactory or the lapse has occurred due to some reasons for which the employee is not directly responsible, the management decides to close the case. But, when the reply to the show cause notice is unsatisfactory the chargesheet should be given to the concerned employee. Actually, the disciplinary procedure starts when the chargesheet is issued.

3. Immediate action

The management should take immediate action against the delinquent as delay in action loses its importance and also conveys message to the general mass that the management is not interested to maintain discipline.

In organizational setting it may not be possible for the management to punish an employee immediately after the act of misconduct is reported, but in this case management should immediately initiate disciplinary action against an erring employee.

4. Adhering to norms of natural justice

The management should ensure that norms of natural justice are followed while taking disciplinary action. That means the erring employee is given the opportunity to know the allegations against him, to produce his own witness, to cross examine the witness(s) brought against him. The punishment should not be disproportionate with the nature of offence.

5. Fair, proper and unbiased action

The management should ensure that the action to be taken against the delinquent is fair, proper and unbiased. So, before punishment decision is taken the management needs to look at extenuating, aggravating factors. The punishing authority should not be biased or influenced by any person at the time of taking decision of punishment against an erring employee.

6. Maintenance of congenial environment in work place

The management should ensure that congenial and harmonious environment exists in the department/shop where the punished person works. The supervisor under whom the punished employee works should express his supportive, facilitative and helping attitude towards such employee. He should behave normally so that the erring employee can improve his behaviour.

Punishment

The organization adopts disciplinary procedures that culminates into punishment. That means, punishment is the ultimate way to maintain discipline. The purpose of imposing punishment is to let the delinquent feel that what he has done is wrong and undesired by the organization and also to give a chance to correct his behaviour. Punishment serves as an example to others that acts as a preventive tool to maintain and promote discipline in the organization.

A delinquent may be punished in many ways. It may start from censuring and may extend to dismissal from service depending on the gravity of misconduct.

Disciplinary authority imposes punishment on the delinquent when all or some of the charges levelled against him are proved in the departmental enquiry. The type/kind of punishment to be imposed needs to be decided by the disciplinary authority from the list of punishment mentioned in the standing orders, service rules, bipartite settlement, staff regulations, etc. For example, the disciplinary authority considers a suitable penalty to be imposed on non-officer employee in banks as mentioned in the bipartite settlement. Such penalties are:

An employee found guilty of gross misconduct may[7]

a. be dismissed without notice or
b. be removed from service with superannuation benefits i.e., pension and/or provident fund and gratuity as would be due otherwise under the Rules or Regulations prevailing at the relevant time and without disqualification from future employment, or
c. be compulsorily retired with superannuation benefits i. e, Pension and/or Provident Fund and Gratuity as would be due otherwise under the Rules or Regulations prevailing at the relevant time and without disqualification from future employment, or
d. be discharged from service with superannuation benefits i.e., pension and/or provident fund and gratuity as would be due otherwise under the Rules or Regulations prevailing at the relevant time and without disqualification from future employment, or
e. be brought down to lower stage in the scale of pay up to a maximum of two stages, or
f. have his increment(s) stopped with or without cumulative effect, or
g. have his special pay withdrawn, or
h. be warned or censured, or have an adverse remark entered against him, or
i. be fined

An employee found guilty of minor misconduct may

a. be warned or censured, or
b. have an adverse remark entered against him, or
c. have his increment stopped for a period not longer than six months[8]

Now, it is felt pertinent to give an idea about the penalties/punishment generally imposed on offenders working with various organizations/ establishments in India. Such penalties/punishments include:

7 Memorandum of Settlement dated 10th April 2002 between the managements of banks and their workers (clause 6)

8 Ibid, clause 8

- Dismissal without notice
- Removal from service with superannuation benefits
- Compulsory retirement with superannuation benefits
- Discharged from service
- Demotion
- Stoppage of increment(s) with or without cumulative effect
- Withdrawal of special pay
- Fines
- Written reprimand
- Oral reprimand
- Warning
- Censure
- Loss of privileges
- Punitive suspension
- Making adverse remark entered against the offender

Punishments are imposed on the delinquent employees by the disciplinary authority looking at the gravity of misconducts the employees resort to. Out of the lists of punishment mentioned above the following two types of punishment are harsh and severe.

- Dismissal
- Discharge

A brief idea on such kind of punishment is given herein below.

Dismissal

Dismissal is a capital punishment imposed by the disciplinary authority that makes the erring employee lose his job. This is removal of an employee from his job. The service of an employee can be terminated either by way of discharge or by dismissal. Dismissal is the extreme form of punishment. This kind of punishment is awarded when it becomes incompatible to continue with employer-employee relations. It also happens that when acts of misconduct resorted to by the delinquent employee are grave, serious; and such acts/omissions are proved by the enquiry officer at the departmental enquiry the disciplinary authority may take decision to punish the chargesheeted employee by way of dismissal. Some of such acts of misconduct include:

- Wilful damage to the property of the company

- Wilful insubordination, disobedience of any lawful or reasonable order of the management
- Riotous or disorderly behaviour during working hours at the establishment
- Theft, fraud, dishonesty in connection with employer's business or property

In case of dismissal the employer can withhold bonus, gratuity, contribution to provident fund, leave encashment, additional retirement benefit if any and also his other dues to make up the loss caused to the establishment by his misconduct.

Management cannot dismiss an employee from his service without issuing chargesheet and holding domestic enquiry. The delinquent employee can be dismissed if the charges are proved. So, issuance of chargesheet and also holding departmental enquiry is a must. It is also essential that the erring employee is informed in writing about the alleged misconduct, is given an opportunity to explain the circumstances alleged against him, to produce his witness(es) in his defence and to cross examine witnesses brought against him.

Since dismissed is a severe punishment, it is rarely inflicted. The management generally tries to avoid such punishment. Before taking dismissal decision management looks at various aspects thoroughly viz., enquiry proceedings, findings of EO, extenuating and aggravating factors, compliance of principles of natural justices at the enquiry, etc.

Discharge

Discharge is termination of service of an employee by the employer. The termination of service may be made in various ways. It may be

- by way of punishment. When an employee resorts to an act of misconduct mentioned in the service rules/standing orders, employer punishes the employee after following prescribed disciplinary procedures.
- on the ground of loss of confidence. When an employer loses confidence in an employee, he may terminate his service provided that order of termination is not punitive or malafide or made to victimize the employee or it does not amount to unfair labour practice. This sort of termination of service is discharge simpliciter.
- by way of agreement or contract of service made between employer and employee. When both parties agree to terminate the contract on a stipulated date by giving notice or by paying

money in lieu of notice, contract of service can be terminated. It is automatic, in the sense, on the expiry of contract period service is terminated if no further contract is made.

The discharge may be presented in the following way:

In the field of industrial jurisprudence, discharge is meant 'discharge by way of punishment'. In such case chargesheet should be issued and departmental/domestic enquiry should be constituted, and after proper enquiry and complying with formalities decision, for termination of service/discharge should be taken. Such discharge does not attach to any stigma, and it does not make the discharged employee disentitled to future employment.

In case of discharge simpliciter departmental enquiry needs not be held. Employee's service is terminated for loss of confidence. Employee may or may not resort to any act of misconduct. Employer can terminate service of his employee on the ground of loss of confidence. The ground of loss of confidence should not be malafide or should not appear to be a colourable exercise of the power conferred on the employer either by the terms of the contract or by the standing orders, or should not be made to victimize the employee and should not amount to unfair labour practice.

Some of the examples of loss of confidence are:

- dishonesty in connection with company's property
- misbehaviour with woman co-worker
- working with other establishment privately after leaving office on a false pretext
- failing to protect the interest of the customers by forging on vouchers[9]

9 State Bank of India VJR Surama, Presiding Officer, Central Government Industrial Tribunal, 2003 LLR124 (Delhi HC)

Difference between Discharge and Dismissal

Difference between discharge and dismissal is given in table 7. 1

Table 7. 1 showing the difference between discharge and dismissal

Dimension	Dismissal	Discharge
1. Concept	It is a termination of service of an employee by an employer in term of service rules, or settlement or standing orders after holding departmental/ domestic enquiry and after compliance with disciplinary procedures.	It is a termination of service of an employee by an employer in terms of service rules or standing orders or agreement/ contract or on the ground of loss of confidence for which departmental/ domestic enquiry may or may not be held.
2. Nature of Punishment	It is an industrial capital punishment. It is very harsh and severe.	It is also a capital punishment but it is not so harsh and severe punishment than dismissal.
3. Use	Such punishment by disciplinary authority is rare. Management generally tries to avoid such punishment.	Such punishment is not rare, particularly when discharge is by way of entering into contract or agreement between employer and employee.
4. Form	Dismissal has no form. It is termination of service when an employee resorts to act of grave misconduct and that disciplinary per rules/standing orders.	Discharge has various forms. Termination of service may be made in terms of agreement or contract between employer and employee or on the ground of loss of confidence or for resorting to acts of misconduct for which disciplinary procedures are followed and complied with.
5. Departmental/ domestic enquiry	Departmental enquiry or domestic enquiry is a must for taking decision of dismissal.	Departmental enquiry or domestic enquiry is a necessity if the decision of discharge is taken by way of punishment (that means when it is a punishment discharge).

6. Issuance of chargesheet	Without issuing chargesheet and holding departmental enquiry/ domestic enquiry such punishment cannot be inflicted.	In-case of discharge by way of punishment issuance of chargesheet and holding departmental enquiry or domestic enquiry is a must.
7. Entitlement	A dismissed employee may not be entitled to provident fund, gratuity and other benefits.	An employee whose service is terminated by way of discharge is usually entitled to such benefit and his dues.
8. Future employment	It may be very difficult for a person who is dismissed from service, to obtain further job.	It may not be so difficult to obtain another employment for a person whose service is terminated by way of discharge.
9. Punishment Perspective	It is always a punishment	It is not always a punishment
10. Immediacy	Its effect is immediate. Immediate action is taken to terminate the service of an employee without notice.	Its effect is not so immediate. A notice may have to be given in terms of service rules or standing orders.
11. Social impact	It affects societal recognition, status and image of the person who is dismissed from the service.	It does not affect to that extent.
12. Substitution of decision	In some cases management shows unwillingness to award punishment of dismissal. It may insist that employee submit his resignation, transfer him to some other unimportant department, or promote to some post without assigning work, etc.	Looking to different perspectives like equity, expediency, rationality, exceptional situation the management may take decision to discharge an employee instead of dismissing him.

Difference between Discharge and Discharge Simpliciter

It is now pertinent to differentiate between discharge and discharge simpliciter and such difference is shown in table 7. 2.

Table 7. 2 showing difference between discharge and discharge simpliciter

Dimension	Discharge	Discharge Simpliciter
1. Meaning	It is a termination of service of an employee by an employer in terms of service rules/tanding orders or agreement/ contract of services or on the ground of loss of confidence.	It is a termination of service of an employee by an employer on the ground of loss of confidence.
2. Coverage	It has wide coverage. Termination of service of an employee for any reason, other than termination by dismissal comes under the gamut of discharge.	Its coverage is narrow, short. Only termination of service for loss of confidence comes under it.
3. Concept	It is a concept in itself.	It is a part of discharge concept.
4. Departmental/ domestic enquiry	In case of termination of service by way of discharge, as a punitive action departmental/domestic enquiry is a must.	Departmental/domestic enquiry is not held to terminate the service of an employee by discharge simpliciter.
5. Act of misconduct	Decision for punitive discharge is taken when an employee resorts to acts of misconduct for which chargesheet is issued and departmental/domestic enquiry is held.	To take decision for discharge simpliciter it is not necessary that the concerned employee should resort to any act of misconduct.
6. Issuance of chargesheet	Issuing chargesheet on delinquent employee is a must in case of punitive discharge.	Chargesheet is not issued on to erring employee.

Ex-Parte Enquiry

The dictionary meaning of 'ex-parte' means 'on one side', 'Partial'. Ex-Parte enquiry means partial enquiry or one sided enquiry. It refers to the enquiry where one party remains present and other party remains absent. It means the enquiry which is held in absence of chargesheeted employee and his representative employee, if any.

It happens that sometimes chargesheeted employee does not turn up for enquiry even after giving due notice, accommodation and reasonable adjournment or he walks out in the midst of enquiry. In such case enquiry is held in absence of the chargesheeted employee. This enquiry is called ex-parte enquiry.

In ex-parte enquiry since enquiry is held in absence of chargesheeted employee, the enquiry officer needs to be more careful, conscious and he should ensure that all formalities, enquiry procedures laid down in service rules/standing orders are followed and complied with.

Some of the important activities that enquiry officer needs to observe, perform in ex-parte enquiry are given below:

- A note with regard to non-attendance of the chargesheeted employee at the enquiry or deliberately withdrawal from the enquiry, despite the opportunities given to him, should be recorded by the enquiry officer in the enquiry proceedings.
- The enquiry officer should ensure that the notice of enquiry is served upon the chargesheeted employee and despite this he has failed to attend the enquiry. For this, enquiry officer should examine the peon who went to serve the notice of enquiry, should go through the peon book to check that notice of enquiry has been duly served upon the chargesheeted employee, should keep the evidence (peon book) of having served the notice upon the chargesheeted employee, should keep the evidence of sending notice of enquiry through registered post or of having published in the local news paper.
- The enquiry officer should follow the steps mentioned in service rules/standing orders for conducting domestic/departmental enquiry. For example,
    - to ask the management representative to lead the evidence and prove the charge
    - to put relevant question to the witnesses and get classifications before coming to his conclusion about the charge
- The enquiry officer needs to be careful to see that all formalities/ procedures are complied with.

- He should demonstrate in a positive way to indicate that during the enquiry no advantage is taken of the absence of chargesheeted employee.
- The enquiry officer should record in the proceedings
  - the opportunities provided
  - the adjournment given to the chargesheeted employee to enable him to take part in the enquiry
  - the reason for conducting ex-parte enquiry by the enquiry officer

Legal Perspectives on Punishment

The various laws discuss the punishment of employees when they violate rules/resort to acts of misconduct. The relevant laws that deal with punishment are

I. Section 8 of the Payment of Wages Act 1936

II. Section IIA and section 33 of the Industrial Disputes Act 1947

III. The Industrial Employment (Standing Orders) Act 1946

Section 8 of the Payment of Wages Act 1936

Under section 8 of the Payment of Wages Act 1936 fines can be imposed for acts and omissions of the employees. This section lays down the following restrictions on the imposition of fines:

- An employed person can be fined only for such acts and emissions which have been approved by the State Government and duly notified to him.
- The list must be exhibited in the place of work.
- Before the fine is imposed, the concerned workman must be given an opportunity of showing cause against the imposition of fine.
- The amount of fine must not exceed 3 (three) percent of the wages payable to him in any wage period.
- Fine cannot be imposed on a workman who is below the age of 15.
- Fine cannot be recovered in instalments, or after the expiry of 60 days from the day on which it was imposed.
- Every fine shall be deemed to have been imposed on the day of the act or omission.
- All fines and the realization thereof shall be recorded in a register to be maintained by the employer in such form as may be prescribed by the State Government.

- amount collected as fine should be spent only for the benefit of the workmen through a committee consisting of the representatives of labour and management.

Section IIA of the Industrial Disputes Act 1947

- The Industrial Disputes Act 1947 empowers Labour Court, Tribunal or National Tribunal as the case may be, to set aside the order of discharge or dismissal of an employee, if the concerned authority before which the dispute relating to discharge or dismissal is referred, is satisfied that the order of the discharge or dismissal was not justified.
- The authority concerned may also direct reinstatement of the workman on such terms and conditions as it thinks fit, or give such other relief to the workman including the award of any lesser punishment in lieu of discharge or dismissal as the circumstances of the case may require.
- The court shall rely on the materials on record and shall not take any fresh evidence in relation to the matter.
- This section has the effect of abridging the rights of the employer inasmuch as it gives power to these courts to differ both on a finding of misconduct arrived at by an employer as well as the punishment imposed by him.

Section 33 of the Industrial Disputes Act 1947

The section 33 of the Industrial Disputes Act 1947 lays down conditions of service to remain unchanged under certain circumstances during pendency of proceedings.

- When a dispute is pending in conciliation, arbitration or adjudication proceedings the employer has no right to discharge or punish, whether by dismisal or otherwise, any workman for his misconduct which is connected with the pending dispute. For example, a workman who has resorted to go-slow in furtherence of some demands covered by the dispute being guilty of misconduct connected with the pending dispute cannot be punished.

Punishment in such cases can be imposed only after obtaining the written permission of the authority before which the proceeding is pending.

- The employer may punish a workman or may discharge or dismiss a workman for any misconduct which is not connected with the pending dispute.

For example, when a workman wilfully damages company's property during the pendency of a dispute about gherao, the employer is free to award any punishment to him. But, in this case dismissal or discharge of the employee can be made only after the employee has been paid wages for one month and an application has been made by the employer to the authority before which the proceeding is pending for approval of the action taken by him.

- The employer cannot discharge or punish whether by dismissal or otherwise a protected workman without obtaining prior permission in writing of the authority before which the proceeding is pending, even when the misconduct is not connected with the pending dispute.
- The protected workmen are executive members of office bearers of registered trade union who are declared as such. They are nominated by the unions and their number is one percent of the total number of workmen subject to minimum number of five and maximum number of one hundred.

The Industrial Employment (Standing Orders) Act 1946

The Industrial Employment (Standing Orders) Act 1946 is applicable to an industrial establishment employing 100 or more workmen, but the Central and State governments can apply the provisions of the Act to any industrial employment employing less than 100 workmen after giving not less than 2 months' notice in the Official Gazette (In West Bengal, Maharashtra, Haryana, Delhi, Gujarat and Andhra Pradesh the Act applies to all establishments employing 50 or more workers).

The object of this Act is to require employers in industrial establishments where it is applicable, to define precisely

- termination of employment
- rules of discipline
- procedure for punishment for discipline activities
- acts or omissions which constitute misconduct
- suspension or dismissal for misconduct and
- other conditions of employment and to make them known to the workmen employed in the establishments.

Procedures of Disciplinary Action

An employer has the right to impose punishment on an employee who violates the rules/resorts to act of misconduct. But, no employer can

punish his employee for his misconduct without holding departmental enquiry as per prescribed rules of natural justice. Such enquiry has gained importance in industrial law. The Supreme Court in a number of cases has observed that a departmental enquiry is not a mere formality but is an essential condition to the legality of disciplinary action. That means, before a delinquent employee can be dismissed as a disciplinary measure for misconduct, the employer must hold a fair, proper and regular enquiry into the misconduct.

Steps

It is concerned with what steps/procedures to be followed for taking disciplinary action are laid down in the Standing Orders or Bipartite Settlements and also in the various States Shops and Establishment Acts. In terms of the provisions of various service rules and in conformity with the principles of natural justice some steps are involved in the departmental action against an erring employee.

Prior to initiating disciplinary action the organization needs to take some steps. They are

a. Investigation/Preliminary enquiry

When an employee violates rules of discipline/commits offence the higher authority should be informed through submission of report by the concerned department/branch. On receipt of the reported offence, Senior officer should thoroughly investigate the matter. The object of such preliminary investigation enquiry is to find out whether there is prima facie case or not and also to make the department equipped with necessary data/information, material for establishing the case. So, all these investigation report, evidence, documents help the management to come to a decision.

b. Issuance of show cause notice

If the management thinks that there is an existence of material fact/ prime facie case he may issue show cause notice on the delinquent. This is an opportunity given to the concerned employee to explain his conduct. That means what he has to say about the allegations.

c. Receipt of reply to show cause notice

On receipt of reply to the show cause notice from the delinquent, the disciplinary authority may decide to close the case by issuing necessary letter to him.

Steps involved in Disciplinary Action

1. Issuance of Suspension order, if warranted

If the management is not satisfied with the explanation given by the concerned employee, he may decide to issue chargesheet on the erring employee. However, in cases of grave misconduct it might be necessary for the management to place the delinquent under suspension (suspension of contract of service means postponement of contract or keeping the contract in abeyance), and accordingly, the suspension order may be issued by the management/competent authority on the offender, pending issuance of chargesheet and enquiry. In such case, there is no necessity to issue show cause notice prior to placing the employee under suspension. It may also occur that an order of suspension is issued along with the chargesheet.

2. Issuance of chargesheet

When the disciplinary authority does not like to put the employee under suspension, he needs to issue chargesheet on the delinquent (chargesheet contains reported allegations/offence, charges, appointment of enquiry officer, permission to avail defence representative service, attendance in the enquiry, exparte proceedings, etc.).

3. Holding domestic/departmental enquiry by enquiry officer

The enquiry officer (EO) appointed by the disciplinary authority should give proper notice to the chargesheeted employee well in advance, indicating the date, time and venue of the enquiry. Domestic/departmental enquiry starts with preliminary hearing (PH) and after preliminary hearing is over, regular hearing (RH) starts.

The purpose of preliminary hearing is to sort out the preliminary objections. All organizations may not have two stages of hearing. Some may have only hearing to start with enquiry.

Preliminary Hearing (PH)

During preliminary hearing (PH) the enquiry officer (EO) explain to the chargesheeted employee (CSE) and the presenting officer (PO) the procedure to be followed in conducting enquiry; and puts the following questions to CSE:

a) Whether he has understood the chargesheet?

b) Whether he pleads guilty of the charges?

If CSE does not admit charges, the EO asks presenting officer (PO) to hand over the list of documents and a list of his witnesses to him and to the CSE.

If CSE pleads guilty of all charges, EO stops enquiry and submits Report to the Disciplinary Authority (DA). In such a case EO takes the signature of all concerned (CSE, DR, PO) in the Enquiry Record Sheet.

c) Whether he accepts the genuineness/authenticity of the documents as mentioned in the list given by PO? If CSE does not admit all or some documents, such documents need to be proved by PO through witnesses.

d) Whether he wants inspection of documents?

If CSE wants inspection of documents EO fixes up the date, time and venue for inspection in consultation with both PO and CSE

EO asks CSE to give his list of documents and witnesss(es) to him and to the PO.

EO asks the PO whether he admits the genuineness/authenticity of documents produced by the CSE?

If the PO does not admit the genuineness of any document, the CSE be asked to inspect those documents for the PO. EO fixes up the date, time and venue for inspection in consultation with both CSE and PO.

The EO disposes of preliminary objections, if any raised by CSE or PO and fixes up the date for regular hearing (RH) and takes the signatures of all concerned. When the date is fixed it should be made clear to both the parities (CSE or PO) by the EO that no adjournment will be given except for compelling/unforeseen reasons and the enquiry will go on from day to day. All this should be recorded in the proceedings.

Regular Hearing (RH)

On the first day of regular hearing (RH) the EO must record the documents submitted by the PO and CSE (if not taken on record at the time of PH) and mark such exhibits as M1, M2, M3 and so on (in case of documents produced by the PO) and E1, E2, E3 and so on (in case of documents produced by the CSE).

Procedure:

Step 1	EO asks PO to call witness
Step 2	PO presents witness
Step 3	EO asks PO to examine witness produced by him
Step 4	PO examines witness presented by him (Examination-in-chief)
Step 5	EO asks CSE/DR to cross examine, if desired
Step 6	CSE/DR cross examines

Step 7 PO requests EO to allow him to re-examine his witness

Step 8 EO allows PO to re-examine

Step 9 PO re-examines

Step 10 CSE requests EO to allow him to cross examine further

Step 11 EO allows CSE to further cross examine

Step 12 CSE cross examines further

After examination and re-examination of witness by PO, cross examination and re-cross examination of management witness by CSE/DR EO takes the signature of PO, CSE, DR and management witness in the enquiry record sheet.

After presenting all management witnesses one after another by PO and after examination, cross-examination, re-examination and re-cross examination of all such witnesses, in the same way, the next chance to present witness(es) is given to CSE. The EO, then asks CSE to produce his witnesses one by one. The procedure followed remains the same as in the case when PO produces his, witness(es) like

Presentation of witness by CSE

Examination of witness by CSE

Cross-examination of CSE's witness by PO

Re-examination of witness by CSE

Re-cross examination of witness by PO

The EO takes the signatures of all concerned viz., CSE, DR, PO and the concerned witness in the enquiry record sheet.

Step 13 EO asks CSE to make statement if he wants.

Step 14 CSE makes statement. It is recorded and read by EO to CSE.

Step 15 EO asks PO to submit written arguments within a stipulated period.

Step 16 PO submits written argument to show how from the evidence the CSE has committed misconduct with which he is charged.

Step 17 EO sends a copy of the argument to CSE to give reply in defence.

Step 18 CSE/DR submits reply in defence to EO

Step 19 EO sends a copy of the reply to PO to give his reply if he desires, and to send back to him

Step 20 PO submits his reply to EO

At the conclusion of the enquiry proceedings the EO thoroughly reads exhibits, considers/assesses evidence, considers argument, makes findings on each allegation separately such as proved, not proved, etc., prepares report and submits the report to disciplinary authority along with all records.

4. Receipt of report from enquiry officer by DA

DA receives the EO's report along with all records pertaining to the enquiry of the concerned CSE.

5. Sending a copy of the EO's report to CSE

On receipt of the report from EO, DA sends a copy of the same to the CSE for making submission on the report, if any, within a stipulated period of time to the DA.

6. Receipt of views/comments on the EO's report from CSE

DA receives back the EO's report with or without comment from the CSE within a stipulated time. It may happen that CSE requests for extension of time for submission of his views or CSE abstains from submitting his views within stipulated period, the EO allows extension of time or sends a reminder letter to the CSE for submission of his views.

7. Issuance of proposed punishment order to CSE by DA

DA issues the order proposing punishment to be imposed on CSE and also gives him an opportunity for personal hearing to show cause against the nature of punishment. (This step is taken if the same is required to be followed in terms of Bipartite Settlement or Standing Orders or Service Rules, etc.)

8. Hearing on the proposed punishment by DA

The DA hears the CSE on the stipulated date, time, venue, if he has anything to say against the order of the proposed punishment.

9. Issuance of the order of punishment to CSE

The DA issues the order of punishment to be served on the delinquent employee. Before imposing penalty the DA bears in mind the following

a. Aggravating or extenuating factors

b. Nature and magnitude of the charge/s established

c. Possible effect of the proposed punishment on the moral and general level of discipline of the organization.

d. Change in behavioural activities of the delinquent after the issuance of chargesheet and during the course of enquiry

e. The nature of punishment usually inflicted for an identical misconduct

f. The desirability or otherwise for retention of the concerned employee in service in the context of charge/s proved against him.

In case of appeal made by the aggrieved employee

Procedure

1. Appeal made by aggrieved employee to the Appellate Authority

The aggrieved employee may submit appeal within the stipulated period against the decision of the disciplinary authority. The right to prefer an appeal and also the time limit for submission of appeal should be mentioned in the standing orders or service rules or bipartite settlement.

2. Sending notice of hearing on appeal

On receipt of appeal from the aggrieved employee, the appellate authority gives him a personal hearing. The notice fixing the date, time and venue for personal hearing is sent to the aggrieved employee who prefers an appeal.

3. Hearing on appeal/order of punishment issued by DA

At this stage the appellate authority hears the aggrieved employee against the order of the disciplinary authority. There is no right to personal hearing in an appeal if there is no statutory rules to the effect[10].

4. Issuance of order of the appellate authority

After the process of personal hearing is over the appellate authority issues the order to the aggrieved employee. He considers whether the findings of the enquiry officer and disciplinary authority are justified or whether the penalty imposed is excessive or inadequate, and passes appropriate order at the earliest or within stipulated period if the rules or standing orders provide a time limit for disposal of appeal.

10 F.N Roy Vs Collector of Customs, Calcutta: AIR 1957 SC 648

Illustrative Disciplinary Action

An illustrative flow chart of disciplinary action case is given in table 7.3

Table 7.3 - Flow Chart of Disciplinary Action

Step	Action	Flow
1.	Complaint	a. Department to unit/ plant head or plant head to Regional/ Zonal Head/HO b. Branch Head/ Depatment to Regional/ Zonal Head/HO
2.	Preliminary Investigation	Unit/Plant Head/ Regional/Zonal Head/HO to Investigating officer
3.	Carrying Investigation and Submission of Report	Investigating officer to Unit/Plant Head/ Regional/Zonal Head/ HO
4.	Issuance of show cause to concerned employee/calling explanation of the employee concerned for reported irregularities/ allegations	Unit/plant Head/ Regional/Zonal Head/ HO to concerned employee
5.	Receipt of reply to show cause/explanation letter from the concerned employee. (If the reply is satisfactory, the matter is dropped).	Concerned employee to Unit/plant Head/Regional/ Zonal Head/HO
6.	Issuance of chargesheet (when reply to show cause notice is unsatisfactory)	Disciplinary Authority (DA) to concerned employee
7.	Appointment of Enquiry Officer(EO)/ Presenting Officer(PO)	DA to EO/PO
8.	Enquiry	EO/PO/CSE/DR
9.	Enquiry Report	EO to DA

10.	Sending a copy of EO's Report to CSE for submission, if any	DA to CSE
11.	Receipt of submission from CSE, on EO's Report	CSE to DA
12. If it is required in terms of Standing Orders or Settlements, etc.	Issuance of proposed punishment order to CSE	DA to CSE
13.	Hearing on proposed punishment by DA	DA/CSE/DR
14.	Issuance of order of punishment to CSE	DA to CSE
	In case of Appeal preferred by aggrieved employee	
15.	Submission of appeal by aggrieved employee	Aggrieved employee to Appellate Authority
16.	Sending notice of hearing on appeal	Appellate Authority to aggrieved employee
17.	Hearing on appeal	Appellate Authority/ aggrieved employee/DR
18.	Issuance of Order of Appellate Authority	Appellate Authority to aggrieved emloyee

Flow Chart of Enquiry Proceeding

In the departmental enquiry, enquiry officer holds enquiry and discharges the quasi-judicial obligations. He needs to maintain an unbiased and objective activity to ensure perfection, fair and impartial proceedings. A flow chart of enquiry proceeding is given in table 7.4 to have an indepth idea on the steps followed in the departmental enquiry proceedings

Table 7. 4

Step	Action	Flow
1. Preliminary Hearing (PH)	Understanding chargesheet	EO to CSE
2.	a. Having got to understand or b. Not having got to understand c. making understood	CSE to EO CSE to EO EO to CSE

3.	Admission/denial of charge(s)	EO to CSE
4.	a. Admitting charge(s) (EO stops enquiry, takes signature of all concerned in the enquiry record sheet and submits report to DA) b. Denial of charge(s)	CSE to EO CSE to EO
5.	Making hand over the lists of documents and witness/es in duplicate	EO to PO
6.	a. Handing over the lists of documents and witness(es) in duplicate b. Handing over the list of documents and witness(es)	PO to EO EO to CSE
7.	Genuineness/authenticity of documents submitted by PO	EO to CSE
8.	a. Accepting genuineness/ authenticity of documents or b. Not accepting genuineness/ authenticity of documents c. Confirm willingness for inspection of documents d. Expression of desire for inspection of documents. e. Fixing up date, time, venue for inspection of documents	CSE to EO CSE to EO EO to CSE, PO CSE to EO EO to CSE, PO
9.	Hand over the lists of documents and witness(es) a. Handing over the lists of documents and witness/es in duplicate b. Handing over the list of documents and witness(es)	EO to CSE CSE to EO EO to PO
10.	Genuineness/authenticity of documents submitted by CSE	EO to PO

11.	a. Accepting genuineness/ authenticity of documents.	PO to EO
	b. Not accepting genuineness/ authenticity of documents.	PO to EO
	c. Getting to know about willingness for inspection of documents	EO to PO
	d. Expression of desire for inspection of documents	PO to EO
	e. Fixing up date, time, venue for inspection of documents	EO to PO, CSE
12.	a. Preliminary objection, if any	CSE, PO to EO
	b. Disposal of Preliminary objection	EO to CSE, PO
EO fixes up date, time, venue for regular hearing (RH) and makes clear to PO and CSE that no adjournment will be given except for compelling/unforeseen reasons, and enquiry will proceed on from day to day. Signature of PO, CSE, DR are taken in the enquiry record sheet.		

REGULAR HEARING (RH)

Step	Action	Flow
1.	Making witness present, if any.	EO to PO
2.	Presenting witness	PO to EO
3.	Permitting examination of witness	EO to PO
4.	Examination in chief	PO to MW1
5.	Permitting cross-examination	EO to CSE
6.	Cross-examination of witness	CSE to MW1
7.	Requesting re-examination	PO to EO
8.	Acceeding to request for re-examination	EO to PO
9.	Re-examination of witness	PO to MW1
10.	Requesting re-cross examination	CSE to EO
11.	Acceeding to request for re-cross examination	EO to CSE
12.	Re-cross examination of witness after presenting all management witnesses one after another and following the same procedures as mentioned above CSE presents his witnesses one after another as per advice of EO and in all such cases same procedure is followed like presentation of witness by CSE, examination of witness by CSE, cross-examination of CSE's witness by PO, re examination of witness by CSE and re cross-examination of witness by PO.	CSE to MW1

13.	Allowing to make statement if desired	EO to CSE
14.	Making statement	CSE to EO
15.	Allowing to submit written argument within a stipulated period	EO to PO
16.	Submission of written argument	PO to EO
17.	Forwarding a copy of written argument	EO to CSE
18.	Making submission on written argument	CSE to EO
19.	Forwarding a copy of reply on written argument	EO to PO
20.	Submission of reply on written argument	PO to EO
	PREPARATION OF REPORT BY EO AND SUBMISSION OF REPORT TO DA	EO to DA

Conceptual Perspectives of Some Important Issues Concerning Disciplinary Action

It is felt pertinent to have clear idea, knowledge on some aspects that have direct or indirect bearing on disciplinary action. Some of such important aspects concerning disciplinary action are discussed in brief.

Show Cause Notice/Letter

Organization frames rules, norms of behaviour in terms of standing orders or bipartite settlement or services rules for compliance of employees. The objective of framing such rules is to ensure that discipline is maintained while running the organizational activities smoothly and effectively. So for this, people should conform to the rules. But, it happens that some employees do not conform to rules, they violate rules. In this situation the organization should improve the conduct of behaviour of employees through discussion, interaction, persuasion, counselling, cautioning and other moulding activities. After taking all such measures, it happens that, some employees may not improve their conduct. In this case, the company needs to issue letter/notice on the concerned employees calling upon them to show cause why disciplinary action should not be taken against them for their conduct and submit written explanation within a stipulated period of time. Such notice or letter is show cause notice/letter.

Show cause notice/letter is notice or letter issued by the management on an erring employee for his reported act of conduct calling upon him to show cause in writing within a stipulated period of time as to why disciplinary action should not be taken against him. In the show cause notice it is also mentioned that if the written explanation is not received by the management within the specific period of time the management may presume that the erring employee does not have any explanation to offer and the management may proceed accordingly.

Before issuance of show cause notice, generally the following steps are followed by the management

1. Receipt of complaint/allegations
2. Assignment of task of making discrete preliminary enquiry/investigation to officer
3. Conducting preliminary enquiry/investigation to find fact of the complaint
4. Submission of report
5. Examination of report and taking decision to issue show cause notice/letter on the erring employee.

The show cause notice or letter contains the following main parts:

First part contains allegations or reported act of conduct.

Second part of the show cause notice gives the opportunity to the delinquent to show cause in writing within a specified period of time as to why disciplinary action should not be taken against him. This part of the letter gives the indication of taking disciplinary action and for that concerned employee needs to submit show cause in writing.

Third part states the period during which the explanation to show cause should be submitted.

Last part of the notice expresses that non-receipt of the written explanation within due time may make the company presume that the concerned employee has no explanation to offer and it may proceed accordingly.

A specimen draft (SD1) is given in a case when an employee remains absent from his seat and misbehaves with his superior officer.

Specimen Draft SD 1

Mr/Ms ______________ Date: ______________

____

____

Dear Sir/Madam,

On 2nd June, 2010 you were unauthorizedly absent from your seat between 1pm and 4pm. At about 4pm you came to the office and went straight to joint manager, Mr AK Roy. You made enquiries about your request for leave from 14th June, 2010. When the Joint Manager informed you that no decision was taken till then, you became angry and started shouting at the Joint Manager and disturbed the working of the office and you left office at about 4. 30pm.

You are called upon to show cause why disciplinary action should not be taken against you for your conduct within three days of the receipt of this letter.

If your written explanation is not received within the stipulated period of time, we may presume that you have no explanation to offer and we may proceed accordingly.

Yours faithfully

Manager

Chargesheet

Chargesheet is a document/sheet containing allegations of misconduct levelled against an erring employee which is issued to him calling upon to submit within a stipulated period of time. The word 'chargesheet' is borrowed from criminal law. It refers to an intimation-formal and written to the offender about the misconduct alleged against him so that he can have thorough understanding and knowledge of the allegations.

After issuance of show cause notice and on receipt of the reply to show cause notice the management may decide to hold departmental enquiry and for that matter chargesheet needs to be issued on the erring employee. However, for issuing a chargesheet it is not absolutely necessary to issue show cause notice before chargesheet is served. If after preliminary enquiry/investigation the management finds that there exists a prima facie case to issue chargesheet and wants to proceed against the delinquent, the chargesheet can be served straight away. But, if the service rules or bipartite settlement or standing orders provide for issuing show cause notice before chargesheet is served, the management needs to issue show cause notice first.

So, the chargesheet is letter/sheet addressed to the delinquent employee, which tells him specifically what are the allegations against him.

Chargesheet is not a piece of evidence, it is the most important document for determination of disciplinary action. So, while framing chargesheet management should follow or adhere to the necessary requirement otherwise the entire chargesheet will become defective. The following points need to be taken into consideration:

- **Allegations/reported irregularities**

The particulars of the statement of facts should be clear. It should not be vague and ambiguous. It should specifically mention what is reported against the employee; and the incident, the date, the time and the place where the incident took place.

- **Acts of misconduct**

The chargesheet should mention the acts of misconduct the employee has resorted to. If the charge relates to abusive language, the exact words uttered by the employee be mentioned.

- **Charges and respective clauses/paragraphs**

It should state clearly the charges and respective clause(s) or paragraph(s) of the standing orders or bipartite settlement or service rules under which they fall. If a vague charge is given it is a fatal defect and it may, if challenged, vitiate the entire proceedings[11].

- **Holding departmental enquiry**

The chargesheet should mention about

i. holding departmental enquiry

ii. enquiry officer

iii. the rights the concerned employee will have in defending himself during enquiry

- **Time frame of reply to the chargesheet**

It should state the time within which the erring employee is required to reply to the chargesheet.

- **Presenting of documentary evidence, witnesses**

The chargesheet should mention the right of the delinquent employee to provide the relevant documentary evidence, witness(es) in support of defence, to cross-examine the witness(es) produced by the company, during the enquiry proceedings.

- **Attendance of chargesheeted employee in the enquiry**

It should clearly specify that enquiry shall proceed ex-parte if the delinquent employee remains absent at the stipulated time, date and venue of the enquiry notified by the enquiry officer from time to time.

A specimen draft (SD2) is given in a case when an employee attached to a bank's branch in Kolkata remained absent unauthorizedly on loss of pay for 105 days on earlier occasions in previous branch and at the present branch he remained unauthorisedly absent continuously since 5th March 2010 (imaginary name of the employee, bank and all other information are taken to give an overall idea on the matter).

---

11 Avinash Chandra Sanjar vs Divisional Superintendent, Central Railway, Jhansi: 1962/ LLJ7

Specimen Draft SD 2

No: RM:WB:STF:25/185 Date: 8. 6. 2010

Mr AK Roy

EC No: 25605

Designation: Sub staff

XYZ Bank Ltd

Patipukur Branch

Kolkata

Dear Sir,

Re: Chargesheet

The following have been reported against you during your posting at our Jadavpur Branch and Surya Sen Street Branch, Kolkata.

1. You were habitual in remaining absent unauthorisedly. You were unauthorisedly absent on loss of pay for 105 days when you were posted at Jadavpur Branch and Surya Sen Street Branch, Kolkata. Thereafter you remained absent unauthorisedly on several occasions. Despite serving various letters you did not improve upon your attendance and you remained unauthorisedly absent continuously from 5th March 2010 at our Patipukur Branch, Kolkata. Branch Authority advised you to resume duties vide following letters

a. PATICAL: SUB STAFF: 2010/25 dated 21. 3. 10 (acknowledged on 25. 3. 10)

b. PATICAL: SUB STAFF: 2010/32 dated 24. 4. 10 (acknowledged on 29. 4. 10)

c. PATICAL: SUB STAFF: 2010/37 dated 22. 5. 10 (acknowledged on 26. 5. 10)

You, however, have not reported for duties till date.

Your unauthorised absence at Patipuker Branch Kolkata on different dates is given below:

Occasions	Unauthorised Absence		Total Number of Days Absent
	From	To	
1.	9. 1. 2010	15. 1. 2010	7

2.	19. 1. 2010		1
3.	27. 1. 2010	29. 1. 2010	3
4.	4. 2. 2010	6. 2. 2010	3
5.	13. 2. 2010	14. 2. 2010	2
6.	17. 2. 2010		1
7.	19. 2. 2010	20. 2. 2010	2
8.	23. 2. 2010		1
9.	25. 2. 2010		1
10.	2. 3. 2010		1
11.	5. 3. 2010	7. 6. 2010	95

d. You remained unauthorisedly absent without intimation continuously for a period exceeding 30 days. In spite of repeated instructions you did not resume duties.

e. You neither obtained prior permission nor informed your reporting authority about your absence.

f. Your above absence has disrupted the smooth functioning of the branch.

Your aforesaid acts, if proved, would tantamount to gross misconduct under the provisions of Memorandum of Settlement dated 10. 4. 2002. You are, therefore, charged as under

1. You have committed acts prejudicial to the interest of the Bank (clause 5 (j) of the Memorandum of Settlement dated 10. 4. 2002).
2. You have remained absent unauthorisedly without intimation continuously for a period exceeding 30 days (clause 5(p) of the Memorandum of Settlement dated 10. 04. 2002).
3. You have willfully disobeyed the lawful and reasonable order of your superior authority (clause 5(e) of the Memorandum of Settlement dated 10. 04. 2002).

In this connection, we write to inform you that a departmental enquiry will be conducted against you in respect of the aforesaid charges by Mr Ranjan Dey, Senior Manager, India Exchange Branch who will advise you directly the date, time and place of the enquiry.

You may, if you so desire, submit to the Enquiry Officer, your written statement of defence at least 3 days before the date of enquiry.

You will be permitted to defend yourself in the said enquiry by the representative of a registered trade union of the bank employees of which you are a member on the date notified by the Enquiry Officer for the commencement of the enquiry. If you are not a member of any trade union of bank employees on the said date, you will be permitted to be represented by any representative of a registered trade union of the employees of the Bank.

You will be entitled to produce relevant documentary evidence and examine relevant witness(es) in support of your defence and you will also be allowed to cross-examine the witness(es) produced by the Bank in support of the charges levelled against you during the enquiry proceedings.

Please note that if you do not attend the said enquiry at the date, time and place notified by the Enquiry Officer and thereafter so directed by him from time to time, the enquiry may be proceeded with, in your absence.

Yours faithfully

Sd/

(AK Chandra)

General Manager (Kolkata Region)

& Disciplinary Authority

Suspension

Suspension means debarring an employee for the time being from holding a function or a privilege. The dictionary meaning of suspension is 'barring for a time for privilege, office or function as a punishment'; the act of debarring from an office or its privilege. So, suspension is temporary deprivation from the office or position. Suspension of contract of service means postponement of the contract or keeping the contract in abeyance. It does not terminate employment relationship or the contract, but merely suspends the contract so far as performance of duties or enjoyment of the privileges attached to the office is concerned[12].

In case of suspension the employee is debarred temporarily from further functioning in the office. It is temporary denial of holding a position or privilege.

Types of Suspension

Suspension is of two types. They are

I. Suspension by way of punishment

II. Suspension on administrative grounds (management suspends an employee pending enquiry).

12 Khemchand vs Union of India and others: AIR 1963 SC 687

Suspension by way of punishment

This is a punitive suspension. After going through the enquiry officer's report, extenuating and aggravating factors, standing orders or bipartite settlements or service rules the disciplinary authority takes the decision to impose punishment of suspension. For giving such punishment it must be mentioned in standing orders or service rules. In the Model Standing Orders framed under the Industrial Employment (Standing Orders) Act, 1946 there is a provision for punitive suspension. A workman maybe suspended for a period not exceeding four days at a time if he is found to be guilty of misconduct.

Suspension on administrative grounds

In some grave cases of misconduct it might be necessary for the management to place the delinquent employee under suspension. This is generally done during the pending departmental enquiry or during the pending criminal investigation and trial.

The competent authority takes the decision for placing an employee under suspension. Following circumstances may warrant suspension of an employee:

- Where the continuance of an employee is likely to seriously subvert discipline at the workplace he is working. (e.g., cases of assault, man-handling, etc.)
- Where the presence of the employee in the office will prejudice the investigation, trial or any enquiry (e.g., where it is apprehended that the employee would tamper and manipulate office records).
- Misconduct involving moral turpitude
- Where the alleged misconduct is of serious nature (e.g., fraud, forgery, theft, misappropriation of funds, misuse of official power for personal gains)
- Where the employee has become a security risk particularly in situations where employee is required to handle cash and other valuables
- Dereliction of duties resulting in considerable loss to the organization
- Rank insubordination
- Cases of graft, bribery, etc.
- Doubtful integrity, honesty

The appointing authority is competent to suspend an employee. The other authorities who are given the power to take disciplinary action under service/conduct rules can also suspend an employee.

Subsistence Allowance

When an employee is placed under suspension, he is prevented from attending to work. Under such situation he is neither permitted to do his work nor is he allowed to work elsewhere. Now, the question is, how will he maintain his livelihood and his family? So, from equity, justice and rationality point of view the suspended employee should be given some allowance to sustain himself and his family. The allowance which is given to an employee during the period of his suspension is subsistence allowance. For the survival of the employee and his family management has to pay subsistence allowance and this is settled position in law[13].

Tamil Nadu and West Bengal have separate laws for regulating suspension and payment of subsistence allowance. As per the West Bengal Payment of Subsistence Allowance Act 1969, the Kerala Payment of Subsistence Allowance Act 1972 and the Tamil Nadu Payment of Subsistence Allowance Act 1981 the subsistence allowance should be equal to fifty percent of the wages which the employee was drawing immediately before suspension, for the first ninety days and seventy five percent of the wages beyond ninety days. The Kerala State Subsistence Allowance Act as amended and the Tamil Nadu Subsistence Allowance Act provide that where the period of suspension exceeds one hundred eighty days, the amount of subsistence allowance for the remaining period shall be equal to wages the employee was drawing immediately before such suspension.

Specimen drafts of suspension order (SD3/SD4) are given in a case where an employee attached to a bank's branch has misappropriated money.

Specimen Draft: SD 3

[DRAFT OF ORDER OF SUSPENSION ON A CASH CLERK OF A BANK BEFORE CHARGESHEET IS ISSUED]

Mr/Ms____________ Date____________

EC No: ____________

Designation: ____________

Branch ____________

Dear Sir,

It is decided to hold a departmental enquiry into your conduct ____ ____________________________ state the fact/nature of conduct in

13 Bidhu Deb Roy vs JM Savery & another, 1993 CLR 51

short and pending issue of chargesheet and enquiry into your aforesaid conduct you are hereby suspended from the Bank's service with immediate effect i.e., from______________________.

During the period of suspension, you will be paid subsistence allowance on the following scale as per para 17.1 read with para 17.14 of the Desai Award:

1. For the first insert 'three' if the enquiry is departmental and 'six' if the enquiry is conducted by outside agency like 'Police' 1/3rd (one-third) of the pay and allowances which you would have got but for the suspension.
2. Thereafter ½ (one-half) of the pay and allowances for the succeeding months.

You should leave with the branch/office your address where the chargesheet and other communication meant for you can be served. You should not leave the headquarters during the period of suspension without prior permission of the undersigned.

You should not enter the branch/office premises during the period of your suspension, except for the purpose of operating your own account. For that purpose you should obtain specific permission of the office/ Branch Manager.

Yours faithfully

Sd/-

Competent Authority

PS: If there is any Central or State Act on subsistence allowance during suspension, and it is applicable to Banks and also to the employee concerned then such Act would be applicable provided it is more beneficial/favourable to the employee concerned.

Specimen Draft: SD4

[ALTERNATIVE DRAFT OF ORDER OF SUSPENSION TO BE ISSUED ON A CASH CLERK OF A BANK'S BRANCH BEFORE ISSUING CHARGESHEET]

ORDER

Date____________

As disciplinary proceedings are contemplated against Mr/ Ms*................, I am of the opinion that circumstance exist, making it is necessary to place Mr/Ms____________ under suspension.

* Mention full name, designation and place of posting

2. Accordingly I hereby place Mr/Ms____________ under suspension with effect from the date of service of this order upon him/her.

3. During the period that this order remains in force

i. Mr/Ms** should not leave his/her headquarters without obtaining the prior written permission of the undersigned.

ii. He/She should not enter the branch premises except for the purpose of operating his/her own account. For that purpose he/she should obtain specific permission of the Branch Manager.

iii. He/She will be paid subsistence allowance on the following scale as per para 17. 1 read with para 17. 4 of the Desai Award.

1. For the first*** 1/3rd (one third) of the pay and allowances which you would have got but for the suspension

2. Thereafter ½ (one half) of the pay and allowances for the succeeding months.

Competent Authority

Disciplinary Authority

The disciplinary authority means the officer empowered to take disciplinary action against an employee who violates rules of the company or resorts to act of misconduct incorporated in the standing orders/ service rules or settlements, etc. In such service rules/standing orders or settlement there is a provision regarding appointment of disciplinary authority. That means it is laid down who can work as disciplinary authority and what is the procedure to make the employees know about the disciplinary authority.

So, the disciplinary authority means the official who is empowered by the competent authority of the organization to take disciplinary action against employees who resort to acts of misconduct. Competent authority is basically Chairman-cum-Managing Director or Principal officer of the organization who decides which officer can be empowered to work as disciplinary authority. In Indian banking organizations clause 14 of the Memorandum of Settlement dated 10. 04. 2002 provides for appointment of disciplinary authority. In terms of the clause the Chief Executive Officer or the Principal Officer in India of a bank or an Alternate Officer at the Head Office or Principal Office nominated by him for the purpose shall decide which officer (i.e., the disciplinary authority) shall be empowered to take disciplinary action in the case of such office or establishment.

** Insert surname only

*** insert 'three' if the enquiry is departmental and 'six' if the enquiry is conducted by outside agency like 'police'

Disciplinary authority is the officer who is authorised by the appropriate authority to take disciplinary action against the delinquent employees.

The disciplinary authority (DA) can himself hold enquiry that means he can work as enquiry officer also or he may appoint another officer to hold the enquiry.

The disciplinary authority has to perform the following activities:

- to issue chargesheet on delinquent employee
- to appoint enquiry officer (EO)
- to appoint presenting Officer (PO)
- to send the following papers to enquiry officer (if the DA is not an enquiry officer)
    - order appointing enquiry officer
    - a copy of the chargesheet
    - a copy of the order regarding appointment of presenting officer
- to send a copy of the EO's report to the chargesheeted employee
- to issue order of proposed punishment (if it is required in terms of standing orders/service rules, etc)
- to give a personal hearing on the proposed punishment
- to issue order of punishment
- to send a copy to the appellate authority.

Disciplinary authority has to act within the framework of set rules laid down for the purpose. He should provide necessary help, assistance support and co-operation to the presenting officer, such as administrative assistance to conduct enquiry, supply of documents including privileged documents like CBI report, report of vigilance officer and other official papers to enable him to prove the charges in an enquiry on behalf of DA.

A specimen draft of order of punishment (SD8) is given in this chapter to facilitate understanding on the subject.

Enquiry Officer (EO)

Enquiry officer means the officer who is empowered to enquire into the charges against an employee. Such officer holds enquiry against delinquent employee. The officer who can work as enquiry officer is decided by the top management of the organization. Generally, the standing orders/

bipartite settlement or service rules provide for appointment of EO. In banking industry it is mentioned in the Memorandum of Settlement that the disciplinary authority may conduct the enquiry himself or appoint another officer as the Enquiry Officer for the purpose of conducting an enquiry[14]. The enquiry officer is in the position of a quasi-judicial tribunal. He should be a person with open mind. He should work impartially, objectively and without bias because justice must not only be done but also appear to be done[15]. He has an important role before the enquiry during the enquiry proceedings and also after the enquiry is over.

A specimen draft of order of appointment of enquiry officer (SD6) is given in subsequent deliberation.

Before the Enquiry

On receipt of the order of the disciplinary authority appointing him as enquiry officer along with other papers/orders he issues notice to the chargesheeted employee with a copy to presenting officer fixing up a date for preliminary/regular hearing.

A specimen draft of notice of enquiry (SD-5) is given in this chapter.

During the Enquiry

i. The EO ensures that congenial and conducive atmosphere exists in the enquiry. That means a state of discipline and order prevails.

ii. He ensures that unauthorized persons or other witnesses do not remain present in the enquiry room.

iii. On every day of the enquiry, when the enquiry begins, the enquiry officer notes down the date, time, names of those present in the enquiry register.

iv. He records the proceedings of the day with sufficient fullness in the enquiry register.

v. He records the oral evidence in question and answer form or in a narration form.

vi. He reads out the proceedings recorded in the register to the parties, make correction, where necessary and get all pages of the proceeding signed by parties including witness.

vii. He ensures that the witness is not threatened by either side.

---

14 Clause 14 of the Memorandum of Settlement dated 10.04.02 between the Management of 52 A class Banks as represented by the IBA and their workmen as represented by the AIBEA, NCBE, INBEE

15 Manak Lal vs Dr Prem Chand Singhvi AIR 1957 SC 425.

viii. He sees that the entire evidence of a witness (i.e., examination-in-chief, cross examination and re-examination) is completed on the same day as far as possible.

ix. He gives his ruling on the points on which objections are raised unbiased or without any favour but using his sense of justice, fairness and practical wisdom.

After the Enquiry

i. The enquiry officer goes through the proceeding of the enquiry, reads exhibits carefully, considers, analyses and assesses evidence on the record.

ii. He considers argument put forward before him with a view to finding the truth.

iii. He writes findings on each charge separately with reasons, mentioning whether the concerned charge is proved or not proved. Recording reasons in support of a decision taken by EO ensures that the decision is reached according to law and is not a result of arbitrariness or expediency[16].

iv. The EO prepares a report containing the charges, statement of allegations constituting the charges, the defence of the chargesheeted employee in respect of each charge, assessment of evidence in respect of each charge and the findings on each charge with reason.

v. He submits the report to disciplinary authority with all records.

A specimen draft of notice of Enquiry (SD5)

XYZ Co Pvt Ltd

Mr/Ms___________ Date___________

____

____

Dear Sir,

Re: Departmental enquiry against you

I have been appointed as Enquiry Officer by the Disciplinary Authority as per order No _________ dated _________ to hold an enquiry against

16 Mahabir Prasad vs State of UP: AIR 1970 SC 1302

you on the charges mentioned in the chargesheet dated __________ and to submit my findings to the Disciplinary Authority.

Please note that I shall hold the enquiry at ______________ on ______________ at ______________

Please remain present at the enquiry on the date, time and place mentioned above and continue to remain present throughout the enquiry on that day and subsequent days and also bring the list of your witness(es) and documents if you propose to plead not guilty to the charges.

Please note that if you fail to appear before the undersigned on the appointed date, time and place the undersigned will proceed in your absence.

Yours faithfully

Sd/

Enquiry Officer

Copy to

1. Mr______________ Presenting Officer on behalf of the management for information. He should remain present at the enquiry on the date, time and place mentioned above with all listed documents and papers
2. The Disciplinary Authority for information

Presenting Officer

Presenting officer is the officer who presents management's case against the chargesheeted employee before the enquiry officer. He is also called prosecution officer or management's representative. He is appointed by the disciplinary authority. A specimen draft of the appointment letter (SD7) is given in this chapter. The presenting officer investigates and presents the case in support of the charges before the enquiry officer as a representative of the management. His job is to establish the charges on the basis of evidence, through witnesses against the chargesheeted employee, cross-examining the defence witness, marshalling his evidence and his arguments.

Role of Presenting Officer

- to study all aspects of a case
- to answer all the queries of the enquiry officer
- to cooperate with the enquiry officer to complete the enquiry at the earliest
- to supply copies of statement of witnesses and documents at the preliminary hearing if not done earlier.

- not to ask unnecessary adjournment
- to attend all hearings
- to arrange for inspection of documents by the delinquent if directed by EO.
- to present his witness(es), examine his own witness/es as examination-in-chief.
- to reexamine his witness(es) if necessary
- to cross examine the witness(es) produced by the chargesheeted employee
- to avoid leading question(s) while examining witness.
- to submit his arguments on behalf of the management to prove the charges highlighting the evidence of the prosecution witnesses which supports the charge and pointing out the contradiction and unsoundness of the evidence of the other side[17]. and also to reply to the points made in the arguments of the defence.
- to meet the management witnesses and discuss with them the strategy that he would like to adopt during the enquiry.
- not to get emotionally involved in the case.

Defence Representative

Defence representative refers to a person who is permitted to work as representative of the delinquent to present the latter's case at a domestic enquiry. The delinquent/chargesheeted employee needs to have permission from the disciplinary authority/enquiry officer with regard to present his case at the departmental/domestic enquiry as his representative. To grant permission is not a must if service rules/ standing orders do not provide for such granting permission. So, a delinquent employee has no right of being represented by a person at the domestic enquiry if there is no such provision in the service rules or standing orders. Refusal to allow representation by any union unless the standing orders confer that right, does not vitiate the proceedings[18].

However, it is observed that most companies are providing such facility to the delinquents to present their cases by the representatives as granting such permission is mentioned in the service rules/standing orders. The Model Standing Orders framed under the Industrial Employment (Standing Orders) Central rules provide that the workman

17 SK Datta, *Guide to Disciplinary Action* (Tata McGraw-Hill Publishing Company Limited, New Delhi, P94, 1994)

18 Dunlop Rubber Co (India) Ltd vs their Worknmen, 1965 I LLJ 426

shall be entitled to appear in person or to be represented by an office-bearer of a trade union of which he is a member. The same facility is given to the delinquent employees working with banks in terms of the clause 12 (a) (i) (ii) and (iii) of the Memorandum of Settlement dated 10. 4. 2002. The clause provides that the chargesheeted employee shall be permitted to be defended.

- by a representative of a registered trade union of bank employees of which he is a member on the date first notified for the commencement of the enquiry
- where the employee is not a member of any trade union of bank emploees on the aforesaid date, by a representative of a registered trade union of employees of the bank in which he is employed
- at the request of the said union by a representative of the state federation or all India Organization to which such union is affiliated

or

- with the Bank's permission by a lawyer

Role of Defence Representative

The important roles of defence representative are

- to defend the chargesheeted employee and to prove before the enquiry officer that the charges are not tenable
- to ensure that the chargesheeted employee is absolved of charges
- to present the chargesheeted employee's case, to examine the witness(es), cross examine the witness(es) produced by the presenting officer
- to give all out efforts to ensure that in the event of charges being established, the punishment should not be harsh
- to raise objections to procedural irregularities/defects, if occurred
- to sum up the case on behalf of the chargesheeted employee.

Examination-in–Chief

The examination-in-chief relates to the examination of witness by the party who produces him. In departmental/domestic enquiry both the parties-the management and the chargesheeted employee need to produce their own witnesses. In order to elicit material facts from the respective witnesses they are examined by the parties who present them before the enquiry officer. This examination of a witness by the concerned party who produces him at the enquiry is examination-in-chief.

Some of the important points in respect of examination-in-chief are given below:

- The examination relates to relevant fact. It needs to be confined to the relevant facts only.
- The examination is made for the purpose of eliciting from the witness all the material facts within his knowledge which tend to prove the case of the party producing him at the enquiry.
- In absence of management representative that means when the management does not send representative, examination-in-chief of the witnesses is done by the enquiry officer; he puts questions to them. This is not objectionable and the enquiry proceedings cannot be impeached as unfair if the due opportunity is given to the chargesheeted employee and his representative to cross examine such witnesses of the company[19].

Cross-Examination

Cross-examination is the second step at the witness-adducing process after examination-in-chief activity is over. Cross-examination means examination of a witness by the adverse party.

The cross-examination relates to the relevant facts, but it is not confined to the fact to which the witness testified on examination-in-chief. Through cross-examination material fact could be found which is not possible in examination-in-chief. In examination-in-chief witness gives the idea of the case that is favourable for the party who brings him.

The cross-examination is an important activity/means that makes the departmental enquiry effective in the following ways:

- to bring out the weaknesses of the witness in the evidence
- to expose the witness that he has given false statement/ evidence
- to make the EO know that reliance on such witness's evidence may yield undesired results in the enquiry
- to discover truth through interrogating witnesses
- to make the EO's findings' process smooth and effective as EO can easily test the veracity of a witness and the correctness and completeness of his statement on the basis of information available during cross-examination

19 Bharat Electronics Ltd, vs K Kasi; 1987 II LLJ 202

Re-Examination

Re-examination is the third step of activity in departmental enquiry when a witness is produced before the enquiry officer. After examination-in-chief and cross-examination re-examination activity occurs. It is the examination of a witness by the party who called him, subsequent to the cross-examination of such witness by the adverse party. The witness is first examined by examination-in-chief, then he is cross-examined by the other party. After cross-examination (if the party who produced such witness desires), the witness is re-examined.

Sometimes it happens that during examination some information remained unexplained or during cross examination the fact of the case does not come out. In such case, further explanation and clarification of the matter becomes necessary. The party may request enquiry officer to allow him to re-examine his own witness. So, the re-examination shall be directed to the explanation of matters referred to in cross-examination. However, if any new matter is introduced in the re-examination, with the permission of the enquiry officer the adverse party may further cross-examine upon that matter.

Re-examination is ordinarily meant for giving an opportunity to the witness to explain any statement which he may have inadvertently made during the cross-examination[20]. But in no case this can be used to cover up any deficiency.

Leading Question

The dictionary meaning of 'leading question' is the question phrased to prompt the answer desired. That means, the question itself contains the reply to it. It is a question suggestive of the answer to it. In the leading question, there are two parts – one relates to the question itself and the other part is suggestion, hint, clue to arrive at the answer. This type of question suggests the answer which the person putting it wants/ expects to receive. So, leading question is question wherein the answer is indicated.

Examples of leading questions:

1. Were you in the department when Mr Chowdhary slapped Mr Basu?
2. Is the signature appearing on the representation that of Mr Roy?

Now, the question arises whether the leading question can be put to the witnesses at the departmental enquiry. To reply to this question it needs to see whether the Evidence Act 1872 is applicable to departmental/

20 SK Datta, *Guide to Disciplinary Action* (Tata Mc-Graw Hill Publishing Company Limited, New Delhi, 1994, P III)

domestic enquiry. It reveals that the departmental proceedings are not judicial proceedings and the provisions of the Evidence Act do not apply to them[21]. So, there is no bar in putting leading questions to the witnesses at the departmental/domestic enquiry and putting such leading question would not vitiate the enquiry nor would it amount to violation of the principle of natural justice.

Under the Evidence Act, leading question must not, if objected to by the adverse party be asked in an examination or in re-examination except with the permission of the court. But, leading question may be asked in cross-examination. However, in domestic enquiry leading questions are admissible depending on its nature. In this case Enquiry Officer should ensure that nobody gets undue advantage of this privilege, and suggested questions are not asked to the witness that may give hint to answers.

Appellate Authority

Appellate authority is the authority before whom appeal is made by the punished employee, against the order/decision of the disciplinary authority. It is quite natural that when an employee is punished he should have the right to make an appeal before some higher authority against the decision of the punishing management.

The right to prefer an appeal is a substantive right. The service rules or standing orders contain such provision of appeal against orders in disciplinary matter. For example, in case of bank employees other than officer employees the clause 14 of the Memorandum of Settlements dated 10. 04. 2002 provides, inter alia, that the Chief Executive Officer or the Principal Officer in India of a bank or an Alternate officer at the Head Office or Principal Office nominated by him for the purpose shall decide which officer or body higher in status than the officer authorized to take disciplinary action shall act as the appellate authority to deal with or hear or dispose off any appeal against orders passed in disciplinary matter.

In the Model Standing Orders under the Industrial Employment (Standing Orders) Central Rules 1946 a workman aggrieved by an order imposing punishment may within 21 days from the date of receipt of the order, appeal to the appellate authority.

The aggrieved employee cannot have any right to personal hearing in an appeal if such right is not given in service rules or standing orders. However, standing orders, service rules of some organizations provide such right to personal hearing in some specific cases. For example, in case of non officers (award staff members) in banking industry, if the punishment

21 Anil Behari vs State of Orissa: AIR 1967 Patna 43

is of dismissal or in a case where after perusal of the proceedings, the appellate authority is considering reduction of punishment a hearing will be necessary. The following procedure generally followed to give a hearing

- to fix a date for such hearing and to issue notice by the appellate authority to PO and appellant employee notifying them the date of hearing of appeal.
- to commence hearing within one month from the date of receipt of the appeal
- to call upon the appellant employee or his representative by the appellate authority on the date of hearing to make his submission first
- to record the arguments by the appellate authority after noting the particular of those present, etc., as in the case of an enquiry
- to ask the PO by the appellate authority to give reply to the arguments of the appellant employee
- to ask the appellant employee or his representative to reply if desired.

Normally, an appellate authority should not take fresh evidence at the appellate stage and should decide the case on the argument of the parties. The appeal judgment should be given within one month from the date of conclusion of such hearings.

In cases where hearings are not required an appeal shall be disposed off within two months from the date of receipt thereof. The aggrieved workman in bank can prefer an appeal within 45 days from the date on which the original order has been communicated in writing to the concerned workman.

Specimen Draft 6

[SPECIMEN DRAFT OF ORDER OF APPOINTMENT AS ENQUIRY OFFICER AGAINST A SUB-STAFF, Mr A. K. ROY OF XYZ BANK, PATIPUKUR BRANCH, KOLKATA]

ORDER

Date: 08. 06. 2010

It has been decided to hold a departmental enquiry against Mr AK Roy, sub-staff, Patipukur Branch of XYZ Bank under the provisions of the Bipartite Settlement dated 10th April, 2002.

2. In exercise, therefore, of power conferred on the undersigned by

the Chairman and Managing Director in terms of clause 14 of the said Settlement, I hereby appoint Mr Ranjan Dey, senior Manager, India Excharge Branch, Kolkata as Enquiry Officer to conduct a departmental enquiry against Mr AK Roy and submit to me his report with the record of proceedings after completing the enquiry.

Sd/

(AK Chandra)

Deputy General Manager (Kolkata Region)

&

Disciplinary Authority

Specimen Draft 7

[SPECIMEN DRAFT OF ORDER OF APPOINTMENT AS PRESENTING OFFICER IN THE DEPARTMENTAL ENQUIRY AGAINST A SUB-STAFF Mr AK ROY OF XYZ BANK, PATIPURUR BRANCH, KOLKATA, BEFORE THE ENQUIRY OFFICER, MR RANJAN DEY]

Date: 08. 06. 2010

Disciplinary proceedings have been instituted against Mr AK Roy, sub-staff, Patipukur Branch of XYZ Bank in terms of Bipartite Settlement dated 10th April, 2002.

2. I have appointed Mr Ranjan Dey, Senior Manager, India Exchange Branch, Kolkata as Enquiry Officer to conduct the enquiry in respect of the charges mentioned in the chargesheet dated 08. 06. 2010.

3. I now hereby appoint Mr PK Saha, Manager (Audit and Inspection) Kolkata Regional Office as Presenting Officer to present the case of the Bank at the said enquiry.

Sd/

(AK. Chandra)

Deputy General Manager (Kolkata Region)

&

Disciplinary Authority

SPECIMEN DRAFT OF ORDER OF PUNISHMENT (SD 8)

ORDER

Disciplinary proceedings were initiated against Mr ______________ ECNO ______________ attached to our ______________ branch, Kolkata by issuance of chargesheet dated ______________ in terms of the provisions of Bipartite Settlement dated 10. 04. 2002.

The chargesheet dated ______________ containing charges framed against Mr ______________ was served on him. Mr ______________ was appointed as Enquiry Officer to conduct departmental enquiry against Mr ______________ in respect of charges contained in chargesheet dated ______________ issued to him.

Mr ______________ Enquiry Officer submitted his report dated ______________ containing his findings on the charges framed against Mr ______________ a copy of which was sent to the chargesheeted employee for his representation/submission, if any, which was received by him on ______________ Mr ______________ did not make any representation/ submission within the stipulated period. His Defence Representative, has submitted written submission on ______________.

I have carefully gone through the nature of charges, findings report dated ______________ of the Enquiry Officer, all records of the enquiry, written submission dated ______________ in reply to findings report dated ______________ and the related papers and documents relating to this enquiry.

The following allegations and charges levelled against Mr ______________ stand 'PROVED'.

Allegations:

a) habitual in remaining absent unauthorizedly

b) continuous absenteeism unauthorizedly for a period exceeding 30 days and not resuming duties in spite of repeated instructions.

c) due to his unauthorized absence smooth functioning of the Branch was disrupted.

Charges

i. remaining unauthorizedly absent without intimation continuously for a period exceeding 30 days [clause 5(p) of the Bipartite Settlement dated 10. 04. 2002]

ii. acted prejudicial to the interest of the Bank [clause 5(j) of the Bipartite settlement dated 10. 04. 2002]

iii. willful insubordination or disobediences of the lawful and reasonable order of the management or superior [clause 5(c) of the Bipartite Settlement dated 10. 04. 2002]

Notice of proposed punishment dated ____________ was served on Mr ____________ and a personal hearing was held on ____________ at Bank's Regional office at Kolkata at 11am which was attended by Mr ____________ and his Defence Representative Mr ____________.

During the course of personal hearing Mr ____________ submitted that he is suffering from cardiac ailment for which he was irregular in his attendance. The Defence Representative Mr ____________ stated that chargesheeted employee was not given reasonable opportunity in course of departmental enquiry and the order of hearing on proposed punishment was served on ____________ where as the hearing was fixed on ____________ with a short notice of 2 days. The proposed punishment is very harsh and not proportionate to misconduct. The submission made by the chargesheeted employee during the course of departmental enquiry was not considered by the Enquiry Officer. The chargesheeted employee requested the Enquiry Officer to allow him to present Medical officer of the Bank as defence witness as mentioned in the order sheet dated ____________ which was denied by the Enquiry Officer. The Enquiry Officer was biased and acted partially. Some original documents were not produced by the Presenting Officer.

The chargesheeted employee also submitted that he belongs to Scheduled Caste Community and his discharge from Bank's Service will surely affect his family members. He requested to reconsider the matter and award punishment which is short of discharge/dismissal.

I have taken into consideration the submission of the chargesheeted employee and his Defence Representative during personal hearing and find no reason to reduce the punishment as proposed vide order dated ____________.

From the past records of the chargesheeted employee I observe the following:

Chargesheet dated __________ was issued to him for his unauthorized absence for __________ days and punishment of stoppage of 2(two) future increments of pay without cumulative effect for a period of 1(one) year was imposed vide order dated__________.

The chargesheeted employee Mr __________ remained absent unauthorisedly for __________ days up to__________. His frequent and continuous unauthorized absence has caused disruption in smooth functioning of the branch.

Considering the charges that proved against Mr _________, findings report of the Enquiry Officer dated _________, the records of the enquiry proceedings, the written submission of the chargesheeted employee in reply to the findings report of Enquiry Officer dated _________, past records and the submission of the chargesheeted employee and his Defence Representative during personal hearing dated _________, Iam of the considered opinion that ends of justice in this case would be met if the following punishment be imposed on Mr _________ as proposed vide order dated _________.

"BE DISCHARGED FROM SERVICE WITH SUPERANNUATION BENEFITS i.e., PENSION AND/OR PROVIDENT FUND AND GRATUITY AS WOULD BE DUE OTHERWISE UNDER THE RULES OR REGULATIONS PREVAILING AT THE RELEVANT TIME AND WITHOUT DISQYALIFICATION FROM FUTURE EMPLOYMENT".

In exercise of the power conferred upon me/hereby impose the following punishment on Mr _________.

"BE DISCHARGED FROM SERVICE WITH SUPERANNUATION BENEFITS i.e., PENSION AND/OR PROVIDENT FUND AND GRATUITY AS WOULD BE DUE OTHERWISE UNDER THE RULES OR REGULATIONS PREVAILING AT THE RELEVANT TIME AND WITHOUT DISQUALIFICATION FROM FUTURE EMPLOYMENT".

The punishment will be effective from the date of this order.

In case Mr _________ desires to prefer appeal against this order, he may submit his appeal to the appropriate authority within 45 days of receipt of this order.

Sd/-

Deputy General Manager (Kolkata Region)

&

Disciplinary Authority

Place:

Date:

Books Recommended

1. SK Datta, *Guide to Disciplinary Action* (Tata McGraw-Hill Publishing Company Limited, New Delhi, 1994)
2. NN Chatterjee, *Management of Personnel in Indian Enterprises* (Allied Book Agency, Delhi, 1978)
3. VG Mhetras, *Dismissal on Misconduct in Industry* (National Institute of Labour Management, Bombay, 1971)
4. SL Agrawal, *Labour Relations Law in India* (Macmillan, Meerut, 1978)
5. YB Bhonsle, Disciplinary Action, *A Handbook for Managers* (S Chand, New Delhi, 1978)
6. LS Kudchedkar, *Aspects of Personnel Management and Industrial Relations* (Tata Mc Graw-Hill, New Delhi, 1979)
7. LC Malhotra, *Dismissal, Discharge, Termination of Service and Punishment with Model Forms* (The University Book Agency, Law Book Publishers, Allahabad, 1974)
8. LB Bhide, *A Banker's Handbook on Discipline and Disciplinary Action*, 1983
9. Arun Monappa, *Industrial Relations* (Tata McGraw-Hill Publishing Company Limited, New Delhi, 2007)

Questions

1. What is misconduct? State some acts of misconduct which are generally resorted to by employees of organizations.
2. State some acts of gross misconduct, and minor misconducts mentioned in the standing orders or service rules of organizations.
3. What is natural justice? 'No person should be judge in his own case' Justify the statement.
4. Explain in brief any five principles of natural justice.
5. 'Some say principles of natural justice need to be followed in the departmental enquiry'. Do you endorse this? Explain.
6. For an effective disciplinary system the organization should follow some guidelines/procedures. What are those procedures? Discuss.
7. What is punishment? State some punishments which are generally imposed on the delinquent employees by the management of various organizations.
8. State and explain the relevant provisions of labour laws that deal with punishment to erring employees.

9. Illustrate procedures from the stage of imposing punishment by the Disciplinary Authority to the stage of issuance of order by the Appellate Authority.
10. What procedures should an enquiry officer follow to hold preliminary hearing in a departmental enquiry?
11. Make a destination between:
    a) Show Cause Notice and Chargesheet
    b) Discharge and Dismissal
    c) Discharge and Discharge Simpliciter
    d) Suspension and Termination of service
12. Explain with illustration as and where needed
    a) Leading Question
    b) Cross Examination
    c) Examination-in-Chief
    d) Ex-Parte Enquiry
    e) Defence Representative
    f) Appellate Authority
13. Mr AK Nath clerk- cum cashier attached to Asansol Branch of XYZ Bank was issued show cause notice on 25.06.2010 for his remaining absent unauthorizedly for 100 days. Mr Nath has replied to the show cause notice on 30.06.2010 requesting the management to excuse him for this time. The Regional Manager, Mr SK Bhattacharyya called Mr SP Sen, Manager (HR), and advised him to issue caution letter to Mr Nath. As Manager (HR) of the above bank prepare a caution letter to be issued to Mr Nath.
14. Mr RN Das, Special Assistant attached to Burdwan Branch, National Bank Ltd. entered into the chamber of the branch manager. Mr RK Bose on 21.06.2010 at 1pm and assaulted Mr Bose. The matter was taken up by the union and it is lying with the conciliation officer who held meeting with the management representative and also with the union on two occasions. The dispute is still pending in conciliation proceeding. Now, the disciplinary authority desires to issue chargesheet to Mr Das and to punish him for his misconduct. As IR Head of the above company give your views with reasons whether disciplinary authority can initiate disciplinary action against Mr Das including imposition of punishment.

Case Study 1

Brabourne Road Branch of Kolkata is a large sized branch which is headed by the Chief Manager. The total staff strength of the branch including officers is 35.

1. On 23rd April 2010 Mr AK Roy a valued customer who has been maintaining a Savings Bank Account with Brabourne Road Branch for the last 20 years came to the branch at 11.30am to withdraw some money from his SB A/C to meet up hospitalization expenses for treatment of his ailing wife. Mr Roy needed the money urgently. He waited for 10 minutes in front of the Payment Counter where some other customers were waiting. Since payment cashier, Mr P Datta was not on his seat, he went straight to the Senior Manager, Mr B Bose who was Accountant of the branch and requested him to arrange for making payment of Rs 20,000 to him as he urgently needed it. Mr Bose tried a lot to find out Mr P Datta but he could not get to know where Mr Datta had gone.

   At 11.45am Mr Datta returned to his seat. After seeing Mr Datta, Mr Roy got furious and expressed about the inconvenience he caused by not rendering customer service for 15 minutes. At this Mr Datta told Mr Roy to 'shut up', 'keep quiet' otherwise he would not give him service. Mr Roy got angry and said, "You are public servant, you are bound to provide service to the customers. Remember, this is not your father's bank". Then Mr Datta got up from his seat and rushed to Mr Roy and said, "Get out from here, I will show you whose bank it is?". Mr Roy got very much furious and threatened Mr Datta to see the consequences.

2. The Chief Manager, Mr LN Mukherjee got to know about the incident from Mr B Das officer and then rushed to the payment counter, He intervened in the matter and pacified Mr Roy as also Mr Datta. After this Mr Datta started making payment to the customers who had been waiting on the queue.

3. The Chief Manager, Mr Mukherjee told Mr Bose, Accountant to submit him the detailed incident that took place today. At about 3pm he called Mr Datta in his chamber and asked him why he was not available at his seat. Mr Datta replied that at about 11.30am he was informed by Mr Narayan Sharma of Cash Credit Department over intercom about a telephone call from his relative. He went to Cash Credit Department upstairs to attend the telephone call and it took about six to seven minutes time.

4. At about 6pm Mr Bose submitted a note to the Chief Manager detailing the incident occurred at the branch. He also took the signature of Mr S Menon, Saving Bank Department In Charge as witness to the incident.

5. Mr Mukherjee informed Mr GA Nayak, Regional Manager of Kolkata Region about the branch incident in the evening over phone and next day, the 24th April, 2010 he sent the detailed report in writing to Mr Nayak.

6. On 26th April, 2010 Mr Roy wrote a complaint to the Chairman and Managing Director of the Bank with regard to the misbehaviour of Mr Datta and non-rendering customer's service with a copy to the Finance Minister and also to the All India Bank Customers' Association.

   Next day i.e., on 27th April, 2010 Mr Roy closed the Savings Bank Account and also Fixed Deposit Receipt Account maintained with the branch and took premature payment of Fixed Deposit Receipts amounting to Rs. 15 lac.

7. Mr GA Nayak, Regional Manager called Mr Roy at his cabin on 28. 04. 10 and assured him of providing best service to him. Mr Roy was so unhappy at the behaviour of Mr Datta that the personal meeting could not yield any result.

   The Regional Manager called Mr Datta on 29. 04. 10 and asked him how the incident had occurred and why he did not provide customer service to Mr Roy. Mr Nayak told him to ensure that such incidents are not repeated in future.

8. The Regional Manager, Mr Nayak received a letter from the Chairman and Managing Director enclosing a copy of the complaint made by Mr Roy, advising to look into the matter and apprise him of the action taken.

The Regional Manager being the Disciplinary Authority decided to issue chargesheet to Mr P. Datta, cash clerk

On the basis of what has been stated above, answer the following questions.

a. Prepare a chargesheet to be issued to Mr P Datta, cash clerk.

b. Draw a suspension order to suspend Mr P Datta, cash clerk pending issue of chargesheet and enquiry

c. Give an outline of the procedure that Mr RR Sharma, General Manager of XYZ Bank Pvt Ltd, and Appellate Authority should follow from the stage of receipt of appeal from Mr Datta to the stage of issue of order by him.

Case Study 2

On 3rd September 2009 Mr Amiya Saha was recruited as an assistant for a small-sized automobile service station in Nagpur. He was required to help the mechanic in performing routine maintenance concerning cars leased out to various local firms from time to time. His duty hours started from 7am to 4pm with a recess for an hour. On 8th May, 2010 Mr Arnab Saxena, Supervisor called Mr Saha at his cabin and told him that after confirmation in service on 3rd march 2010 he started coming late for work frequently and during April, 2010 he was late for work on 9 days. He was told about the necessity of reporting on duty on time. It is needed for maintaining discipline and also to create a work culture in the organization. Mr Sexena showed his willingness to help him if he needs so that he can attend to his duty on time.

Mr Saha replied that he would be very happy if he is allowed to report for duty at 8am instead of 7am as he needs to travel 20 Km daily for work. Mr Saxena agreed to help Mr Saha. So, he recommended for favourable consideration of the request of Mr Saha for change of duty hours. The request of Mr Saha was acceded to by the higher management.

Looking to the late attendance of some employees of the organization, in a regular way, management decided to permit an employee to report for duty late (up to maximum 30 minutes) for 3 times a month and to take disciplinary action against an employee if he reports late for work more than thrice in any one particular month.

From the study of the punctuality/attendance records of employees it was found that Mr Saha was habitual late in his attendance.

In the month of June, 2010 he was late for work for 9 times which was much more than the permissible occasions.

In terms of standing orders, 'habitual late' is one of the acts of misconduct.

So, it was decided by the Manager of the Service Station, Mr JR Pandit to give him an advisory letter to improve his attendance. On 5th July 2010, Mr Pandit called Mr Saha into his cabin and gave him a letter advising to be punctual and report for work on time. Mr Saha acknowledged receipt of the letter. On 6th July 2010, at about 2pm Mr Saha along with general secretary of the union entered into the cabin of Mr Pandit when Mr Pandit was doing some paper work. Then Mr Saha shouted at Mr Pandit, threw away visiting chairs from the cabin, broke the table glass, threatened him for dire consequence if disciplinary action was taken against him. Then both union representative and Mr Saha left the office premises.

On the basis of what has been stated above answer the following questions:

a. Prepare a show cause notice and also a chargesheet as a step for taking disciplinary action against Mr Saha. You may use imaginary name, place, date, etc., as and where required.

b. As manager (HR) of the company prepare a suspension order on Mr Saha when decision is taken by the Disciplinary Authority issue such order before chargesheet is issued.

c. Give an outline of the procedures that Enquiry Officer should follow to conduct the regular hearing (Imaginary names of Presenting Officer, Enquiry Officer, Defence Representative, witnesses, etc., should be used)

Case Study 3

Mr LN Roy has been working as Manager (HR) of a medium size factory at Rishra. He has received a complaint from one departmental head with regard to some acts of misconducts resorted to by Mr RN Karfa, clerk.

Case details

The office hours of the department where Mr Karfa, works start from 10am and end at 6pm with half an hour's recess. Mr Karfa, takes his lunch recess between 1pm and 1.30pm.

On 17th December 2009 Mr Karfa, went out of the office during his lunch recess. He did not return at 1.30pm as he should have normally done. He returned to the office at about 4.30pm and was quite drunk. On entering the office he went to Mr SP Lahiri, Deputy Manager. Mr Lahiri was in fact, waiting for Mr Karfa, to return to the office and wondering why he was so late. When Mr Lahiri found Mr Karfa, returning at 4.30pm in a drunken state, he was a little upset and asked Mr Karfa, the reason for his coming late. On hearing this Mr Karfa, got annoyed and said something to the effect that the Dy Manager was unnecessarily questioning him and was harassing him. To this Mr Lahiri tried to explain to Mr Karfa, that he was merely doing his duty which was to see that office work did not suffer due to such absence of an employee. At this Mr Karfa, got upset, shouted at Mr Lahiri and called him a 'rascal'. Mr Lahiri realized that Mr Karfa, was quite drunk and therefore tried to point out to him that he should not behave in that manner. The whole incident lasted for about 10 minutes.

Hearing the shouting of Mr Karfa, the Manager, Mr PS Jha came out of his cabin. Two other employees of the factory who had come on the scene by that time took Mr Karfa, away to his department. Mr Karfa, then left the office, without permission at 5pm. The Manager Mr Jha got in touch with Mr LN Roy, Manager (HR) and narrated the incident.

Read the above case and answer the following

a. Prepare a chargesheet which is required to be issued by Mr Himadri Guha, Factory Manager and Disciplinary Authority against clerk Mr RN Karfa.

b. If you work as Manager (HR) in place of Mr LN Roy in the above organization how would you deal with such case?

c. Draw an outline of the procedures the enquiry officer should follow to conduct departmental enquiry. You must use the imaginary names of PO, EO, DR, CSE's witnesses, Management witness, for such purpose.

d. Explain the factors the Disciplinary Authority should consider before deciding the nature of punishment.

e. Can DA terminate the service of Mr Karfa as a fit case for discharge simpliciter? What are the differences between 'discharge' and 'dismissal'?

VIII

Introduction to Industrial Relations

Concept of Industrial Relations

In narrow sense, the term 'industrial relations' means relations between parties in industrial establishments. That means, nature of relationship established amongst the parties in the industry. Dictionary meaning of industrial relations is the relations between management and employees in industrial concerns. In short, the term, 'industrial relations' means the relations between employees and management arising out of day to day work in industry.

Different authors, experts have expressed their views on the concept of industrial relations. Dale Yoder (1948) views industrial relations 'as a whole field of relationship that exists because of the necessary collaboration of men and women in the employment process of an industry'. From the analysis of Dale Yoder's opinion it is revealed that the employees work in industry as per terms and conditions of employment and in the process of working in collaborative system both management and employees develop relations with each other and this relationship as a whole is industrial relations.

International Labour Organization has stressed upon the relations among state, employers' organizations and workers' organization or the relationship among occupational organizations. John T Dunlop (1958) has expressed his views on the concept of industrial relations as the relations among three actors– employer, employees and government.

In a wider sense, industrial relations are the collective relations between management, trade unions, government and industrial and non-industrial organization. Sometimes the terms 'labour management relations', 'union management relations', 'employment relations' and 'industrial relations' are used interchangeably. 'Labour management relations'/'union management relation' is the collective relations between union and management. The Employment relations is used to denote the relationship arising out of the employment condition between individual and management or between trade unions and management. That means it is either individual relations or collective relations.

We may have clear idea about industrial relations from following:

- Industrial relations is the relations between management and employees.
- The relationship may be positive or negative or mixed.
- Pattern of IRs is influenced by people's value, belief, perception, aptitude, personality, attitudes, ethics, etc.
- State acts as regulator, facilitator in shaping IRs pattern in industry.
- The relationship is based on economic, non-economic issues arising out of terms and conditions of employment as also practices not covered under the terms.
- Means of IRs are HR/IR policies, procedures, rules, regulations, legislations, etc.
- Collective bargaining is the effective mechanism of shaping the pattern of industrial relations.
- Changing economic scenario, technological advances, organization mission, strategic approach, trade unions' role contribute a lot to influence IRs pattern.

Figure 8.1: A conceptual model of industrial relations system

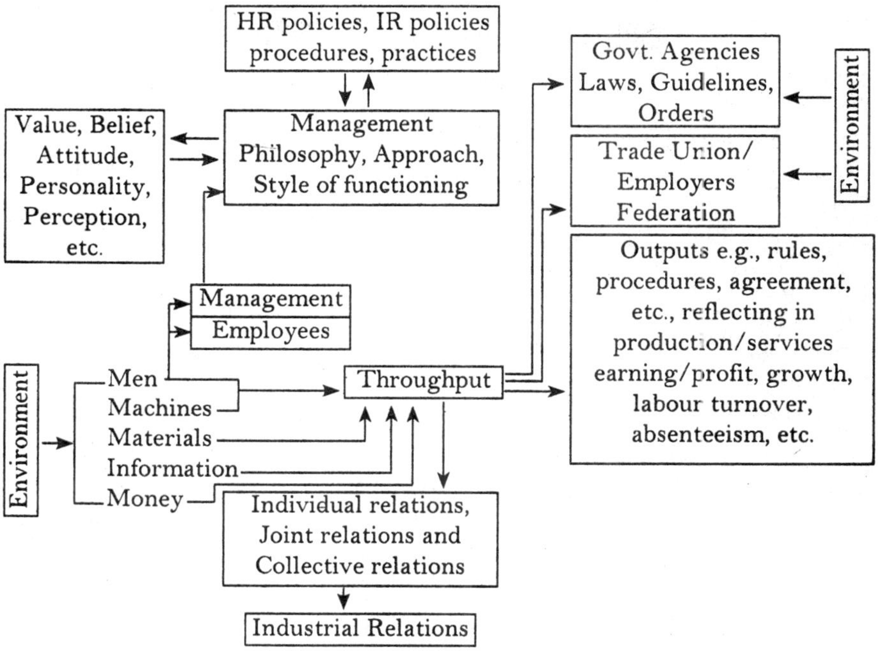

Characteristics of Industrial Relations

The salient characteristics of industrial relations are discussed herein below:

1. Parties in the industrial relations activities

Basically two parties-workers and management are involved in the process of establishing relations. However, the government agencies regulate/maintain industrial relations.

2. Interactive Process

Industrial relations arise out of interactions between different persons/parties. They are supervisors, workers trade unions, employers' associations. So interactive process takes place between

- Supervisors and industrial workers
- Supervisors and group/team members
- Management and trade union leaders
- Employers' federations and workers' unions

3. Two-way communication

IRs is a two-way communication process. One party gives stimuli, other party responds to the stimuli. So, the transaction occurring through such mechanism is either complementary or cross. More the complementary transactions, better will be the industrial relations situations.

4. HRM Practices

Effective human resource planning system, identification and stimulating prospective employees, designing the most suitable selection technique to choose the right kind of people help the organization to get a committed and willing workforce that wants to grow, develop and achieve. Such employees in the process like to develop better relations with their bosses. So HRM practices influence IRs pattern in the industry.

5. Approaches to IRs

Various approaches contribute to shape IRs pattern in industrial organizations. These approaches include sociological, psychological, socio-ethical, human relations, Gandhian, system approaches, etc.

6. State intervention

State plays a vital role to influence industrial relations situations through its activities as facilitator, guide, counsellor for both the parties in the industry.

7. Role of trade union

Behavioural manifestations of workers are mostly governed by the trade unions to which they belong. Hence trade union's perception, attitudes towards management influence workers to form their mindset that regulates/promotes interaction with the management.

8. Organizational climate

If congenial and conducive organizational climate prevails, workers feel homely, interact spontaneously, communicate to boss about their problems, difficulties directly and come close to him to exchange/share the views with each other in respect of work, change of job design, introduction of any operative system, process, etc. Under such situation possibility of establishing healthy human relations develops and it influences industrial relations pattern of the organization.

9. Dispute settlement process

If the management personnel belive in the philosophy of settling workers' grievances/disputes through bi-lateral negotiation process, they give much more emphasis on mutual talk, sharing responsibility, collaboration, partnership dealing and mutual trust. In the process changes in workers' atitudes, behaviour and thought pattern are likely to occur which effect industrial relations.

10. Outcomes of IRs

Outcomes of IRs are reflected in production both in quantity and quality, services, mandays lost, wastes, accident rate, productivity, labour turnover rate, absenteeism rate, number of bipartite negotiations, company's image, growth, development, etc.

11. Competence development

Healthy industrial relations help develop workers' skill, knowledge, ability, aptitude and change their attitudes, perception to enable them to participate in collaborative activities/collective bargaining process effectively.

12. Issues in IRs

Industrial relations climate/situation is greatly influenced by the issues-economic, non-economic governed by service contract/terms and conditions of employment. Besides, the issues not covered under service rules, viz., behavioural, and attitudinal issues influence IRs pattern.

Evolution of Industrial Relations

Industrial relations contribute a lot to the achievement of organizational goals. No organization can run smoothly and effectively if industrial relations of that organization are unsound, unhealthy. Today, in the changing and stiff competition, industrial relations play a preponderant role to make the organization competent to face challenges and obtain competitive advantage. It is possible for the organization to remain in the market and make a place there if it can supply quality goods and services to the customers at a competitively lesser price and at the time they desire. For this it needs congenial, conducive and harmonious industrial relations. So, better industrial relations is a necessity for growth and development of organizations. It is now felt pertinent to have a clear idea about industrial relations in India that has passed through several stages. These stages are

1. Industrial Relations: Early Period (The period upto 1918)
2. Industrial Relations in the Pre-Independence Period (The period from 1919 to 1946)
3. Industrial Relations in Post-Independence Period (The period from 1947 till date)

Industrial Relations: Early Period (The period upto 1918)

This period is basically the period that starts from pastoral and agrarian economy to the end of First World War. Industrial relations during this period was very bad. 'Hire and fire' was a routine activity of the managerial staff. The slave concept/master-servant concept was predominantly prevalent in industrial settings that indicated the pattern of industrial relations. Such state of uncongenial and unconducive industrial relation emerged from accumulated feelings of sufferings, emotions of the people at work that generated from deprivation of just and reasonable wages, benefits due to the workers for a long period. The economic conditions of the workers were very bad. The wage rate was appallingly low. The working conditions were very unhealthy. There was no labour law existing to protect the workers' interests except the Employers and Workmen (Disputes) Act, 1860 that looked at the settlement of wage disputes. All this resulted in poor labour management relations. There was no trade union existing during the period till 1875 when Sorabjee Shahpurjee Bengali led a movement in Bombay for legislative measures against the sufferings of the workers.

In 1890 the Bombay Mill Hands Association was set up under the leadership of Mr NM Lokhande for amending the Factories Act 1881 and also for improving the working conditions of employees.

During this period there was no trade union activity in the true sense. The unions like the amalgamated Society of Railway Servants of India, 1897, the Printers' Union Calcutta, 1905, the Bombay Postal Union, 1907 and the Kamgar Hitvardhak Sabha, 1909 worked as labour welfare associations to improve the workers' conditions through government measures. No major strike occurred except the weavers' strike in Ahmedabad in 1895, jute mill strike in Calcutta in 1896, mill workers' strike in Bombay in 1897 and strikes in Madras Press in 1903.

Industrial Relations in the Pre-Independence Period (The period from 1919 to 1946)

After the First World War the industrial relations climate was worsened. Industrial workers felt the necessity of forming union to improve their bargaining strength to make the management agree to their demands. Formation of International Labour Organization in 1919 generated a new spirit amongst the working class to show their solidarity and unity by forming unions. All India Trade Union Congress (AITUC) was formed in 1920 with the principal objectives to ameliorate the economic and social conditions of the working class, to promote, safeguard and further the interests, rights and privileges of the workers of the workers in all matters relating to employment. The Workmen's Compensation Act, 1923 was enacted to protect the workers against injury during employment. Enactment of Trade Unions Act, 1926 that provides legal protection to the workers inspired them to form unions. There had been instances of numerous strikes and disturbances in 1928-29[1]. The then Government enacted the Trade Disputes Act, 1929 in line with the British Industrial Courts Act, 1919. The Royal Commission on Labour appointed in 1929 to make a thorough study of labour problems, submitted report in 1931. This gave much emphasis on industrial peace and harmony through settlement of issues. The enactment of the Bombay Trade Disputes Conciliation Act, 1934 was a significant attempt for the settlement of industrial disputes and for bringing peace and harmony in industry through making provisions for appointment of Labour Officers, Special Conciliators. In 1938 this Act was replaced by the Bombay Industrial Disputes Act to provide for an elaborate machinery to promote peaceful and amicable settlement of industrial disputes.

During the Second World War the employers made a lot of profits. The workers demanded a share in it. Bonus and dearness allowance were granted to them but as the money wages did not increase in proportion to the rise in price, the Government tried to check this dissatisfaction and consequential strike activity by prohibiting strike under the Emergency Rules (Rule 81A of Defence of India Rules)[2]. The Rules empowered the government to refer any dispute to conciliation or adjudication and to prohibit any strike and lockout if resorted to without notice. The tripartite Indian Labour Conference and Standing Labour Committee were set up in 1942 with the objectives of discussing the matter of national importance between employer, employees and government and laying down procedures for the settlement of industrial disputes. The unanimous decision taken in this tripartite committee on labour matters was greatly influenced by government's labour policy and also the industrial relations pattern of Indian industries.

This period was very significant from the point of establishing a culture of mutuality in industrial settings as Industrial Employment (Standing Orders) Act was promulgated in 1946. The Act makes it compulsory for the establishments having 100 or more employees to get the standing orders certified by the appropriate government official. The standing orders contain the issues relating to employment, terms of employment and condition of labour; and before standing orders is certified trade union/employees are given chance to present their suggestions/comments in the matter. The Bombay Industrial Relations

1 VV Giri, *Labour Problems in Indian Industry* (Asia Publishing House, Bombay 1960)

2 CB Mamoria, S Mamoria, and SV Gankar, *Dynamics of Industrial Relations* (Himalaya Publishing House, Mumbai, 2000 p 234)

Act was promulgated replacing the Bombay Industrial Disputes Act 1938 with the objectives of generating a climate of peace and harmony in industry through settlement of issues by the parties.

Industrial Relations in Post Independence Period (The period from 1947 till date)

This period showed a significant change in industrial relations situation as a large number of labour laws were enacted to protect the interest of the working class with the objectives of developing country's economy by generating a climate of peace and harmony in industry that could ensure smooth and effective functioning of industrial activities. The labour laws enacted in the post-Independence period include:

- The Industrial Disputes Act 1947
- The Factories Act 1948
- The Minimum Wages Act 1948
- The Dock Workers (Regulation of Employment) Act 1948
- The Employees State Insurance Act 1948
- The Employees' Provident Fund and Miscellaneous Provisions Act 1952
- The Plantations Labour Act 1951
- The Mines Act 1952
- The Employment Exchanges (Compulsory Notification of Vacancies) Act 1959
- The Maternity Benefit Act 1961
- The Apprentices Act 1961
- The Payment of Bouns Act 1965
- The Contract Labour (Regulation and Abolition) Act 1970
- The Payment of Gratuity Act 1972
- The Equal Remuneration Act 1976
- The Child Labour (Prohibition and Regulation) Act 1986

The Industrial Disputes Act 1947 was enacted to provide for the establishment of permanent machinery for the settlement of industrial disputes and to make these awards legally binding and enforceable. Immediately after Independence a tripartite conference was convened in 1947 at which Industrial Truce Resolution was taken to lay greater importance to the maintenance of peace and harmony in Indian industries.

A growth in trade unionism and trade union activities occurred during the period as revealed in the Table 8.1. It was due to change in the attitude of workers who realized the necessity of trade unionism and also the trade union leaders.

Table 8.1

Showing number of registered unions (workers and employees) and membership of unions submitting returns.

year	No of registered trade union	Membership of unions submitting returns in (000)
1947-48	2766	1663
1950-51	3766	1757
1997	59968	7408

Source: *Government of India, Ministry of Labour, Various Issues of Indian Labour Year Book and Pocket Book of Labour.*

This period witnessed the formation of various central trade unions at different time, namely

- The Indian National Trade Union Congress (INTUC) in 1947
- The Hind Mazdoor Sabha (HMS) in 1948
- The United Trade Union Congress (UTUC) in 1948
- The Bharatiya Mazdoor Sangh (BMS) in 1955
- The Centre of Indian Trade Union (CITU) in 1970
- The National Labour Organization (NLO) in 1972
- The United Trade Union Congress – Lenin Sarani (UTUC-LS)
- The National Front of Indian Trade Union (NFITU)
- The Trade Union Coordination Committee (TUCC)

The formation of central trade unions that gave an indication to the employers for settlement of labour issues through collective bargaining mechanism encouraged the employers to strengthen their associations. All this enhanced the importance of bipartite settlements at different levels, viz., plant level, industry level and national level. Some important collective agreements were made viz., the Bouns Agreement for plantation workers in 1956, the Agreement reached in Ports and Docks in 1977, 1981, 1994, the Bata Shoe Company Agreement in 1955, 1958, 1982, and so on.

Five Year Plans (1951-1956) stressed upon the necessity of bringing peace and harmony in industries to promote sound industrial relations in organizations. The First Five-Year Plan gave much importance on the following to develop healthy industrial relations in industry:

- to set up tripartite body consisting of representatives of employers, employees and government to sort out problems/issues through discussion, negotiation, and reaching an agreement
- to use arbitration machinery in case of disputes arising out of interpretation of agreement
- to set up mutually agreed grievance procedure at the plant level as also in the industry level
- to use collective bargaining as an effective tool for reaching agreement
- to set up conciliation machinery by the state in case of failure to reach an agreement

The Second Five-Year Plan (1956-1961) laid emphasis on promoting sound labour management relations through

- setting up wage boards for need based minimum wage
- introduction of voluntary code of discipline, code of conduct to counteract the unhealthy trends of litigation and delays
- introducing scheme for workers' participation in management
- use of voluntary arbitration
- setting up model grievance procedure, evaluation and implementation machinery

Under the Third Five-Year Plan Industrial Truce Resolution was adopted in 1962 when emergency was caused by Chinese aggression. At that crisis period employers and employees took pledge to give maximum production and not to disturb effective running of industrial activities. Joint Consultation Machinery was given much more weightage as a measure to reduce problems of employees to promote a better labour-management relation.

During the Third and Fourth Five-Year Plans industrial relations pattern was regulated mostly by protective labour laws. A large number of labour laws were enacted during those periods of time covering two Five Years Plans. The Government of India set up National Commission on Labour in the month of December 1966 to make a detailed study on various aspects of labour viz., working condition, wages, welfare, trade union deployment, labour-management relations, etc., and to submit recommendations in the matter. The Commission submitted recommendations in 1969 some of which were implemented. This period was also significantly important for nationalization of some banks, sick textile mills, sick steel plants, collieries, etc. The participation of workers of the nationalized banks in the boards got a statutory footing in term of Bank Nationalisation Act. The Fifth Five-Year Plan (1974-1979) stressed much for the establishment of a climate of sound industrial relations through

- promotion of productivity oriented profit sharing scheme linked with performance of employees
- developing collective bargaining machinery for settlement of issues jointly by the representatives of employers and employees
- strengthening conciliation machinery and voluntary arbitration system for resolution of conflicts
- creating a spirit of industrial democracy at all levels
- setting up of shop councils and other similar bodies involving participation of representatives of employees and management to sort out problems in a mutually agreed way.

The period of Emergency (1975 and 1976) made an impact on industrial relations as strikes, lockouts or any sort of work stoppages were prohibited. The Sixth Five-Year Plan (1980-1985) laid emphasis on collective bargaining machinery as a tool for settlement of labour problems/issues, promoting cooperative attitude amongst employers and employees in the organizations for maintenance and development of sound industrial relations, inducting and promoting professional management in industrial settings to create a culture of peace and harmony in industry.

The late 1970s and the early 1980s were remarkable for lawlessness, violence in industrial belts that worsened the industrial relations situation. For instance, the President of the HMS Workers' union was beaten and murdered on 29th June, 1981 and on the same day another worker was murdered[3]. On July 24, 1981 the Managing Director of Bombay Tyres Company was assaulted. In another incident a worker of Wellman India, a company in the Thana area, was murdered[4].

To face the situation emerged from industrial strife and to ban strikes, lockout, layoffs in essential services the government promulgated the Essential Services Maintenance Act through issuing ordinance on 26th July, 1981.

The Indian economy in the post-independence period prior to globalization (upto 1990) was controlled, regulated and protected. The

3 *India Today*, July 1-15, 1981, p 26

4 *Business India*, September 28, October 11, 1981, pp 40-51

working class got the judgments from the judiciary system in their favour. After introduction of New Economic Policy (NEP) by the government in 1991 there has been a paradigm shift of economy from CRP (controlled, regulated and protected) economy to LPG (liberalization, privatization, globalization) economy that affects industrial relations system in the country. In the globalized economy MNCs and TNCs enter into the market and create a stiff and fierce competition amongst the market players. In the changing situation, those companies that want to remain in the market need to face challenges. This is possible through delivery of quality goods and services at a competitively lesser price, according to the requirement of the customers. So, the employees need to be involved in the organizational activities to give their best to delight the customers. The employers need to ensure that organizations function smoothly and effectively in a congenial and conducive climate created through mutual understanding, mutual faith and mutual responsibility between labour and management. The situation generated is like 'either perform or perish.' It establishes a new industrial relations climate where unions' role is to help the organizations to remain in the market, to stay with the organizations and grow. If this is not done, consequences affect not the employees only but the employers, society and the country as well.

Significant Aspects of Industrial Relations

There are two significant aspects of industrial relations. They are co-operation and conflict.

Cooperation

Cooperation refers to as working together for a common goal and for mutual benefit. The most essential element of cooperation is common goal. It means one person's achievement of goal facilitates the achievement of other's goal. Other element is mutual benefit. That means one seeks an outcome that benefits all participants.

In industrial settings labour and management are expected to work together to achieve organizational goals. It happens that employees give their best to produce quality goods, render quality services to attain organizational excellence when they feel happy, satisfied and contented. All these are manifested in the process of working between employees and management. This is an ideal situation that gives an indication of sound industrial relations in organizations. This generates a climate of co-operation arising out of working together for a common objective and for mutual benefit.

Cooperation brings a congenial and conducive atmosphere of working in organization based on mutuality i.e., mutual understanding, mutual faith and mutual trust between labour and management.

In practice union-management cooperation is a function of two forces. The behavioural pattern of union and management, and the balancing of union rights with management rights. This requires a tough exercise in the demarcation of joint and exclusive areas of two parties.[5]

Conflict

Conflict is a mutual antagonism as of ideas, interest. Conflicting situation arises in industrial organizations when both parties, union and management, do not reach to an agreeable term. Union submits charter of demands, grievances to the management and presents the employee issues for settlement by the management, but the management does not pay heed to the problems of the employees and does not show interest or willingness to solve problem. In such a situation differences between management and union crop up that disturb the industrial relations climate in the organization.

Workers have a lot of expectations, desires, needs. They may want more wages, more benefits, social security measures, job security, good working conditions, etc. When they do not get all these, they develop unhappiness, dissatisfaction, a bad image about the management and the company as well. All these affect production, productivity, quality, customer delightment, smooth functioning of organizational activities. High, dysfunctional level of conflict leads to lower level of organizational performance and disturbs peace and harmony in the organization.

However, a moderate amount of conflict is functional and benefits an organization. Without conflict, problems might not be attended to. Some degree of conflict is inevitable and a goal should be to keep conflict to the level that leads to optimum performance[6]. But, the conflict should not be allowed to exist; necessary measures should be taken immediately on its recurrence to ensure that the industrial relations climate remains unaffected.

Participants in Industrial Relations System

Industrial relations in wider perspectives refer to the relationship established between employees and their associations/trade unions, employers and their associations, and the government. The employees and their trade unions, employers and their associations and the government are the participants in industrial relations system. John T Dunlop has called the participants as actors who jointly determine the output of the system which consists of rules, regulations relating to terms and conditions of employment, to a great extent. These three

5 Raj K Agarwala: *"Union-Management Cooperation: A Framework"* Indian Journal of Industrial Relations, 13(3) January 1978 pp 321-337

6 VO Jenks, *Human Relations in Organizations* (Harper & Row Publishers New York, 1990, p 295)

actors play their role differently in an industrial relations system which is discussed below:

Employees and their organizations

Employees nurtured in formative childhood under different family systems having different level of education, pattern of nurturing, thought process develop a different values, attitudes, beliefs, mindset. Some may have positive beliefs, attitudes, values, some others may have negative values, attitudes, beliefs. So, in the organizational setting when the employees and management (boss and subordinates) with positive values, attitudes interact each other on any issue they develop mutual understanding, trust and a relationship that results in healthy industrial relations. Reverse is the case when the employees and the management with different values, beliefs, attitudes interact with each other.

So, the personal characteristics of employees viz., level of education, culture, mindset, values, beliefs, attitudes towards management, commitment to work and to the organization play important roles in industrial relations system. Employees form unions to satisfy their physiological and psychological needs. The main objectives of trade unions are

- to ensure that wages/salaries and other benefits are given to the employees in term of agreement, laws
- to protect from unfair labour practices by employers
- to protect from exploitation, victimization by employers
- to make aware of rights and duties
- to enhance standard of living of the employees
- to raise status in the organization and in the society

Trade unions make all-out efforts and strive hard to achieve those objectives by putting pressures on the management. They play important role in establishing industrial relations in an organization. The extent of influence of the unions to shape industrial relations pattern in an organization depends on its strength, degree of unionization, inter-union rivalry, values and the attitudes towards the management.

Employers and their Associations

One of the participants in industrial relation system is employers/ management. They provide employment to the employees, lay down terms and conditions of employment, and sanction various welfare and social security measures, introduce career planning and developmental programmes in organizations. The employers/management want maximum production, higher productivity, quality production and services from the employees. It happens that the employees give their best, look at the organizations as their own organizations and try hard to satisfy employers if they get what do they want to get from the employers. The employee's unrest affecting industrial relations arises when their demands, expectations are not fulfilled by the employers. Here, lies the employers' attitudes towards employees' and their unions, their style of functioning, strategic decision, use of machineries to settle industrial disputes, to dispose off individual grievances, climate created for performance, growth and development of employees. All this has a direct bearing on industrial relations system.

In order to increase the bargaining strength employers join associations at the local or national level. The associations on behalf of the member employers put pressure on trade unions and government in various ways. The employers' associations also participate in tripartite bodies to decide vital issues relating to labour. This way association regulates the industrial relations system in the organizations.

The Government

The government plays an important role to regulate the industrial relations system in organizations. Till nineteenth century the government did not in intervene in the labour issues that affected industrial relations. Employers and the employees were given freedom to settle IR issues by themselves. That means the government adopted laissez faire policy. In the late nineteenth century the conflicts between employers and employees started increasing, and even disputes cropped up on the issues which were triffling in nature. During this time the social philanthropists like Robert Owen, Ruskin and others in the UK, and Lokhandey, Bengalee and Wadia and others in India started agitation. Then the government changed its attitude and intervened on IR issues.

In the early forties of the twentieth century the government of India constituted tripartite bodies like Indian Labour Conference (ILC), Standing Labour Committee (SLC), Industrial Committees (ICs) for deliberation and consultation among labour, management and the government on the issues relating to labour and management. All this made an impact on the country's labour policies and legislation.

Now, in the recent time the government's intervention in IR systems in organizational settings is highly remarkable. It regulates the relationship of employers and employees through enacting various labour laws and setting up adjudicating machineries (i.e., Labour Courts, Tribunals at the state and national level) for resolving industrial disputes. The labour courts and tribunals intervene in the solution of labour problems referred to them. So, they go through the IR issues and give their judgment.

Objectives of Industrial Relations

The main objective of industrial relations is to create congenial, conducive climate, healthy environment, enabling organizational culture so that individual goals, team goals and organizational goals are achieved. The other objectives of IRs are discussed herein below:

1. Uninterrupted production and increased productivity

The objective of IRs is to keep the production process/services running so that target of production/services set by the organization is attained and also to increase productivity to enable the organization to grow and develop.

2. Less/Zero conflict

If better industrial relation is established both management and workers develop mutual understanding and put in their best efforts to resolve disputes through bilateral discussion, negotiation. So, conflicts are minimized if not reduced to zero.

3. Industrial peace and harmony

The sound industrial relations bring industrial peace and harmony while unsound industrial relations create situation/climate of disharmony, industrial unrest, conflict.

4. Contented and committed workforce

The objective of industrial relations is to create a contented and committed workforce by way of increasing their wages, providing fringe benefits, social secutiry measures, opportunities to develop, grow, etc. This is done through establishment of healthy industrial relations.

5. Dynamic workforce

Sound industrial relations create a dynamic workforce to get acquainted with the changing scenario, to know the organization needs, demands to place in the competitive race and to help the organization survive, grow and develop. IR policies, procedures are framed to give emphasis on workers' involvement, participation in decision making process, to develop competencies through training, education, counselling.

6. Management of organizational complexity

In view of liberalization, privatization and globalization (LPG) organization has to face a tough competition as multinational companies

(MNCs), transnational companies (TNCs) occupy a place in the market. For producing quality product and also a variety of products different sophisticated machines, devices with complicated operation processes are installed which need workforce to accept changes, update knowledge, skill. Sound industrial relations through developing human relations, understanding, mutual confidence and enriching knowledge, imparting training to enhance the level of competence and skill, manage the organizational complexities.

7. Developing Trade Unions

If union leaders, active members are educated, aware of changing environment, position of the organization where rank and file work and also rights, duties and responsibilities of the workers, most of the workers' problems are solved by themselves. So, it is one of the objectives of IRs is to educate trade union people and to support and develop them to act as real trade unions for the right cause of the workers and for growth and development of the workers and the organization as well.

8. Cordial human relations

One of the objectives of IRs is to promote employer-employee relations i.e., human relations through effective interaction and communication process. Organization philosophy, climate, management approach, style of functioning facilitate to develop mutual understanding, mutual faith between boss and subordinates.

9. Educating workers

Because of illiteracy, ignorance workers are unable to judge the specific situation, issues and give consent or agree to take recourse to action which is unjustified, unwarranted and uncalled for. IRs' objective is to educate the workforce, to develop their skill, ability to perceive the situation rightly, to make them aware of their strength and weaknesses so that they can negotiate their grievances, issues, problems with their boss and can resolve them.

10. Promoting trust, creativity, cooperativeness

Sound industrial relations create a conducive and congenial climate in the organization which promotes trust, creativity, cooperativeness amongst the workers. Under such organizational milieu workers develop a sense of 'belonging', 'we-ness', 'together-ness' which drive them to undertake any job for making things happen. Workers become loyal, committed, particular about their job role, and make no/less wastes, accident. Labour turnover and absenteeism rates are reduced.

Factors influencing Industrial Relations

The term 'industrial relations' means the relationship between labour and management which arises through interactive processes.. Both labour and management interact with each other on different issues, may be the issues relating to employement, terms and conditions as specified in the standing orders/bipartite settlement, HR practices or the issues concerning court judgement, legal implications, government orders, instructions. Origin/development, representation, settlement of the issues depend on various factors which indicate/influence the pattern of industrial relations. These factors are socio-ethical and cultural, ideological, technological, psychological, political, governmental, international, economic/financial, market conditions and enterprise related factors. Details of these factors are discussed. Factors influencing industrial relations are shown in Figure 8.2.

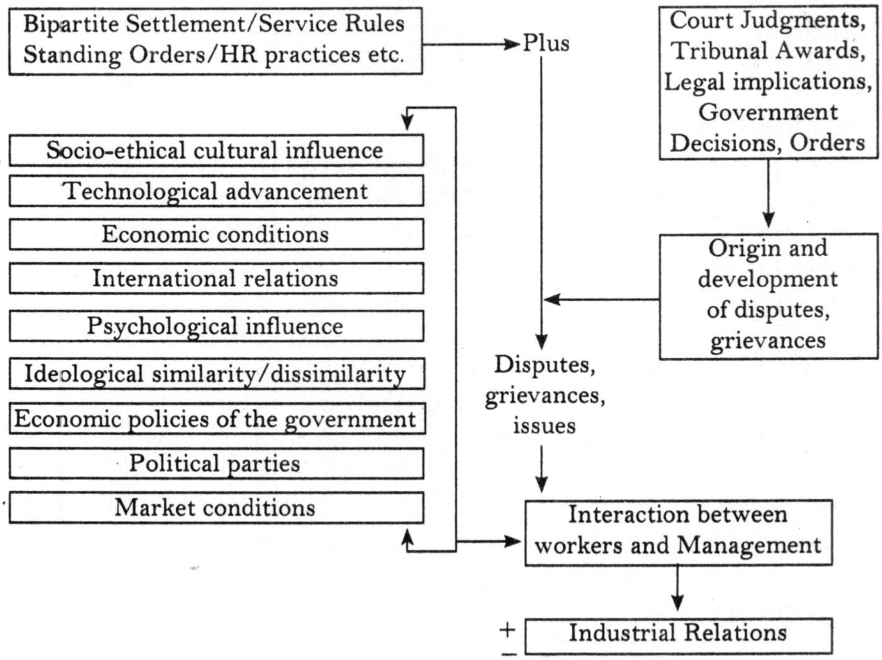

Figure 8.2: Factors Influencing Industrial Relations Pattern

Socio-ethical and cultural factor

Interaction between workers and management personnel becomes effective and complementary when both the parties possess positive thought process, values, beliefs that facilitate to develop a state of collaborative approach, willingness to help, desire for accepting risk, responsibilities to function in a joint venture and application of rational, judicious approach on the issues. All these traits and attributes develop mostly from social, ethical and cultural activities. So, the positive social, ethical and cultural values influence interaction between labour and management in a positive way. In such a situation human relations will be cordial and industrial relations will be better.

Technological advancement

In case of advancement of technology production is increased, quality of the product is improved, extent of defective product is minimised, cost of production is reduced, productivity is increased. All this increases the wages of the employees and makes them happy. The contented and happy workers are much more willing to keep the production activities running than to disturb the system; and for this they establish good relations with their bosses. So, advanced technology influences the industrial relations pattern of the industry.

Market conditions

Product market plays an important role to judge company's strength to run the production activities. If the market condition is uncomfortable, production is affected, worker's earnings get reduced; and in the process discontented, unhappy workforce is created. Under such circumstances labour-management relations are disturbed and reverse is the case when market conditions improve.

Economic conditions

If the workers are well paid and can satisfy their physiological need to the extent they desire, they feel contented and develop positive impression about the management. In such situation workers mainfest effective behavioural activities and establish better relations with boss through complementary transactions. Hence, economic health of the workers influences the pattern of IRs.

International relations

Relations with foreign countries indicate the prospect of marketing the products in the foreign market. Better relations open up avenues for marketing the goods and increase volume of sales. Besides these, the benefits of technological advancement are available. In such a condition production is increased, profit is enhanced, workers' earnings are increased. Workers develop better relations with their supervisors. So, human relations are established. But, if there is global conflict, the country may not have trade relations with the foreign country. Production is hampered as demand for goods in foreign market is reduced. Workers' earnings are affected, industrial relations are disturbed.

Psychological factor

Mindset, perception, attitudes of both workers and management determine outcome of their interaction. Conflict arises when perception level differs, attitudes vary, Mindset is dissimilar and all this disturbs the labour management relations. Better human relation develops when positive attitude prevail in all these psychological areas.

Ideological factor

Since labour-management relations arise out of interaction between labour and management the influence/guidelines of the government or governmental machineries/agencies, the ideological similarities, dissimilarities amongst workers, trade union leaders, government also affect interactive processes. So, greater the similarity in ideology the concerned parties possess, better are the industrial relations.

Economic policy

Economic policies of the government manifest its philosophy, approach towards workers, employers and affect employer-employee relations. Economic policies concerning liberalization, privatization and globalization (LPG) accept the concept of 'global village' where MNCs, TNCs have free access to carry on business/industrial activities in any country of the world. Under such situations small, weak and medium-size organizations are unable to face competition and find difficult to survive. Hence, labour-management relation is affected. Even the workers in MNCs, TNCs feel unhappy, discontented as they remain under the threat of losing their jobs.

Political Parties

Political parties influence government to formulate labour policies, to enact laws, to issue instructions, orders to industrial organizations on different aspects. They also dominate trade union people and rank and file to behave and manifest activities in a way they desire. In the process labour-management interaction is controlled by political parties and whole industrial pattern is influenced.

Conditions for Sound Industrial Relations

Sound industrial relations are essential to achieve individual goals, team goals and organizational goals. Absence of congenial labour-management relations creates an atmosphere of disharmony, labour unrest, conflict, disturbance in production activities, piling up workers' grievances, higher rate of labour absenteeism, fall in productivity and profit. This situation tends towards virtual collapse of the functional activities of the organization. Hence, healthy/congenial industrial relations are must for survival, growth, development of the people and the organization as well. For promoting sound industrial relations the following conditions are required to exist in industrial setting:

1. **Management attitudes**

   Management personnel must treat the workers as part and parcel of the organization. Better industrial relations are established when workers realize that the attitudes of the management are supportive, helping, positive, and management considers them as members of the organization.

2. **Organization Culture**

   Organization should have the culture to generate and develop enabling and proacting capability of the people at work so that number of disputes becomes less and the disputes/grievances which crop-up are settled mutually at the shortest possible time. Positive organization culture helps establish sound and healthy industrial relations of an organization.

3. **Management philosophy, approaches and style of functioning**

   Sound industrial relations are established when top management personnel are liberal, participative, facilitative, enlightened and are concerned for people and work. They practice both theory 'X' and theory 'Y' at the time of necessities. Their philosophy, style of functioning, approaches are for growth and development of the people and the organization as well.

4. **Collective bargaining, grievance procedures as methods for settlement of disputes**

   Congenial industrial relations are possible if the management people accept, encourage collective bargaining process, grievance procedure as methods for settlement of disputes and do not force/compel the workers for adjudication of the issues. In such organization it occurs that practice is already in vogue to dispose off grievances/issues through mutual discussions/negotiations. Regular structured meetings with union representatives are held at different levels to discuss and sort out the agenda issues bilaterally. Day-to-day issues which require immediate solutions are dealt with promptly and in case of need workers'/unions' suggestions are sought. It also happens that Erie Vance redressal procedure is used to find solutions for individual grievance. These sorts of organizational functioning helps in promoting industrial relations.

5. **Collabourative/cooperative organization climate**

   Existence of collabourative/cooperative climate helps develop human relations. Under such conditions both management and workers come close to each other and establish mutual understanding, mutual trust and mutual faith. So, in an organization where conducive climate exists for establishment of mutuality of relationships, it is possible to develop better industrial relations.

6. **Existence of educated, conscious and positive trade union**

   Existence of educated, conscious and positive trade unions help the management to increase production, to improve quality, to reduce labour turnover rate through making workers aware of their rights, duties, responsibilities and their role as individuals, members of the team and members of the organization; and this way they achieve organizational goals. Educated, conscious and positive leaders show their convincing, compromising activities in the collective bargaining process/negotiation as they develop an impression that they grow with the growth of the organization and they lose everything when the organization loses. They do not resort to unfair, restrictive practices and expect fair, unbiased treatment from the management. Prevalence of such condition in the organization facilitates establishment of healthy industrial relations.

7. **Initiative by top management**

   If the top management of the organization takes initiative or indulges in encouraging activities for introduction and implementation of workers' welfare/benefit schemes, these are implemented uninterruptedly. This stimulates the workers to develop positive mindset, a positive impression about top management and the organization as well. This situation helps nurture a comfortable climate to establish sound industrial relations.

8. **Attitudinal, job satisfaction survey**

   If the organization develops practice/system to study employees' needs, satisfaction, morale, aspiration, expectations, demands in a planned and continuous manner through attitudinal, job satisfaction survey and takes appropriate measures to satiate their needs, workers feel involved, contented, committed and intended to reciprocate. In such condition, workers develop sense of 'we-feeling', 'togetherness', 'being in the family' which facilitate congenial climate for the improvement of industrial relations.

9. **Fair and rational management**

   If the management is fair, rational, and gives honour to implement court order, government directions, orders, guidelines, regulations, bipartite settlements, tribunal awards, agreements, a climate of mutual trust, confidence and faith is estasblished which is one of the prerequisites for sound industrial relations.

10. **Positive, stimulating HR policies, procedures and practices**

    If positive and stimulating policies, procedures are formulated and practised in the organization in the area of wage and salary administration, human resource planning, recruitment, selection, reward management, training, career planning and development, performance appraisal, potential appraisal, counselling, quality circles, workers' involvement, TQM, QWL, welfare, social security measures, discipline management, etc., workers feel proud of being the members of the organization. This feeling indicates expression of maintaining healthy human relations and conveys the message of performing all kinds of activities for achieving goals. All this helps establish healthy industrial relations in the organization.

11. **Use of HRD mechanisms**

    If the organization introduces HRD techniques for development of skill, knowledge, abilities of workers for performing present job, future job through training and education, workers get acquainted with the operative processes, work methods, etc. and thus enrich their knowledge, upgrade skills and competence These training and education mechanisms are also applied for development of knowledge, ability and skills of supervisors that help develop trust, understanding and confidence between management and employees. All these help generate a climate for establishing better industrial relations in the organization.

Importance of Harmonious Industrial Relations

Industrial relation is the creation of an atmosphere of relationship between labour and management. Such relationship arises out of interaction between two parties. If the interaction makes fruitful outcome which pleases both labour and management, it brings harmony and peace in the industry and reverse is the case when interaction generates differences and creates a state of disagreement. Harmonious industrial relations bring prosperity while disharmonious industrial relations stand in the way to progress. Hence, harmonious industrial relations are very important for growth and development of the organization. Importance of harmonious industrial relations can be judged from the following:

Benefits to workers

Sound industrial relations may provide a lot of benefits to workers in an organization. Some important benefits to workers include:

- It makes the functioning of the industrial activities of the organization smooth and effective and keeps workers' deployment process uninterrupted/unaffected.
- It increases production and productivity as workers find congenial atmosphere at work.
- It creates a climate of cooperation where both labour and management come close, develop understanding, solve disputes and grievances mutually.
- It enhances workers' wages and allowances, provides welfare amenities, introduces reward system and satiates the need, aspiration and expectation of workers.
- It makes the employees contented, happy, committed, loyal through formulation of employee-oriented IR/HR policies, procedures and practices.
- Satisfaction of workers' physiological and psychological needs is possible as both workers and management personnel work for growth and development.
- It develops a sense of 'we-feeling' 'togetherness', 'involvement' amongst the employees which drive them to ensure perfection, completeness, accuracy in all sorts of functional activities and delivery of world class quality of products and services to customers.
- Level of job satisfaction and morale of employees is increased in a climate of harmonious industrial relations.
- Collective bargaining mechanism is accepted as a tool of settling disputes and grievances of the employees. Day to day grievances, problems are sorted through direct negotiation, discussion and also through grievance procedure machinery. All this is possible when harmonious industrial relations exist.
- In an atmosphere of sound industrial relations workers may find improvement in quality of work life (QWL), participative system in decision making, introduction of quality circles, interest of management to solve their problems, design of career planning and development, unbiased evaluation of performance and action orientation by management.

Benefits to Management

Management personnel may have ample benefits from a healthy industrial relations system. Benefits are discussed below:

- Industrial conflict becomes less/zero.
- Production and productivity tend to be on the higher side as workers participate in the organizational activities as members of the team and intend to grow with the growth of the company.
- Since workers co-operate spontaneously organization can compete with the competitors and can grow and develop.
- Customers' delightment is possible through delivery of quality goods and personalised services.
- Industrial peace prevails as mutual understanding, faith and confidence between labour and management are established and both the parties avoid conflict.
- Management can make the people dynamic through creation of changed environment and application of OD mechanism to improve/develop core areas of human resources – skill, knowledge, competences, talent, attitude, aptitudes, values, beliefs, perception, etc. Such organizational environment creates a ground for workers to accept changes to show their worth, values in a state of dynamism.
- Organization can have a reservoir of talented, committed human resources.

Benefits to Society

- Societal members are benefited if sound industrial relations prevail in industries. Benefits to society include:
- Instances of lay-off, retrenchment of workers are remote.
- No adverse behavioural activities are manifested by the employees in the society as they feel high degree of QWL.
- Production and distribution system remain uninterrupted. Supply of goods is ensured. Price is not increased, rather it shows a decline.
- Climate of lawlessness that arises out of industrial disputes viz., strike, dharna, closure, lockout does not prevail in the society.
- Societal peace prevails.

From the above discussion it is observed that harmonious industrial relations benefit workers, employers (management) and society. Hence, importance of sound industrial relations cannot be exaggerated, particularly in the present changing scenario (i.e., change in economic policies, change in technology, change in job requirement, change in markets and the like.) which needs dynamic HR and dynamic organization to face competition against MNCs, TNCs, and this is possible if a state of harmonious relations between labour and management exist.

Perspectives of Industrial Relations

Attempts have been made by industrial sociologists, psychologists, economists, industrial relations authorities and the authorities in allied disciplines to explore the genesis, origin of industrial relations and to develop a theoretical framework on solid foundation. Such authorities have made an indepth analysis in the matter and developed theoretical perspectives from different approaches. There is no single theory developed to give a concrete exposition and perfect view of industrial relations. Some of the important approaches to industrial relations are discussed in brief.

1. Sociological Approach to Industrial Relation

People work in the organizations in different cadres and capacities. Some work in managerial cadre, and some work in non-managerial cadres. They work together, interact with each other on various issues relating to work, employment, conditions of work and non-employment issues. They interact individually or in a group, and in the process they develop understanding, a relationship that tends towards establishing industrial relations.

According to industrial sociologists people at work including managers who come from different families, societies are likely to have different values, attitudes, culture, beliefs, perception, mindsets which are formed in different situations and through different processes.

It occurs that a person's values, beliefs, mindset, perceptions, attitudes are formed in his formative childhood in the family where family environment, parental level of education, values, beliefs of parents/parent substitutes, culture, family relationship, nurturing process contribute a lot to such formation.

Society, on the other hand plays an important role to influence family environment, culture, norms, etc., that affect growth and development process of individuals.

Industrialization process also affects the society and subsequently to the family and the members of the family. All this differs from person to person, family to family and society to society. So, when the people with some positive values, beliefs, culture, etc., interact on any issue with each other they may express their identical/similar views. This may help develop understanding, relationship between them resulting in healthy industrial relations. Reverse is the case when the people with divergent values, culture, beliefs, etc., interact with each other.

The industrial sociologists are of the strong opinion that industrial relations can be viewed form the sociological perspectives.

A diagrammatical presentation of such societal process activities is shown in Figure 8.3.

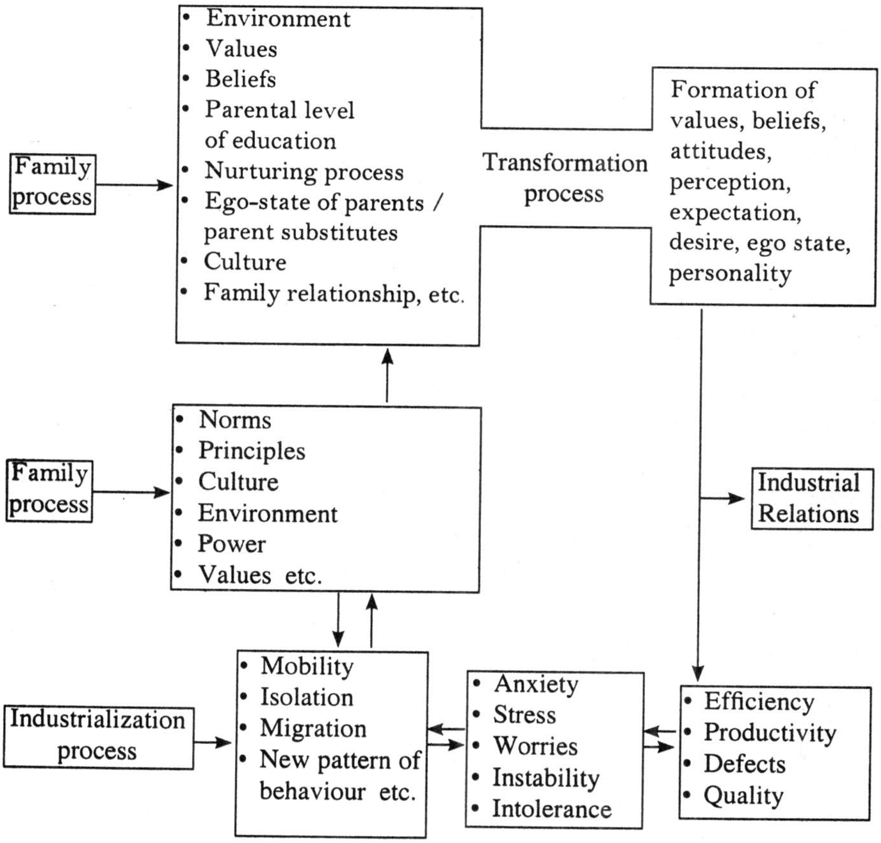

Figure 8.3: Sociological Approach to Industrial Relations

2. Human Relations Approach to Industrial Relations

There are various approaches to industrial relations. This is one of such approaches. The behavioural scientists, human relations theorists claim that industrial relations are based on human elements of the people. People are resources/assets. They are much more important than any other physical resources in the organization. They have emotions, sentiments, feelings, perceptions, needs, desires, expectations, etc. They interact with each other concerning various aspects and in the process they develop relations. Keith Davis (1967) the main proponent of this theory believes that human relations are the integration of people into a work-situation that motivates them to work together productively, cooperatively and with economic, psychological and social satisfaction. So, an important factor in all conflicts is the dissatisfied needs of the individuals. In a situation when people feel satisfied, contented, happy, they develop a sense of 'belonging', 'togetherness', 'we-feeling' and a 'feeling of accomplishment,' and in the process they promote a state of mutuality – mutual confidence, mutual trust, mutual responsibility and mutual understanding. All this helps develop healthy industrial relations. Reverse is the case when the people become unhappy, dissatisfied. Regarding the goals of human relations Keith Davis has expressed that they are to

- get people to produce
- cooperate through mutuality of interest and
- gain satisfaction from their relationship

A schematic presentation of linkages between human needs/desires, use of HR tools/instruments, outcome variables and effects is made in Figure 8.4 to indicate that sound industrial relations can be established where healthy human relations exist; and this is possible in situations where HR needs are satisfied through use of appropriate HR tools, techniques/instruments.

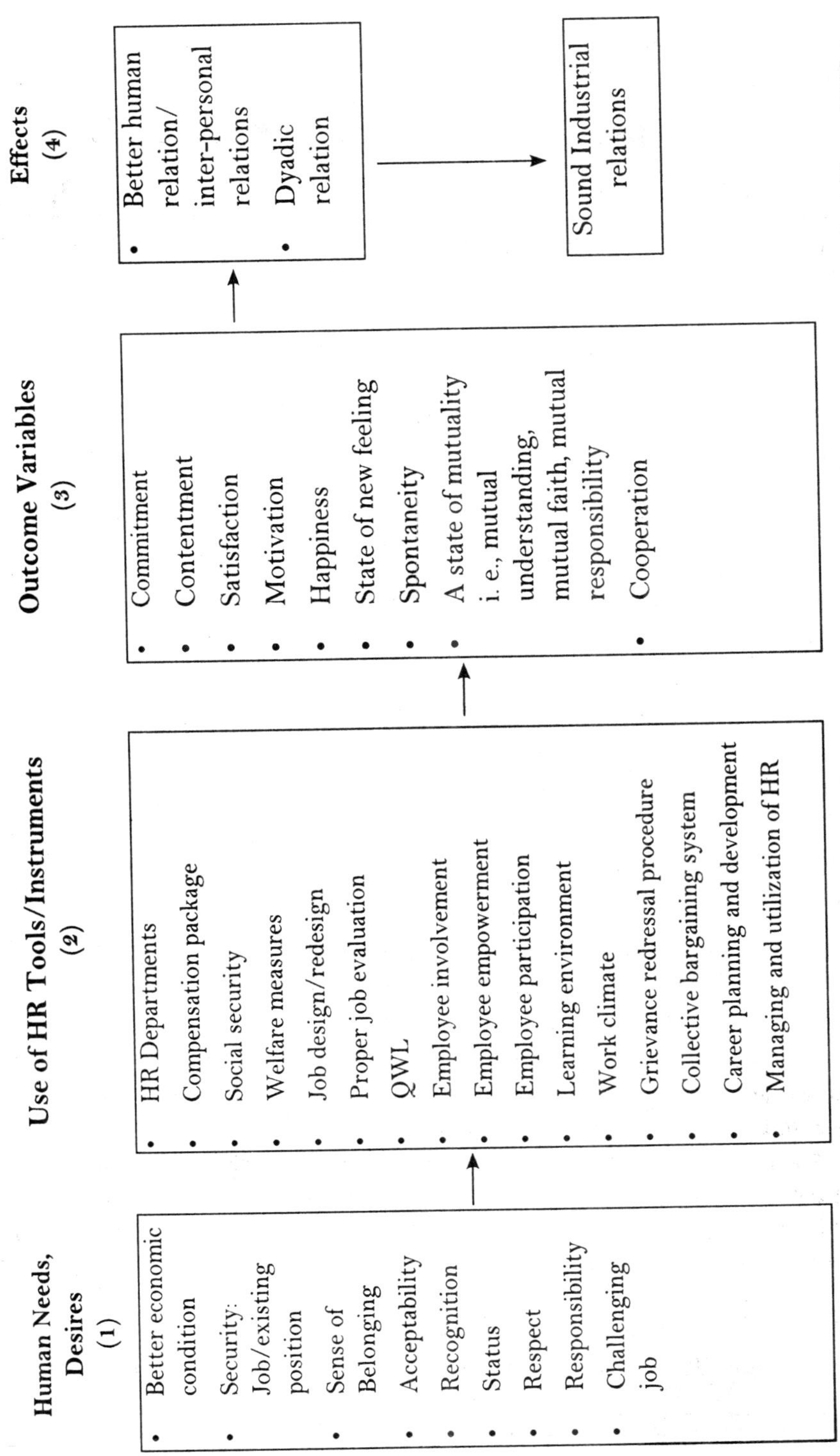

Figure 8.4 A Schematic Presentation of Linkages between Human Needs/Desires, Use of HR Tools/Instruments, Outcome Variables and Effects

3. Systems Approach to Industrial Relations (Dunlop's System Theory/Dunlop's System Model)

John T Dunlop has developed system concept to industrial relations. Dunlop analysed industrial relation system as a subsystem of society. "An industrial relations system at any one time in its development is regarded as comprised of certain actors, certain contexts, an ideology which bind the industrial relations system together and a body of rules created to govern the actors at the workplace and work community [7]".

The basic elements of the systems approach include:

i. Actors or participants in the system

Three actors/participants are

- Workers and their organizations
- Management and their representatives
- Specialized government agencies (like labour courts)

These actors/participants interact with each other within the social and economic framework

ii. Context or environment

Context or environment is the ground in which actors or participants interact. The significant aspects of environment which are relevant to industrial relations are

- Technological characteristics of the organization and the workplace
- Market or economic constraints
- Locus and the balance of power existing in the society

Technological characteristics

The organization's production, productivity, quality of production depend largely on the technology it uses. The use of sophisticated and latest technology in a production system increases production, reduces cost (in a situation where production is made on large scale), improves quality, enhances profit, increases earnings of workers. All this makes the employees happy. Reverse is the case when obsolete, primitive technology is used in the organization.

Market/Economic constraints

The market/economic constraints influence the industrial relations

7 John T Dunlop, *Industrial Relations System* (Henry Holt and Company, New York 1958)

pattern of an organization. Wider market for the product, smooth supply of fund make the production system running at a full swing. All this increases production, enhances earning, promotes standard of living of the employees.

Locus and balance of power

The locus and balance of power in a society in the form of power centres – the workers' organizations, the employers and the government influences the relationship between labour and management. It occurs that workers' organizations submit their issues/demands before the employers' association/management and to further interests both parties demonstrate their strength of power. In such case government plays an important role to regulate the situation and influences the pattern of industrial relations. Dunlop has expressed that 'a conflict emerges when the parties are less mature, are power-conscious and, therefore, aggressive. Contrarily, the conflict tends to recede from the scene when the parties become more mature, responsible and discreet in the use of power and learn to accommodate themselves with each other[8]'.

iii. Ideological linking

Ideological linking of actors influences considerably to shape the industrial relations pattern in the organizations. According to Dunlop an ideology is a set of ideas and beliefs commonly held by the actors that helps build or integrate the system together as an entity.

Output

Output is the result of interaction the actors/participants make in given contexts. The network of web of rules, country's labour policy, labour agreements, etc., are established. All this facilitates a fair deal to workers.

Dunlop's Industrial Relation's system approach is explained in Figure 8.5

IRs = f (a, c. i)

Industrial relations is the function of a, c. i when, 'a' stands for actors,

'c' stands for contexts i.e. technological context, market/budgetary constraints context, power context, and

'i' stands for ideological linkage

8 ibid

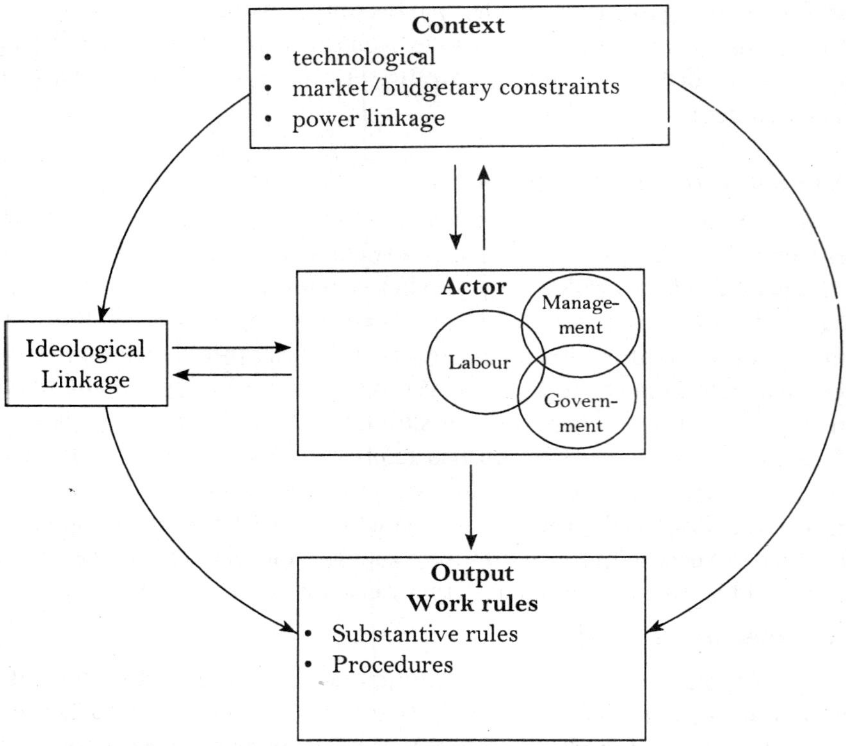

Figure 8. 5: Dunlop's System Approach to Industrial Relations

Dunlop's system approach is not without limitations.

1. Dunlop has not considered the informal relations, rules and group processes that influence industrial relations system.
2. It may happen that under some situations ideological linkage may not yield results in the process of developing sound industrial relations.
3. Some actors' charisma, personalities, acceptability may facilitate development of industrial relations; but all these have not been taken into consideration in the systems approach.
4. It is not clear from the Dunlop Model how inputs are converted into output; that means how transformation process works in the system.

4. The Trusteeship Approach of Mahatma Gandhi/the Trusteeship Theory of Mahatma Gandhi

Industrial relations can be viewed from the principles, thought process of Mahatma Gandhi. Truth, non-violence and non-possession which are the fundamental principles of Gandhiji form the base of industrial relations in an organization. Out of these principles evolved the concept of non-cooperation and trusteeship on which the philosophy of industrial relations rests. This philosophy presumes the peaceful co-existence of capital and labour, which calls for the resolution of conflict by non-violence, non-cooperation (i.e., satyagraha) which actually amounts to peaceful strike in ordinary parlance. Gandhiji accepted the workers' right to strike, but remarked that this right is to be exercised in a just cause and in a peaceful and non-violent manner and it should be resorted to only after employers fail to respond to their moral appeals[9].

With regard to trusteeship Gandhiji held the view that the individual does not have any right to hold or use wealth for his own purpose in disregard of the interest of the society. The capitalist is expected to hold industry in trust for the society and the individual workers are expected to be co-trustees with the employers. It indicates that the wealth belongs to society morally though it belongs to the owners legally. In such situation there cannot be any scope to create conflict between the capitalists and workers. However, if the capitalists do not pay minimum living wages to workers, conflicts may crop up.

The theory states that the workers should represent their case with factual data, information before the employers. If the employers do not pay heed to this, the workers should resort to non-cooperation in a non-violent way. In such a case workers need to be united (that means they should strengthen unity among themselves) and there must have awakening among them. With regard to awakening among workers Gandhiji meant developing and nurturing faith in their moral strength and their awareness of its existence. This means workers should realize the fact that without their co-operation, capitalist cannot work and when the workers resort to non-cooperation, their exploitation by capitalists would stop.

In short, Gandhiji's view in respect of redressal of grievances/ settlement of disputes leading to establishment of industrial relations is given herein below.

- The disputes should be resolved peacefully.
- The industrial disputes should be settled through mutual negotiation. The workers and the management should dispose off grievances through discussion, negotiation jointly.
- As far as possible the workers should take recourse to voluntary arbitration where efforts at direct settlement have not succeeded.

9 KG Mashruwala, *Gandhi and Marx* p 79

- After exhausting the available means of resolving differences the workers can go for strike on the following conditions:
  a. the cause of the strike must be just and based on facts, data and information,
  b. there should be no violence during strike,
  c. there should not be strike without a genuine grievance,
  d. the trade union should seek authority from all workers in respect of decision to go for strike,
  e. the workers should resort to strike in a peaceful manner,
  f. the workers should avoid strike as far as possible in essential services.

Books Recommended

1. John T Dunlop, *Industrial Relations Systems* (Henry Holt & Company, New York, 1958).
2. Keith Davis, *Human Relations at Work, The Dynamic of Organizational Behaviour* (Mumbai, Tata McGraw Hill, 1967).
3. Dale Yoder, *Personnel Management and Industrial Relations* (New York, 1948).
4. FH Harbison and R Dubin, *Patterns of Union-Management Relations* (Science Research Associates, Chicago, 1947).
5. NP Dufty, *Industrial Relations in India* (Allied Publishers, Mumbai, 1964).
6. RD Aggarwal (ed), *Dynamics of Labour Relations in India: A Book of Readings* (Tata McGraw-Hill, Mumbai, 1972).
7. P Verma, *Management of Industrial Relations* (Oxford IBH, New Delhi 1981).
8. VB Singh, *Climate for Industrial Relations: A Study of Kanpur Cotton Mills* (Allied Publishers, Mumbai, 1968).
9. CB Mamoria and S Mamoria, *Dynamics of Industrial Relations in India* (Himalaya Publishing House, New Delhi, 1995).
10. EA Ramaswamy, *Industrial Relations in India* (Macmillan, New Delhi, 1995).
11. VV Giri, *Labour Problems in Indian Industry* (Asia Publishing House, Bombay, 1960).
12. VO Jenks, *Human Relations in Organization* (Harper & Row Publishers, New York, 1990).

13. AK Ghosh, *Human Resource Management (With Cases)* (Manas Publications, Daryaganj, New Delhi, 2006)

Questions

1. Define the term 'industrial relations'. State the salient characteristics of industrial relations.
2. The term 'industrial relations' has been expressed 'as a whole field of relationship that exists because of the necessary collaboration of men and women in the employment process of an industry'. How would you justify this?
3. Do you think an organization can achieve its goals even when unhealthy industrial relations climate exists? Discuss in support of your views.
4. State and explain the objectives of industrial relations?
5. 'For promoting congenial industrial relations some conditions require to exist in industrial setting'. Discuss in this context the pre-requisites for healthy industrial relations.
6. 'Some factors influence the industrial relations of an organization'. What are these factors? Discuss.
7. Explain the importance of harmonious industrial relations.
8. 'Industrial relations situation in India has passed through various stages'. What are those stages? Discuss.
9. State and explain the different stages in industrial relations.
10. 'There are two significant aspects of Industrial relations'. Explain those aspects.
11. Explain in brief the actors who are the participants in industrial relations.
12. State the approaches to industrial relations and explain any one of them.
13. Explain in brief
    a. Sociological approach to industrial relations
    b. Significant aspects of industrial relations
14. Can any single Model/Theory give a perfect view of industrial relations? Explain. Also discuss how does Dunlopian Theory work in Indian industrial relations system?
15. 'Advance in technology influences industrial relations patterns of an industry? How can you justify this statement? Also state other factors that influence industrial relations.

16 a. As an IR specialist of a company how would you explain industrial relations?

b. Do you think government machineries can play any role to shape industrial relations pattern of an industry? If so, how?

17 a. How does an industrial relations system affect functioning of organizational activities? Discuss.

b. Do you feel that promoting sound industrial relations in an organization is a necessity? If so, why?

Case Study

Mr SP Bhatia is an executive of a big organization. He is an Area Manager of the North Eastern States and posted in Guwahati. He is a biased personality. He does not like people. He is not acceptable to the people at work. People do not pay him respect. He is afraid of Mr PK Chatterjee who happened to be union leader, now head of one department working under him.

Mr Chatterjee is also a biased person. His acceptability by his colleagues is not worth mentioning. He is vindictive like Mr Bhatia. Both personalities are the same as regards to their activities, role character, ego pattern and behavioural manifestations.

Mr Bhatia discusses problems with Mr Chatterjee pertaining to other departments and seeks suggestions from him in presence of the head of the concerned department. It also happens that Mr Bhatia sometimes gives importance on those issues of other departments raised by Mr Chatterjee with an intention to apparently strengthen understanding with him.

One day Mr Bhatia expressed his feeling to Mr SP Gupta head of HRM Department, in the matter of interference of Mr Chatterjee on the issues and problems pertaining to his department. Mr Bhatia emphasized that Mr Chatterjee's entry to the HRM Department should be minimized and no information which is confidential in nature would be supplied to him, if requested.

Mr Bhatia elaborated the dubious character of Mr Chatterjee and advised Mr Gupta to refrain from discussing or seeking suggestions on any matter relating to his department. Mr Gupta got surprised and tried to find out the real cause of such behaviours as he observed that his boss, Mr Bhatia would give much more importance on Mr Chatterjee and on vital aspects including those of confidential in nature the boss would discuss with him.

The conversations between Mr Gupta and the boss Mr Bhatia which took place on that day are given hereunder:

Mr Bhatia : Mr Gupta, does Mr Chatterjee come to your department frequently?

Mr Gupta : Not frequently, Sir. Occasionally, and that too on urgent work.

Mr Bhatia : How is the important and confidential information divulged? Mr Chatterjee gets all information and supplies to the right person/s before our official communication reaches.

Mr Gupta : Sir, 1 confirm that no information is leaked through our department staff.

Mr Bhatia : I have information that staff members of your department have established a good rapport and understanding with Mr Chatterjee. Is it true?

Mr Gupta : Sir, it is quite usual that staff members build up good human relations and understanding amongst all the staff members of the office. But, in no way does this relation affect department secrecy and privacy. Sir, I have a small appeal to you.

Mr Bhatia : Yes, Mr Gupta, come on, tell me.

Mr Gupta : Sir, you attach undue importance on Mr Chatterjee. In my presence you ask suggestions from him on vital and confidential issues pertaining to our department and you act upon his suggestions.

Mr Bhatia : Mr Gupta, it is not that. I do not want his intervention on matters not related with his department.

Mr Gupta : It is fine. Sir, then why do you discuss with Mr Chatterjee those issues pertaining to our department?

Mr Bhatia : I discuss those with him just to study his mindset on the matter and sometime I also consider his suggestions to appease his sentiment. You know, all these are outward shows. I make him understand that he is an important person which he is not and I take decision on vital issues after consultation with him.

Mr Gupta : That's right. I assure you sir, no information pertaining to our department be given to Mr Chatteriee without your permission.

Read the above case thoroughly and answer the following questions:

i) What sort of relationship between Area Manager and other officers exists in the organisation? If such relationship continues what will happen in future?

ii) Under the situation as revealed from the above case how will Mr Gupta deal with the problems as pointed out by Mr Bhatia?

iii) If you were HR Manager of that factory what would be your suggestions to promote healthy human relations vis-à-vis sound industrial relations?

iv) Point the strengths and weaknesses of Mr Bhatia.

IX

Industrial Disputes

Industrial Conflicts - Concept

In narrow sense industrial conflict means conflict between parties in industrial establishments. Dictionary meaning of 'conflict' is 'disagreement', 'mutual antagonism as of ideas, interests etc.'. So, industrial conflict is disagreement/mutual antagonism as of ideas, interests, etc., between parties in industry. In industrial setting, parties are invariably workers and management. In the process of working, workers express their need, expectation, desire for fulfilment and satisfaction. They want more money, i.e., attractive wages, allowances, monetary incentive which the management may not agree to pay. Workers demand better fringe benefits, health benefits but management may provide less than their requirement. They want recognition, status, power, advancement, higher quality of work life but management may be reluctant to provide. Under such situation a state of disagreement/mutual antagonism between workers and management develops which gives birth to industrial conflict. So, industrial conflict is a general concept and this conflict gets the shape of industrial dispute in a specific dimensional situation. Basically, there is no difference between 'industrial conflict' and 'industrial dispute', variation lies only in scope and coverage.

According to section 2(k) of Industrial Disputes Act 1947, 'industrial dispute' means any dispute or difference between employers and employers or between employers and workmen, or between workmen and workmen, which is connected with the employment or non-employment or the terms of employment or with the conditions of labour, of any person.

Analysis of the provision of the Act reveals the following:

- Industrial dispute is a dispute or difference
  i. between employers and employers, or
  ii. between employers and workmen, or
  iii. between workmen and workmen
- Industrial dispute is connected with
  i. employment, or
  ii. non-employment, or
  iii. terms of employment, or
  iv. conditions of labour of any person

However, under Section 2A of the Industrial Disputes Act 1947 (by an amendment in 1965) a dispute between an employer and individual workman is also an industrial dispute if it relates to discharge, dismissal, retrenchment or termination of a worker's services.

Some of the issues which are held by different courts as industrial disputes are mentioned below:

- Re-instatement of a dismissed workman [Western India Automobile Association vs Industrial Tribunal, M'bai, AIR (1949) FC iii]
- Employer's failure to reply to a letter of demand sent by the workmen [Triangular Motors Ltd.; M'bai vs Their workmen, (1949) LLJ 79]
- Profit bonus [FW Heiglers & Co Ltd vs NC Chakravarty, AIR (1949) FC 142]
- Rejecting a polite request of the employees by an employer [Sree Minakshi Mills vs State of Madras, AIR (1954) Mad. 143]
- Declaration of lockout by an employer and workers' entitlement to wages or compensation for the lock out period [Shamnugger Jute Factory Co Ltd vs SM Modak, AIR (1949) FC 150]
- Dispute in respect of two workmen's designation espoused by the Delhi Union of Journalists having 25% of the working journalists of the newspapers establishment as members [Workmen of Indian Express Newspapers (Pvt) Ltd vs Indian Express (Pvt) Ltd (1970) 2 LLJ 132]

Forms of Industrial Conflicts/Disputes

Industrial conflict may take different forms starting from the phase of showing protest, demonstration, deputation during recess period to the culminating phase of cessation of work, gherao, etc. These forms of industrial conflicts/disputes are the reflection/manifestation of group/ concerted action of the employees. Employers use lockout weapon as a form of industrial dispute when magnitude of the conflict is very serious.

Sometimes the workers go for strike to express their sympathy, moral support that strengthens the solidarity of the working class. In such case workers do not have any grievance against their employer. It also happens that workers cease to work for political cause or for a common cause involving entire working community. From these perspective the strike may have some other forms like sympathetic strike, political strike and general strike.

The different phases of workers' activities for redressal of their grievances/ settlement of industrial disputes are shown in Fig. 9.1. It may happen that workers in some organizations do not follow the forms of disputes/phases of activities in seriatim, they may resort to some form of dispute superseding other. It depends on the type of leadership, nature of dispute, issues involved, management attitude, environmental situations, etc.

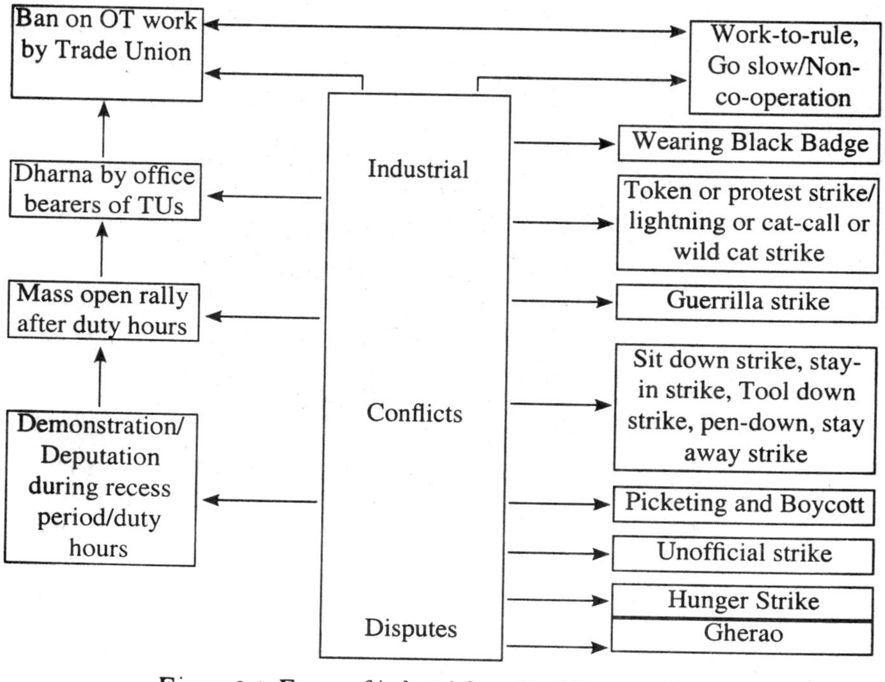

Figure 9.1: Forms of industrial conflict/disputes: Phases of workers' activities for redressal of disputes

Different forms of industrial conflicts are briefly discussed herein below:

i. Demonstration/Deputation during recess period/duty hours

Workers or some executive members of trade union show their unhappiness over some issues which remain unsettled or are disposed off irrationally, whimsically through demonstration, deputation during recess period before head of the department or head of the personnel/human resource management department, factory manager or demonstrate in front of their chambers/office. Such workers may give deputation, demonstration during recess period or working period. Initially, in most cases they carry on such activities during recess period.

ii. Mass open rally during holiday/after office/factory hours

Workers participate in the open rally during holidays or after factory/office hours where next course of agitational programme is decided. This rally is arranged and conducted by trade union to appraise extent of workers' support and consent for the next phase of agitational programme as also to send message to the management about their solidarity and action programmes decided by them.

iii. Dharna by office bearers of trade union

Workers who are office bearers of trade union stage dharna in front of the main entrance of the executive's/chamber or in the main gate of the factory/office to protest for immediate settlement of their issues. In some cases during dharna some workers manifest their emotional feeling and use abusive, filthy languages against executive/s while shouting.

iv. Ban on overtime work (OT) by trade union

It is decided by trade union to which workers belong that workers will not perform overtime work if they are directed by the management to do so. When the workers find that excessive/accumulated work requires overtime work for immediate clearance, they resort to such action to express their reluctance/unwillingness to work beyond scheduled hours. The intention is very clear. Workers create pressure on management to clear the pending order of goods/pending job in order to deliver goods and services to customers.

v. Work-to-rule

Work-to-rule is resorted to by the workers when the management does not pay heed to their problems/issues. Workers perform their work strictly as per rule. They keep the job incomplete and pile up till their demands are settled. In some industries like banking, life insurance companies, post and telegraph and others the nature of some work and the rules prescribed to perform the work are such that lead to slowing down the speed of performance if the rules are followed strictly. In such case workers use this weapon to ventilate their grievances.

The intention of the workers is to exert upon the management to agree to their demands and to solve the issues. Work-to-rule is a misconduct as per Standing Orders/Bipartite Settlement of the company.

vi. Go-slow

Go-slow is a device used by the workers to slow down their rate of production/service with the intention to make the management agree to solve their problems/issues. This is a concerted action of the workers to give less production/service than scheduled/usually performed. Apparently, this is not a strike, but in reality this is more than a strike as this keeps the production and all sorts of activities running for which company bears establishment and running expenses but produce much less than targeted/scheduled. Such sort of agitational programme is resorted to by workers in factories, offices during the period when workers' smooth and speedy functioning is a necessity to complete the process activities, for example, in sugar factories during crushing period, in docks during the period when the work pressure is heavy for unloading goods from ships.

Go-slow is a misconduct under Bipartite Settlement/Standing Orders of the company and punishment is imposed on the delinquent worker in terms of company rules.

vii. Non-cooperation

Non-cooperation is a tool adopted by the workers to protest against management decision. They want immediate settlement/disposal off their issues and for redressal, they start non-cooperation with the management by not agreeing to their request for doing overtime work, or other specific job beyond stipulation of their job role, by slowing down performance, by doing work strictly as per rules.

viii. Wearing black badge

This step is taken by the workers to condemn management decision/ activities and exert upon management to settle/dispose off their issues immediately. Workers wear black badge to convey message to the management about their solidarity and unity over the issues.

ix. Strike

Strike is one of the forms of industrial disputes. Employees resort to strike to get their demands settled by the management. Strike is a cessation of work by the employees. According to **section 2(q)** of the

Industrial Disputes Act, 1947 strike means:

i. a cessation of work by a body of persons employed in an industry acting in combination or,

ii. a concerted refusal of any number of persons who are or have been so employed in any industry to continue to work or to accept employment, or

iii. a refusal under common understanding of any number of such persons to continue to work or to accept employment.

So, the important characteristics of strike include

(a) It is a cessation of work by a group of persons.

(b) It is a concerted refusal to continue to work or to accept employment.

(c) It is a refusal under a common understanding to continue to work or to accept employment.

Strike has different forms. The important/commonly used forms of strike are discussed here.

a. Token/Protest Strike

Token strike is a short duration strike and has all the characteristics of strike. Through token strike workers convey the message to the management to ventilate grievances/settle issues immediately. This token strike is first stage for indefinite strike/long duration strike. It is also called protest strike.

b. Lightning Strike or Cat Call Strike

Lightning strike is one form of strike. It is like a lightning in the sky which appears all of a sudden without giving any intimation or giving some indication to occur immediately before its appearance and disappears quickly. This form of strike is of short duration. It happens that sometime some workers resort to such strike due to provocative action taken by the management. Such workers without intimation or with short intimation to management cease work for a short period of time. It contains all the characteristics of strike. This strike is also called cat-call strike or wild cat strike.

c. Guerrilla Strike

It is that form of strike which comes suddenly without warning/ communication. It may last for a few hours, a day, or an indefinite period. It has all the characteristics of strike. The difference between lightning strike and guerrilla strike is in the matter of communication. In case of guerrilla strike no indication/communication is given for resorting to strike but in case of lightning strike a short notice may be given.

d. Sit Down Strike

Sit down strike is a form of strike. In such form of strike all the characteristics of strike as mentioned in section 2(q) of Industrial Disputes Act, 1947 are present. Workers resorting to such form of strike sit down in the work place, they do not work and do not allow others to enter into the premises for work. Executives are also not allowed to come inside the workplace. In such form of strike an element of trespass upon the property of the employer is involved. Strikers remain in the factory till settlement of their issues/demands is made.

e. Stay Away Strike

Stay away strike is a form of strike when workers do not enter into premises but cease work and protest against the management through organizing/participating rally, demonstration.

f. Pen-down Strike

This is one form of strike that contains all the characteristics of a strike under section 2(q) of the Industrial Disputes Act 1947. Under such strike employees working in offices remain present in offices, down their pens and refrain from doing work.

g. Tools-down Strike

Tools-down strike is one kind of strike. Under such form of strike workers remain present at the workplace at prescribed time, down their tools and refrain from doing work.

h. Picketing

Picketing is a form of strike, which is used by workers during industrial conflict situation. Some workers remain posted in front of the premises of the employer and request others not to enter into the work place for work. Some workers march and patrol the area with banners/placards mentioning their demands, reasons for going for strike, employer's attitude and inaction, etc. Picketing is 'watching and dissuading those who go to work, during a strike'[1]. The main objective of picketing is to draw attention of the public about the grievances of the workers and to obtain public support/sympathy and also to urge upon the management to accede to their demands. Picketing may be peaceful or violent. When the striking employees posted at the gate of the factory/office persuade the non-strikers not to enter the premises but to join the strike such sort of picketing is said to be peaceful. But, it happens sometime that striking employees use physical force, create obstruction, prevent non strikers from entering the premise. This sort of picketing can no longer remain to be peaceful and may take the form of violence.

---

1 BEST Undertaking, Bombay vs Mushaffe Ahmed Khalil, 1961 ICR 845 IC Maharashtra

i. Boycott

Boycott is a form of industrial conflict. It aims at dysfunctioning of industrial activities by withdrawing cooperation. Trade unions use this weapon against the management for settlement of disputes. The process may start from non-cooperation activities but it may culminate with refusal to work.

j. Unofficial Strike

This is a form of strike resorted to by some workers in the organization without approval of their trade union leaders. The decision to cease work is taken by striking workers themselves. In such a situation workers have no confidence on their leaders and also on the management personnel. It occurs that workers resort to such form of strike when procedure for grievance settling is exhausted.

k. Hunger Strike

This is a manifestation process for showing anger, unhappiness, displeasure by the workers on remaining on fast during duty hours/ beyond stipulated hours of work in front of management chamber/ premises or main entrance of the premises. Workers resort to such strike weapon in batches or sometime it happens that only trade union leaders go for hunger strike. The main objective is to put pressure on management to come to their terms by means of creating public sympathy/support. This measure is adopted by the workers in very serious situation when some workers are at peril or may be, that their genuine demands remain unsolved/unsettled for a long period.

Hunger strike is strike within the definition of strike under section 2(q) of the Industrial Disputes Act. In Katkona Colliery Western Coal fields Ltd vs Central Government Industrial Tribunal (CGIT) cum Labour Court, the Hon'ble High Court of Madhya Pradesh held that if hunger strike is not simply refraining from taking food but is also accompanied by cessation of work by a body of persons employed in any industry the same would obviously come within the definition of strike.

l. Gherao

Workers use this technique in extreme situation when they feel to achieve their gain through keeping the management personnel in a state of physical discomfort, inconvenience and hardship for some period, maybe for some hours, days. Gherao is an encirclement/confinement of management by some workers for settlement of disputes/grievances. In most cases blockade is created by 'gherao makers' so that nobody can have an access to the place of gherao or can move from the 'gherao-place'. Gherao is illegal and is a grave/serious misconduct Under Sections 339 and 340 of Indian Penel Code wrongfully restraining any person or wrongfully confining him during a gherao by the workmen is a cognizable offence for which they would be liable to be arrested without warrant and punishable with imprisonment or with fine or with both. The National Commission on Labour deprecated the technique of gherao instrument of coercion and expressed that if such means are to be adopted by labour for realization of its claims, trade unions may come into disrepute. It is the duty of all trade union leaders, therefore, to condemn this form of labour protest as harmful to the interest of the working class itself.

m. Lockout

Lockout is one of the forms of industrial conflict. Employer uses this device when production suffers due to industrial unrest, workers' agitation, strike, go-slow, work to rule, etc. Employer keeps the industrial activities suspended for some period and so, closes temporarily the place of employment. Section 2(1) of the Industrial Disputes Act 1947 defines lockout as the 'temporary closing of a place of employment, or the suspension of work, or the refusal by an employer to continue to employ any number of persons employed by him'. So,

- A lockout is a temporary closing of an industrial undertaking
- It is the suspension of work
- It is the refusal by an employer to continue to employ people employed by him
- It is used by employer to coerce, force workmen to agree to his terms.

Causes of Industrial Disputes/Conflicts

Industrial dispute is a dispute or difference between employer and workers. Such dispute arises when workers want to satisfy their physiological and psychological needs and management fails to satiate such needs. In other words, workers want more wages, allowances, incentive, better housing accommodation, medical benefits, transport facilities, canteen facilities, good working conditions, better welfare amenities, fringe benefits, social security measures, challenging job, authority, responsibilities, promotion, status, recognition, good treatment, etc. But management fails or shows unwillingness to meet their requirements. In such a situation, interactions between management and workers create difference/dispute between them which, in turn, takes the shape of industrial dispute.

Pocket Book of Labour Statistics indicates the following factors responsible for work stoppages:

i. Wages and allowances
ii. Indiscipline
iii. Personnel
iv. Charter of demands
v. Standing Orders/Rules/Service Conditions/Safety measures
vi. Bonus
vii. Non-implementation of agreements
viii. Better amenities
ix. Leave, hours of work and shift
x. Inter/intra union rivalry
xi. Retrenchment and lay off
xii. Violence
xiii. Work load
xiv. Suspension/change of manufacturing process
xv. Other factors

To give a clear idea in the matter the industrial disputes by causes are shown in table 9.1

Table 9. 1 Percentage Distribution of the factors leading to industrial disputes

Year	Factors Leading to Industrial dispute					
	Wages and allowance	**Bonus**	**Personnel (Dismissal, retrenchment etc)**	**Leave and hours of work**	**Indiscipline & violence**	**Other**
1921	42. 2	18. 9	17. 2	2. 7	-	18. 9
1935	62. 8	1. 4	14. 5	6. 8	-	14. 5
1939	57. 1	0. 6	18. 2	2. 9	-	21. 2
1961	30. 4	6. 9	29. 3	3. 0	-	30. 4
1970	37. 1	10. 6	25. 6	2. 1	3. 8	20. 8
1980	28. 4	7. 3	24. 3	2. 2	8. 9	28. 9
1991	24. 5	4. 0	17. 4	1. 0	18. 8	34. 3
1995	30. 9	7. 6	19. 8	2. 0	15. 3	24. 4
1999	21. 9	9. 0	14. 9	1. 0	21. 9	31. 3

Source: Government of India, Ministry of Labour. Various issues of India Labour Year Bank, Pocket Book of Labour Statistics.

'Other factors' as mentioned in this table inter alia include charter of demands, standing orders/rules/service conditions/safety measures, non-implementation of labour awards and agreements, inter/intra-union rivalry. The causes of industrial disputes are shown in six categories. They are:

- Wages and allowance
- Bonus
- Personnel (dismissal retrenchment, etc.)
- Leave and hours of work
- Indiscipline and violence
- Other.

Industrial Disputes Act 1947 prescribes the causes of industrial disputes. In terms of section 2(k) of the Act causes of industrial disputes are:

i. Employment causes
ii. Non-employment causes
iii. Terms of employment causes
iv. Causes concerning conditions of labour of any person.

From the survey conducted by the author in the sampled collieries in West Bengal during 1970-72 it is revealed that the following factors contribute to the causes of strike as expressed/opined by the workers, union leaders and management personnel of those sampled collieries:

i. Economic factor
ii. Employment conditions
iii. Promotion
iv. Working condition
v. Welfare measures
vi. Living condition
vii. Unionism
viii. Management/supervisor's attitude
ix. Social Security
x. Others viz., political causes, individual interest, instigation by management.

The survey conducted by the author indicates that the following factors contribute to the causes of lockouts in sampled collieries of West Bengal

i. Counter measure

ii. Union attitude

iii. Management attitude

iv. Contingent factor

v. Economic factor

vi. Others viz., conflict between partners, investment of capital from one venture to other, employers' arbitrary decision to close down mines, etc.

VB Singh (1968) mentioned the following as causes of industrial dispute:

a) Income that includes wages, time and piece rate, dearness allowance, bonus, minimum and basic wages, provident fund, gratuity, pension, pay for night, overtime work, etc.
b) Employment that includes items like holidays and leave, shift duty, hours of work, welfare activities, recruitment, dismissals, retirement, permanency, reinstatement, lay off, lockouts, strike, standing orders and others
c) Technological changes. Under this, factors relating to workload, rationalization of schemes, modernization of plants and others are included.

In the present changing scenario tough competition for survival, growth and development amongst indigenous companies and MNCs/ TNCs is evident in the market. Hence, expectations, demands, needs, requirements of workers, trade unions and management change considerably.

Now, the factors that contribute to the causes of industrial disputes/ conflicts are discussed below in short:

1. Economic Factor

Economic factors affect largely in creating disputes/differences between labour and management in the organization. The issues which are directly involved in compensation, investment required to provide welfare, social security and any benefits/services to employees are covered under such factor/group. Some of the important economic factors that generally cause industrial disputes are:

i. wages and allowances (higher wages and allowances to meet up physiological needs)

ii. Monetary rewards, incentives

iii. Welfare benefits (both statutory and non-statutory) like subsidized canteen facilities, creches, drinking water, house accommodation, transport facilities, supply of articles through co-operative societies at a reasonable price, medical benefits, hospitalization facilities

iv. Bonus, gratuity, retrial benefits, additional retirement benefits

v. Fringe benefits e.g., leave encashment, leave travel concession, paid holidays, education allowance, canteen allowance, customary benefits

vi. Working facilities, improvement of working conditions

vii. Introduction of new machine, computers, technology

2. Factors Relating to Management Activities, Practices

Management attitudes, treatment, behaviour style of functioning, approaches thought process, various management practices cause industrial dispute/conflicts. They are:

i. Unfair labour practices

ii. Management's reluctance to deal with labour problems, casual approach of the management to solve disputes

iii. Ill treatment, ill-behaviour of the supervisor/management, strained dyadic relation between boss and subordinates

iv. Autocratic management style, treating workers as commodities

v. Whimsical and arbitrary decision in respect of promotion, sanctioning special increment, nomination for training, posting

vi. Stubborn attitudes of management regarding recruitment, transfer, promotion and their insistence on handling those issues by themselves ignoring trade union to play any role

vii. Non-implementation of award, settlements, court orders

viii. Non-disposal of grievances, pending issues

3. Factors relating to trade union activities, practices

Trade unions' attitudes, behaviour practices in organization cause industrial disputes and disturb smooth and effective functioning of organizational activities. The main issues under this category are

i. Inter-union, intra-union rivalry

ii. Unfair practices of union

iii. Violent attitudes, physical assault, resorting to agitational programmes to disrupt organizational activities

iv. Adopting non-cooperative approach

v. Formation of trade unions, non-recognition of trade unions, multiple unions
vi. Membership verification
vii. Check off
viii. Collective bargaining

4. Factors Relating to Maintenance of Discipline

It happens that management takes disciplinary action against delinquent employees for maintenance and promoting discipline in the organization. The workers/trade union leaders go against management action and disturb the organizational activities. Some of the issues that cause industrial disputes are mentioned herein below:

i. Issuance of show cause notice, chargesheet, suspension order
ii. Orders of punishment
iii. Discharge, dismissal, discharge simpliciter
iv. Issuance of warning letter, caution letter
v. Indiscipline, violence
vi. Rules of discipline
vii. Retrenchment, lay-off of workmen

5. Legal Factors

Government is one of the actors in establishing industrial relations in organizations. Government discharges its functions through enactment of labour laws and by helping organizations to function effectively through setting of various machineries. But, disputes arise on some grounds under legal factors. Some of such causes of industrial disputes are given below

i. Multiple labour laws
ii. Ineffective labour laws because of their improper, inadequate implementation
iii. Loss of relevance in labour laws which have been enacted long back, in the context of changing scenario
iv Difficulties in monitoring the various activities/working of labour laws by the employers
v. Accumulation of labour issues in conciliation
vi. Ineffectiveness of conciliation officers to dispose off disputes referred to them

6. Other factors

Sometimes Industrial disputes occur because of other reasons. They are

i. Political interference. Different political parties create disputes to exhibit their political strength through their affiliated trade unions in organizations.

ii. Mushroom growth of political parties and intervention in organizational activities functioning through their trade unions.

iii. Economic policy of the country governing industrial activities viz., policies on liberalization, privatization and globalization (LPG)

iv. Price hike of essential commodities making the workers conscious for appropriate price for labour.

v. Political instability, centre-state relationship affecting industrial activities that result in industrial disputes.

From the above it becomes clear that various factors are responsible for occurrence of industrial dispute. The analysis of data given in table 9.1 gives the idea that most common factors that lead to industrial disputes in our country are economic factors. But, the most alarming fact the table depicts is indiscipline activities of the workers for which management has to take disciplinary action against them. If such situation continues, it will generate a state of mistrust, misunderstanding, 'no confidence', 'no faith' amongst the labour and management that will make the industrial relations unhealthy and unsound. All this will arrest the growth of industry and the country's economy as well.

Impacts/Effects of Industrial Disputes

Industrial disputes manifest in the form of strike, lockout gherao, go-slow and in other forms that disturb the production and other activities of the organization. If the disputes continue for a long period whole organization activities get paralyzed. This affects, to a great extent, the employees, employer, society and the country as well. It also happens very much in basic industries. The stoppage of production activities of such industries makes a terrible impact on the people of all quarters of the society viz., employees, employers, customers and the stakeholders of the organizations. The effect of industrial disputes in basic industries is like the effect caused to form ever widening waves when a big stone is thrown into a pond, till they touch the entire pond.

The impact of industrial dispute is far reaching. It is not that the disputes affect the workers only. The employers, the society and the country as a whole are affected due to industrial disputes. The effects of disputes are discussed in short.

Effects of Industrial Disputes on Workers

Industrial disputes make a lot of impact on the workers. The workers suffer heavily due to industrial disputes.

1. Loss of earning

Industrial disputes affect production, productivity resulting in less earning or no earning for workers. In such a situation workers find it difficult to maintain their families.

2. Standard of living

In a situation where workers cannot earn or earn less due to industrial dispute, they become compelled to lower their style of maintaining families, standard of living. It also happens in some cases when workers have to stop children's education or to change the school where children are studying for lowering the expenses to be incurred for continuing with education.

3. Disturbance in family peace

Understanding between family members gets disturbed particularly when the workers cannot earn money to maintain livelihood, to afford expenses needed to meet social rituals/activities and other daily necessities of the families.

4. Generating a state of anxiety, worries and mental agony

If the situation emerged due to industrial disputes continues for a long period some workers may have to face a state of terrible hardship, suffering which they may find very difficult. All this generates a state of anxiety, worries and mental agony.

5. Job insecurity

Prolongation of industrial disputes may compel the employers/ owners of industrial establishments to close down establishments or to retrench or terminate the services of some workers. This makes some workers lose their jobs. So, the workers suffer from a feeling of insecurity, uncertainty of job that may further weaken their mental strength to carry on with a normal life.

6. Losing public sympathy

In situation when strike continues for a long period and the general public feels that the strike is unwarranted and there is no genuine ground for strikes, the striking employees lose public sympathy.

7. Affecting social status, recognition

The pecuniary strength of workers is adversely affected when they do not earn due to industrial disputes. It occurs that after some period of time when the workers do not have any savings to afford family needs/expenses, they may be required to borrow money, take loans from the relatives, friends and other people in the society by mortgaging ornaments, properties, etc. All this affects the social status, recognition and image in the society that demoralizes them.

8. Incidence of kidnapping

A fierce and unhealthy situation may crop up in industrial settings when the kids and close/near relatives of activist workers, trade union leaders are kidnapped by social miscreants, vested people who may be involved in industrial disputes.

9. Worsening dyadic relationship

A strained relationship between labour and management is created during the period of strike, lockout even after the settlement of industrial dispute the chance of restoring normalcy may not be bright. This may affect the dyadic relationship that results in uncomfortable, uncongenial and unconducive atmosphere in the work place.

10. Slackness in application of HRD tools

Very few employers/owners may go for developing and promoting competence of human resources through introducing HRD techniques in organizations when their establishment activities remain disturbed/affected due to industrial disputes. So, a casual approach to employee development by employers through HRD tools may be observed.

Effects of Industrial Disputes on Employers

Industrial disputes affect employers to a great extent. Impact of industrial disputes on employers can be ascertained from the following:

1. Loss of production

The industrial establishments suffer from loss of production when the workers go for strike. There may be no production if complete strike occurs, and less production if there is partial strike.

2. Loss of profit

The industrial dispute may affect profit and profitability of the organization. Due to strike the whole sphere of organizational activities is disturbed resulting in situations like no production, less production, no turnover, less turnover, no profit, less profit.

3. Image of the organization

In a situation when company's production and other activities are disturbed due to strike or other forms of industrial dispute, the company cannot be able to deliver its products to the customers on the scheduled date as agreed upon earlier. This may affect maintaining and promoting mutual relationship established between management and the valued clients through business transactions made for a long period. Frequent occurrence of industrial disputes tarnishes the image of the organization before the customers and the people in the society.

4. Customers' delight

Today, customers' delight is one of the effective means used by most of the organization to make a place in the competitive market; and this the companies make it possible through delivery of the quality goods and services at a comparatively lesser price and at the time the customers need them. But, in a situation when the companies' activities remain disturbed due to industrial disputes, it become difficult for the organizations to provide such services to the customers.

5. Industrial peace and harmony

Industrial disputes generate a climate of mistrust, misunderstanding amongst the workers and management that affects peace and harmony in industry. There is no denying the fact that industrial growth and people development which are interrelated and interwoven to each other, cannot be made in a situation when industrial disharmony and labour unrest prevails in the industry.

6. Forced expenses

The organizations are forced to incur expenses toward safety and security of the men, machines and properties of the organization during the period of strike. The companies may also be required to spend money towards cost of advertisement to make the society people aware of the whole incidence/situation of strikes.

7. Competitive advantage

Every company wants to survive, grow, develop and make a place in the competitive market. So, it needs to confront challenges against competitors. But, it becomes very difficult for the organizations to face challenges and obtain competitive advantages in a situation when production and delivery of the products are stopped due to industrial disputes. For obtaining competitive advantage the companies must ensure that there is no interruption in organizational activities, and quality products and services are rendered smoothly to the satisfaction of customers.

8. Industrial relations

Industrial disputes disturb the workings of the organizations and affect production, distribution and profit of the companies. In such situation a strained relationship between labour and management prevails in the organizations. All this makes the climate of industrial relations unsound and unhealthy in the organizations.

9. Retention Problem

Companies may face a problem of retention of their competent and effective employees. It occurs that industrial disputes make the organization's environment unhealthy, unconducive and uncomfortable for work. In such situation competent and effective employees do not intend to continue with the organizations. They search for alternative employment and quit their present jobs when they get them.

Effects of Industrial Dispute on Society

Industrial disputes make an impact on the people of the society. The effects of industrial disputes on society can be ascertained from the following:

1. Non-availability of products

Industrial production suffers to a great extent due to industrial disputes resulting in shortage of supply of products in the market. That means, smooth supply of products is disturbed. In this situation, societal people may not get products according to their need/demands.

2. Price of products

Since the goods are not easily available in the market according to the demands of the people, in some cases dishonest businessmen charge higher price for the products. So, due to industrial disputes societal people need to pay higher price for the products.

3. Employment crisis

Industrial disputes that continue for a long period may create a situation when the employees lose their jobs. This situation in fact adds to the unemployment problems of the country which already exists in greater magnitude. All this affects the environment of the society.

4. Law and order problem

If the employees remain without work for a long period due to industrial dispute, they may not be able to maintain their families in honest and proper way. In such case they may be required to earn money in some other way which may invite law and order problems. This may disturb the peace and harmony of the society.

5. Social evil

In a situation when industrial disputes exist for a long period workers get frustrated, demoralized and develop a state of mental agony, anxiety, worries. All this makes them addict to social vices/evils which affect congenial climate of the society.

Effects of Industrial Dispute on National Economy

Industrial dispute affect the country's economy. The effects of industrial disputes are mentioned below.

1. National income

Industrial disputes affect the earning/revenue of the country. In a situation when the production activities are affected because of industrial disputes, the employees and employers may have no earning or less earning. All this reduces the per capita income and makes the nation lose earning/revenue.

2. Developmental activities

The developmental activities of the country get disturbed in a situation when the country's revenue/earning is decreased due to industrial disputes.

3. Utilization of human resources

Industrial disputes weaken the economic strength of the nation and stand in the way of development of the country. In such situation, when strikes/lockouts make the people unemployed, affect the prosperity, growth of the country, problem arises about utilization of human resources in the country.

Roles of IRs/HR Specialists/Executives to Deal with Strike

Strike is a workers' weapon used to get their demands settled by the management. It is the last resort of the workers/trade union to make the management agree with their demands. So, in a concerted effort workers strive their best to compel the management to agree to their terms. In some cases, they may resort to such activities during strike which are unusual and unwarranted in normal situation in the organization.

In organization the whole perspective of HR activities starting from recruitment to maintenance of industrial relations belongs to the domain of the professional people who work as HR/IR managers or executives. So, such officers need to play important roles before the strike occurs, during continuance of strike and after it is over, roles are discussed in short.

Roles of HR/IRs Executives before the Strike Occurs

When the date of strike is declared by the trade unions the following steps may be taken:

1. Action plan

The HR/IR manager must study the nature, attitudes of trade unions, their past activities and collect information regarding the action plan decided by the unions to be taken during strike. The HR manager should verify the information regarding unions' decision on any matter if obtained for some other reliable sources like damage of men, machines, properties of the companies.

On collecting information the HR manager should prepare action plan for the strike period, in consultation with his boss or with the advice of his boss in respect of

- Running operative function
- Making normal production
- Rendering normal service
- Deployment of workers, officers for different activities
- Safety, security of the property and people
- Maintenance of record of production
- Procedure of collecting strike information
- Posting of officers in different points if untoward incident is apprehended
- Arranging photographer if required
- Involving security officer, assigning the job of security to a responsible officer to ensure that no untoward incidence occurs.

2. Seeking approval from higher authority in respect of police help/service

Sometimes, police help may be required to maintain law and order situation in the enterprise. When HR/IR manager or unit head feels/

apprehends that agitating workers may create nuisance in the company premises or may damage the properties of the company or may put the lives of non-striking employees into danger, the police assistance/help may be a necessity. In such case higher management should be informed and, if required, approval may be sought for taking police assistance in the organization for such purpose. If it is decided that police help will be taken, the local police authorities should be informed in writing seeking their assistance, cooperation for such purpose.

3. Obtaining approval from higher authority for seeking injunction/rules of order from the appropriate court

It happens that in some organizations one or two departments do not function due to strike while other departments function. In such case the striking employees/trade unions create problem for smooth running of those departments that function. The strikers intimidate the non-strikers to stop work. Sometime, the trade union leaders coerce the non-striking employees to join strike. To ensure smooth running/functioning of departmental activities the HR/IR manager may seek approval from higher authority to obtain injunction/rules of order from the appropriate court to restrain strikers/activists from entering into the work place. The HR manager may also advise the higher management to take disciplinary action against the concerned employees.

4. Rejecting leave application of employees/trade union leaders for joining strike

It is observed some employees submit applications for sanction of leave to join strike/trade union activities on the date of strike declared by the trade unions. In such case the leave application should immediately be rejected and the concerned employees be informed in writing that the leave has not been sanctioned because the reason for sanctioning leave is not convincing.

5. Issuance of notice for not resorting to strike

Notice may be issued from the Personnel/HRM department under the signature of unit Head/Factory Head requesting the concerned employees not to go for strike as decided by them. It should also be mentioned in the notice that those employees who will resort to strike will not be entitled for the wages of that day/s, and also they will be subject to disciplinary action as the management thinks fit.

6. Notice for the Customers/Public

If the strike called by the trade union is for more than one day and the customer service will be greatly affected, the HR department may advise the higher management to arrange for giving intimation/

information to the public in the daily local newspapers with regard to their inability to provide normal service on the strike day/s.

7. Forming a committee to combat the strike situation

A committee consisting of reliable, dependable and committed officers should be formed to overcome the strike situation. The committee members should be taken into confidence and the tasks should be allocated to them.

Role of HR/IRs Executives During the Period of Strike

The HR/IRs executive should take the following steps during strike period

1. Issuance of 'Notice' to the employees who resort to strike

The HR/IRs manager should ensure that the notice is displayed at the Factory gate/entrance of the office stating the employees who go for strike are not entitled for the wages/salaries for the day/s. It should also be mentioned in the 'notice' that the management may take disciplinary action against those employees who resort to strike, as it deems fit.

2. Issuance of 'Notice' to customers

If the concerned organization is a service organization, or an organization that has direct dealing with public a notice for customers should be given at the entrance of the office stating its inability to render customers' service for the day due to strike resorted to by some workers/a section of workers belonging to some union. The notice should mention the management's regret for inconvenience caused to the customers/ public due to strike and its request to bear with.

3. All round help and support to non-striking employees

In a situation where a section of workers stop work/cease work and another section of workers continue to work, there remains a possibility to coerce, intimidate non-strikers to join strike or abstrain from work, by the striking employees. This makes the non-strikers afraid of carrying on activities. The HR/IRs manager should motivate, encourage the working employees and provide all round help, assistance, support to them. He should develop a mutual understanding with them and make them feel that the management is always with them

4. Ensuring that no untoward incident does happen

There is a possibility for occurrence of untoward incident by the strikers to create a panicky situation in the organization so that non-striking employees may feel insecure, unsafe and unprotected and subsequently may decide to remain absent rather than attending to work. In such situation the management may arrange for continuous and persistent vigil by security personnel, and may ensure that at some vital/ danger points security personnel is posted. This can check the occurrence of unusual incident and improve the mental strength, courage of the non-striking employees.

5. Police help

The HR/IRs manager or some officer who has been assigned the specific task, should call the police personnel if the situation warrants. It happens that when the police officials come to the factory, office for providing service, officer who calls the police personnel denies of having called them. The HR manager should ensure that such situation does not occur.

6. Recording the activities

The HR/IRs manager should keep a detailed record of activities, production/service of different departments, details of untoward incidents, if occurred, property damaged; and arrange for taking snaps of all those activities.

7. Collecting information regarding participation in strike

The HR department should collect information in respect of number of employees participated in strike (department wise), mandays lost, number of employees not participated in strike, number of employees worked, number of employees remained on sanctioned leave/unauthorized absence, etc.

8. Informing the higher authority regarding strike

The HR/IRs manager should keep in close contact with higher authority and furnish information/data regarding strike to them. He should inform them if any development crops up, untoward event occurs and how the situation tackled.

9. Submission of information in 'N' form

If the organization comes under Public Utility Service, information of strike is required to be submitted to the appropriate authority (i.e., Asstt. Labour Commissioner/Dy Labour Commissioner). It happens that some organization makes a practice to collect information from regional/ zonal office and submits the compiled information in prescribed Form 'N' to the appropriate authority.

Roles of HR/IRs Executives after the Strike is Over

The Industrial Relations/Human Resource Manager should take the following steps after the strike is over.

i. Preparation of a list of strikers and submission to the wages/ Accounts Department

The HR/IR Department should prepare a list of employees who participated in the strike and submit it to the Wages/Accounts Department under the signature of the Factory/Unit Head with the instruction for deduction of wages/salaries for the strike period from the current weekly/fortnightly or monthly payment of wages/salaries of the concerned employees. A copy of the instruction should be displayed on the notice board for communication to the concerned employees.

ii. Confirmation of deduction of wages/salaries for the strike day(s)

The HR/IR manager should ensure that deduction of salaries/wages for the strike day/s has been made from the current weekly/fortnightly/ monthly payment of salaries/wages of the employees who participated in strike.

iii. Disciplinary action

The HR/IR manager may advise the higher authority to take disciplinary action against striking employees who resorted to violent activities, coerced, intimidated any non-striking employees on the day/s of strike.

iv. Submission of a detailed report regarding strike to the higher authority

The HR/IR manager should submit a detailed report to the higher authority regarding strike mentioning

- Employees involved in strike
- Extent of work/production suffered
- Number of employees not participated in strike
- Number of employees remained on authorized/unauthorized leave
- Untoward incident, if occurred, (details should be given)
- Steps taken to provide normal service/to run normal activities
- Reasons of strike and recommendations for further course of action
- Damage of property made by strikers (photos to be enclosed), if any

Roles of IRs/HR Specialists/Executives Before Gherao

Ghereo is a physical blockade of a target by a group of persons by encirclement. The target, may be a place, a person or persons. In industrial settings the target is usually the managerial/supervisory personnel. A group of employees encircle such sort of executive/s and make a physical blockade with the objective of getting their demands settled forthwith. In such case, HR manager/IR manager has a role to deal with ghereo situation. If the HR/IR executive can have confirmed information regarding gherao to be resorted to by some workers, he may take some steps; but in most cases it happens that gherao information is not divulged and it is very difficult to obtain information regarding gherao. In such case, the HR manager has got nothing to do prior to gherao. However, if the management has information that some workers may resort to gherao tactic on any day, the following steps can be taken, as guideline, prior to gherao.

1. Gathering information about gherao

On receipt of some confidential information from some source regarding gherao to be made by some workers/trade union leaders of the organization, the HR/IR manager should check, cross check the information, and should get confirmed about the gherao plan of the union/s workers.

2. Action plan

The HR/IR manager should prepare the action plan in consultation with his boss or with the advice of his boss, to face the gherao situation. The action plan may include

a) To take some officers into confidence and to assign different jobs to different officers. For example, some officers may be given the duty to list out the slogans and also the names of the person/s who use slogans, abusive language and damage properties during gherao, someone may be given the responsibility to remain present in the chamber of the executive/s targeted by the union people/ workers, prior to gherao. Some officer may be assigned to call the police if the situation turns out to be ugly, someone may be given the duty to take the snaps of the chairs, tables and other furniture if damaged/broken by the employees who gheraoed the executive/s.

b) To allocate duty/task to some officers for keeping a continuous vigil on the situation.

c) To inform the local police station concerning that there is a likelihood of a gherao and request them to send police personnel when assistance is sought.

d) To develop a rapport with the police personnel.

e) To inform secretly the departmental heads regarding the gherao and also to make them know how the matter is to be dealt with.

3. The HR/IR manager should ensure that the executive who is targeted to be gheraoed should not be left alone in the department.

4. To confirm the 'gherao' and also the police assistance sought

It happens when the police officials come to the factory/office for providing service, factory head/other officers deny of having called them. The HR manager should ensure that factory head/officer assigned the special duty shall not deny when the police personnel come and enquire about gherao and also the police assistance sought by the factory/office.

Roles of HR/IR Specialists/Executives During Gherao

HR/IR executives need to take the following steps during gherao:

1. Ensuring smooth and prompt activities of officers who have been assigned duties to deal with gherao situation

As per action plan already made earlier the particular officers should start their activities and the HR manager should ensure that all are working smoothly, promptly.

2. Police assistance

If the situation turns out to be serious and violent, police assistance should be taken immediately. The HR manager or the officer assigned to the job of calling the police personnel should call the police immediately and confirm them of having gheraoed.

3. Ensuring that names of the employees who participated in gherao are noted

The HR manager should ensure that names of the employees who gheraoed the executive(s) and also the names of the employees who used abusive languages along with the exact wordings/phrases used in slogans are noted down. The HR manager should also ensure that the snaps of the furniture and other properties of the factory/office damaged/broken by the employees who gheraoed the executive(s) are taken. Such job should be performed by the officers who were assigned as such.

4. Advice to the departmental heads to prepare list of names of employees who participated in the gherao and also not to give them any job if they come back to the department.

The HR manager should advise departmental heads to prepare the list of names of employees of the departments who have left the departments and participated in gherao. The time of leaving the respective departments and coming back to the departments should be mentioned. He should advise the departmental heads not to give any work/job to those who participated in gherao and came back to the department to work.

5. Behavioural manifestations of the executive(s)

The HR manager should ensure that the executive/s who has/have been gheraoed by the employees of the organization maintain/s the following

a) Maintain/s calm and cool state of mental activity

b) Not bowing down to pressure, not being afraid of gherao situation

c) Not entering into argument/discussion

d) Not withdrawing any office order, instruction, decision of the management

e) Noting down the problems, issues raised by the people who gheraoed him/them

f) Not agreeing to talk to higher authority immediately over phone on their issues/problems

g) Telling them to convey their sentiments, problems to the higher authority

6. Informing the higher authority

The HR manager should immediately inform the higher authority over phone when some employees of the factory/office gheraoed the executive(s). He should inform about the action taken by them, and should seek advice for any other action/steps if required to deal with the situation.

Roles of HR/IR Specialists/Executives after Gherao

Roles of HR/IR executives after gherao include the following:

1. Ensuring that the employees who participated in gherao have not been given job/work

The HR manager should ensure that the employees who gheraoed the executive/s have not been given any job/work after they came back to the department.

2. Snaps of articles damaged

The HR manager should collect the snaps of articles, furniture damaged/broken by the employees from the officer who was given such assignment earlier.

3. Collecting information from the departments

The HR department should collect the details of information from different departments duly signed by the departmental heads. The information should relate to

- Names of employee who participated in gherao
- Date, time at which employees left department for participating gherao and came back to the department for work
- Languages, slogans, wordings/phrases of slogans used by employees: the names, employee code numbers, designation, department of such employees should be given.

4. Collection and verification of information by the HR manager

The HR manager should collect the information in respect of slogans, languages, word/phrases, etc., used by the employees who gheraoed the executive(s), from the officer(s) assigned for such purpose. All these should be duly signed by the concerned officer(s). He should check, cross check and verify the details of information with the information collected by the HR department.

5. Wage deduction

The HR department/HR manager should prepare a list of names of employees who participated in gherao and submit it to the Wages/Accounts department under the signature of factory head/unit head with the instruction to deduct full day's wages/salaries from the current weekly/fortnightly/monthly payment of salaries/wages on the principle of 'no work, no pay', if the incident/gherao was made by such employees during their working hours. The HR manager should ensure that deduction of salary/wage has been made.

6. Collection of information from the department regarding work suffered due to gherao

The HR department should collect detailed information regarding work/production suffered due to gherao by employees, from the department duly signed by the concerned department head.

7. Submission of report to the higher authority

The HR manager should submit detailed report under the signature of factory head/unit head to the higher authority mentioning

- names of employees who participated in gherao (employee code number, department attached, designation should be given)
- work suffered due to gherao

- damage made by the employees during gherao (the photos of the damaged articles, furniture, etc., should be enclosed)
- action taken by the factory/office to deal with gherao situation
- slogans, word, languages, phrases used by the employees during gherao
- names of employees of other organizations/units if any participated in gherao activities.
- wage deduction for full day made on the principle of 'no work, no pay'
- the details of incident
- recommendations for taking disciplinary action against some employees who resorted to gherao, damaged furniture and properties, created violence, used abusive languages, shouted slogans, assaulted executive(s).

Methods for Prevention and Settlement of Industrial Disputes/Conflicts

Industrial dispute arises from a situation of disagreement, difference between labour and management in an organization. Both employer and employees become unhappy, feel discomfort, develop misunderstanding, mistrust. Human relation is disturbed. Industrial scenario manifests different forms of conflicts/industrial disputes like go-slow, work to rule, gherao, dharna, strikes, lockouts, etc., resulting in decrease in production, profit, non-supply or less supply of goods and services, loss in business, market, creation of unemployment, pathetic economic conditions of workers, lawlessness, disorderly behaviour of workers, loss in national income and the like. Such situation affects employers, employees and society. Country's development is disturbed. So all these are manifestations of unhealthy and unsound industrial relations that deter achievement of organizational goals. Hence, for establishing harmonious industrial relations and for growth and development of the employees vis-a-vis organization, some preventive and curative/remedial measures are required to be taken so that industrial disputes do not crop up, and in the event of raising some disputes arrangement is made to settle those disputes immediately.

Methods for Prevention of Industrial Disputes

Industrial disputes do not occur in an organization when both employer and employees are happy, contented and develop mutual understanding, mutual faith and confidence in each other. Workers remain happy and satisfied when they get better wages, allowances, incentives, welfare benefits, fringe benefits, social security, higher quality of work life, lucrative career planning and development, status, recognition, job responsibilities, involvement, participation in decision making, good treatment from the management and the like. Management in order to make human resources dynamic to produce world class quality of products and also to face stiff competition needs to create a state of congenial and healthy industrial relations through formulation and implementation of HR policies, procedures, practices and also changing philosophy, approaches and style of functioning concerning employees in the organization.

The following are preventive methods of industrial disputes generally adopted by the management in the organization.

A. Standing Orders

It is one of the methods used by the management to develop mutual understanding, confidence, faith between them and workers through framing clearly defined rules and regulations that govern terms and conditions of employment. Workers want just and fair conditions of employment and also their participation in the process of preparing terms and conditions of employment. The rules made in this regard are 'standing orders'. In terms of the provisions of the Industrial Employment (Standing Orders) Act 1946 the industrial establishments employing 100 or more employees shall have standing orders which covers the matter like hours of work, holidays, pay days, wage rates, shift working, attendance, termination of employment and others as mentioned in the schedule given below.

The Schedule

Matter to be provided in the Standing Orders

1. Classification of workmen, e.g., whether permanent, temporary, apprentices, probationers or *badlis.*
2. Manner of intimating to workmen, periods and hours of work, holidays, pay-days and wage rates.
3. Shift-working
4. Attendance and late coming
5. Conditions of procedure in applying for, and the authority which may grant leave and holidays.
6. Requirement to enter premises by certain gates and liability to search.

7. Closing or reopening of section of industrial establishment, temporary stoppage of work and the rights and liabilities of the employer and workmen arising therefrom.
8. Termination of employment and the notice thereof to be given by employer to the workmen
9. Suspension or dismissal for misconduct and acts of omission which constitute misconduct.
10. Means of redress for workmen against unfair treatment or wrongful exaction by the employer or his agents or servants.
11. Any other matter which may be prescribed

    The certified standing orders are the terms and conditions of service between the employer and his employees. Before certification of the standing orders, the certifying officer sends a copy of the draft standing orders received from the employer, to the trade union of the workmen if any, or where there is no trade union to the workmen in such manner as may be prescribed along with a notice for submission of objection if any, in the prescribed manner to be submitted to him within 15 days from the receipt of the notice. The certifying officer gives the opportunity to the trade union or such other representative of the workman of being heard of objection for addition/modifications to the standing orders. After this, the certifying officer certifies the draft standing orders with the modifications, and sends within 7 days thereafter copies of the certified standing orders authenticated in the prescribed manner, and of his order to the trade union or other prescribed representatives of the workmen, if any.

The standing orders act as preventive method of industrial disputes for the following:

i. Most of the issues that generate industrial disputes relate to terms and conditions of service of employees which are incorporated in the standing orders. If the terms and conditions of service are conducive and favourable to the employees, they heartily accept them. Employees become happy and contented with the standing orders.
ii. Trade union is given opportunity of being heard of concerning suggestion/objection for modification, addition before certification is made. So, workers develop a sense of involvement, partnership feeling and participation in the process of formulating rules and regulations by the management.
iii. Standing orders make the employees committed, loyal to the

organization as this manifests employer's positive intention towards employees.

iv. Workers' level of job satisfaction and morale are enhanced as they feel satisfied on the matter like job, promotion, working conditions, pay, etc., which are incorporated in the standing orders.

v. Better terms and conditions of service of employees promote quality of work life (QWL), provide scope for advancement, develop systematic/rational evaluation of performance, improve core components of human resources and create changes in attitudinal dimensions of employees. All this makes a dynamic workforce to face, accept and confront challenges for betterment and development of people vis-a-vis organization.

vi. In a situation when workers are provided comfort, convenience, amelioration through formulation of excellent standing orders, congenial and conducive state of organizational climate prevails. This brings industrial harmony and peace.

vii. Interactions between employer and employees become positive/ comfortable when employees find favourable standing orders. Both the parties come close and develop mutual understanding, faith and confidence. This makes the employer-employees relations/human relations solid and healthy.

B. Code of Discipline

Code of discipline is a set regulations or principles that control and promote discipline. It is a preventive method used to bring harmony and peace in industry, (A detailed discussion on Code of Discipline has been made in an earlier Chapter 'Employee Discipline').

C. Tripartite bodies

Tripartite bodies are formed with the representatives of employers' organizations, employees' organizations and Government to study the industrial relations climate of different industries and help ensure peace and harmony in industries. Such tripartite bodies include Indian Labour Conference (ILC), Standing Labour Committee (SLC), Committee on Conventions, Industrial Committee and other tripartite committees like Steering Committee on Wages, Central Implementation and Evaluation Machinery, Central Board of Workers' Education, National Productivity Council and others.

i. Indian Labour Conference (ILC)

This is the highest tripartite body that deliberates upon the issues relating to labour-management relations jointly and finds solution to advise the central government in the matter referred by the government. The objectives of ILC are

- to develop mutual understanding between the members of employers' organizations and employees' organizations and to establish rapport with the government
- to eliminate differences between parties and to work effectively as a team to suggest the government to take measures for bringing healthy industrial relations
- to consider the issues referred to it by the government from the overall view point of country's economic development that mostly depends on uninterrupted production arising out of a situation of congenial and conducive industrial climate
- to study the different aspects of industrial relations and to evolve measures in industry.

ii. Standing Labour Committee (SLC)

This tripartite body makes discreet study of the issues referred to it and gives suggestion to the government keeping in view the necessities of maintaining and promoting peace and harmony in industry and healthy industrial relations as well. Some of the issues for which it submitted suggestions in the recent past include bonded labour, employment, vocational training, child labour, etc.

iii. Committee on Convention (COC)

This committee helps prevent industrial disputes through different measures like providing various benefits of international standard to the workers. Its main function is to see which ILO conventions remain unratified by the government and to submit suggestion for ratification and implementation.

iv. Industrial Committee (IC)

This committee is constituted with the representatives of employers' organizations, employees' organizations and government. It has equal number of representatives from the employers' organization and employees' organization. Indian Labour Conference acts as coordinator between industrial committee and the government on the issues referred to this committee. The main objectives of industrial committee include

- to give suggestion on the specific issues to the ILC
- to make thorough discussion/deliberation and give its view on the proposals for legislation and other policy and administration issues

- to see the aspects that prevent industrial disputes on the issues referred to it and to submit suggestions

I. Other Tripartite Committees

Some of the tripartite committees are discussed below:

A. Steering Committee on Wages

This committee is formed with the representatives of employers, workers, state governments and an economist. Its main function is to study the price structure of different products, production aspects, wage matter, etc. It acts as a research body and prepares report through survey work. Different authorities appointed for wage fixation and other bodies, institutions may take the help from the findings of the survey work carried by this committee. This committee helps prevent disputes arising of wage issues by way of giving the real situation/actual information with regard to production, price of goods and the wages paid by the organization. Employers' capacity to pay and also the rationality/justifiability of workers' demand for wages can be ascertained from the report of this committee.

B. Central Implementation and Evaluation Machinery

The necessity for setting up Implementation and Evaluation Division in the Centre was felt at the Standing Labour Committee Session in 1958 as industrial harmony and peace was disturbed due to non-implementation of some settlements, awards by some employers in industries. In order to prevent disputes and to establish congenial industrial relations Implementation and Evaluation Division in the centre was set up under the Ministry of Labour. So, tripartite committee was constituted with equal number of representatives (i.e., 4 representatives from each party) from the employers' organizations and workers' organizations and government.

Area of functioning:

The activities of this machinery include

- to see the extent of implementation of awards, code of discipline, settlements etc and ensure implementation
- to find out causes of non-implementation of agreed issues and to take measures for implementation
- to ensure settling long pending issues
- to find out genesis of strikes, lockouts and other forms of industrial conflicts and to fix up the responsibilities
- to ascertain efficacy of labour laws, policies, settlements, etc. and to suggest measures to remove the weak areas

- to build up harmonious industrial relations through avoidance/ prevention of disputes.

Implementation and Evaluation Division and tripartite committees are also set up in the states with the objectives of preventing disputes in state industries.

C. National Productivity Council (NPC)

This council is constituted with the members of workers' organizations, employers' organizations, some independent experts and the government. The objectives of NPC are given below:

- to study the trend of production and productivity of workers
- to give the information as to the level of production of workers and to suggest measure to improve production
- to encourage workers to increase production and productivity
- to help strengthen collective bargaining process by supplying correct information of production to workers, trade unions
- to help increase wages so as to avoid disputes arising out of wage issues.

D. Central Board of Workers' Education

This tripartite body headed by a chairman (nominated by the government) consists of representatives from central trade unions, employers' organizations, central government, state governments, university grants commission, Indian adult education association, and one independent trade union nominated by the ministry of labour and employment.

The main objective of the board is to educate the workers and trade union leaders so that they can realize their duties, rights and responsibilities and develop understanding between them and their superiors.

The board's area of activities include:

i. to change the attitudes of worker to accept/adopt the work environment through education and training

ii. to acquaint them with organization culture, philosophy, policies, procedures, rules, regulations so that they can perform better

iii. to make the workers know their job roles, leave rules, standing orders, disciplinary matter, etc.

iv. to develop 'a sense of belonging', 'we feeling', 'togetherness' amongst the workers through counselling, participation in workshops, interactive processes

v. to educate the workers so that they are not biased to union decision and can judge the real situation

vi. to impart training to the trade union leaders to improve their ability, skill to understand their importance as representatives of workers in the organization and also as role players to develop the organisation

vii. to make the workers/trade unions understand the fundamentals that they grow with the growth of the organization, and they exist if the organization exists

viii. to motivate the workers so that they can feel the importance of trade union and can take part in constructive activities.

The board, thus, plays an important role to prevent industrial disputes.

E. Preventive Method through Industrial Disputes Act

Industrial disputes arise out of interaction between management and trade union/workers and such disputes can be prevented if their interaction is positive and complementary. Industrial Disputes Act 1947 restricts the arbitrary activities of both trade unions and employers and drives them to develop better relations between them. Such activities are:

- Change in condition of service governed by section 9A of the Industrial Disputes Act 1947
- Lay-off governed by section 25C, 25M of the Industrial Disputes Act 1947
- Retrenchment governed under section 25F, 25G, 25N of the Industrial Disputes Act 1947
- Closure governed under section 25FFA, 25Ff(i) and 25 (O) of the Industrial Disputes Act 1947
- Strikes and lockout governed under sections 22, 23, 24, 26, 27 and 28 of the Industrial Dispute Act 1947
- Unfair Labour Practices governed under 25T and 25U of the Industrial Disputes Act 1947

Unfair Labour Practices

I. On the Part of Employers and Trade Unions of Employers

1. To interfere with, restrain from, or coerce, workmen in the exercise of their right to organise, form, join or assist a trade union or to engage in concerted activities for the purposes of collective bargaining or other mutual aid or protection, that is to say,
   (a) threatening workmen with discharge or dismissal, if they join a trade union
   (b) threatening a lock-out or closure, if a trade union is organised
   (c) granting wage increase to workmen at crucial periods of trade union organisation, with a view to undermining the efforts of the trade union at organisation
2. To dominate, interfere with or contribute support, financial or otherwise, to any trade union, that is to say
   (a) an employer taking an active interest in organising a trade union of his workmen; and
   (b) an employer showing partiality or granting favour to one of several trade unions attempting to organise his workmen or to its members, where such a trade union is not a recognised trade union
3. To establish employer sponsored trade unions of workmen
4. To encourage or discourage membership in any trade union by discriminating against any workman, that is to say
   (a) discharging or punishing a workman, because he urged other workmen to join or organise a trade union
   (b) discharging or dismissing a workman for taking part in any strike (not being a strike which is deemed to be an illegal strike under this Act)
   (c) changing seniority rating of workmen because of trade union activities
   (d) refusing to promote workmen on higher posts on account of their trade union activities
   (e) giving unmerited promotions to certain workmen with a view to creating discord amongst other workmen, or to undermine the strength of their trade union

(f) discharging office-bearers or active members of the trade union on account of their trade union activities

5. To discharge or dismiss workmen,
   (a) by way of victimisation
   (b) not in good faith, but in the colourable exercise of the employer's rights
   (c) by falsely implicating a workman in a criminal case on false evidence or on concocted evidence
   (d) for patently false reasons
   (e) on untrue or trumped up allegations of absence without leave
   (f) in utter disregard of the principles of natural justice in the conduct of domestic enquiry or with undue haste
   (g) for misconduct of a minor technical character, without having any regard to the nature of the particular misconduct or the past record or service of the workman, thereby leading to a disproportionate punishment
6. To abolish the work of a regular nature being done by workmen, and to give such work to contractors as a measure of breaking a strike
7. To transfer a workman mala fide from one place to another, under the guise of following management policy
8. To insist upon individual workmen, who are on a legal strike to sign a good conduct bond, as a precondition to allowing them to resume work
9. To show favouritism or partiality to one set of workers regardless of merit
10. To employ workmen as "badlis", casuals or temporaries and to continue them as such for years, with the object of depriving them of the status and privileges of permanent workmen
11. To discharge or discriminate against any workman for filing charges or testifying against an employer in any enquiry or proceeding relating to any industrial dispute
12. To recruit workman during a strike which is not an illegal strike.
13. Failure to implement award, settlement or agreement

14. To indulge in acts of force or violence
15. To refuse to bargain collectively, in good faith with the recognised trade unions
16. Proposing or continuing a lock-out deemed to be illegal under the Industrial Disputes Act 1947

II. On the Part of Workmen and Trade Unions of Workmen

1. To advise or actively support or instigate any strike deemed to be illegal under the Industrial Disputes Act.
2. To coerce workmen in the exercise of their right to self-organisation or to join a trade union or refrain from joining any trade union, that is to say,
   (a) for a trade union or its members to picketing in such a manner that non-striking workmen are physically debarred from entering the work places
   (b) to indulge in acts of force or violence or to hold out threats of intimidation in connection with a strike against non-striking workmen or against managerial staff
3. For a recognised union to refuse to bargain collectively in good faith with the employer
4. To indulge in coercive activities against certification of a bargaining representative
5. To stage, encourage or instigate such forms of coercive actions as wilful "go-slow", squatting on the work premises after working hours or "gherao" of any of the members of the managerial or other staff
6. To stage demonstrations at the residence of the employers or the managerial staff members
7. To incite or indulge in wilful damage to employer's property connected with the industry
8. To indulge in acts of force or violence or to hold out threats of intimidation against any workman with a view to prevent him from attending work

Violation of the above provisions under Industrial Disputes Act is punishable with imprisonment or with fine or with both.

F. Other Preventive Measures

1. Trade Union Activities

Trade Unions play the key role in shaping the pattern of industrial relations through their activities. The attitudes of trade union leaders, their beliefs, values structures, financial position of trade unions, leadership competencies, unity and solidarity amongst members, degree and extent of unionism, etc., decide the conditions of work culture as also labour-management relations in the industry. Sound and solid trade union, positive mindset of the union leaders, dynamic leadership, attitude to accept changes, constructive and 'as-the-situations demand trade unionism' help the leaders develop rapport with the management. All this facilitates to establish harmonious industrial relations and avoid conflicts in industry.

2. Employers'/management Activities

Employers' attitude, philosophy, style of functioning, perception, value structure, approaches to IRs, etc., reflect in dealing with workers' problems, grievances. Dynamism in employers' thinking process and activities, formulating and developing positive HR/IR policies, welfare and social security measures, introduction of HRD mechanism, etc., manifest conducive, comfortable climate and activities in the industrial set up.

Under the above situations both workers and management do not resort to unfair labour practice. Further, cases of strikes, lockouts, lay offs, retrenchment, withdrawal of any concessionary benefits, changing service conditions of workers do not occur. However, workers'/trade unions' and management/employer's activities that tend to occur such above situations are regulated by the provisions of Industrial Disputes Act 1947. This Act helps the parties to change their behavioural pattern and establish good relations between them.

3. Works Committees

This committee is constituted in the industrial establishments where 100 or more workers are employed. This is a statutory committee setup under the Industrial Disputes Act 1947 with the equal number of workers' and employer's representatives. Though the setting up of this committee is statutory obligation, recommendations of the committee are not legally binding. The main objectives of the works committee are given below.

i. to create a climate of mutual understanding, mutual faith and mutual confidence so as to establish harmonious industrial relations

ii. to see that industrial disputes do not occur

iii. to remove the differences between management and workers/trade unions in respect of issues/problems

iv. to develop clear perceptions on the issues so that no disputes arise out of misperception

v. to promote better human relations between the representatives

vi. to introduce a system of industrial democracy where both parties interact/participate

vii. to settle disputes through joint discussion, open deliberation

This committee discusses/deals with day-to-day issues and other issues like bonus, welfare and social security, terms of conditions of service, employment conditions, working conditions, etc., and develops congenial and conducive atmosphere of work that prevents disputes to crop up.

4. Joint Management Council (JMC)

It is one of the methods used to prevent disputes in industry. This is a joint consultative/deliberative body constituted with the equal representatives of workers and management with the objectives of maintaining peace and harmony in industry through disposal of grievances/issues of the workers at the earliest possible time. In this council workers' representatives are taken from recognised union.

(A detailed discussion has been made in chapter - 10)

Methods for Settlement of Industrial Disputes

Industrial disputes arise out of differences between labour and management on different issues like employment, terms of conditions, discipline, management and labour attitude related issues and others. If the issues are not settled expeditiously there will be labour unrest and workers will resort to agitational programmes in the form of strike, gherao, go-slow, dharna and the like resulting in loss of production, loss of market, reduction of profit, tarnishing goodwill, reputation of the company. So, for smooth and effective functioning of the organization and for achieving organizational goals settlement of disputes is a necessity.

For immediate and amicable settlement of disputes the following methods are used in industrial setting.

A. Collective Bargaining

Collective bargaining is one of the mechanisms used in organization to make an amicable settlement of industrial disputes between the parties (i.e., workers' representatives and employer's representatives). It helps develop healthy industrial relations through generating a climate of mutuality that is, mutual understanding, mutual responsibility, mutual confidence and mutual trust.

(Already discussed in Chapter 5)

B. Grievance Procedure

It is the method for disposal of grievance of the employees of the organization. It is natural that the employees want to get their grievances redressed by the management within the shortest possible time. They don't like to keep pending their day-to-day issues/grievances like employment conditions, welfare, social security, fringe benefits for days together. So, they manifest their feeling of dissatisfaction/resentment in their behavioural activities which make their relations with the management unhealthy, bitter, and unpleasant. This sort of relations stands in the way of achieving individual goals, team goals and organizational goals and deters growth and development of people at work and the organization as well. So, in order to settle/dispose off the issues speedily the need for grievance procedure is felt. That means there is a need for introduction of a system for redressal of grievances within a reasonable period of time through different authorities/hierarchies.

The necessity for introduction of grievance procedure in Indian industries can be felt from the following:

i. The Factories Act 1948 provides for employment of welfare officer in factories where 500 or more workers are employed. The state government has framed rules in this respect requiring welfare officers to look after workers' complaints and grievances and also the implementation of different labour legislations.

ii. Under the Industrial Employment (Standing Orders) Act 1946 every establishment employing 100 or more workers requires to frame standing orders which, inter alia, contains provisions for introduction of methods/means for redressal of workers grievances against unfair treatment or wrongful exactions by the employer or his agents or servants.

iii. The Industrial Disputes (amendment) Act 1982 provides for setting up of grievance settlement authority for the settlement of industrial disputes connected with an individual workman employed in the establishment where fifty or more workmen are employed.

iv. The Code of Discipline lays down for establishment of a grievance procedure on mutually agreed basis to ensure a speedy disposal of issues/grievances to promote sound relations between labour and management.

v. The Indian Labour Conference, 1958 suggests for a model grievance procedure for disposal of grievances in a phased tier system.

A detailed discussion has been made in the preceding Chapter 5 on Management of Grievance.

C. Conciliation Officer

It is one of the statutory methods for settlement of industrial disputes. Settlement of disputes is made by the third party who is called conciliation officer appointed by the government, through persuasion and establishing mutual understanding between trade union people and management representatives attending the conciliation. Normally, conciliation process starts when either party (management or employee) refers the dispute not settled/discussed in the collective bargaining to the conciliation officer or when industrial disputes are already in existence/apprehended. Role of conciliation officer is to act as mediator, facilitator, advisor, guide, helper, pathfinder, solution-explorer for amicable settlement of the disputes. The appointment and duties of conciliation officers are provided in the Industrial Disputes Act 1947. The objectives of conciliation include:

- bridging the gap/differences between management representative and worker/worker representative.
- establishing mutual trust, understanding between parties through creation of congenial environment for discussion/conciliation.
- manifestation of unbiased behavioural activities of the conciliation officer in order to establish confidence amongst the parties.
- putting in efforts to avoid strikes, go-slow, lockout through amicable settlement of disputes.
- bringing harmony and peace in industry.

D. Board of Conciliation

This is a tripartite body constituted by the government for settlement of disputes. The necessity for setting up this board is felt when the disputes referred to conciliation officers are not settled by them. Hence, for disposal of such issues, chairman is appointed by the government to head the board consisting of equal number of nominated members of the parties to the disputes. The board endeavours to bring about a settlement of the disputes through persuasion. The board sends report to the government in respect of settlement signed by the parties to the dispute. In case of failure to reach an agreement, failure report is sent to the government together with a full statement, recommendation for determination of dispute, etc.

E. Court of Enquiry

The appropriate government is empowered to constitute a court of enquiry to inquire into any matter appearing to be connected with or relevant to an industrial dispute. It is the duty of the court of inquiry to inquire into the matters referred to it and submit report in writing, duly signed by all the members of the court to the appropriate government ordinarily within a period of six months from the commencement of the enquiry. The court is a fact finding body. Its object is to inquire into, ascertain and reveal the cause of an industrial dispute. It has no power to make an order/to impose any settlement upon the parties.

F. Voluntary Arbitration

It is one of the methods used for settlement of industrial disputes. The salient features of voluntary arbitration are mentioned below:

i) Arbitration award is a third party judgement/decision.

ii) When the conciliation fails, reference to arbitration is made by the parties to the disputes under persuasion of the conciliation officer.

iii) The arbitrator is appointed by the parties.

iv) Cost of arbitration (arbitrator's fees) is borne by the parties.

v) Arbitrator submits his judgement to the government who, in turn, publishes it within 30 days from the date of its submission.

The voluntary arbitration is an effective method for settlement of disputes as

a) arbitrator's appointment is made spontaneously by the parties. No compulsion is imposed to accept any person as arbitrator.

b) arbitration award is easily implemented by the parties.

c) it brings both the parties together, removes the area of their differences and helps develop understanding between the parties.

d) it is an acceptable mode for solution of the problems.

e) possibility of biased judgement is remote.

f) award within time frame is possible.

g) it is a process for settlement of disputes amicably through their own person.

G. Adjudication

It is one of the methods of settlement of disputes. It is done through intervention of a third party appointed by the government. This third party is Labour Court or Industrial Tribunal or National Tribunal. The adjudication process starts on reference of industrial disputes by the government in case of failure of conciliation proceeding or on reference by the government when in its opinion industrial dispute exists or is apprehended, or on reference of industrial dispute mutually by the parties.

The adjudication award is binding on all parties to the industrial disputes. The main features of adjudication are as follows:

- It is a method of settlement of disputes by third party intervention.
- Parties are under compulsion to contest the case/dispute referred to the adjudication machinery and to accept the award.
- It creates a climate of bitter feeling/understanding between the parties.
- Settlement by third party is not accepted spontaneously by the parties and they honour the adjudication award as they cannot escape.
- The issues or disputes not settled in the collective bargaining/conciliation process but decided/settled by the adjudication machinery creates a climate of win-lose situation in the organization which is not a sign of healthy industrial relations.
- The adjudication machinery under Industrial Disputes Act 1947 consists of Labour Court, Industrial Tribunal and National Tribunal.

Labour Court

It is one tier under three-tier adjudication machinery constituted for settlement of disputes. It consists of one person appointed by the government. The concerned person is/has been a judge of a High Court or has been a District Judge/Additional District Judge for a period not less than 3 years or has held any judicial office in India for 7 years or more. The Labour Court deals with following matter for settlement of disputes:

i. the propriety or legality of an order passed by an employer under the standing orders

ii. the application and interpretation of standing orders

iii. discharge or dismissal of workmen including reinstatement of, or grant of relief to, workmen wrongfully dismissed

iv. withdrawal of any customary concession or privilege

v. illegality or otherwise of a strike or lockout, and

vi. all matters beyond the jurisdiction of Industrial Tribunal

Industrial Tribunal

This dispute settlement machinery is constituted with one person appointed by the government. This person who acts as presiding officer is or has been a judge of High Court or has for a period of not less than three years been a District Judge or an Additional District Judge. The Tribunal may get the advice of two assessors if appointed by the government, in the matter of the proceeding before it.

The Industrial Tribunal may adjudicate upon the industrial disputes relating to any matter which are within the jurisdiction of Labour Court as specified in the Second Schedule under the Industrial Disputes Act 1947 and also the industrial disputes relating to any matter specified in the Third Schedule under the Act as mentioned below:

1. Wages including the period and mode of payment
2. Compensatory and other allowances
3. Hours of work and rest intervals
4. Leave with wages and holidays
5. Bonus, profit sharing, provident fund and gratuity
6. Shift working otherwise than in accordance with standing orders
7. Classification by grades
8. Rules of discipline
9. Rationalization
10. Retrenchment of workmen and closure of establishment
11. Any matter that may be prescribed

The Tribunal adjudicates upon a dispute when the government refers the dispute by order in writing for adjudication. The government refers the dispute to adjudication under the following situations:

i. where the parties to the dispute apply in the prescribed manner either jointly or separately for reference to the Tribunal and the government is satisfied that the persons applying represent majority of each party
ii. where in its opinion industrial dispute exists or is apprehended
iii. where the dispute relates to a public utility service and a notice of strike or lockout has been given under section 22 of the Industrial Disputes Act and it considers that the notice has not been given frivolously or vexatiously

As a machinery for settlement of dispute Industrial Tribunal is useful when trade union is weak and cannot have collective bargaining power to settle problems.

National Tribunal

It is constituted to adjudicate in industrial disputes which in the opinion of the Central Government, involve questions of national importance or are of such a nature that industrial establishments situated in more than one state are likely to be interested in or affected by such dispute.

It consists of one person appointed by the Central Government and this person who is or has been a judge of High Court works as Presiding officer of the National Tribunal. The Central Government may appoint two persons as assessors to advise the National Tribunal in the proceeding before it.

National Tribunal initiates adjudication process on obtaining reference in writing from the Central Government to adjudicate upon the disputes relating to any matter specified in the Second Schedule or Third Schedule under the Industrial Disputes Act. It holds its proceeding expeditiously and submits its award to the Central Government within the period specified in the order of reference. The maximum time limit for submission of award in case of individual dispute is three months.

Books Recommended

1. VB Singh, *Climate for Industrial Relations: A Study of Kanpur Cotton Mills* (Allied Publishers, Mumbai, 1968)
2. Pramod Verma, *Management of Industrial Relations* (Oxford IBH, New Delhi, 1981)
3. CB Mamoria, S Mamoria and SV Gankar, *Dynamics of Industrial Relations* (Himalaya Publishing House, Mumbai, 2003)
4. EA Ramaswamy, *Industrial Relations in India* (Macmillan, New Delhi, 1981)
5. SC Jain, *Productivity and Discipline* (Allied Publishers, New Delhi, 1988)
6. H John Bernardin and Joyce EA Russel, *Human Resource Management* (McGraw-Hill, New York, 1993)
7. AM Sarma, *Industrial Relations - Conceptual and Legal Framework* (Himalaya Publishing House, Mumbai, 1989)
8. John B Miner and Mary Green Miner, *Personnel and Industrial Relations* (Macmillan, New York, 1985)
9. Dale S Beach, *Personnel - The Management of People at Work* (Macmillan, New York, 1980)
10. SL Agarwal, *Labour Relations Law in India* (Macmillan, New Delhi, 1980)

11. CS Srivastava, *Industrial Relations Machinery* (Deep and Deep, New Delhi, 1983)

Questions

1. What is industrial dispute? Discuss different forms of industrial disputes.
2. What is industrial dispute as per Industrial Disputes Act 1947? Are industrial disputes and industrial conflicts the same? Discuss any two forms of industrial conflicts.
3. What is strike? Explain different forms of strike.
4. Is there any difference between 'go-slow' and 'work-to-rule' ? Can management take any disciplinary action against an employee if he resorts to 'go-slow' activities?
5. State the differences between 'strike' and' lock-out'
6. What is 'guerrilla strike'? Do you find any difference between 'guerrilla strike' and 'lightning strike'?
7. Is there any difference between 'unofficial strike' and 'hunger strike'?
8. Do you think 'economic cause' is the only cause of strike? State the causes of strike in Indian industries.
9. What is Code of Discipline? Is there any necessity of Code of Discipline in industry?
10. Discuss three important tripartite bodies that contribute to promote peace and harmony in Indian Industries.
11. Explain the machinery that facilitates prevention and settlement of industrial disputes in India.
12. What is grievance procedure? As a student of MBA do you think grievance redressal is a necessity in an organization? Give your views in the matter.
13. As HR manager of an organization how will you deal with strike situation?
14. Explain the roles of an Industrial Relation Manager before strike, during strike and after strike.
15. What is gherao? As HR manager of a company what steps will you take during gherao and after gherao.
16. Discuss in detail the consequences of industrial disputes.

Case Study 1

Aviskar Pharmaceuticals Private Ltd. was set up by Mr AP Jain, scientist in 1995 at Bangalore.

It had 6 working days per week making 26 working days per month and was running smoothly. There was no workers' union till 1999. In April 2000 some workers formed union with an outsider Mr LN Mirdha who was made General Secretary of the union. The attitudes of office bearers were rough, violent and aggressive. The industrial relations situation started deteriorating making it difficult for the company to survive. Mr Jain and other partners of the company sold their shares to ABC Pharmaceuticals Limited in May 2001. After taking over, ABC Pharmaceuticals made many changes and the major ones were:

- They increased the salaries of executives and staff of the unit to reduce the gap in the pay structure of the executives and staff of this unit and their other units.
- They shifted from 6 days' working per week to 7 days' working per week to imporve the productivity and enhance cost-effectiveness of the unit.

The shift from 6 days to 7 days working without any financial gains made workers resist the change. At this juncture, Mr Manohar Vaid, Corporate Manager (IR) intervened and promised the workers that they would be paid for all 30 days instead of 26 days, but Mr AR Srivastav, Director (Personnel) and Mr JN Tandon, GM (Operations) refused to agree to this since they were not involved when Mr Vaid made the commitment. This issue kept lingering for 9 months. No decision could be taken because of the difference of opinion among senior executives. In June 2002 the workers gheraoed Mr Tandon to pressurise the management to take the decision. They were successful to some extent as it led to the agreement of management with workers that financial benefit would be given with retrospective effect of 4 years making it one additional year over and above 3 years of normal agreement. The workers gave a notice of change in August 2002 demanding an increase of Rs. 2000/- per month. In September, 2002 a notice of change was given by management. In October 2002 the negotiation started and continued till February 2003. The first two rounds of meeting did not lead to any outcome as none of the parties was ready to sacrifice. This made Mr LN Mirdha withdraw as he was not happy with the rigid stand taken by the union leaders.

The third meeting was held without Mr Mirdha wherein the union leaders came down to Rs 1000 from Rs 2000 pm. The minutes of the meeting were jotted down but the union leaders refused to sign. Taking advantage of the occasion some management personnel attached to

Personnel Department had a secret meeting with Mr Mirdha in a hotel. Mr Mirdha advised the representatives of the management to maintain a low key for a few months during which workers would be compelled to reduce their level of expectations. It was observed by the management representatives that there were perceptual differences between senior and junior union leaders. Taking cue from this, they adopted a policy of divide and rule and took Mr Hiralal Ram, the senior union leader into confidence and had a secret meeting with him to explore the last settlement amount and apprised him that the management could go only upto Rs. 400. They also took Mr Dhiman Kumar, the junior union leader into confidence and convinced him that management was not going to accept their demands and ultimately the workers were going to suffer. Besides this, they spread the message that no wages would be given retrospectively. The next day meeting resumed in which union representatives came down to Rs. 700 (because of the pressure from the workers) beyond which they were not ready to come down. It was decided that instead of having meeting with all the members, only two members, one senior union leader Mr Hiralal Ram and one junior union leader, Mr Dhiman Kumar would sit in the negotiations. Immediatly a meeting among GM (Operations), new Corporate Manager (IR), Mr Hiralal Ram and Mr Dhiman Kumar was held and it was resolved that Rs 500 average per month would be given for 4 years retrospectively. An MOU was drafted by legal consultant at the corporate office and was duly signed by GM (Operations), Corporate Manager (IR) and the union representatives who participated in the negotiation. In the evening a dinner was hosted in which all the negotiators were invited. When the papers were sent to Mr Srivastav, Director (Personnel), he objected to the MOU on two points:

First, the other plants were having 30 days pay system leading to less average pay per day and in Bangalore plant it was to be given for 26 days leading to higher average pay per day. Second, the canteen allowance was sanctioned for Bangalore unit employees only. It took GM (Operations) and new Corporate Manager (IR) two months to convince Mr Srivastav, Director (Personnel) about the agreement and therefore, implementing the same. This way the issue was settled.

On the basis of what has been stated above, answer the following questions.

i) Was it proper for Mr Manohar Vaid, Corporate Manager (IR) to make a commitment to the workers to give higher average pay per day to them? Give reasons for your answer.

ii) Was it ethical to use the tactics used by management in the case? If yes, why? If not, why not?

iii) Should Directer (Personnel) have raised objections after MOU was signed? Explain with reasons.

iv) Was it right for the General Secretary of the union to withdraw half-way during negotiations?

v) In view of the information given in the case, suggest the strategic measures that the company could make for promoting healthy industrial relations in the organization.

vi) How was the human relations situation in the Company?

vii) Give your detailed views on this narrating the incidents mentioned in the case.

viii) As a student of MBA(HR) critically analyse the company administration and discipline management from IRs perspectives.

Case Study 2

Mr AR Sengupta is the Chief Manager (HRM) of the Eastern Region of Universal Bank Limited. The Eastern Regional office of the Bank is in Kolkata. Mr GA Nayak, Dy General Manager is the Regional Head of the Bank.

Some information

1. The bank has 100 branches, 1500 employees including officers, clerks and subordinate staff under eastern region.
2. The union composition looks like this:
   - Three unions namely Universal Bank Workers' Union, Universal Bank Employees' Union and Universal Bank Workers' Solidarity Union are having members in branches and regional office in Kolkata.
   - The Universal Bank Workers' Solidarity Union is majority union of the Bank. The Corporate management has recognised this union as a sole collective bargaining agent but this union is minority union in Eastern Region from the membership point of view.
   - The Universal Bank Employees' Union ranks third from the view point of union membership in the Bank as a whole, but in Eastern Region it has about 60% membership.
3. Some of the Bank's salient activities are given below:

a) The Eastern Regional Authority in consultation with Head Office made an agreement with Universal Bank Employees' Union (minority union in terms of all India union membership strength) in 1985 to provide canteen facilities to employees at branches and administrative office. Under this agreement the Bank requires to appoint canteen boys (on permanent employee roll), provide utensils, furniture, room spaces, fuel at free of cost and arrange to serve the employees food, tea, snacks at subsidised rate on 'no profit, no loss' basis. Mentionably, only the bank employees of Eastern Region are enjoying such benefits. The other unions started agitation to extend such benefit to all the bank employees in other regions. Looking into different perspectives top management agreed to provide a canteen allowance for all employees of the Bank at different rates (Rs. 20 per day per officer, Rs. 15 per day per clerk and Rs. 10 per day per subordinate staff) linked to attendance of employees in a month. The payment of such allowance came into effect from April, 2009. The Universal Bank Employees' Union was called by the management of eastern region in May, 2009 for discussion on the 'canteen boy' issue in the context of having introduced a similar benefit scheme for the employees of the Bank. The management informed them about justification for discontinuance of 'canteen boy engagement' system and told them that existing canteen-boys would be converted into peons. The management expressed their views that this practice of engaging/recruiting canteen boys would be stopped forthwith. The Union leaders vehemently protested over the management's desire/intention to discontinue the system of appointing canteen boys in Bank. They informed management that if, such practice is discontinued they would cease work for indefinite period.

b) The Universal Bank Ltd. has introduced a system of holding discussion/negotiation on the issues raised by three unions separately in structured meetings twice a year in Regional Office and once a year in the Head Office.

c) The branches developed a practice to hold staff meeting on the personnel and non-personnel issues of the branches where free and open discussions are held to sort out differences/problems and promote understanding, faith amongst them.

d) For cleaning, sweeping the branch/office premises the bank has permanent sweepers at different time rate (viz., 1/3, 1/2. 3/4, full rate of scale) depending upon the floor space of the premises. The bank engages casual sweepers (from the enlisted panel of casuals) on a temporary basis when permanent incumbents go on leave.

On the basis of what has been stated above, answer the following questions.

(a) Is it a right decision of the management to provide canteen facilities only to the employees of eastern region ? Give reasons for your answer.

(b) What would have happened if management would not have agreed to reach such an agreement meant for a section of employees of the bank?

(c) Do you think management's proposal to stop engaging canteen boys is justified and proper particularly in the light of the agreement that still exists?

(d) Do you think 'structured meeting' as practised by bank, and 'collective bargaining process' are the same? Produce your arguments in support of your views.

(e) Name the central trade unions and employers' federations that can participate in the negotiation held for settlement of industrywise issues under collective bargaining system.

(f) Do you think appointment of sweepers on permanent basis at different time scales is justified in the context of LPG? Submit your views.

(g) What are other alternatives to appointment of permanent part time sweepe

X

Employee Empowerment, Quality Circle and Workers' Participation in Management

Introduction

In the liberalized, privatized and globalized economy competition in the market reveals an aggressive, fierce and stiff exposition. To remain in the market, to make a place in the market, organization needs to deliver quality product and service to customers at a reasonable price, and at the time customers need them; and this can be possible if the organization can have a reservoir of committed, dynamic and motivated workforce that can take quick and immediate decision to serve the customers and provide customers delightment. Employee empowerment, in this case helps the company to prepare such workforce. All this makes the organization to face challenges and obtain competitive advantages.

Empowerment is the process of shifting authority and responsibility to others in the organizational setting. Empowerment takes place when higher management transfers the power, authority, and responsibility to lower level employees. Shifting of authority and responsibility to the workers is made to take over the charge of the work they do. The concept of shifting of power, authority is very simple in the sense that the person who has been doing some job for years together develops thorough idea, knowledge, competence over the job and keeps everything under his grip. Now, if such person is given overall charge of the work he does, with adequate authority and responsibility he can take decision on his own for accomplishment of the job. He performs quality work and at the same time he gets motivated and develops a sense of commitment and a 'feeling to reciprocate in consideration of the power shifted. It generally occurs that most human beings desire recognition, power, status, authority, and responsibility and when they achieve they exert drives to utilize their full energy, abilities, and competences to excel their performances. Such people prepare their mindsets to achieve, to perform, to win, to succeed and to strive their best to go ahead in that direction as projected. Empowerment is such a mechanism that helps achieve individual goals, team goals and organizational goals through handing over the charge of the job to the employees to perform the job with authority to take decision on their own. So, empowerment relates to individual development and the development of the organization as well. Empowerment as a process of passing authority and responsibility to lower level employees is introduced in organizations like GE, Medical Systems, Tata Information System, Asea Brown Broveri and others.

Meaning and Definition of Employee Empowerment

The dictionary meaning of the verb "empower" is 'to give the means, ability or authority'. So, the empowerment in work setting means to give the people means, ability and authority to do something which they have not done before. Wellins et al (1991) defines empowerment as the process of passing authority and responsibility to individuals at lower levels in the organizational hierarchy. Randolph (1995) states that employee empowerment is a transfer of power from the employer to the employees. So, empowerment involves the people at the lower echelon in the work activities through delegation of power with responsibility. This makes a different kind of people with a different mind frame to serve the organization.

Mohammed et al (1998) expresses that empowerment is a state of mind. An employee with an empowered state of mind experiences feelings of

i) control over the job to be performed

ii) awareness of the context in which the work is performed

iii) accountability for personal work output

iv) shared responsibility for unit and organizational performance and

v) equity in the rewards based on individuals and collective performances

Most authors agree that before empowering the lower level individuals managers must be sure that such employees have the right mix of information (about process, quality, customer feedback and events), knowledge (of the work, the business and the total work system), power (to act and make decisions about the aspects of work) and rewards (tied to business results and growth in capability and contribution) to work autonomously or independently of management control and direction (Lawler, et al 1989, Lawler, 1992).

Newstrom and Davis (1998) have defined empowerment as any process that provides greater autonomy through the sharing of relevant information and the provision of control over factors affecting job performance.

The core element of empowerment involves giving employees a discretion (or latitude) over certain task related activities. (Bowen and Lawler, 1992; Conger and Kanungo, 1988; Schessinger and Heskete, 1991)

So, empowerment is a process of transferring authority with responsibility to the individuals at lower level. It takes place through sharing information, autonomy in making decisions and improving competence.

Salient Features of Empowered Organization

Salient features of empowered organizations are discussed in short.

1. Organizational hierarchy

The organizational hierarchy of the companies is flat. They do not have a large structure with a series of levels that command and control the one immediately beneath them.

2. Hiring of people

The hiring process of the companies is very systematic. The companies pay a lot of time and effort in hiring to make sure new recruits can handle workplace freedom. The recruiters ensure that 'accept errors' and 'reject errors' in recruiting people do not occur.

3. Span of management

They appoint fewer managers with wider responsibilities. The span of management is well above twenty in which a manager's role shifts from controller to coach and mentor. (Lorenz, 1993)

4. Accountability

A great deal of importance is given on accountability of the empowered individuals. It is felt that accountability world instil discipline in utilizing scarce resources to benefit the stakeholders and the organization as well.

5. Guidelines

The companies make unstructured guidelines that can make the empowered employees know the decision making parameter.

6. Climate of openness, trust and collaboration (OTC)

A climate of openness, trust and collaboration between subordinates, between boss and subordinates prevails in the organizations. The employees are encouraged for developing a spirit of mutuality – mutual understanding, mutual confidence and mutual trust.

7. Job satisfaction and commitment

The companies put emphasis on job satisfaction and commitment to work and to the organization. The organizational culture activities make the employees feel that they are valued in the organization, they are part and parcel of the system, and their satisfaction is the core value of the organization.

8. Quality of performance

One of the characteristics of empowered organization is to ensure that quality of performance is excellent. The people should keep in mind the concept of zero-defect while they are in the process of performance.

Principles for Empowering People

The organizations with high level of job autonomy follow some principle for transferring authority and responsibility to their employees. The companies like Xerox, Cadilac, Telco, Toyota, Honda, Maruti Udyog, IBM, etc., follow some principle while empowering their employees. The principles include:

1. Tell people what their responsibilities are

People to whom the authority will be given, should know their responsibilities. They should be aware of the responsibilities, not the authority only.

2. Give them authority equal to their responsibility

The people should be delegated authority along with the responsibility. The responsibility should not be less than authority given. Both authority and responsibility should be equal.

3. Set standard of excellence

What standard of performance the people are required to attain, should be set/fixed. The standard to be set should be excellent. In no way the standard should be average, below average, it should always be excellent.

4. Provide them with training that will enable them to maintain standards

The people to whom the authority and responsibility will be delegated should be given training to make them conversant with the standard and also to make them competent to perform excellently by enhancing their skill and abilities.

5. Give them knowledge and information

The people should have adequate knowledge and information with regard to the activities they will be required to perform. So, the companies should give them training to enhance their understanding, knowledge in respect of their authority and accountability.

6. Provide them with feedback on their performance

The following queries are highly relevant for quality performance:

- How the people are performing?
- Is there any mistake or wrong doing?
- Are the people at the below level or average level or above level of standards of performance?

Management should get to know all these and provide feedback to the employees.

7. Trust them and create trustworthiness in the organization

The organization should develop the culture of mutuality – mutant trust, mutual faith and mutual understanding between people, between boss and subordinates.

8. Allow them to fail but guide and counsel them when needed

The organization should not take it seriously when the people fail, cannot perform as desired. Management should encourage employees to try out new ideas and take decisions. If the employees fail in their attempts management should appreciate their attempts, guide them.

9. Treat them with dignity and respect

Management should pay the employees proper respect. Each and every job should contribute to the achievement of organizational goals. So people feel that their work is dignified.

Conditions Necessary for Empowerment

Empowerment is a process of transferring authority and responsibility to the lower level people by the higher management. So, it is a delegation of authority and responsibilities. The lower level people get autonomy to the job, can make decisions at their ends. To introduce such system in an organization it is required that the following basic conditions exist in the organization.

1. Top management's desire, willingness

Top management of the organization spontaneously and from core of the heart must want to introduce empowerment system in the organization. It is not that top management gives his lip service for introduction and implementation of such policy. He should keep close watch, look at the matter and show his interest for implementation of the system.

2. Congenial and conducive work environment

The working environment of the organization should be highly congenial and conducive. The dyadic relationship between boss and subordinate should be healthy and sound to establish a state of mutuality i.e. mutual understanding, mutual trust and mutual confidence between boss and subordinates in the organization.

3. Participation

In an empowered organization workers need to give their best to learn the basic activities for quick disposal. They should be encouraged to take initiative to improve their daily work processes. The organization must arrange to conduct empowerment training for participation of the employees where they can be able to share their ideas, and thought process for quality performance. It happens that organizational bureaucratic system prevents employees from seizing initiatives. In such case the organization should take proper steps so that the spirit of employees' initiative, enthusiasm is not lost, and the employees can effectively participate in the training (JH Dobbs, 1993).

4. Healthy industrial relations

Labour–management relations in the organization should be sound and healthy so that the organizational activities can run smoothly without any interruption. In such healthy industrial relations situation employees may feel comfortable to work and show their effective and worthy activities.

5. Innovations

Empowerment encourages innovation for quality performance. The management must encourage employees to try new ideas and make decisions that help explore new ways of doing things. Sometimes, it may happen that employees fail even after putting a lot of efforts. In such case management must encourage their innovative efforts so that they can feel that failures are the stepping stones to success, and with such supportive management the employees will be able to achieve, win, succeed (JH Dobbs, 1993).

6. Access to Information

Empowerment assumes that employees have free access to information to do their jobs and improve their productivity. The information may be relating to profit and loss statements, purchasing procedures, manufacturing process and the like. The management must provide employees free access to information and resources to enhance their willingness to cooperate and use empowerment. Further, if the employees want additional training, this should be offered readily, even if it is peripheral to their main jobs (JH Dobbs, 1993).

7. Accountability

In empowered situation, the employees are held accountable for results. However, this step is not intended to identify the black spot and take disciplinary action against the employees. The intent, instead, is to see that the empowered employees are giving their best efforts, working toward mutually agreed goals and behaving responsibly toward each other. When employees manifest such behaviour, employees should be encouraged to go at their own pace and in their own way (JH Dobbs, 1993)

8. Feedback

Empowered employees need to know their level/quality of performance from the stakeholders. That means they need feed back from the boss, peers, subordinates, customer and other persons who are directly or indirectly related to the activities of the empowered employees. The management of the empowered organization must develop a regular practice to provide feedback to the employees.

Perspectives of Employee Empowerment

Employee empowerment makes the people happy, contented and committed that helps contribute to the achievement of organizational goals. This is possible through delivery of quality product and services to the higher satisfaction of customers, by the employees. So, the employee empowerment can be viewed from different perspectives which are discussed in short.

1. Growth Perspective

Employees are recruited in organization to perform, to give their best to attain excellence. Organization introduces various nurturing methods to make them excel in their performance. It happens that the people cannot manifest their peak performance even when they are technologically sound to operate activities. It occurs that the employees need autonomy in their job to enable them to take quick decision and respond to any change in environment without loss of time and perform excellently. In such situation they may feel a sense of accomplishment as they can do their best looking at their goals and also the goals of the company.

2. Social Perspective

People in the organization have their social base formed during formative childhood through nurturing process. In the process of rearing and bringing up they developed a feeling to 'perform job by being involved, sharing responsibilities and active participation' when they observed that the family activities viz., ritual performances, marriage ceremony, family festivals, etc., were performed by the family members through a process of involvement, participation and sharing responsibilities to form a strong and effective family with loyal, disciplined and committed members. All these are recorded in their ego-states. They feel the urge to play back their desire for involvement, sharing responsibilities and giving opportunity to take decision on their own when they are grown and required to perform activities. So, to satiate social needs employees are empowered to take decisions by themselves without consulting their boss in the organization. In this perspective empowerment is linked to a belief in a democratic polity where power resides in individuals at all levels of a system (Prasad, 2001).

3. Psychological Perspective

An employee can perform well when his esteem need is satisfied. He wants recognition, status, existence in work-setting as an effective personality, some kind of work which is distinctive, meaningful and specific to his level of mindset, perception held to influence work. This can be possible if the person is given authority and responsibility in his work. In such situation he gets autonomy to design work activity compatible to changing environment, make quick decision in his performance, provide customer's delightment through quality product and service. Thomas and Velthouse (1990) state that employee empowerment is based on four dimensions that affect a person's intrinsic motivation for the job. They are meaningfulness (meaning of the value of a task goal or purpose judged in relation to individual's own ideals of standard), competence (individual's belief in relation to his knowledge, skill, abilities to perform task activities), self-determination and perception of the degree to which an individual can influence some outcomes of the work activities.

4. Organizational Perspective

Every organization intends to survive, grow, develop and make a place in the market. Today, in the changing scenario it is not an easy task for an organization to stay, continue its operational activities and capture substantial position in a market. Organization needs to face fierce, aggressive competition, confront to very difficult challenges to obtain competitive advantages. For attainment of business excellence, achievement of employees and organization peak performance what is required is to create a more focus on the customers' community in respect of the product, and also deliver the value added services to them with a distinct quality in product and all other modes of activities till delivery is made. This may be possible by the empowered employees who can be able to ensure quality product and quick delivery to the utmost delightment of customers. Ketchum and Trist (1992) assert that employee empowerment helps achieve organization performance. Empowering teams should be central concept for managers who wish to improve their organization's performance.

Employee empowerment can be viewed from different dimensions. The whole concept of empowerment cannot be based on single approach/ perspective. Linda (1997) opines that various dimensional approaches need to be studied, only one approach is not enough to view employee empowerment.

Empowerment Stages

Empowerment is a process of transferring authority with responsibility to the individuals at lower level. The empowerment process is a long term, complex process involving five stages (Hogan, 2000).

Stage 1. Recalling de-powering and empowering experiences

The empowerment decision is not taken all of a sudden; it evolves over a period of time with experience. So, for empowerment it needs to recall events that show both de-powering and empowering.

Stage 2. Discussing reasons for de-powerment and empowerment

After getting to know the events that show de-powerment and empowerment, it is required, at this stage, to identify the reasons for depowerment and empowerment. The reasons may be due to organizational processes and activities viz., communication, span of control, delegation of authority, etc. The reasons for empowerment and depowerment may lie with individual depending on his locus of control (meaning the belief whether he is in control of events or events control him), level of his self-esteem (meaning the extent to which an individual thinks he is capable of making things happen).

Stage 3. Choosing one issue, problem or project to work on

After identifying the reasons of depowerment some steps need to be taken to overcome them. It is possible that the depowering events happen in several areas and all these areas cannot be covered at a single step of empowerment. So, the best strategy is to choose a problem or project which is easier to work on, and after this is done, the more difficult problems/issues are to be taken.

Stage 4. Identifying potential power bases

At this stage, potential power bases need to be identified. French and Raven (1959) have classified power bases into five categories viz., legitimate power (i.e., the power derived from the position that one holds in organization), reward power (i.e., the power derived from ability to grant rewards – financial rewards, non-financial rewards), coercive power (i.e., the power derived from one's ability to inflict punishment or block an opportunity), expert power (i.e., the power arises from specialized knowledge or expertise of a person) and referent power (i.e., the power derived from one's attractive personality, charisma).

5. Developing and implementing action plans

Identification of power bases will not help the organization to empower if action plans are not developed. At this stage, it is a great necessity to develop and implement action plans for empowerment. The power should be used in proper ways. There are four ways of using the power:

i) Increase one's own power base.

ii) Enact power to make things happen through others.

iii) Challenge the power basis of others.

iv) Increase the power basis of others.

Now, it becomes obvious that power bases are found to be existing at individual level and also at the organizational level. So, necessary steps need to be taken to make the empowerment process smooth and easy. For example, at individual level employee's power base can be improved through training and development measures so that they can assume more power; and at the organizational level, factors responsible for depowerment can be removed through initiating appropriate changes.

Benefits of Employee Empowerment

Today, in fierce and aggressive competitive market, employee empowerment plays a crucial role to make the organization confront challenges, face the competitions and achieve goals. Empowerment benefits the employees and the employer as well.

Benefits to the Employees

Employees' benefits from empowerment are discussed below in short.

1. Satisfaction of esteem need

Most employees desire to satiate their needs for recognition, status, authority, responsibility and challenging job when their physiological needs are fulfilled. Empowerment gives the autonomy to the employees to exercise their power in their work activities along with responsibility.

2. Job satisfaction

Empowerment makes the employees develop a better image of the company, management; and attaches high value to the job. All this enhances the level of job satisfaction of the empowered employees.

3. Dyadic relationship

A sound dyadic relationship is established between boss and subordinates when some authority is delegated. Empowered employees develop a better feeling about their boss that helps establish a state of mutual understanding, mutual faith and mutual confidence.

4. High degree of morale

The empowerment process makes the people feel that the work they do is meaningful, significant and contributes to achieve organizational objective/goals. This enhances the level of morale of empowered employees.

5. Developing a feeling of self-efficiency

Empowerment is the process that enhances the feeling of self-efficiency among the employees (Conger and Kanungo, 1988).

In empowered organization employees have free access to information which they can use to make decision on their own without consultation with or guidance of the boss. This makes them efficient and develops a feeling of mastery over the job.

6. A sense of accomplishment

When the decision of empowered employee makes an effect to contribute to organizational success and the higher management considers it an achievement and also appreciates the employee's efforts, the employee develops a sense of accomplishment, achievement that may lead him towards performance at its peak.

7. Substitute to career path and development

Every person desires to go up in the ladder of career progression and development to enjoy power/authority and also responsibility. It happens that in the limited layered organization scope of promotion to the next cadre is unavailable or restricted. In such situation empowerment may act as a substitute to career path and development.

8. Self-growth and development

In empowered organization employees can have a high degree of involvement, participation and a learning environment opportunity. All this drives him to try new ideas, thought process to make decision. This generates self-confidence, determination to promote self-growth and development.

9. Use of latent talent

It happens that the empowered employees attain excellence in performance through value addition to their activities. For such activities they are required to have creativity, innovative ideas, avenues, alternatives through use of talents the employees possess in active or latent form. So, the empowered organizations provide lot of opportunities to fully utilize the talents of the people.

Benefits to employer

Employers are benefited from the empowerment in several ways. Some of the important benefits the employers get are mentioned below.

1. Increase in production and productivity

Since the empowered employees feel happy, contented they give their best to produce maximum products and quality products. They use their skill, attitudes, talent in the best possible way to make quick and peak performance that may result in reduction in cost of product and also warranty costs.

2. Higher degree of customers' delightment

The customers want quality products, quality service at competitively lower price and at the time they desire. This is possible in empowered organizations where the employees can make quality and rapid decisions in respect of price, product, delivery of the articles. So, a higher degree of customers' delightment can be provided by the organizations.

3. Obtaining competitive advantages

It is possible for the empowered organization to face challenges, compete against competitors as the employees can be able to attract customers through prompt, rapid delivery of the quality goods and services at a lesser price. In the process the organization can make a place in the market and obtain competitive advantages.

4. Sound industrial relations

In empowered organization a state of mutuality (i.e., mutual understanding, mutual trust and mutual responsibility between boss and subordinates) is established resulting in creation of comfortable and congenial atmosphere in work place. This makes the employees develop a feeling of 'we-ness' 'togetherness' and 'belongingness' and give their best for smooth and effective functioning of organizational activities. All this helps promote sound industrial relations in the organization.

5. Reducing stress of higher management

A large portion of work activities of the manager is delegated to the lower level employees to perform with responsibility. This power transferring process relieves the higher management from stress activity. Lack of employee empowerment is considered as a stressor to the individual and members of the management team (Parker and Slaughter, 1995); and employee empowerment acts as a stress reducer of the management.

6. Reservoir of loyal, dynamic, motivated and committed people

The empowered organization can have a reservoir of employees who become loyal, motivated, committed and dynamic to the company. Such employees with their proacting, enabling and 'face-the-situation' mindset, qualitative attributes can confront emerging market challenges and make a place in the market for its survival, growth and development.

7. 'Kaizen' culture

In changing environment the empowered employees make continuously a series of experiments, innovations for new ideas to find how value added products and services can be provided to the customers so that business excellence can be attained. In such situation the employees remain engaged to give excellent services, performance under continuous improvement process. This helps develop a 'continuous improvement culture' ('Kaizen' culture) in the organization that gives a strength to the organization to 'survive and compete' in the economy.

8. Image

In empowered organization

- Customers' delightment becomes prominent
- Employee-customers relationship becomes very healthy
- Instances of work-stoppages, agitations by employees remain absent
- Increasing trend of market share is noticeable
- Increasing trend of profit is revealed
- Dyadic relationship becomes healthy
- Sound industrial relations exist

All these make the image and stature of the organization very high.

9. A motivational tool

Empowerment process acts as a tool to motivate employees to make prompt, rapid decisions to produce and deliver quality products and services, accept changes, confront challenges and achieve organizational goals.

10. Other benefits

a. Empowered employees make quick decisions and suggestions that improve quick service delivery in the operational activities. All this saves a lot of money and time in organizations.

b. In empowered organizations optimum utilization of human resources is made.

c. It is possible for the empowered organization to make strategic change in policies and objectives suiting emerging environment.

d. Since empowered organizations can have employees with high degree of job satisfaction, involvement and morale, the rate of absenteeism and employee turnover becomes insignificant.

Factors Affecting Empowerment Process

Employee empowerment is a process of transferring authority with responsibility to the lower level employees. It benefits the employees who are empowered and also the employer who delegates the power with responsibility. But, in reality it happens that effective empowerment does not occur in organizations. There are various factors that affect adversely the empowerment process. These factors include

- Organization related factors
- Management related factors
- Employee related factors

Organization Related Factors

Some organization related factors create barriers in employee empowerment. They are:

i. Organizational Approach

Organizations function based on some approaches like participative approach, autocratic approach, etc. If the organization's approach is autocrat centric the delegation of authority is restricted. In such organization authority is centralized and it is exercised by the higher level management; the lower level employees are required to implement. Here, the employee empowerment process cannot work.

ii. Organizational working environment

If the organization's working activities are continuously disturbed due to demonstration, deputations, go-slow, work-to-rule, strike, gherao by workers, trade union leaders, empowerment process cannot work. Existence of congenial and conducive working environment is one of the prerequisite for effective empowerment.

iii. Industrial relations situation

For effective employee empowerment sound and healthy industrial relations in the organization are essential. But, unhealthy industrial relations make a barrier in empowerment process.

iv. Lack of organizational policies towards training and other aspects

It happens that some organizations do not have policies to arrange for empowerment training to the employees identified for empowerment and also employees already empowered. Such organizations do not have a planned system to help the empowered employees to have access to information required for performance. All this creates a lot of problems for the empowered employees to perform excellently and also conveys a message to the employees about the difficulties to be faced for discharging functions if empowered. Under such environment empowerment process cannot work effectively.

Management Related Factors

In some organizations management personnel create barrier to effective empowerment. The management related factors that adversely affect empowerment process include:

i. Power addiction

Some managers are addicted to authority, power. They get satisfaction when they exercise authority. They want subordinates to come for guidance, advice and for any work and make them busy all the time. Such managers become reluctant to delegate power to their subordinates and create obstacles to employee empowering process.

ii. Management ineffectiveness

The managers who are not effective in performance and are considered to be non-achievers show their unwillingness to implement empowerment programme on the ground

- that they may be distinctly exposed to the peers, subordinates and higher management regarding their performance activities.
- that their qualitative attributes can be reassessed and evaluated by the higher management and compared with that of those lower level employees who are empowered.
- that their importance in the area of functional activities will be lessened.
- that they may not be able to perform the work assigned to them in absence of effective subordinates if empowered.

These sorts of managers do not like to delegate power/authority to their subordinates, rather they make efforts to ensure that empowering system is not introduced.

iii. Management's attitudes, disposition

It happens that in some organizations employee empowerment programme cannot work well due to negative dispositions, attitudes of managers. Such managers may feel that their subordinates are not competent to perform higher job as they have attitudinal problems. These kind of managers do not want to establish and promote better dyadic relationship. They do not allow subordinates to come close to them and develop a better understanding between themselves. They make a strict and close supervision of the job assigned to the subordinates. Such managers do not have trust, confidence on their subordinates. So, climate of mutuality (i.e., mutual understanding, mutual trust and mutual confidence between boss and subordinates) is absent in such work-setting. All this creates hindrance to the empowerment process in the organization.

Employee Related Factors

It happens that in some cases employee related factors make barriers to effective empowerment. Such factors include:

i. Lack of confidence in employees

It occurs that some lower level employees do not have confidence over their competence to perform the higher job responsibility. They think that they are not competent to excel performance in higher level job. So, they express reluctance to accept higher level job with responsibility.

ii. Lack of expectation of employees for career advancement

Some employees' level of expectation, mind-frame, disposition towards career advancement creates a barrier in effective empowerment. Such employees want to remain in the same position, carry on activities as assigned for present performance. They have no expectation, desire to go up, build up their career advancement and they do not intend to take up higher responsibility.

Quality Circle (QC): Meaning and Characteristics

There are different forms and methods of participative management. Quality Circle (QC) is one of the participative methods used in industrial settings. The term 'quality circle' means a small group formed with employees working in the same department, on voluntary basis to identify, prioritize, discuss and analyze problems and suggest solutions in the work related issues in the regularly held meeting on company time. So, it is a small group of employees who work together and meet voluntarily to analyze and resolve work related problems.

The main characteristics of quality circle are as follows:

i. **Size:** It is a small group. The total member of group members is generally 4 to 12 depending upon the size of the department/work area.

ii. **Voluntary group:** It consists of volunteers. Employees on their own join the group. Management does not force them to join the circle.

iii. **Meeting:** It holds regular meeting generally once in a week/ fortnight or month for a specific period, during working hours. The meeting is held on company time. The period of time spent in the meeting is treated as being on duty.

iv. **Group leader:** The leader of the group is elected by the group members.

v. **Use of latent talent:** It is an employee-talent search process for effective and smooth running of departmental activities. The members can be able to utilize their latent talent through it.

vi. **Process of activities:** It identifies problems, prioritise problems, analyses problems, recommends solution, implements accepted proposals, reviews results and takes follow-up action.

vii. **Approach:** It is a bottom-up approach, not a top-down approach. It has a structure with various constituents. They are non-members, members, leader and deputy leader, facilitator, coordinator, steering committee and top management committee/top executive committee.

viii. **Focus:** Its focus is on quality product, quality service and quality activities to enable the organization to attain business excellence and achieve organizational goals.

Quality Circles in India

Quality circles concept originated in Japan in 1962. It has made a tremendous contribution to the success of large number of industrial, commercial and service organizations in Japan and this state of affairs has encouraged many organizations in various countries in the world including India to implement the quality circle programmes for excellent organization performance. In India Qcs were first initiated in Bharat Heavy Electricals Limited (BHEL). It started five Qcs in various shops in January 1981 in Ramchandrapuram unit. Subsequently it spread to other shops; and by October, 1983 as many as 228 Qcs were operating in BHEL, 121 of them were in the Hyderabad division (BR Dey, 1984). Now, Qcs have been introduced in various organizations like Chemical, Jute, Pharmaceuticals, Steel, etc. Some of the companies which are operating Qcs are

- Hindustan Antibiotics
- State Bank of Hyderabad

- National Textile Corporation
- Indian Airlines
- Shriram Fibres Ltd
- Crompton Greaves
- Durgapur Steel Plant
- Bank of Baroda
- State Bank of India
- TELCO, Jamshedpur
- Bajaj Auto
- TVS
- Hindustan Aluminium
- Hindustan Machine Tools

The activities, performance, success stories of quality circles operating in various organizations are focused through quarterly journal, 'Quality Circle in India', booklets entitled 'Quality Circle at a Glance', 'Quality Circle Manual', 'Training for Quality Circles', etc. All these are published by Quality Circles Forum in India (QCFI) which was formed as a non-profit professional body in April, 1982.

Qcs in Different Nomenclatures

Quality circles are operating in India and other countries by different names. In India different companies use different names for Qcs. Some of them are:

- Small Group Activities (SGAs) at Telco, Eicher
- Guna Vretha at some companies in Bangalore
- Quality Control Circles
- Thinking at Work Circles (at JK Synthetics)
- Productivity Circles
- Shop Improvement Teams (in some PSUs)

In the USA some companies use different names for quality circles like the Quality Seekers, Action Circles, Mac Circles, Human Resource Circles, Employees Circles, etc.

Objectives of Quality Circles

S Ingle (1985) has identified objectives of quality circles which are related to people and task. The principal objective of Qc is to ensure delivery of the quality goods and services to confront challenges against competitors so that organization can survive, grow and develop. So the objectives of Qc include:

- Self development
- Mutual development
- Satisfaction of psychological needs
- Improvement in communication and attitude
- Problem identification and problem prevention
- Team building
- Linkage among people
- People improvement
- Participation
- Reduction of absenteeism and grievances
- Improvement in quality
- Reduction of wastes, scraps
- Reduction of cost
- Improvement in productivity
- Safety improvement
- Problem solving
- Promoting human relation between managers, supervisors and employees
- Reduction of error
- Creation of talent bank
- Promoting sense of belonging
- Promoting consciousness among employees about quality, safety and cost of production
- Improving employee motivation
- Developing leadership among potential employees
- Improving quality of work life (QWL)
- Promoting sound industrial relations

Structure of Quality Circle

The structure of quality circle in Indian organizations consists of several levels viz., non-members, members, leader, deputy leader, facilitator, coordinator, steering committee and top executive committee or top management committee. The organizational structure is shown in Figure 10.1

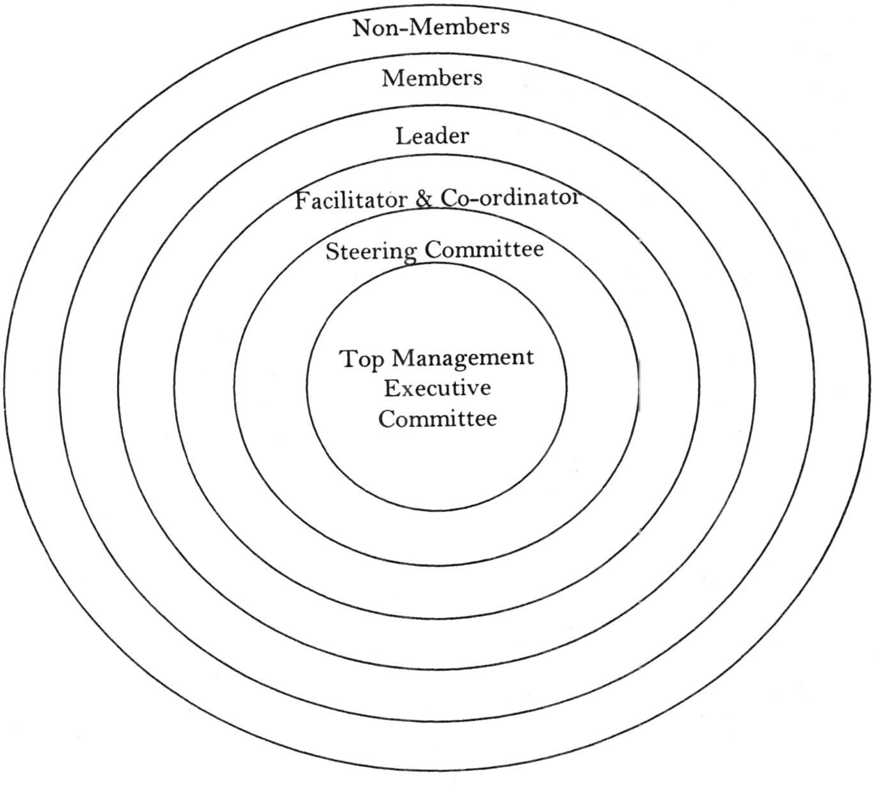

Figure 10.1: Organizational Structure of Qc

Non-members

Non-members are those employees of the concerned department who are not directly involved in circle activities but play important role to implement approved suggestions/recommendations of the circle members. It is well-nigh impossible to implement members' suggestions if non-members do not extend cooperation.

Circle Members

Members are those workers of work area/department who volunteer to form circle to discuss and propose ways of improving quality and solving other work related problems in their areas. Total number of circle members may vary from 4 to 12 depending upon the size of the work area. Membership to Qc is not a compulsion or binding on the workers; it is totally a voluntary form of participation. Once a quality circle is formed, circle members remain as permanent members of the circle for a certain period of time as decided.

The main functions of a circle member are given herein below:

i) Attend meeting regularly.

ii) Actively participate in the meeting.

iii) Cooperate with the leader and to perform roles assigned to him.

iv) Pay respect to other members and cooperate with them.

v) Catalyze generation of cohesive team working in the work area.

vi) Listen, appreciate, accommodate and assimilate others' view points, opinions.

vii) Make all out efforts for peak performance of the circle.

viii) Share Qc team's goals and objective.

ix) Identify issues deterring improvement.

x) Analyse issues/problems.

xi) Involve in the improvement of the organization as a wlole.

xii) Submit suggestions for improving quality and solve problems arising in work related areas.

xiii) Participate in the mid-term and top management presentation.

xiv) Helping leader to prepare report.

Circle Leader

Quality circle is headed by the leader who is elected by the member of the circle. It may happen that line management takes the charge of the circle in the initial stage if it is newly set up in the department. He needs to conduct meeting where members threadbarely discuss problems creating barrier in smooth functioning of the departmental work and also for improving quality of the product. Leader motivates the members to contribute their views/suggestions for digging out the inhibiting areas and for offering solution to overcome the problematic situation. The leader may have such assignment for a particular project and after the concerned project work is over, members may elect any other member as leader.

In some circle the deputy leader may be chosen by the members so that circle activities can be performed in absence of leader. When the supervisor or the leader of the department/work area performs the job of a leader, another worker of the circle acts as deputy leader. The leader plays an important role to contribute to the achievement of circle goals. So, the success of the Qc depends upon how the leader leads the circle members. The leader should possess some qualities. Some of the qualitative attributes expected of a Qc leader include

- Cooperative
- Accommodative
- Ready to help, assist members
- Ready to take responsibility
- Transparent in activities
- Acceptable to members and non-members
- Tolerant
- Coordinates
- Has a knowledge of group dynamics/interactive behaviour for performing group activities
- Task-cum-people oriented
- Self-disciplined
- Delegates responsibility
- Ability to persuade
- Energetic
- Very much friendly to department people
- Ability to plan and organize circle activities

The leader needs to perform a lot of activities. The important functions of a leader are:

i. conducting circle meetings regularly
ii. Maintaining records of circle activities, registers of the circle meetings
iii. Preparing project report for management presentation
iv. Training members with the help/assistance of the facilitator/ coordinator
v. Involving members in circle activities
vi. Inspiring members to give their best so that circle goals as fixed, can be achieved
vii. Bringing about a consensus approach in problem solving
viii. Catalyzing non-members to join existing circle

ix. Monitoring the circle activities in respect of formulated work programme

x. Generating a climate of mutuality i.e., mutual understanding, mutual faith and mutual confidence between members and leader

xi. Developing a sense of belonging amongst the members, in the circle

xii. Reviewing progress of the circle activities at regular interval

xiii. Maintaining a high degree of cohesiveness to make the members generate a feeling of 'we-ness' and 'togetherness' in the circle

Facilitator

The facilitator is generally management personnel having a good position in the organization. He is selected by the top management to facilitate smooth and effective functioning of circle activities. He acts as an ideal role player and a value shaper. He is guide, friend, adviser, coach, teacher to the circle members. He is a link personality between leader and steering committee. He takes the stock of operational activities, helps in smooth functioning of Qc activities. He develops healthy relations amongst the members. The facilitator can be rotated once in 2 years, or as may be decided by the higher management looking at various perspectives of the organization.

The facilitator of Qcs should have some qualities. The important qualitative traits of a facilitator include:

- Acceptable to the member
- Friendly
- Should be of reasonable standing and position
- Patient
- Should have positive values
- Committed
- Having excellent communication skill
- A good listener
- Persevering
- Innovative
- Integrity
- Tender, affectionate and caring – like a parent
- Facilitative, supportive

- Energetic, dynamic
- Having faith in Qc movement and in the philosophy associated with it
- Ability to guide, advise and inspire

Facilitator needs to perform a lot of functions. Some of his important functions are given below:

i. Attending Qc meetings. If he cannot remain present during the whole period of meeting, he should attend meeting at least for a short period of time

ii. Ensuring that meetings are held regularly, members attend meeting and meetings are conducted smoothly and effectively

iii. Assisting the leader in maintenance of records of circle activities, proceedings of meetings

iv. Assisting in clarifying and defining problem, goal setting and planning

v. Helping to select and use application of problem solving techniques

vi. Giving proper feedback to leader and circle members for improvement

vii. Coordinating with training officer for organizing need based training programmes for circle leaders and members

viii. Taking initiative for setting up of Qcs by persuading supervisor, by imparting training to circle leaders and members

ix. Evaluating and reviewing Qcs operations and programmes

x. Working closely with the steering committee

xi. Helping prepare report and arranging management presentation

xii. Encouraging, motivating members, non-members to participate in Qc contests

xiii. Ensuring that circle activities are on the right track

xiv. Collecting and arranging dissemination of literatures concerning Qc activities elsewhere

xv. Implementing the work programme through three committees such as promotion committee, training committee and evaluation committee

xvi. Recommending the persons for different committees, supervising these committees and evaluating their performance

xvii. Obtaining support and assistance from other departments

Coordinator

The coordinator coordinates the activities of the quality circle in an organization. Generally senior executive of the organization is assigned the job of coordinating Qc operations in the organization.

The coordinator is an important personality to ensure that Qc activities excel in performance. So, to achieve quality circle goals the coordinator needs to perform various activities. The important activities/ functions include:

i. Registering quality circle in the work areas/departments or in the organization
ii. Concerning periodical and regular meetings of steering committee.
iii. Having liaison with the facilitators to ensure that the Qc meetings are held regularly
iv. Circulating record notes of the meetings of the steering committee
v. Interfacing with all the structural elements of Qcs
vi. Appraising steering committee on the progress and development of quality circles activities in the organization
vii. Organizing systematic documentation of case studies made by various circles and publishing them regularly
viii. Maintaining records of steering committee meetings systematically
ix. Arranging for top management presentation in coordination with facilitators
x. Organizing training programmes for facilitators, circle members, leaders in collaboration with training department and providing service as a resource person
xi. Establishing rapport with other organizations for promoting Qc activities
xii. Providing assistance to the quality circles as and when required
xiii. Preparing training materials for leaders, facilitators in consultation with training department
xiv. Arranging to provide facilities for holding quality circle meetings at regular intervals
xv. Organizing exposure programmes for workers and different levels of executives to the concept of quality circles in a planned and systematic manner

xvi. Publishing periodicals, pamphlets, etc., for the promotion of quality circles

xvii. Organizing social get-together of quality circle members, facilitators, steering committee members once or twice in an year

xviii. Organizing conventions of quality circles within the company

xix. Organizing workshops, seminars, lectures, conferences on quality circles

xx. Dealing with the matter in respect of starting new quality circles

xxi. Conducting survey at regular interval on the health of Qcs and presenting the findings to the steering committee with suggestions

xxii. Arranging presentation of case studies in sister units and outside as and when requested by them.

Steering Committee

This committee is formed with the top management personnel and departmental heads of the unit/plant. Since quality circles need to be started in all departments of the organization it is advisable to include all departmental heads in the steering committee as its members. It formulates guidelines for smooth working of Qcs and also review the functioning of Qc activities. It makes the functional heads accountable for smooth and effective functioning of quality circles in their areas. Functional heads, in turn, make the facilitators accountable.

Steering committee provides infrastructure, resources to strengthen Qcs, designs/formulates objectives, goals, strategy of Qcs.

The meeting of the steering committee is convened by the coordinator/facilitator who is also the member of the steering committee. Such meetings are usually presided over by the chief executive officer of the plant.

The chief executive officer and coordinator/facilitator act as chairman and secretary of the steering committee respectively.

The steering committee performs various functions for promotion of quality circles in organization. Some important functions of steering committee include:

i. Providing financial resources needed for smooth and effective functioning of quality circles

ii. Establishing the objective of the quality circle function in an organization

iii. Providing policy guidelines and direction

iv. Ensuring that quality circle activities become a way of life in an organization.

v. Providing moral support to the facilitators

vi. All members of the steering committee attend management presentation

vii. Taking decisions for implementation of recommendations of Qcs

viii. Members of the steering committee participate in the social get-together of the quality circle members along with facilitators/ coordinator

ix. Rating the project reports of the quality circles for awards

x. Designing and developing a transparent, un ambiguous guidelines for Qc operations

xi. Studying the application of quality improvement techniques

xii. Obtaining feedback and reviewing Qc activities

xiii. Reviewing the overall working of Qcs

xiv. Promoting quality circles in the organization

Top Management Committee or Executive Committee

This committee is constituted with chairman and management director (CMD) and 2-3 top level management personnel to formulate company policies and procedures with regard to quality circles of the organization.

Top management support is highly needed to operate any scheme. So for effective functioning of Qc activities, role of executive committee (EC) is important. The more the EC takes interest in Qcs, the higher will be the degree of successful performance of Qcs.

The functions of the top management committee include

i. Laying down policy incorporating Qcs as an integral part of management activities

ii. Demonstrating its faith, belief in the concept of quality circles

iii. Implementing policy, reviewing the policy implementation and results thereof

iv. Spelling strategies and systems for the achievement of results

v. Working as advisory committee to guide steering committee members, facilitators

vi. Assisting employees at various levels to make the Qcs movement a self-sustained success

vii. Attending management presentation of different Qcs

viii. Encouraging healthy growth through competition between quality circles of various departments

ix. Responding to circle recommendations in a positive way

x. Deputing members to outside seminars/conferences or workshop

xi. Reviewing Qc activities periodically at regular interval.

Operations Process of Quality Circles

Quality circle operations pass through different stages of activities. Such stages of operations include

- Finding problems
- Selection of problems
- Analysis of problem
- Solution of problem
- Management presentation
- Implementation
- Follow up and review

Finding problems

This is the first stage of the quality circle operations. The members are asked to give their views regarding the problems they face, come across in the process of their discharging activities in the work area. This is done through the use of brain-storming technique. This technique is carried out for such period of time when all problems are identified and the members express their inability to identify further problems. That means, more problems can be identified.

Selection of problems

After identification of problems it is now seen which problems are very much important that need immediate solution. So, efforts are made to select the problems on the basis of priority. The leader facilitates discussion and asks the members to identify the most pressing problems that need to be dealt with immediately and to pick up one problem at a time in order of priority by each member. To generate such views/idea the leader organizes brain storming session.

Analysis of problem

In this stage all the problems are analyzed thoroughly. Since problems have effects on the organization, each problem is analysed to find the genesis/cause of the problem, that means to get to know the 'why' of such problem. For digging out the cause of the problem and for making a thorough analysis of such problem various data, information may be required. The facilitator helps the circle to get the necessary data/information to carry the analysis. It is highly important to ascertain the causes of the problem and its likely impact on the organization. For establishing cause and effect relationship the circle uses various techniques/methods like line graph, bar graph, stratification, scatter diagram, etc.

Solution of problem

After analyzing the problem and its likely effect on the organization the leader goes for the next step, that is, solution of the problem. Since solution comes from the members who are well aware of the problem because of their deep involvement in the work area activities, the leader of the circle conducts brainstorming exercise in a congenial and conducive atmosphere and encourages members to effectively participate in the exercise. In the process of exploring solution some suggestions are put forward. Now, from amongst suggestions final decision is taken after a thorough analysis, thorough consensus.

Management presentation

The quality circle members and the leader need to present the problem, its solution suggested and the benefits anticipated from solving problem by them. The presentation to management may be made orally or in the from of project report presentation by the members/leader. Such presentation helps the members develop their communication skill, confidence in work activities and establish a cordial relationship with the management personnel. This also recognizes the group members for the efforts they make for effective functioning of the circle activities.

Implementation

On receipt of the approval from the higher management with regard to the problem for which solution/suggestion was prescribed through presentation, the circle leader takes necessary steps for implementation like:

- generating a climate of mutuality in the department/work areas
- establishing a good understanding and rapport amongst all the employees of the department/work areas

- developing a feeling of 'we-ness', 'togetherness' amongst the members and non-members
- preparing a schedule for implementation
- assigning the task to the member/s for performance
- seeking cooperation and assistance from non-members for speedy disposal of the activities
- taking the help of facilitator as and when needed to direct the other department/s to assist, if required/involved
- assigning the job of monitoring to some member/s.

Follow-up and review

This step is very important as the circle needs to know the progress of the activities relating to implementation. It may happen that for implementation of the approved suggestion/s some changes may be required. So, proper review of the results and also the follow-up action need to be ensured so that timely implementation can be made.

Hindrances/Barriers to the Growth of Quality Circle Activities in Indian Organizations

Quality circle is an effective tool to increase production, productivity, to solve problems that stand in the way for smooth functioning of departmental activities, to enhance quality of products, services, to attain business excellence and to achieve organizational goals. Though utility and usefulness of quality circle is admitted, the growth and development of quality circle in Indian organizations has not reached the benchmark level as expected because of some constraints. The important factors that create a barrier in the growth of quality circles in India are explained below in brief.

1. Top management attitude, faith in Qcs activities

Top management attitude needs to be positive for introduction of quality circles in various departments/work areas of the organization. It is a fact that there cannot be any difficulty to launch quality circle programmes and operate smoothly in an organization if the top management desires spontaneously from the core of the heart; only lip service cannot yield results. It happens that quality circles in some Indian organizations cannot perform effectively because of negative, apathetical attitudes of the higher management and also their lack of faith in Qcs activities.

2. Resistance of trade unions

One of the obstacles to the growth of Qc activities in Indian organization is the resistance made by trade unions continuously for operations of Qcs. The trade union leaders may feel that they are ignored by the management for discussion/solution of problems as quality circles take necessary steps for identifying, analyzing and solving problems in work areas.

3. Ineffectiveness of leaders

Most of leaders of Qcs cannot run Qcs in proper way as they do not have thorough knowledge, skill, understanding of Qc operations, and in the process they become ineffective.

4. Incompetent facilitators

It happens that facilitators do not have required knowledge, skill and ability (KSA) for smooth functioning of Qcs activities. In some cases facilitators lack interest in Qc operations and they take these assignments casually.

5. Lack of communication skill of members

In heterogeneous employee composition members speak different languages that are not understandable. In Qc meetings they cannot express their views properly because they lack communication skill. So, the activities like problems identification, analysis, solution and management presentation cannot be performed which are very much important for growth and development of Qcs in organizations.

6. Irregular meeting

In some Indian organizations Qcs meetings are not held regularly, and as a result no steps can be taken to find out problems and its solution for smooth and effective functioning of departmental activities. Besides, implementation of the approved suggestions cannot be made timely. All this creates hurdles for effective functioning of Qc activities.

7. Irregular attendance in meeting

It happens that a significant number of members of Qcs in Indian companies do not attend Qc meetings; may be that they are not interested in Qc activities or they feel that they may not be able to contribute to Qc operation through participation in the meetings. All this deters the growth of quality circles in India.

8. Proper records not maintained

For each and every Qc activity records need to be maintained so that Qc operation can be performed in a planned and systematic way. In many Indian organizations records of Qc activities are not maintained properly. Non-maintenance of records makes the whole operation process of quality circles dysfunction, ineffective and standstill.

9. Inadequate training facilities and ill-designed training system

Members, leaders and facilitators of Qcs need training so that they can have thorough idea, understanding regarding concept, philosophy, operation of quality circles. Training makes the participants effective, performers, creates interest, generates desire and motivates them to excel in Qc activities. In large number of Indian organizations training facilities provided to the trainees are not adequate. There may have a lot of loopholes/limitations in the training system like lack of competent, experienced and dynamic trainers, ill-designed training modules, Programmes, contents, use of obsolete tools, devices for presenting deliberations, absence of a congenial, conducive learning environment in the training place, lack of seriousness and interest in training amongst trainees, use of imaginary data, information that does not have any relevance in real life situation, and others.

10. Non-members' attitudes, faith in Qcs activities

If the non-members develop faith in Qc activities, consider members as performers, good in behaviour, honest, hardworking they will extend their cooperation, assistance, help to members, facilitators for smooth and effective functioning of Qcs operation. But, in many Indian organizations it does not happen. Qc members keep themselves aloof from non-members, create a division between members and non-members, think that they are superior in various qualitative traits than non-members. All this results in generating a feeling of 'we' 'they', 'antagonism' 'bitterness' amongst the non-members; and they dissociate from circle activities. This creates hurdles in the growth of Qc operations.

Implementation Procedures of Quality Circle

Quality circle is an effective tool to help the people grow, develop and deliver peak performance. It makes the people able to face challenges in the competition and obtain competitive advantages. It is, therefore, a necessity to implement quality circles in various work areas/departments of the companies. For implementation of quality circles in any organization definite plans, programmes and procedures are required to be made. Some of important plans/procedures include:

1. Chief Executive of the company should be convinced with regard to the usefulness of the Qc in the company. Necessary measures should be taken so that he develops faith in the concept, philosophy and operations of the quality circle, and feels the necessity for implementation of Qcs in his company.
2. Attempts need to be taken to develop understanding and knowledge of the senior executives of the company with regard to the quality circle through proper presentation to them, and also to generate a positive feeling, idea for its application in the organizational setting.
3. Middle management grade personnel should be made aware of Qc concepts, philosophy, utility through detailed presentation, and then a thread-bare discussion, interaction should be carried on between the participants to explore the work areas/departments where quality circle can be introduced. In the interactive session selection of work areas or departments should be made.
4. Since quality circle operations are done with and through the employees they should be given a broad idea, understanding and knowledge about the Qc and its effect on their production, earnings and quality of working life (QWL). Awareness development programme should be organized by the HRM department of the company and the initiative should be taken by the HR head to ensure that employees are inspired, motivated; and they express their keen interest for launching Qc programmes in their work areas.
5. After identification of the work areas/departments the facilitator should be appointed. The head of HRM department should be nominated as facilitator to facilitate the Qcs activities in the organization. Then, the coordinators for respective departments/work areas should be nominated by the facilitator.
6. The steering committee should be formed. This committee should be headed by the head of the company along with functional heads as members.

However, for an organization that has different units functioning at different places, steering committee should be formed and this committee should be headed by the unit head along with the functional heads. But, a central steering committee should be formed at the head office or at the corporate office headed by the head of the organization and with unit level heads as members. This committee should meet regularly after short intervals and review the Qc activities operating in the organization as a whole.

7. The Executive committee/top management committee should be constituted with head of the organization and 2/3 top level management personnel.
8. The facilitator would be the convener of the steering committee and should ensure that the steering committee's meetings are held regularly. The head of the organization will be the chairman of the steering committee.
9. People should be aware of the total support and the commitment the top management extends to the development of Qcs in the organization.
10. The members of the circle would elect their leader.
11. Training Programmes should be organized for leaders, coordinators/ supervisors for smooth and effective functioning of Qcs.
12. Initially the company should start organizing one or two quality circles and subsequently the number should be increased.
13. Formal inauguration of the quality circles should be made by head of the organization/unit declaring the names of the members.
14. Quality circle meeting must be held regularly once in a week initially and then once in a fortnight/month. In the first meeting the circle members should select a name for the circle to work as leader.
15. The HRM department should be given additional assignment to ensure that the records of the Qcs are preserved in the department.
16. The facilitator should brief the steering committee members and the top management committee with regard to the functioning of Qcs in the organization.
17. The coordinator should be given the responsibility to ensure that 'log book', 'minute book' are maintained by Qcs operating in his work areas. He should also be given the responsibility to conduct periodical survey on the health of Qcs and suggest measures for discussion in the steering committee.
18. The coordinators should have direct access to facilitator.
19. The suggestions given by members affecting circle's objectives/ goals should be discussed threadbarely.
20. Team members must be motivated to effectively contribute in circle meetings.

Some Problem Solving Tools for Qcs

Brainstorming

Brainstorming is a process/mechanism that stimulates to generate new ideas, thought on any matter. It is a group technique used for generating new and useful ideas. VO Jenks (1990) defines brainstorming as a group technique for uncritically generating more innovative alternatives in the decision-making process. It is frequently used in Qcs operation for identification of problems, selection of problems and for solution of problems. The technique consists of involving members of QC, assigning them a task (generally phrased as 'how to') and fixing a time limit. At the end of the time limit, the ideas generated are closely scrutinized, evaluated to make decision for solving problems.

For an effective brainstorming session the under mentioned guidelines should be followed:

1. The number of participants preferably should be between four to twelve.
2. The participants should be made aware of the subject on which brainstorming is done.
3. Some time should be given for incubation.
4. Each participant should give one idea at a time.
5. Participants should not be criticized for the ideas presented by them. Each participant should be encouraged to think freely and creatively without any constraint of what others will think of this.
6. It should be ensured that all participants contribute to the session as the objective of brainstorming is to get maximum number of ideas.
7. Participants should be explained the importance of brainstorming for generating creative ideas and also the use of five Ws (when, where, what, who, and why) and one H (How) for bringing creativity.
8. Each and every participant's contribution should be clarified.
9. Decision should be taken on evaluation criteria.

Pareto Analysis

Pareto analysis is a technique used to arrange data according to priority. That means it separates the important, vital problems from minor, trivial problems. It helps in identification of the 'vital few' from the 'trivial many' for problems selection. When projected using the column graph named after Pareto, Italian economist is termed as Pareto diagram.

Pareto diagram can be drawn after collection of data. The steps used for constructing Pareto diagram may include:

- Use of checksheet or brainstorming to obtain data
- Rearranging the data in descending order
- Calculating total of each category
- Computing percentage of the total that each category represents
- Computing cumulative percentage
- Scaling the vertical axis for frequency from zero to hundred
- Constructing a bar for each category (from left to right)
- Drawing a vertical scale on the right to indicate the percentage
- Plotting a cumulative percentage line

Example

Sunshine Company Limited obtained 100 complaints from the customers during 2009. The complaints were made in respect of quality, personnel, delivery, packaging and invoicing. The total number of complaints categorywise were involved as

Personnel	25
Delivery	15
Invoicing	30
Quality	20
Packaging	10
Total	100

A Pareto Diagram can be constructed in the following manner.

Category of complaints	No of complaints	Cumulative	% to total	Cummulative %
Invoicing	30	30	30	30%
Personnel	25	55	25	55%
Quality	20	75	20	75%
Delivery	15	90	15	90%
Packaging	10	100	10	100%
Total	100			

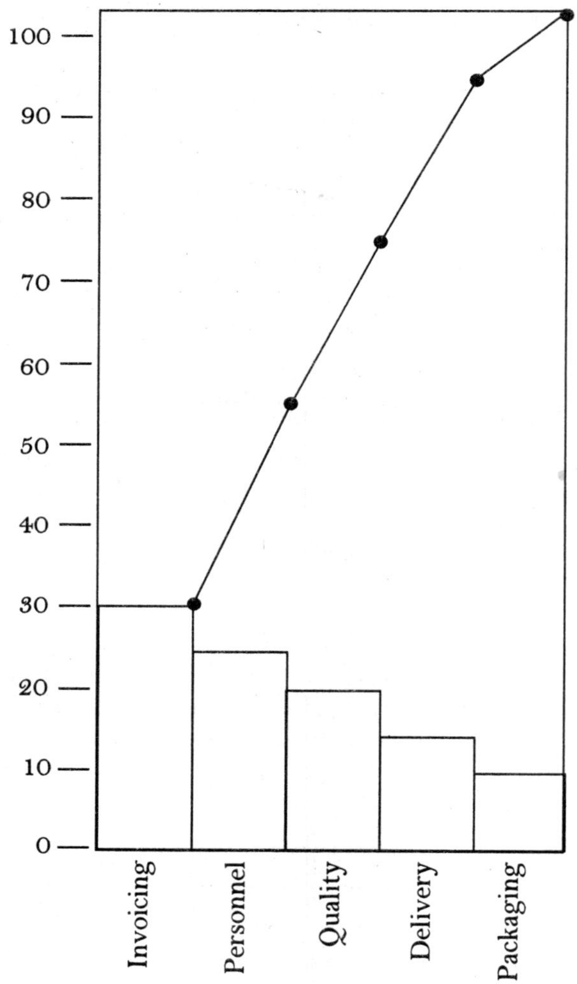

Fig. Pareto Diagram for customers' complaints

Cause and Effect Diagram/Fishbone

The objective of any organization is to achieve its goals and this is possible if the organization functions smoothly and effectively. But, in reality, it happens that organizational activities are disturbed as some problems stand in the way of organization's effective functioning. So, for uninterrupted and smooth running of organizational activities some tool/mechanism needs to be used for finding out reasons/causes of the problems. Such tool/mechanism is cause and effect diagram.

The cause and effect diagram is an explorative tool which can be used to find reasons/causes of problems that disturb functioning of organizational activities. This 'diagram' is called Ishikawa Diagram since Dr K Ishikawa invented and popularized its use. This is also called Fishbone Diagram as the shape of the diagram is like fishbone.

Importance

The cause and effect diagram is highly important in organizational setting. Its importance can be ascertained from the following:

1. It helps to know the genesis of problems.
2. The organization can be able to take suitable measure to solve problems.
3. It helps organization to take preventive measure so that such problems do not occur in future.
4. Since causes/reasons of problems are identified and solution is arrived at, the organization can function effectively and smoothly.
5. Absence of problems generates a climate of mutuality. That means mutual understanding, mutual faith and mutual trust between boss and subordinates are established.
6. Organization can be able to prepare strategy, policy effectively as probable problems, its genesis, efforts and solution, in given situations are known.
7. It enhances team spirit as the process for finding causes of any problems brings the people in the team together and develops team spirit.
8. It generates a sense of accomplishment amongst the members of the team when, through brainstorming the members can explore/identify the causes of problems and also give solution of problems.
9. Preparation of cause and effect diagram needs a thorough understanding, knowledge on the work related activities. So, it makes the people self-learned which subsequently tends toward self-growth, self-development.
10. This method not only helps the management to get to know the causes of problems but also lets the management know the sub-causes of problems like the situation, why do such causes occur? So, this can act as a fool proof technique to solve problems.

Steps for Using the Tool

Some steps are required to be taken to use the cause and effect diagram. They are:

1. Identification of problems: Problems need to be identified by the members preferably, through brainstorming. Efforts should be made to ensure that maximum number of problems/ideas are generated; and it is possible if each and every participant contributes to the problems-hunting exercise.
2. Selection of problems: After problems are identified, it is a great necessity to prioritize problems. That means, to select problems on the basis of priority. Since initially one problem is taken for solution, it needs to select the problem which requires immediate solution/disposal. For selecting problems priority wise, factors like importance, frequency of problems, urgency, cost and time involved in implementation are taken into consideration; and the problem is selected by giving weightage on all the problems.
3. Enumeration of cause(s) sub-cause(s) of problem: The cause(s) of the problem need to be ascertained/found out through brainstorming exercise. After finding the cause it is a necessity to ascertain the sub-cause, that means, to know why does it happen?

Example

ABC Bank Private Ltd situated in Kolkata introduced Quality Circle in its Fixed Deposit Department. Five clerical staff members of the department formed the Qc with department-in-charge as leader of the team Through the use of brainstorming technique on different dates in 2009 the following problems were identified by the members:

1. Shortage of chairs
2. Delay in customer service
3. Cleanliness of the Fixed Deposit Department

Selection of problems was made through brainstorming exercise and the factors like importance, frequency of problems, urgency, cost and time involved in implementation were taken into consideration. For this, weightage was given in the following manner:

High:	3
Medium:	2
Low:	1

Selection of problem was made as follows:

Problems	Urgency	Frequency	Implementation cost	Implementation time	Importance	Total
1. Delay in customer service		2	2	2	3	9
2. Shortage of Chairs	2	3	1	1	1	8
Cleanliness of the Fixed Deposit Department	3	3	2	2	3	13

Cleanliness in the Fixed Deposit Department of the Bank's branch was given priority to solve it. For solving this problem causes and sub-causes were identified through brainstorming exercise as shown below:

Problems	Causes	Sub-causes
Cleanliness	1. Inattentive sweeper	i. Badli/casual sweeper ii. Lack of supervision
	2. Stationery kept in haphazard and casual manner	i. Shortage of sub-staff ii. No space available in the department to keep stationery in a systematic way.
	3. Bad habit of customers	i. Spitting at the corner of the department. ii. No spitting pot

Causes and Effect Diagram/Fishbone Diagram can be constructed with the above information like problem, causes, sub-causes identified by the Qc members of the Fixed Deposit Department of ABC Bank Private Ltd, Kolkata.

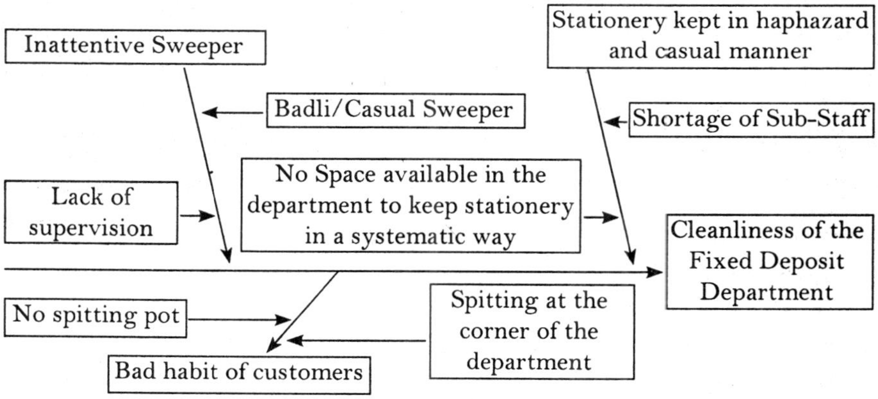

Fig: Cause and Effect Diagram

Workers' Participation in Management: Introduction

Change, continuous change and radical change is a regular phenomena. It is prevalent in every walk of life viz., social, economic, cultural and political activities. The abrupt change in industrial activities has started after the implementation of the new industrial policy in July 1991 that brought a significant departure from controlled, regulated and protected (CRP) economy to the liberalized, privatized and global (LPG) economy.

In the LPG economy hyper competitive environment exists as a lot of MNCs and TNCs enter into market and strive hard to show their strength and competence to face challenges and capture market through delivery of goods and services to the delightment of customers.

Competitors know that customers demand for quality goods and services at a reasonable price, as they are highly aware that today's market is 'buyer's market' not 'seller's market'. In order to face challenges and survive in the market and to obtain competitive advantages, the organizations need a different kind of employees who will be committed to work and to the organizations and will contribute to the achievement of business excellence.

Types of people required:

- Satisfied and contented people
- People having high degree of morale
- People that can provide customers' delightment
- People having a sense of 'belonging', 'togetherness' and 'we-feeling'
- People who have developed a spirit of co-operation and collaboration.

For attaining business excellence, achievement of organizational goals the above referred kinds of people is a necessity for the organizations and it is not difficult to have such kind of people as per requirement if participative management is accepted and implemented in true spirit by the actors of the industrial relations system.

Meaning and Concept of Participation

Participation is an overworked word in business and government, but an under worked activity. The idea sounds good to most managers, but they are frequently unsure of what to do with it. Some grossly misinterpret what it is, so that when they say, "participation is great", they are really talking about something else; others are not sure when to apply it or how far to go with it. So, clear ideas and understanding on the term 'participation' is a necessity. Participation is an individual's mental and emotional involvement in a group situation that encourages him to contribute to group goals and to share responsibility for them. This contains three key ideas - (a) First, participation means mental and emotional involvement of a person's self, rather than just his skill (b) Second, participation motivates contribution. Individuals are given an opportunity to direct their initiative and creativity toward the objectives of the group. (c) Third, participation encourages people to accept responsibility for an activity. Because they are self-involved in the group, they want to see it work successfully.

It is now obvious to say that workers' participation in management means mental and emotional involvement of workers in a group situation that encourages them to contribute to group decision making goals and to share responsibility for them. Mc Gregor Douglas defines workers' participation as a formal method of providing an opportunity for every member of the organization to contribute his brain and ingenuity as well as his efforts to the improvement of organizational effectiveness. So, it is a mechanism or method that gives an opportunity to the workers to express their views in the decision making process of the organization.

The term 'Workers Participation in Management' has been perceived by different people in different ways.

For management, it is joint consultation prior to decision making; for workers, it is just like co-decision or co-determination and for trade union it is the ushering in of a new order of social relationship and a new set of power equations within enterprise.

For sociologists, workers' participation is an instrument of varying potentialities to improve industrial relations and promote industrial peace. For economists, workers' participation is a means for higher productivity of labour and utilization of effective experience of workers towards promoting qualitative and quantitative conditions of production. For lawyers, workers' participation is a legal obligation upon the management to permit and provide for involvement and participation of workers in the decision making process of management.

Participation is a sort of involvement of individual in group activities to contribute to group goals. In organizational context, participation refers to involvement of employees as representatives of the employees' community in the decision making process of the management. Stevens (1990) believes that 'participation is about employees playing a greater part in the decision making process'.

The concept of workers' participation in management is a sort of industrial democracy which gives the rights to the employees' representatives to participate in decision making process. The term 'participation' is also extended to forms of financial participation such as profit sharing.

Levels of Participation

Workers participate in decision making at various levels.

VG Mhetras (1966) has suggested five levels of participation in decision making viz.,

(i) Information participation that refers to sharing information in respect of sales programme, balance sheet, production, economic conditions of the firm, etc. Here the workers have no right to scrutinize the information provided.

(ii) Consultative participation that refers to sharing of views on such matters as working conditions, welfare programme, work and safety methods, etc. Here, the joint council works as an advisory body. Management may or may not accept suggestions and final decision is taken by the management.

(iii) Associative participation. In such case management accepts and implements the unanimous decision of the council.

(iv) Administrative participation. Here, the degree of sharing authority and responsibility of administrative work is much more than in other cases.

(v) Decisive participation. Here, decisions are taken jointly on matters relating to production, safety, welfare, etc. This is the highest form of participative activities.

Importance of Workers' Participation in Management

The existence of organization without people cannot be thought of. So, workforce is a necessity in the organizations. Organizations cannot run, cannot function without people. Now, only the functioning of organization is not sufficient to stay in the market in changing competitive scenario. Organizations need to face competition and win over challenging situations. For that it needs a reservoir of different kinds of people that helps companies to exist, grow, develop and achieve excellence. And this is possible through participation. Participation on the part of employees exerts profound effects on quality of work, acceptance of changes, and on overall morale, loyalty, and productivity. Furthermore, employees who are psychologically and mentally involved in their jobs display a much greater degree of identification with the company and its goals, thereby creating a climate conducive to individual growth and development. In turn, it is this very growth and development that so vitally affects the expanding company and the business economy as well.

Workers' participation in management has become increasingly important over the past few decades. This benefits the employees and the organizations as well. These include

- **Creating a state of mutuality**

  Participation helps generate a climate of mutual understanding, mutual faith and mutual confidence amongst the employees and the management.

- **Helping to identify the real problems that stand in the way of taking quality decision**

  Through participation by employees much more information may be available that can help get out of the standstill position and make decision.

- **Promoting sound industrial relations**

  Participation brings both the parties (management and workers) close, promotes interpersonal relations, reduces industrial conflict and develops healthy industrial relations in the organization.

- **Helping the people grow and develop**

  In participative management employees get the opportunity to question and suggest instead of having to follow a rigid set of instructions. This makes the employees grow and develop.

- **Generating a sense of self-respect and dignity amongst employees**

  Participation process allows the employees to express themselves in their work rather than being absorbed into a complex system of rules, procedures, and formalities. This helps the employees promote a feeling of dignity, self-respect.

- **Changing paradigmal state of employees**

  Participation makes it easy for the management to change the mindset of the people. In the discussion forum of the participation Committee/Board members virtually accept the change in the organization.

- **Increasing quality of work and services**

  Participation makes the employees committed to work and to the organization that results in increase of quality work and quality services.

- **Ensuring increased production and productivity**

  Participation generates a feeling of 'we-ness', 'togetherness' resulting in creating a spirit of 'must do', 'must achieve' amongst the employees, as they feel that they are part and parcel of the company.

Workers' Participation in Management in India

The need for workers' participation in management was advocated by the philosophers, thinkers like Comte, Owen, Webs and Cole. The management pioneers like Rand Black, Rensis Likert, Mc Gregor through findings of their research work popularized the belief that participative management could bring a change in performance activities of the workers.

Today, the scheme of workers' participation in management decision-making process has been implemented by a large number of countries in the world in various forms like:

- Joint committees in Great Britain
- Workers' council in Yugoslavia
- Joint consultation in Japan
- Workers' assemblies in China
- Codetermination in Germany
- Joint management councils and works committees in India

The workers' participation in management is not a new concept in India. The initiation of the scheme through the formation of joint consultation was made in Textile industry around 1910. At Jamshedpur, Tata Iron and Steel company set up Works Committee consisting of representatives of management and workers immediately after the first world war. The Tisco works committees, however could not achieve results because of inter union and intraunion rivalry. Some companies set up works committees in Bengal and in other parts of the country. Buckingham and Carnatic Mills in Chennai was one of the first industries that set up Joint Committee. The Royal Commission on Labour set up in 1929 recommended Works Committees at the plant level as also at the industry level for redressal of grievances through participation process. But, the system of joint consultation did not make much headway due to affect of economic depression of the thirties. After 1940 a national tripartite machinery was set up in the form of Indian Labour Conference that was modeled after the International Labour Organization and it came into effect in 1942.

The scheme of workers' participation in management got a legal footing and a strong base when the Government of India enacted the Industrial Disputes Act 1947 with the primary objectives of prevention and settlement of industrial disputes. The Act made it obligatory for all units employing 100 or more workers to constitute Works Committee with equal representation of workers and the management.

In the same year i.e., in 1947 the Industrial Truce Resolution that was adopted at the Industries Conference recommended inter alia, the formation of Unit Production Committee in industrial establishment. In 1948, the Government of India accepted in principle the establishment of bipartite production committees under Industrial Policy Resolution. Subsequently, a model constitution for the formation of Unit Production Committees and also for smooth and effective functioning of Works Committees as Production Committees, was adopted. Since then the Government has introduced various schemes of workers' participation in management like Joint Management Councils (1956), Board-Level participation (1970), Shop Councils and Joint Councils under the old 20-point Programme (1975), Unit Councils and Joint Councils in commercial and service organizations in the public sector (1977), Institutions of Employees' Participation in Management for Public Sector Undertaking (1983), Sector Undertaking (1983), Workers' Share in Equity (1985), participation of Workers in Management Bill (1990).

Works Committee (1947)

The institution of works committee was introduced in 1947 under the Industrial Disputes Act 1947.

Application: Section 3 of the Industrial Disputes Act 1947 provides that in the case of an industrial establishment in which one hundred or more workmen are employed or have been employed on any day in the preceding twelve months, the appropriate Government may, by general or special order, require the employer to constitute a Works Committee. The Committee shall consist of representatives of employers and workmen engaged in the establishment. The number of representatives of workmen on the committee shall not be less than the number of representatives of employer.

Objectives: The objectives of the works committee include:

- to promote measures for securing and preserving amity and good relations between the employer and workman
- to comment upon matters of their common interest or concern
- endeavour to compose any material difference of opinion in respect of such matters

The recommendations of the Works Committee are recommendatory and not binding. So, these are purely of advisory nature.

Functioning

From the perusal of the Table 10.1 it is revealed that workers' participation in establishments is not encouraging, rather depicts unsatisfactory picture regarding involvement of workers and also dealing with their issues.

Table-10.1 Showing the Works Committees formed, required to be formed

Year	Works Committees formed	Works Committees required to be formed	% of WCs formed to WCs required to be formed
1959-60	2574	4730	54. 65
1970-71	2124	3826	55. 5
1993	1346	2118	63. 5

Source: Various Reports of Ministry of Labour and Handbook of Labour Statistics, 1993

The same picture, rather a bit different picture on workers' participation in central sphere establishments is evident from the Table-10.2. It is generally expected that Government organizations should have Works Committees in all its organizations as a measures to promote harmony and create a state of mutuality in organizations. But, in reality it does not happen.

Table 10. 2 Showing the Works Committee formed, to be formed and percentage of W.Cs formed to W Cs to be formed in Central Sphere Establishments

Year	Works Committees (WCs) formed	WCs required to be formed	Workers involved	% of WCs formed to WCs required to be formed
1997	869	1131	11, 79, 577	77. 7
1999	881	1287	8, 70, 000	68. 5

Source: Government of India, Ministry of Labour, Annual Report 1997, 1998, p 29

Joint Management Councils (1956)

- The Government's Industrial Policy Resolution of 1956 emphasized greatly over the workers' participation in management.

- The Second Five-year Plan recommended the establishment of joint councils of management consisting of representatives of workers and management.
- The 15th session of the Indian Labour Conference in 1957, after considering the report of the study group, accepted in principle the idea of setting up joint management councils in India and appointed a tripartite sub-committee to work out details of the new scheme.

Objectives

The main objectives are

- to promote cordial relations between management and workers
- to increase operational efficiency of workers
- to generate a climate of mutual understanding, trust and confidence between them

Functioning

There is no definite data available regarding the number of JMCs and their functioning, but on perusal of literatures available on the working of JMCs, it becomes clear that the progress of JMCs is far from satisfactory. The Table 10.3 shows declining trend of growth of JMCs activities. The study conducted by the Joint Director, Labour, Employment and Rural Manpower, Planning Commissions revealed that the scheme did not make headway and it had never reached the target fixed for JMCs. The National Commission on Labour has expressed displeasure on the working of JMCs. The Commission is of the opinion that JMCs have failed to achieve their objectives of promoting joint consultation in industry.

Table 10.3 Showing number of JMCs working in Indian enterprises

Year	No of JMCs in public sector	No of JMCs in Private sector
1963-64	25	55
966-67	43	97
1968-69	34	55
1972-73	31	49

Source: (i) The figures are based on a reply to a question in the Rajya Sabha by the Deputy Minister of Labour on June 4, 1971

(ii) PRN Sinha, IB Sinha & SP Sekhar: *Industrial Relations, Trade Unions and Labour Legislations* (Pearson Education, 2008, Delhi)

Board-level Participation (1970)

- In 1970 the Government of India accepted the recommendation of the Administration Reforms Commission to appoint workers' representatives on the Board of Directors of public sector undertakings and introduced a scheme of workers' representation on Board of Management of selected public sector enterprises and nationalised banks.
- The Nationalised Bank (Management and Miscellaneous Provisions) Scheme 1970 was passed which required, each nationalized bank to have employee directors on its Board - one representing employees and other representing officers having tenure of 3 years.
- The Organizations like Hindusthan Antibiotics Ltd, BHEL, NTC, Rashtriya Chemicals and Fertilizer Ltd Port Trust, Hindusthan Organic Chemicals Ltd and others have workers' director on the board.

Objectives

Some of the important objectives include

- to generate a feeling of 'self-respect', 'belonging', 'we-ness' amongst the workers.
- to identify workers' problems and to sort out at the earliest possible time.

Functioning

The contribution of worker-director in the decision-making process is not appreciable. Lack of thorough knowledge and experience and also paradigmal pattern of worker-director makes the participation process ineffective.

Participation under Old 20-Point Programme/Workers' Participation Scheme (1975)

The Constitution of India was amended in 1975 and Section 43A was corporated in the Directive Principles of the Constitution. The Section provided that, "The State shall take steps by suitable legislation or in any other way to secure the participation of workers in the management of undertakings, establishments or other organizations engaged in any industry". Accordingly, the Central Government adopted through a resolution a new scheme of workers' participation in management, on October 30, 1975. This is a voluntary scheme covering all manufacturing and mining industries whether in public, private or co-operative sector which employs 500 or more persons. The scheme provides for the setting up of shop councils at the shop floor level and joint councils at the plant level.

Shop Councils

The salient features of shop councils are discussed below:

- There shall be one shop council for each department or shop, or one council for more than one department or shop considering the number of employees in the department or shop.
- Each shop council shall consist of an equal number of representatives of employers and workers.
- The total number of members may not generally exceed, 12. However, the number of members of each council may be determined by the employer in consultation with the recognized union or registered unions of workers.
- The employer's representatives to be nominated by the management shall be from the unit concerned, and the representatives of workmen shall be from among workers of the department or shop concerned.
- The chairman of council is nominated by the management and vice-chairman is elected by the worker-members of the council.
- The council shall function for a period of 2 years.
- The council shall have regular meeting to discuss matters like welfare, social security measures, working conditions, production, and safety measures, smooth functioning of the department/ shop, discipline, attendance aspects, etc.
- The decisions of the council are taken on the basis of consensus.
- The main objective is to increase production, productivity and overall efficiency of the department/shop.

Joint Council

The main features of the joint council are given herein below:

- The joint council shall function for a period of 2 years.
- The chief executive of the unit is its chairman, and vice-chairman is nominated by workers' members of the council.
- The members of the joint council shall be from the unit.
- The secretary is appointed by the joint council from amongst the

members of the council. He is responsible for smooth functioning of the council.

- The joint council meets once in a quarter to discuss:

i. matters remaining unresolved by shop council

ii. matters relating to fixation of productivity norms, training and development of employees, preparation of working hours and holiday schedules, optimum utilization of raw materials, quality of products, health, welfare, safety measures for the unit/plant and so on.

Functioning

The scheme started working with great zeal and enthusiasm. It showed effective functioning with great success immediately after the operation of the scheme. It is gathered from a Report of the Ministry of Labour that initially as many as 162 central public sector undertakings implemented the participative scheme. Table 10. 4 indicates the great response the undertakings made at the beginning of the operation of scheme.

Table 10.4 Showing number of units implementing the scheme

Year	No. of Units Implemented by				Total
	Central Govt. Undertakings	State Public Sector	Private Sector	Co- operative Sector	
1976	466	NA	NA	NA	466
1977-78	545	167	1131	99	1943

Source: KL Gupta, Industrial Democracy in Public Enterprises in India, Navman Prakashan, Aligarh, 1979.

The reason for smooth implementation and functioning of the scheme may be due to imposition of Emergency Rules in the country.

Scheme of Workers' Participation in Management (1977)

- A new scheme of workers' participation in Management in commercial and service organizations in the public sector having 100 or more employees was announced by the Government of India on 5th January 1977.
- The objective of introducing the scheme was to improve customer service.
- Instead of Shop Councils, there will be Unit Councils at the unit level and Joint Councils at the divisional, regional or zonal level.

- There is no basic difference with regard to features between 1975 scheme and 1977 scheme except the fact that these councils can be constituted by units employing 100 or more workmen.

Scheme of Workers' Participation in Management (1983)

After thorough overhauling the functions of participative activities and progress of various scheme in organizations a comprehensive scheme for workers' participation in public sector undertakings was prepared and notified by the Government on 30th December 1983. The important features of the scheme are briefly mentioned below:

i. The scheme is applicable to all public sector organizations irrespective of number of workers employed in the organizations.

ii. Participation is at the shop floor level, plant level and also at the board level.

iii. There shall be equal representation of workers and management in shop level forum and plant level forum. The size/extent of representation and also the mode of representation of workers are determined through consultation by the management with the unions.

Coverage for shop level forum

To discuss the matters relating to storage facilities, production, wastage control, welfare measures, hazards, health, safety, cleanliness, etc.

Coverage for plant level forum

- To discuss the matters not resolved at the shop level or concerning more than one stop.
- To deliberate the matter relating to house keeping, quality improvement, material supply, review of monthly targets of production, storage, productivity, economic and financial aspects, welfare, personnel matters, etc.

The decisions at shop floor level and plant level are taken on the basis of consensus.

Coverage for board level forum

To review the work activities of shop and plant level forums.

A standing tripartite committee was set up by the Ministry of Labour for submission of report and suggestions for corrective measures to the Government. The implementation of the scheme was left to the administrative ministries concerned. Barely half of the Central Public

Sector enterprises introduced the scheme over the next decade and several of these atrophied subsequently.

Workers' Share in Equity (1985)

The Government of India expressed intention to provide shares to employees upto 5% of the total shares and that was reflected in the 1985-86 Budget. This sort of provisions of stock options had positive intention of the government to make the workers shareholders of the company.

The Participation of Workers in Management Bill (1990)

The Central Government introduced Participation of Workers in Management Bill in the Parliament on 25th May, 1990. The salient features of the Bill are as follows:

i. The Bill provides for setting up of Shop Floor Councils, Establishment Councils and Board of Management at shop floor level, establishment level and board level respectively.

ii. The Bill suggests for three-tier participation of workers in management at shop floor level, organization level and board level.

iii. The shop floor council and establishment council will consist of equal number of representatives of employer and workmen.

iv. The Bill provides for the principle for electing the workers' representatives through secret ballot.

v. The council shall function for a period of 3 years from the date of constitution of the council.

vi. The Bill provides that in the Board of Management the representation of workers and other workers shall be 13% and 12% of the Board strength respectively, with minimum of one workers' representative in the Board.

vii. The Bill provides for choosing chairperson of shop floor council and establishment council by and from amongst the member thereof.

viii. The powers of shop floor council and establishment council have been extended to have a wide coverage of activities.

ix. The Bill provides for constitution of a monitoring committee to review and advise upon matters arising out of the scheme.

x. The Bill extends the coverage of the scheme to all corporate establishments.

Prerequisites for Effective Workers' Participation in Management

Workers' participation in management is a process of involvement and participation of workers' representatives in the decision making of the management. The principal activities of participative management include effective involvement, sharing views, meaningful participation and contributing to management decision making of the organization. To perform such activities and to make participation effective some conditions are required to exist. They are:

i. Culture of mutuality

Organization should have a culture of mutuality where people feel free, open to perform their job, develop a team spirit for cohesive working, establish healthy human relation, find a congenial place to show their worth and develop a sense of belonging, 'we-ness' and togetherness. Such climate helps make the participation effective.

ii. Top management thinking and desire

It is very much important to know as to what top management desires/thinks about permitting workers' representatives to participate in the company's vital decision making process. If top management sincerely wants workers' involvement and participation in the system workers feel the seriousness of such process. Under such situation it is possible to carry on effective decision making in the organization.

iii. Level of morale and job satisfaction of workers

The high level of morale and job satisfaction of workers indicates a favourable situation for effective workers' participation in management.

iv. Existence of educated, strong and positive trade union

The educated, positive and strong trade union is a necessity to make the participation scheme effective in an organization. Such union motivates the people to cooperate with the management for smooth functioning of the participation activities. So, to make the participation effective, there must be such union in organization.

v. Workers' perception, thought pattern about management

Workers' high thinking, image, impression about management approach, style of functioning, method of dealing with problems create a soothing, congenial climate for successful workers' participation in management.

vi. Workers' attitudes, values, beliefs

Positive attitudes, values and beliefs of workers prepare a ground for effective participation in management decision making. Such workers develop confidence, faith on the efficacy of participative system.

vii. Training System in the organization

If the company develops a training system and the workers are given training, education to make them acquainted with company's mission, philosophy, strategy participation may be meaningful. Under such situation workers can actively participate and effectively contribute to the discussion.

viii. Management attitudes

If the management recognizes the role of workers for growth and development of the organization, it satisfies the psychological need of the workers that contribute to effective participation in management decision making.

ix. Participative Culture

If there exists a cultures of participation in the organization where both the parties (union and management) spontaneously develop a feeling of essentiality for joint participation in decision making, it is possible to make the participative system effective.

Evaluation of Participation Schemes

In India, we have different forms of workers' participation in management, of which works committee is constituted under law (Industrial Disputes Act 1947) and all other participative forms are voluntary. On overhauling and detailed perusal of participative schemes operating in Indian organizations it becomes apparent that none of such schemes is found to be successfully working, barring a few private organizations where schemes show greater success. The principal reasons for non-attainment of desired result may be:

i. Not accepting the schemes by the parties-workers and management from the core of the heart. Neither party takes the participation system spontaneously in real spirit.

ii. Reluctance of trade unions to operate the scheme thinking that their importance will be curbed if their members are taken in various committees to discuss problems and give suggestions to solve problems ignoring the existence of trade unions.

iii. Non-cooperative attitudes of the management to invite workers in different committees as they feel their participation will undermine their status and authority. Management also does not like to leave a fraction of the decision-making authority to other party, that too, to subordinates working under them.

iv. Lack of appropriate effort by the Government machineries in the workings of works committees in various organizations.

v. Illiteracy and also lack of proper sense to understand the importance of participative system amongst the workers. Workers lack competence to gauge the importance and recognition given to them through various participation schemes and also to explore different perspectives to identify problems and submit suggestions.

vi. Non-existence of conducive climate to develop mutual understanding, trust and faith. Most of the Indian organizations barring few fail to generate a climate of mutuality mutual trust, mutual dependence, mutual responsibility and mutual confidence. Both the parties do not consider themselves belonging to a family resulting in creations of mistrust, misunderstanding among themselves.

Effective Participation: How to Make?

This is an important area that needs to explore the possible means to make the workers' participation process effective. At this backdrop some ideas are presented. Those here indicated are suggestive rather than fully definitive.

1. Optimum/balanced ego-state of executive community

Executives should have strong belief that participation by workers is essential and a dire need of the day. And this can be done through moulding process of ego-states of those executives who need it.

2. Decentralized organization structure

If the companies are highly decentralized managers may have power to invite workers for participation in various activities, which is not possible in centralized companies. So, the need arises to change the structure of organizations.

3. Mature attitude of unions

Workers are led by unions. It happens loyalty of workers towards unions is much more than the loyalty they have towards companies where they work. If union executives hold dynamic, positive, mature, constructive thought process, it may be possible to generate awareness amongst workers regarding the necessity of workers' participation in management. This can be possible by providing appropriate training to the identified union leaders and also by creating a congenial climate for interactions between management and union leaders.

4. Ensuring employees' job security and continuance of existing benefits and services

Workers may think the process of participation may create a situation of insecurity of a job and depriving benefits, services they are getting. Under such eventuality participation process gets disturbed. Hence, necessary steps need to be taken to develop understanding among the workers to feel that in no circumstances participation process will make their jobs insecure and disturb the continuance of providing existing benefits and services.

5. Communications channel

A well planned and effective practice of communication between management and workers may facilitate smooth functioning of participation activities.

6. Education

Illiteracy makes the workers incapable to understand the usefulness of participation in the organisations. Sometimes they think this participation process may not do better for their wellbeing than to harm their job activity. So, workers need to be given proper education through sponsoring/conducting training programmes to understand the participation process in the organizations.

7. Generating a climate of openness, cooperation, trust, authenticity, collaboration and autonomy (OCTACA)

Participation process can be effective if the workers' community feel that the organization belongs to them and they are part and parcel of the organizational system. This sort of feeling workers may develop if a state of mutuality and also a climate of openness, cooperation, trust, authenticity, collaboration and autonomy (OCTACA) is generated in the organizations. So, importance is given to generate and inculcate a culture of OCTACA, not through imposition by statute.

Books Recommended

1. AK Ghosh, *Human Resources Management* (with cases) (Manas Publications, 2006, New Delhi)
2. Mc Gregor Douglas, *Human Side of Enterprise*, 1960,
3. SG Huneryager and IL Heckmann, *Human Relations in Management* (DB Taraporevala Sons & Co. Private Limited, Bombay)
4. BD Singh, *Industrial Relations: Emerging Paradigms* (Excel Books, New Delhi, 2005)

INDEX

5. K Ganapatty, *Quality Circle Hand Book for the New Millennium* (Quality Circle Forum of India, Secunderabad)
6. Gerald Ferris, *Research in Personnel and Human Resource Management* (JAI Press, Stanford, 2000)
7. D Katz and R. Kahn, *The Social Psychology of Organizations* (John Wiley and Sons, New York, 1978)
8. J Hyman and B. Mason, *Managing Employee Involvement and Participation* (London, Sage, 1995)
9. K Legge, *Human Resource Management: Rhetorics and Realities* (Macmillan, London, 1995)
10. SR Udpa, *Quality Circles - Progress Through Participation* (Tata McGraw Hill, New Delhi, 1992)
11. BR Dey, *Quality Circles* (Macmillan, New Delhi, 1988)
12. BR Virmani, *Workers Participation in Management* (Macmillan, New Delhi, 1978)
13. D Dewar and JF Beardsley, *Quality Circles* (International Association of Quality Circles, USA. 1980)
14. KC Alexander, *Participation Management: The Indian Experience* (Sri Ram Centre, New Delhi, 1972)
15. Michael Armstrong, *A Hand Book of Human Resource Management Practice* (Kogan Page Limited London, 1999)
16. Jack Halloran, *Applied Human Relations - An Organizational Approach* (Prentice-Hall of India Private Ltd., New Delhi, 1978)
17. VG Mhetras, *Labour Participation in Management* (Manaktalas, Mumbai, 1966)
18. S Ingle, *Quality Circles Master Guide* (Prentice Hall of India, New Delhi, 1985)
19. John W Newstrom and Keith Davis, *Organizational Behaviour: Human Behaviour at Work* (Tata McGraw Hill Publishing Company Ltd. New Delhi 1998)
20. LM Prasad, *Human Resource Management* (Sultan Chand & Sons, New Delhi, 2001)
21. C Hogan, *Facilitating Empowerment* (Kogan Page, London, 2000)

Journals/Periodicals Recommended

1. J Sundbo, "*Empowerment of employees in small and medium sized service firms*", Employee Relations, 1999, 21(2): 105-27.

2. RS Wellins, WC Byham and JM Wilson, "*Empowered Teams: Creating Self-Directed Work Groups that improve Quality, Productivity and Participation*", Jossey-Bass. SanFrancisco, CA, 1991

3. NA Randolph, "*Navigating the Journey to Empowerment*". Organizational Dynamics, 1995, 23(4) 19-50

4. R Mohammed and KA Pervaiz, "*A contingency model for empowering customer-contact services employees*". Management Dewsion, 1998, 36 (10): 686-693

5. DE Bowen and EE Lawler, "*The empowerment of service workers: what, why, how and when?*' Sloan Management Review, 1992, 33(3): 31-39

6. JA Conger and RN Kanungo, "*The empowerment process: integrating theory and practice*", Academy of Management Review, 1988, 13(3): 471-82

7. LA Schlessinger and JL Heskett, "*Breaking the cycle of failure in services*". Sloan Management Review, 1991, 17-28

8. C Lorenz, "*Uphill Struggle to Become Horizontal*". Financial Times, November 5 1993

9. JN Dobbs, "*The Empowerment Environment*". Training and Development Journal, Jet 1993, 55-57

10. KW Thomas and BA Velthouse, "*Cognitive elements of empowerment*". Academy of Management Review. 15(4) 666-681. 1990

11. LD Ketchum and E Trist, "*All Teams Are Not Created Equal: How Employee Empowerment Really Works*". 1992, Sage, Newbury Park, and CA 106

12. John RP French and Bertram Raven, "*The Bases of Social Power*" in Dorwin P Cartwright (ed), Studies in Social Power, Ann Arbor: University of Michigan, 1959

13. M Parker and J Slaughter, "*Unions and Management by Stress*" in S Babson (Eds), Team Work: Empowerment and Exploitation in the Global Auto Industry, Wayne State University Press, Dotroit

14. David J Glew et al, *Participation in Organizations: A Review of the issues and proposed Frame Work for Future Analysis*". Journal of Management, vol 21(3), 1995, 395-421

Questions

1. What do you mean by the term 'workers participation in management'? Discuss the objectives of workers' participation in management.

2. Discuss in brief different forms of workers' participation in management.
3. Discuss the main features of shop council and joint council.
4. Explain the term 'empowerment'. Discuss importance of employee empowerment in organization.
5. Some say empowerment is a process of transferring authority with responsibility to the individuals at lower level. Do you justify this statement? Give reasons.
6. State and explain briefly the important characteristics of employee empowerment.
7. 'Empowered organizations follow some principle for empowering people'. What are those principles? Explain them in brief.
8. What are the prerequisites for employee empowerment? Explain.
9. The whole concept of employee empowerment cannot be based on single approach/perspective. Do you endorse this statement? If yes, why? If not, why not?
10. Discuss in brief the different stages of employee empowerment.
11. Employee empowerment plays crucial role to make the organization confront challenges, face competitors and achieve goals. Do you justify this? Give reasons for your answer.
12. State and explain the factors that affect empowerment process in an organization.
13. Quality circle operations pass through different stages of activities. What are those stages? Discuss them in brief.
14. Discuss in brief, the factors that create barriers to the growth of quality circle activities in Indian organizations.
15. Prepare an implementation plan of quality circle in an organization.
16. What is Quality Circle? Discuss organizational structure of quality circles.
17. Explain the term 'Quality Circle'. Discuss the objectives of quality circles.
18. State briefly the prerequisites for effective workers' participation in management.
19. What, according to you, are the reasons for not working successfully of the workers' participation schemes in Indian organizations? Explain them.

20. Give your suggestions to make the workers' participation process effective.
21. Write short notes on
    (a) Brainstorming
    (b) Pareto Analysis
    (c) Cause and Effect Diagram
    (d) Benefits of employee empowerment
    (e) Prerequisites for employee empowerment
    (f) Organizational Perspective of employee empowerment
    (g) Facilitator
    (h) Coordinator
    (I) Steering Committee

Case Study

XYZ Bank Ltd has 1200 branch across the country. It has five Zonal offices which are situated in Mumbai, Delhi, Chennai, Lucknow and Kolkata. Each Zonal office has its Regional offices that control and monitor the branch activities. The Head office of the bank is in Mumbai. The Regional offices are headed by Regional Managers who report to respective Zonal Managers. The overall control of the Regional offices is made by the concerned Zonal office headed by Zonal Manager. The Regional Managers are directly accountable to their Zonal Managers for the business activities of the respective regions. The Zonal Managers of different Zones, in turn, are accountable to Chairman and Managing Director for business performance, activities of their respective zones.

Additional Information

1. The Bank has received award for Excellent Performance and Quality Services from various Institutions in 2004, 2005, 2006 and 2007.
2. The market share of the company has increased considerably from 10% in 2000 to 25% in 2007.
3. The company's profit has shown an increasing trend (20% in 2000, 40% in 2004, 50% in 2005, 75% in 2006 and 125% in 2007).
4. The performance of the Kolkata zone is not satisfactory. The zone reveals a very dismal performance record all through the years. It is now felt by the zonal authority that staff involvement in customers services which has declined needs to be strengthened.

So, for running smoothly and effectively of branch activities it is a necessity to develop a team spirit of rendering quality customer service, amongst the staff members. The matter has been discussed threadbarely in a meeting between the Zonal Manager of Kolkata zone and four Regional Managers under Kolkata zone; and in the process of discussion the idea emerges to make an experiment with quality circle (Qc) initially in Savings Bank Department of India Exchange Branch under west Bengal Region. The administrative set up of India Exchange Branch is like as shown in the chart on p-420.

On the basis of what has been stated above answer the following questions.

1. Draw an organizational structure of Quality Circle for Savings Bank Department of India Exchange Branch under West Bengal Region of XYZ Bank Ltd. The imaginary names of members, leader, coordinator, facilitator, Steering committee members and Executive committee members are to be taken.
2. Identify problems and also select problems which may appear to be relevant.
3. Point out the procedures to be adopted for identification of problems and prioritization of problems.
4. Prepare a Fishbone Diagram to indicate problem, its causes and sub-causes, assuming that the problem needs to be solved immediately looking at its degree and extent of impact on the overall functioning of the department and the branch as well.
5. Make a list of suggestions given by the members for solving the problem and also prepare a report for management presentation mentioning the causes(s), subcause(s) and measures recommended for solution.

As HR Manager of the West Bengal Region of XYZ Bank Ltd do you think implementation of quality circles in different branches can be of great use? Give your views.

The Administrative set-up

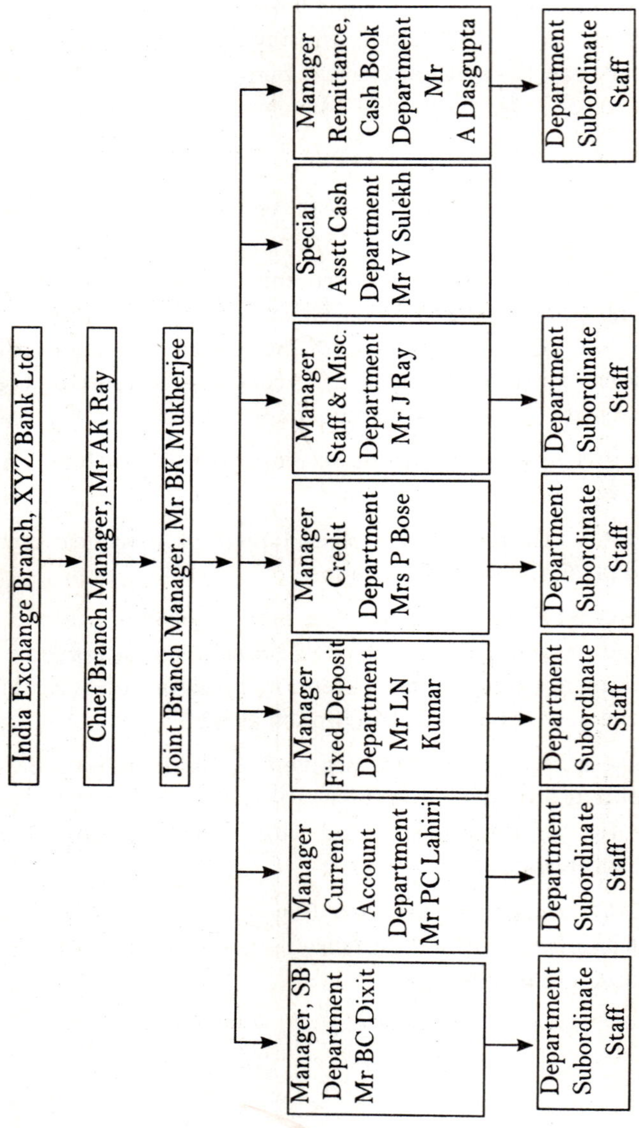